ABUSE OF DISCRETION

Best Wishes !

Clarke

ABUSE OF
DISCRETION

The Inside Story of *Roe v. Wade*

CLARKE D. FORSYTHE

ENCOUNTER BOOKS
New York · London

First American edition published in 2013 by Encounter Books,
an activity of Encounter for Culture and Education, Inc.,
a nonprofit, tax-exempt corporation.
Encounter Books website address: www.encounterbooks.com

Manufactured in the United States and printed on
acid-free paper. The paper used in this publication meets
the minimum requirements of ANSI/NISO Z39.48–1992
(R 1997) (Permanence of Paper).

FIRST AMERICAN EDITION

LIBRARY OF CONGRESS CATALOGING-IN-PUBLICATION DATA
Forsythe, Clarke D., 1958–
Abuse of discretion : the inside story of Roe v. Wade / Clarke D. Forsythe.
     pages   cm
Includes bibliographical references and index.
ISBN 978-1-59403-692-7 (hardcover : alk. paper) —
ISBN 978-1-59403-693-4 (ebook)
1. Abortion—Law and legislation—United States. 2. Abortion—
Government policy—United States. 3. Political questions and
judicial power—United States. 4. Trials (Abortion)—United States.
5. Roe, Jane, 1947– —Trials, litigation, etc. 6. Wade, Henry—
Trials, litigation, etc. I. Title.
KF3771.F67 2012

                                        342.7308'4—dc23
                                         2013003349

PRODUCED BY WILSTED & TAYLOR PUBLISHING SERVICES

For Karen

· CONTENTS ·

· THE JUSTICES AND THE ADVOCATES ·

The Justices

Justice Hugo Black (1886–1971) United States Senator from
Alabama (1927–1937), appointed by President Franklin D.
Roosevelt in 1937; retired due to ill health and died in
September 1971, three months before the first oral
arguments in *Roe v. Wade* and *Doe v. Bolton*.

Justice Harry Blackmun (1908–1999) Federal appeals judge
before nomination to the Supreme Court by President
Richard M. Nixon in 1970; author of the opinions in *Roe
v. Wade* and *Doe v. Bolton*.

Justice William J. Brennan, Jr. (1906–1997) New Jersey
Supreme Court Justice (1951–1956), appointed by President
Dwight D. Eisenhower in 1956; voted with the majority in
Roe v. Wade and *Doe v. Bolton* to strike down the Texas and
Georgia abortion laws.

Chief Justice Warren E. Burger (1907–1995) Appointed
by President Richard M. Nixon in 1969; voted with the
majority in *Roe v. Wade* and *Doe v. Bolton* to strike down
the Texas and Georgia abortion laws; distanced himself
from the abortion decisions at the time of his retirement
in 1986.

Justice Tom C. Clark (1899–1977) Attorney General of
the United States (1945–1949), appointed by President

Harry Truman in 1949; joined the majority in *Griswold v. Connecticut* in 1965 to strike down the Connecticut criminal prohibition on the marital use of contraception; retired in 1966 and published a very influential law review article in 1968, arguing that abortion laws should be repealed.

Justice William O. Douglas (1898–1980) Appointed by President Franklin D. Roosevelt in 1939. Upon his retirement in November 1975, *Time* magazine called Douglas "the most doctrinaire and committed civil libertarian ever to sit on the court"; voted with the majority in *Roe v. Wade* and *Doe v. Bolton* to strike down the Texas and Georgia abortion laws.

Justice John Marshall Harlan (1899–1971) Federal appeals judge before nomination to the Supreme Court by President Dwight D. Eisenhower; retired in September 1971 one week after Justice Black due to ill health, three months before the first oral arguments in *Roe v. Wade* and *Doe v. Bolton.*

Justice Thurgood Marshall (1908–1993) The leading civil rights lawyer in the United States in the 1940s and 1950s who argued and won *Brown v. Board of Education* in 1954; appointed by President Lyndon B. Johnson in 1967; voted with the majority in *Roe v. Wade* and *Doe v. Bolton* to strike down the Texas and Georgia abortion laws.

Justice Lewis F. Powell (1907–1998) Appointed in 1971 by President Richard M. Nixon to replace Justice Black; voted with the majority in *Roe v. Wade* and *Doe v. Bolton* to strike down the Texas and Georgia abortion laws; later called the abortion opinions "the worst opinions I ever joined."

Justice William H. Rehnquist (1924–2005) Appointed by President Richard M. Nixon in 1972 to replace Justice Harlan; one of two dissenters in *Roe v. Wade* and *Doe v. Bolton*; became Chief Justice when Warren Burger retired in 1986.

Justice Potter Stewart (1915–1985) Appointed by President Dwight D. Eisenhower in 1958; voted with the majority in *Roe v. Wade* and *Doe v. Bolton* to strike down the Texas and Georgia abortion laws.

Justice Byron White (1917–2002) Deputy U.S. Attorney General, 1961–1962; appointed by President John F. Kennedy in 1962; one of two dissenters in *Roe v. Wade* and *Doe v. Bolton*.

The Advocates

Dorothy Toth Beasley (1937–) Assistant Attorney General for Georgia who defended the 1968 Georgia abortion law, arguing both the first and second arguments in the Supreme Court in *Doe v. Bolton*; later Chief Judge of the Court of Appeals of Georgia.

Sandra Cano (1951–) The Georgia plaintiff who filed suit in 1970 under the pseudonym "Mary Doe" to strike down the Georgia abortion law enacted in 1968; she eventually opposed the abortion decisions and sought a rehearing of her case to get it reversed; in 2005, she testified before Congress against the abortion decisions.

Robert C. Flowers (1923–2009) The Assistant Attorney General for Texas who argued the defense of the Texas abortion law in the second oral argument in *Roe v. Wade* on October 11, 1972; later the Executive Director of the Texas State Commission on Judicial Conduct.

Jay Floyd (1923–1996) The Assistant Attorney General for Texas who argued the defense of the Texas abortion law in the first oral argument in *Roe v. Wade* on December 13, 1971.

Margie Pitts Hames (1934–1994) The Atlanta attorney for Sandra Cano (Mary Doe) who challenged the Georgia abortion law and won; argued the first and second arguments in *Doe v. Bolton* in the Supreme Court.

Roy Lucas (1942–2003) Lawyer who filed many of the state and federal court cases challenging state abortion laws that led to the abortion decisions; co-counsel with Sarah Weddington in the Supreme Court in *Roe v. Wade*.

Norma McCorvey (1947–) The Texas plaintiff who filed suit in 1970 under the pseudonym "Jane Roe" to strike down the Texas abortion law; like Sandra Cano, McCorvey eventually opposed the abortion decisions and sought a rehearing of her case to get it reversed, and filed briefs in the Supreme Court in subsequent abortion cases to overturn *Roe v. Wade*.

Sarah Weddington (1945–) The attorney for Norma McCorvey (Jane Roe) who challenged the Texas abortion law; at the age of twenty-six, she argued both the first and second arguments in *Roe v. Wade* and won.

ABUSE OF DISCRETION

· INTRODUCTION ·

Solving the
Puzzle of *Roe v. Wade*

And in Roe v. Wade *and* Doe v. Bolton, *when the Court had its most dramatic opportunity to express its supposed aversion to substantive due process, it carried that doctrine to lengths few observers had expected, imposing limits on permissible abortion legislation so severe that no abortion law in the United States remained valid.*

—LAURENCE TRIBE[1]

Thus, in one bold, cataclysmic move the Court undid about a century of legislative action. It swept away every abortion law in the country.

—LAWRENCE FRIEDMAN[2]

Tuesday, January 16, 1973, was, looking back, the calm before the storm. But Justice Harry Blackmun was a constant worrier, and nothing worried him more than the two abortion decisions that the Supreme Court was set to release on Monday, January 22. After a solid career as a lawyer in Minnesota and a decade as a respected federal judge, Blackmun had been nominated to the Supreme Court in 1970 by President Richard Nixon. Chief Justice Warren Burger, Blackmun's boyhood friend, had recommended him to Nixon after Nixon's first two nominees to the Court, Clement Haynsworth and G. Harrold Carswell, had been rejected by the Senate. Blackmun often doubted his own ability to do the job, and suspected that other Justices, like Hugo Black, Potter Stewart, and William O. Douglas, shared his doubts. Even his most sympathetic biographers referred to Justice Blackmun as "ever the martyr" because of his frequent complaints about the burden of the job.[3]

After the two abortion cases—*Roe v. Wade* and *Doe v. Bolton*—were first argued in December 1971, Burger had assigned the opinions to Blackmun to write, for reasons that Blackmun never entirely understood. He had spent the previous thirteen months working on multiple drafts of the opinions, pressured by Justices Douglas, Brennan, and Stewart to change and expand the scope of the decisions.[4]

Chief Justice Burger, too, was concerned about the abortion decisions, but for different reasons. He was due to swear in Richard Nixon for a second term as president on Saturday, January 20. Contrary to the president's antiabortion position, the Court was about to strike down the abortion laws of all fifty states based on a broad "right of privacy" that was nowhere in the words of the Constitution nor the Bill of Rights. Despite his reputation as a "strict constructionist" that got him named Chief Justice, Burger was going to sign onto Blackmun's opinion, along with a third Justice whom Nixon had named to the Court, Lewis Powell. Concerned that the decisions, joined by three Nixon-appointed Justices, would embarrass him or the president, Burger kept telling Blackmun that Burger was writing an additional, concurring opinion, which he was able to delay until after the inauguration.

Having more than once shared with his colleagues his fears that the Court would be criticized for the decisions, Justice Blackmun crafted a statement that Tuesday explaining the decisions that he proposed to release to the press. But when Blackmun distributed the draft among his fellow Justices, Justice William Brennan, known as a liberal champion of the Court, warned him that the Justices didn't issue "press releases" that might be confused with the written opinions they issued. So Blackmun simply read his statement from the bench on Monday, January 22.

When Blackmun was finished, and the opinions were released, the two abortion decisions took on a life of their own. The political, social, and medical turmoil caused by the decisions has lasted for forty years and shows no signs of abating.

Roe v. Wade[5] is considered the "most controversial" decision of the modern Court era.[6] Even sympathetic legal academics have described *Roe* as an "engine of controversy."[7] A decade after the decision, one law professor referred to *Roe* as "a unique decision" in the Supreme Court's history: "No other case . . . caused such a loud and sustained public outcry."[8] Others have admitted that it is "unquestionable that *Roe* has become . . . the preeminent symbol of judicial overreaching."[9] It "handed abortion rights advocates a vastly more far-reaching victory than they ever could have attained through the legislative and political process."[10] *Roe* "generate[d] long-term controversy [and] upheaval."[11]

The impact of the abortion decisions was immediate.

- All of the abortion laws, across all fifty states, were rendered unenforceable, thereby lifting the threat of prosecution against abortion providers.[12]
- Though abortion was legal in some states before January 1973, *Roe* enabled abortion clinics to open in every state.
- By February, abortion clinics—some run by former "back alley abortionists"—opened in major cities like Chicago.[13]
- *Roe* barred public health officials from enforcing health and safety regulations in the first trimester.
- By invalidating Georgia's hospitalization requirement, the Justices encouraged the movement of abortion practice from hospitals to stand-alone clinics.
- The federal courts were given continued oversight of any new regulations that might be passed by state or local governments.
- *Roe* empowered abortion practitioners to challenge any abortion regulations, including health and safety regulations, in federal court.

The outcome in *Roe* surprised even abortion activists. Lawrence Lader, one of the key abortion-rights leaders of the 1960s, wrote that the abortion decisions were "far broader in scope than anyone expected" and "even more conclusive than any of us dared to hope."[14] Legal historian Lawrence Friedman wrote that "*Roe v. Wade* belongs to a very select club of Supreme Court decisions—those that sent shock waves through the country, affecting every aspect of political life."[15] The morning they were released, *Time* magazine, based on a leak from one of Justice Powell's clerks, pronounced the outcome, "Abortion on Demand."[16]

Thirty-two years later, *New York Times* columnist David Brooks described the impact:

> When Blackmun wrote the *Roe* decision, it took the abortion issue out of the legislatures and put it into the courts. If it had remained in the legislatures, we would have seen a series of state-by-state compromises reflecting the views of the centrist majority that's always existed on this issue. These legislative compromises wouldn't have pleased everyone, but would have been regarded as legitimate.
>
> Instead, Blackmun and his concurring colleagues invented a right to abortion, and imposed a solution more extreme than the policies of just about any other comparable nation. . . .
>
> The fact is, the entire country is trapped. Harry Blackmun and his colleagues suppressed that democratic abortion debate the nation needs to have. The poisons have been building ever since. You can complain about the incivility of politics, but you can't stop the escalation of conflict in the middle. You have to kill it at the root. Unless *Roe v. Wade* is overturned, politics will never get better.[17]

What *Roe* Said

The Court that decided the abortion decisions in January 1973 consisted of Chief Justice Warren Burger and Justices William O. Douglas, William Brennan, Potter Stewart,

FIGURE 1. *The nine Justices who decided* Roe v. Wade *in January 1973. Seated, left to right: Potter Stewart, William O. Douglas, Warren E. Burger, William J. Brennan, Jr., Byron R. White. Standing, left to right: Lewis F. Powell, Jr., Thurgood Marshall, Harry A. Blackmun, William H. Rehnquist.* Collection of the Supreme Court of the United States.

Byron White, Thurgood Marshall, Harry Blackmun, Lewis F. Powell, Jr., and William H. Rehnquist.

What the Supreme Court actually says and how the media reports it are often quite different. Supreme Court decisions are typically reported by the media in two ways: as a vote split between "liberals" and "conservatives" (5–4, 6–3, 7–2), or as a verdict that the Supreme Court "approved" or "disapproved" some policy. These two methods of reporting cases tend to be misleading. They portray the Justices as no different than politicians voting on bills, and they obscure the essential legal "holdings" or "rulings," interpreting and applying existing laws, from which the impact of the decisions flows.

Roe had two essential rulings based on interpretations of

the Fourteenth Amendment to the U.S. Constitution, which declares, in part, that no state shall deprive any "person" of "liberty." First, the Justices interpreted "liberty" to include a "right to privacy" and held that abortion is part of the right to privacy—the "right of privacy ... is broad enough to encompass a woman's decision whether or not to terminate her pregnancy."[18] Second, the Court held that the "unborn" are not included with other "persons" protected by the Constitution—"the word 'person,' as used in the Fourteenth Amendment, does not include the unborn."[19]

Not only did the Justices nullify the abortion laws of all fifty states, but—in a break from the traditional function of judges—they also prescribed what would be permissible by drafting their own national abortion standard. They outlined a three-trimester division of pregnancy, which ostensibly allowed different levels of permissible regulation, with virtually no regulation in the first trimester (the first twelve weeks), some regulation in the second trimester designed to protect the health of the mother, and some regulation in the third trimester to preserve the "potential life" of the unborn child.

The Significance of *Doe v. Bolton*

What we know as "*Roe v. Wade*" is actually two cases from two states: *Roe v. Wade* from Texas, and *Doe v. Bolton* from Georgia. The two cases were argued together, decided together, and issued on the same day. The Court held that *Roe* and *Doe* "are to be read together."[20] The *Doe* decision has been relatively ignored over the past forty years, despite its significant impact on abortion policy in the United States.

In *Roe*, the Court implied that the states could prohibit

abortion after fetal viability, "except where it is necessary, in appropriate medical judgment, for the preservation of the life or health of the mother."[21] "Viable" traditionally meant "able to live." Thus, a "viable pregnancy" meant a pregnancy that was progressing. But the Justices defined "viability," for the purposes of abortion law, as the ability of the unborn child to survive outside the mother's womb. In that sense, viability in 1973 was thought to generally occur at twenty-eight weeks of pregnancy.

In *Doe*, the Court added a significant "health exception" after fetal viability that is often overlooked. The Justices defined "health" in abortion law as "all factors—physical, emotional, psychological, familial, and the woman's age—relevant to the well-being of the patient."[22] The way the Justices defined that "health" exception proved critical.

"Health," in abortion law, means emotional well-being without limits. Any potential emotional reservation a woman has about being pregnant can be deemed, at the discretion of the abortion provider, as a threat to her "health," and thus a reason to ignore any abortion prohibition after fetal viability.

This "health" exception in *Doe* swallowed the supposed ability of the states to prohibit abortion after fetal viability. This exception also eventually led to the issue of "partial-birth abortion" in the 1990s and the scandal of live-birth abortions in Dr. Kermit Gosnell's clinic in Philadelphia in 2010.[23]

Where *Roe* prevented any prohibition on abortion before viability, the *Doe* "health" exception eliminated prohibitions after viability as well.[24] While some realized immediately that the states could no longer prohibit abortion in the first trimester, the full implication of the Supreme Court's decisions only became clear over time as the lower federal courts decided hundreds of cases in the following decades.[25]

> The Justices defined "health" in abortion law to mean "emotional well-being" without limits, left to the discretion of the abortion provider.

Roe eliminated the laws in thirty states that prohibited abortion except to save the life of the mother; *Doe* eliminated the rest, including the new abortion laws adopted by approximately thirteen states between 1967 and 1971, which had canceled or replaced traditional abortion prohibitions. As Harvard law professor and comparative law expert Mary Ann Glendon has emphasized, "It was *Doe* that set the United States on a far more extreme course than that taken in most other liberal democracies, where the regulation of abortion has largely been left to be worked out through the ordinary democratic processes of bargaining, education, persuasion and voting."[26]

The sweeping scope of *Roe* and *Doe* isolated the United States as one of approximately nine countries that allow abortion after fourteen weeks and one of only four nations (with Canada, China, and North Korea) that allows abortion for any reason after fetal viability.[27]

Although the abortion decisions were sweeping in their scope, the Justices did not decide all aspects of the abortion issue in January 1973. The Justices said, in effect, "henceforth, we will decide the abortion issue, but not all of it today." The Court left to be decided—in more than twenty-nine cases stretching over forty years—dozens of additional medical and legal issues. Though it was clear in January 1973 that no legal prohibition of any abortion before viability could stand, it became apparent only over several years that a prohibition even after viability was unenforceable.

What *Roe* Did

When the abortion decisions were publicly released on January 22, 1973, the Justices lost significant control of them, and the decisions developed a political and social dynamic of their own.

The Justices nationalized an issue that, until *Roe*, had been a state issue. By nationalizing abortion, they nationalized the politics of abortion. Within days, constitutional amendments were introduced in Congress to overturn the decisions, and a vigorous congressional debate over proposed amendments continued for ten years. Hearings were held in 1974–1975 and again in 1981–1983. Between 1973 and 2003, approximately 330 constitutional amendments on abortion were introduced in Congress.[28] But the one and only vote in the U.S. Senate on a constitutional amendment failed on June 28, 1983, by a vote of 49–50, lacking the two-thirds needed.[29]

The Justices also abruptly changed American medicine. Abortion was declared to be a *constitutional* right—the only medical procedure to ever have that status—which shielded abortion and abortion providers from the regulation to which medical procedures and doctors have been traditionally subjected.

Furthermore, the decisions caused considerable confusion across a broad spectrum. The Justices wrote "that the right of personal privacy includes the abortion decision, but that this right is not unqualified and must be considered against important state interests in regulation."[30] But if the "right" was "not unqualified," just what "qualifications" were permissible has remained in doubt. And while *Roe* left state abortion laws unenforceable, it did not answer many questions that parents and doctors and women and men and public health officials were soon asking. Did girls of any age have a right to abortion, too? Did parents have a say in the matter? Did fathers or husbands? Could the states restrict or regulate abortion? How could cities regulate the new clinics? What kind of regulations were enforceable after fetal viability? The answers to some of these questions took years, until the Justices reviewed new laws and decided additional abortion cases.[31] Some have still not been answered.

Further public confusion arose because the decisions were initially reported—and are still described—as having legalized abortion only "early in pregnancy" or only "in the first three months."[32] Since *Roe*, however, numerous Supreme Court and lower federal court decisions have reaffirmed that *Roe* and *Doe* legalized abortion throughout pregnancy for any reason.[33] Even so, the Justices have often been reluctant to be frank about the scope of *Roe* as the courts have applied it,[34] referring to the "right" as though it only existed in the "early stages" of pregnancy.[35] That misleading description has continued for forty years in court decisions and media reporting.

The Justices centralized what had previously been decentralized. Since colonial times, abortion had been a local public health issue and crime, determined by state legislatures, state governors, state courts, local prosecutors, and state public health officials. Federal governmental involvement in abortion had been rare, strictly limited to the powers of Congress expressly stated in the federal Constitution, such as prohibiting abortion ads from being sent through the mail.

The Justices effectively ended an active public debate, in the sense that the American people could no longer decide the issue. The Justices, along with federal courts in every state across the country, would henceforth control the issue. Until the 1960s, all but a few of the fifty states prohibited abortion except when necessary to save the life of the mother.[36] These abortion laws were enforced and updated and strengthened during the nineteenth century as medical understanding progressed.[37] As of January 1973, however, thirty states permitted no other exception than to save the life of the mother, and most states actively enforced their abortion laws.[38] Prosecutions against abortionists were pending in many states on the day *Roe* was issued.

The abortion decisions effectively bound Congress and the president and all state and local governments across all fifty states. The Supremacy Clause in Article VI of the original Constitution, ratified in 1789, states:

> This Constitution, and the laws of the United States which shall be made in Pursuance thereof . . . shall be the supreme Law of the Land; and the Judges in every State shall be bound thereby, any Thing in the Constitution or Laws of any State to the Contrary notwithstanding.

While there continues to be considerable academic debate over the "supremacy" of Supreme Court decisions in controlling the decisions of the Congress and the president, few doubt that the decisions of the Supreme Court supersede state law, including state supreme court decisions, state constitutions, and state statutes. As a practical matter, federal judges obey even the most controversial decisions of the Justices and apply those against the states. In the immediate aftermath of the abortion decisions, state officials from Connecticut, Louisiana, Missouri, and Rhode Island sought to reject, or limit, or clarify the abortion decisions, and asked the Justices to reconsider. Rhode Island, in particular, immediately sought to reenact abortion prohibitions, but its law was quickly struck down by the courts.[39]

Of course, the most obvious effect of the abortion decisions was the increase in abortions. Although the biggest *percentage* increase of abortions in America actually occurred before *Roe*, after thirteen states had legalized abortion in certain circumstances between 1967 and 1970, the nationwide legalization in January 1973 significantly increased the number of abortions performed in America. In 1972, the year before *Roe*, about 550,000 legal abortions were recorded. After *Roe*, abortions increased, reaching an annual high of 1.6 million in 1992, before declining to 1.2 million in 2006.[40]

Finally, in the *Roe* and *Doe* decisions the Justices sided with a minority of the public who supported abortion *for any reason, at any time of pregnancy.* Already a minority position at the time of the decisions, by 2009 that minority had shrunk to just 7 percent of Americans.[41]

Although the *New York Times* praised the abortion deci-

sions on January 24, 1973, as "a sound foundation for final
and reasonable resolution" of the abortion issue, the Justices
could not resolve, by a judicial edict, an issue of such complexity and such a long legal and cultural history.

Why So Sweeping?

How could the Supreme Court have issued such a sweeping,
unprecedented decision, with such serious consequences for
public health, which has produced forty years of unending
legal, political, medical, and social turmoil?

> Why did the Justices not leave the issue to the state and
> local public health officials?
>
> Why did the Justices expand the right beyond viability?
>
> Why did the Justices expand the right beyond what the
> public supported?
>
> Why did the Justices stake out a position broader than
> almost any other nation in the world?

There are no simple, easy answers to these questions.
There were many reasons, which came together to influence
the Justices at the end of the tumultuous decade of the 1960s.

But solving the puzzle of *Roe v. Wade* and *Doe v. Bolton*
is the aim of this book. The controversy over the abortion
decisions has hardly subsided, and the reasons why are to be
found in the deliberations of the Justices in 1971–1972 that
resulted in their unprecedented decisions.

PART I

MISTAKES

· CHAPTER ONE ·

The Road to *Roe*

INSIDE THE SUPREME COURT

Potter [Stewart] pressed for Roe v. Wade *and* Doe
v. Bolton *to be heard and did so in the misapprehension
that they involved nothing more than an application of*
Younger v. Harris. *How wrong we were.*

—JUSTICE HARRY BLACKMUN,
LETTER TO CHIEF JUSTICE REHNQUIST[1]

*Should we spell out—although it would then necessarily
be largely dictum—just what aspects are controllable by the
State and to what extent?*

—JUSTICE HARRY BLACKMUN,
MEMORANDUM TO THE CONFERENCE (MAY 1972)[2]

A Mistake from the Beginning

Roe and *Doe* began, in the Supreme Court, as a serious
procedural mistake that left the Justices without any
factual record to consider the complex historical, legal, medical, and constitutional issues surrounding abortion. At least

some Justices decided to hear the cases under the "misapprehension" that they were dealing merely with procedural issues.

Justice Blackmun related this mistake to at least two people, and it is confirmed by the briefs in the abortion cases, the Justices' papers, and the oral arguments. Blackmun told the story to Chief Justice William Rehnquist in July 1987, as the Supreme Court confirmation hearings for Judge Robert Bork were heating up in the U.S. Senate. In a July 16 letter to Blackmun, Rehnquist shared his concerns that the Court would be short-handed without a full bench of nine Justices in the fall, if Bork wasn't confirmed or the hearings were prolonged.

Blackmun wrote back on July 20 to allay Rehnquist's concerns with his story of how *Roe* was selected in 1971 by a subcommittee of Justices that Chief Justice Burger assembled to avoid "controversial cases" while the Court was shorthanded with two vacancies after the sudden retirements of Justices Hugo Black and John Harlan in September 1971.

> I remember that the old Chief [Warren Burger] appointed a screening committee, chaired by Potter [Stewart], to select those cases that could (it was assumed) be adequately heard by a Court of seven. I was on that little committee. We did not do a good job. Potter pressed for *Roe v. Wade* and *Doe v. Bolton* to be heard and did so in the misapprehension that they involved nothing more than an application of *Younger v. Harris*. How wrong we were.[3]

Blackmun repeated his story to James Simon four years later in a May 1991 interview for Simon's book, *The Center*

Holds, calling the decision to hear the abortion cases "a serious mistake":

> The chief justice was concerned that the remaining seven members of the Court would have to decide controversial cases on the docket, such as *Roe v. Wade* . . . without a full court. . . . The committee, chaired by Potter Stewart and which included Harry Blackmun, let *Roe v. Wade* and *Doe v. Bolton* go forward. "It was a serious mistake," Blackmun later said. "We did a poor job. I think the committee should have deferred them [the abortion cases] until we had a full Court."[4]

With *Younger v. Harris,* Justice Blackmun was referring to a controversial case decided on February 23, 1971, sixty days before the Justices voted on April 22 to hear *Roe* and *Doe*. For two years, while Justices Hugo Black and John Harlan were still on the Court, the Justices had been immersed in *Younger v. Harris*, which involved the politically delicate issue of federal court intervention in state court criminal proceedings. Argued three times before it was finally decided, *Younger* put limits on the power of federal courts to interfere with *pending* criminal prosecutions in state courts.

Younger intersected with the abortion cases filed in federal court against state laws from 1969 to 1972 because a doctor who was prosecuted for abortion in state court might file a case in federal court to block the state prosecution—the kind of scenario with which *Younger* was concerned. Thus, *Younger* overshadowed the abortion cases filed in federal court at a number of points between 1970 and 1972.[5]

In fact, Bob Woodward and Scott Armstrong—in their

controversial 1979 book *The Brethren*, which shed more light on the inner workings of the Supreme Court than ever before—briefly reported the same story. But they told it in such a casual way that its significance was probably lost on most readers, and they told the story from the perspective of Justice Douglas, who had a long-standing desire to eliminate the abortion laws, and who had strongly opposed the Court's result in *Younger*. They wrote:

> Douglas had long wanted the Court to face the abortion issue head on. . . . Douglas realized, however, that a majority of his colleagues were not likely to give such a sweeping reading to the Constitution on this increasingly volatile issue. He knew also that the two cases now before the Court [*Roe v. Wade* and *Doe v. Bolton*] did not signal any sudden willingness on the part of the Court to grapple with the broad question of abortions. They had been taken only to determine whether to expand a series of recent rulings limiting the intervention of federal courts in state court proceedings. Could women and doctors who felt that state prosecutions for abortions violated their constitutional rights, go into federal courts to stop the state? And could they go directly into federal courts even before going through all possible appeals in the state court system? Douglas knew the Chief wanted to say no to both these jurisdiction questions. He knew the Chief hoped to use these two cases to reduce the number of federal court cases brought by activist attorneys. The two abortion cases were not to be argued primarily about abortion rights, but about jurisdiction. Douglas was doubly discouraged, believing that his side was also going to lose on the jurisdiction issue.[6]

Blackmun's scenario helps explain why the nine Justices (Black and Harlan were still on the Court) agreed to hear *Roe* and *Doe* in April 1971 and why they took two cases without any factual record addressing the difficult legal, historical, or medical questions involving abortion that the Justices would eventually face. Other abortion cases with such trial records had been, or would be, decided between 1970 and 1972. But deciding the procedural application of *Younger* to *Roe* and *Doe* in 1971 would not require an extensive factual record.

Blackmun's story is confirmed by the plaintiffs' briefs. For years, attorney Roy Lucas had pursued a court strategy to eliminate the abortion laws. In October 1970, Lucas and co-counsel Sarah Weddington filed their thirty-three-page appeal (called a "Jurisdictional Statement") in the Supreme Court in *Roe v. Wade*. It focused on the procedural questions, and did not forecast the extensive medical, historical, and sociological questions that would eventually be addressed. Joining Lucas and Weddington on the appeal was Professor Norman Dorsen (a good friend of Justice William Brennan),[7] who would argue the abortion rights side in January 1971 in a case involving the District of Columbia's abortion law, *United States v. Vuitch*.

Blackmun's recollection of the Justices "misapprehension" is also confirmed by the Justices' papers. One of the earliest memos in Blackmun's files on the abortion cases is a memo from a law clerk, dated January 5, 1971, a week before *United States v. Vuitch* was argued and six weeks before *Younger* was decided.[8] The memo focused on the procedural questions.[9] Later in 1971, just before the first arguments in *Roe* and *Doe*, another Blackmun clerk wrote a thirty-two-page "bench memo" to Blackmun on December 10, referring to the "procedural complexities of this case [*Roe*]."[10]

The procedural complexities were not something to be lightly dismissed. Indeed, they were asking some of the biggest questions about *Roe*: Should the Justices decide this issue? Should they decide it without any factual record? Or without review first by a federal appellate court? Could Jane Roe or Mary Doe clearly and accurately represent the facts of the abortion controversy? Could they represent the "class" of women seeking abortion? Should the Supreme Court sweep away an important area of criminal law and public health?

Roe started with all these procedural questions, until several Justices found a way to get around them. Justice Brennan suggested a way, after the first oral argument, in a December 30, 1971, memo to Justice Douglas:

> [T]here would seem to be a number of threshold issues that are of varying difficulty. Some, I think, must be expressly addressed, while others perhaps require no discussion or should be simply finessed. None, in my opinion, forecloses decision on the crucial questions here—the existence and nature of a right to an abortion.[11]

The procedural complexities meant that the lawyers and the Justices spent so much time on procedure during the first round of arguments in December 1971 that precious little time was left for the substantive, constitutional questions.

In the first argument in *Roe* on December 13, 1971, Justice Stewart posed the second question of the morning to Sarah Weddington, emphasizing that "a good many threshold questions . . . of jurisdiction" needed to be addressed.[12] According to Woodward and Armstrong's account, the jurisdictional issues didn't take a backseat to the question of a right to abortion until after the first oral argument, when the Justices met in conference* to vote on Thursday, December 16, 1971. *Mitchum v. Foster*,[13] a case with a "similar question of jurisdiction," was argued on the same Monday as the abortion cases, and the Justices discussed *Mitchum* before *Roe* and *Doe* that Thursday. The discussion of *Mitchum* among the seven Justices present at that conference (Justices Powell and Rehnquist did not join the Court until January 1972) ended with a vote of Stewart, Douglas, Brennan, and Marshall for "taking jurisdiction" in *Mitchum*. Woodward and Armstrong recorded what was apparently Douglas's conclusion that day:

> Since the jurisdiction question here was the same as in the abortion cases, the Court had effectively decided the abortion jurisdiction issue as well. The Court *did* have jurisdiction. Suddenly, unexpectedly, the Court found itself faced with the underlying constitutional issue in the abortion cases. Did women have a right to obtain abortions?[14]

If the Court had jurisdiction, and such federal challenges to state laws could be filed in federal court, the Justices should have limited the decisions in *Roe* and *Doe* to the jurisdictional issue, and looked for new abortion cases with a factual and medical record.

Though this oversight seems minor, it was a blunder that skewed the Justices' consideration of abortion for the next

---

*"Conference," as used at the Supreme Court, refers both to the meeting at which the Justices vote on cases and to the entire group of judges, as in "distribute to the Conference."

thirteen months. By brushing aside these procedural questions, and deciding the abortion issue with no factual record, the Justices stumbled into an enduring controversy.

The Marital Foundation of
Griswold v. Connecticut

The desire of a 4–3 bloc of Justices—Douglas, Brennan, Marshall, and Stewart—to sweep aside the procedural issues to create a right to abortion in December 1971 is better understood by three cases that preceded *Roe v. Wade*: *Griswold v. Connecticut*, *Eisenstadt v. Baird*, and *United States v. Vuitch*.

Before considering abortion, the Justices had faced the issue of contraception. They eliminated state restrictions on contraceptives in two major cases in 1965 and 1972, an action that provoked little public opposition in the midst of the sexual revolution. The ease with which they were able to eliminate those laws likely gave some of the Justices a sense that the abortion laws were simply another set of laws that could be eliminated as an "invasion of privacy." They saw contraception and abortion laws as one and the same intrusion on "privacy."

The Justices first seriously addressed the issue of contraception in 1961 in a case called *Poe v. Ullman*,[15] but in a very limited way. The Connecticut statute in *Poe* was unique, the only one of its kind in the country to *criminally prohibit* the *marital use* of contraception.[16]

Although a majority of the Justices dismissed the *Poe* case—Justice Brennan complained about "this skimpy record"[17]—two influential dissents by Justices William O. Douglas (a "liberal") and John Harlan (a "conservative") kept the issue alive. Both dissents emphasized marital privacy as the reason for striking the Connecticut law.[18] Harlan made clear in *Poe* that "[t]he right to privacy most manifestly is not an absolute. Thus, I would not suggest that adultery, homosexuality, fornication and incest are immune from criminal enquiry, however privately practiced. So much has been explicitly recognized in acknowledging the State's rightful concern for its people's moral welfare."[19]

The same Connecticut statute came back to the Court in 1965 in a similar test case, then called *Griswold v. Connecticut*.[20] The Justices struck down the Connecticut criminal prohibition on *the marital use of contraception* and announced, for the first time, a general constitutional right of privacy. *Griswold* quickly became the Supreme Court precedent that spurred the litigation campaign against state abortion statutes, led in large part by attorney Roy Lucas, who authored one of the first major law review articles attacking state abortion laws on constitutional grounds in 1968.[21]

> The Court's 1965 decision in *Griswold v. Connecticut* created, for the first time, a general constitutional right of privacy that emboldened judges to strike down state laws that inhibited individual autonomy.

Although the Court's opinion in *Griswold* contained broad language about privacy, the Justices in *Griswold* based their decision specifically and expressly on marital privacy and on the historical fact that marriage was deeply rooted in Anglo-American law and history.

In Justice Douglas's opinion for the Court in *Griswold*, he emphasized the words "*married persons*" in his statement of the facts.[22] Douglas used the term "married people," "married couples," "rights of husband and wife," "marital bedrooms," "marriage relationship," and "relationship" at least seven times and ended with a paragraph specifically on marriage:

> Marriage is a coming together for better or for worse, hopefully enduring and intimate to the degree of being sacred. It is an association that promotes a way of life, not causes; a harmony in living, not political faiths; a bilateral loyalty, not commercial or social projects. Yet it is an association for as noble a purpose as any involved in our prior decisions.[23]

Beyond the marital context, Douglas denied a broader basis for the decision:

> We do not sit as a super-legislature to determine the wisdom, need, and propriety of laws that touch economic problems, business affairs, or social conditions. This law, however, operates directly on an intimate relation of husband and wife and their physician's role in one aspect of that relation.[24]

Justice William Brennan also pushed marital privacy as the basis for the decision. In fact, *Griswold* turned into a marital privacy opinion because of Brennan. Though Douglas wrote the majority opinion, Brennan played a significant role behind the scenes, as his biographers, Seth Stern and Stephen Wermiel, make clear: "There was no better example of the silent hand of Brennan shaping an opinion dur-

ing this period than the case of *Griswold v. Connecticut. . . ."*[25]
As soon as Brennan got Douglas's first draft, he sent along
a three-page letter on April 24, 1965, drafted by his clerk,
suggesting a major shift from basing the decision on "the
right of association . . . in the First Amendment context" to
"the privacy of married couples."[26] Douglas "largely adopted
Brennan's approach."[27]

Justice Arthur Goldberg, writing his own opinion in
Griswold, also framed the issue at stake as "marital privacy."
Goldberg mentioned marriage, marital privacy, or privacy
in marriage at least twelve times.[28] Chief Justice Earl Warren
and Brennan joined Goldberg's opinion. Goldberg also emphasized an important limit to the Court's decision: that the
decision "in no way interferes with a State's proper regulation of sexual promiscuity or misconduct." This necessarily
limited their understanding of the scope of *Griswold*.[29]

The contrasts between marital privacy in *Griswold* and
abortion in *Roe* and *Doe* are striking. *Griswold* emphasized
marriage—a right and a relationship protected by the law
for centuries. American law never recognized a "right" to
abortion before some states legalized abortion between 1967
and 1970.[30] And marriage was never considered in American
law or tradition to include a right to abortion, any more than
marriage included a "right" to infanticide or adultery. *Griswold* was about the marital bedroom; abortions aren't done
in bedrooms.[31] The Connecticut statute prohibiting *marital
use* was one-of-a-kind; no other state prohibited the *marital use* of contraception. But in 1972, after virtually all fifty
states had seen legislative and public debate, thirty states retained their prohibitions on abortion except to save the life
of the mother, and the other twenty retained abortion laws

that did not allow abortion as broadly as the "right" eventually created in *Roe*. Many states had rejected "reform" laws, and nearly all had rejected "repeal" laws.

The attorney for *Griswold*, Yale Law School Professor Thomas Emerson, told the Justices at oral argument on March 29–30, 1965, that the right to privacy would not include abortion, because abortions were not done in the bedroom. In response to a question by Justice Black, Emerson told the Justices—repeatedly—that "the right to privacy" would not touch the state prohibitions on abortion:

JUSTICE BLACK: Would your argument concerning these things you've been talking about relating to privacy, invalidate all laws that punish people for bringing about abortions?

MR. EMERSON: No, I think it would not cover the abortion laws or the sterilization laws, Your Honor. Those—that conduct does not occur in the privacy of the home.

[. . . .]

JUSTICE BRENNAN: Well, apart from that, Mr. Emerson, I take it abortion involves killing a life in being [or "killing the life of a being"], doesn't it? Isn't that a rather different problem from conception?

MR. EMERSON: Oh, yes, of course.[32]

Nevertheless, Emerson was soon forecasting that the *Griswold* decision *could* be used against abortion laws. By the end of 1965, Emerson had even given a paper at a Michigan Law School symposium that described how *Griswold* could be used against abortion laws.[33]

The First Bridge from *Griswold*

If *Griswold* was expressly based on marriage, how could it be cited as a precedent for abortion? One attempt to build a bridge from *Griswold* to abortion that proved very influential was a law review article advocating legalized abortion published in the fall of 1969 by retired Supreme Court Justice Tom Clark.[34] Clark had been attorney general in the Truman Administration and then served on the Court from 1949 to 1967. He had joined Douglas's opinion in 1965 to strike down the Connecticut contraception law in *Griswold* before retiring in 1967.

Clark's article was cited by numerous lawyers and lower court judges.[35] It was quoted to the Justices by Professor Norman Dorsen in January 1971 during his oral argument against the District of Columbia's abortion law in *United States v. Vuitch*. It was quoted by Justice Douglas in his dissent in *Vuitch*,[36] and by Justice Brennan in his December 30, 1971, letter to Douglas outlining Brennan's view that the right of privacy included abortion. And Justice Douglas cited the article in his concurring opinion in *Doe v. Bolton*.[37]

The reasons for its influence, however, are somewhat baffling. Clark's article was brief and published in the second volume of *Loyola of Los Angeles Law Review*, an obscure journal. He claimed that "the demand for abortions has increased astronomically" without citing any statistics. He spent paragraphs on religious debates about "ensoulment," a topic irrelevant to American abortion law since colonial times. He cited the *New York Times* for many sociological assertions. And Clark gave no thought whatsoever to the possible risks to women from abortion. There was very little *law* in the article—just a few Supreme Court precedents and several citations to the *Griswold* case. Clark admitted that the Supreme Court "has not, however, dealt directly with the problem under discussion [abortion], nor do the decided cases cast much light on its solution."[38] Clark didn't discuss the extensive enforcement experience with American abortion statutes, or the case law across fifty states applying abortion statutes, and he only touched on the developing law of prenatal injury and wrongful death involving the unborn child.

Clark confused the common law of abortion (which never placed emphasis on viability) with tort law developments in the twentieth century (when some judges adopted viability as a marker). His claim that "[n]o prosecutor has ever returned a murder indictment charging the taking of the life of a fetus"[39] showed his utter misunderstanding of the criminal law and its practical application: injuries inflicted on a child *in utero* could be prosecuted as homicide as long as the child died outside rather than inside the womb. As a legal matter, that necessarily meant that the child injured inside the womb was the same child who died outside the womb— the same entity inside as outside. In fact, in March 1969 (just a few months before Clark's article was published), a prosecutor in the *Keeler* case indicted a California man for brutally beating his ex-wife and killing her unborn child *in utero*.[40] Such cases had been prosecuted in other states, and statutes that treated abortion as homicide existed in several states.[41]

Clark's article was long on rhetoric ("The law . . . began to emerge from its quagmire and rid itself of the archaic restraints on abortion.") but short on reasoning. The quality of his reasoning is captured in three passages.

First, he argued that "there is no proof of life [with a fetus] in the sense that the law contemplates proof of fact."[42] That would have surprised the English and American courts that applied two common-law evidentiary rules: the quickening rule (as first evidence of life) and the born-alive rule (for proof that a *criminal* act had *caused* the death). It also would have surprised the prosecutor in the *Keeler* case, who proved beyond a reasonable doubt that the perpetrator killed the child while unborn.

Second, Clark asked: "Does it therefore follow that voluntary destruction of the fetus is also [prevented] from interference by the State? Perhaps—unless life is present. . . ."[43] The entire motivation of the movement to eliminate the quickening rule across the states in the mid-nineteenth century—led by the medical profession—was the biological evidence that the life of each child began at conception, not quickening, and the state statutes were explicitly amended to adopt conception.[44]

Third, Clark's most famous sentence—quoted by Justice Brennan to Douglas in December 1971 and by Justice Blackmun in *Roe*—begged the evidentiary question that the nineteenth-century state legislatures expressly decided: "To say that life is present at conception is to give recognition to the potential, rather than the actual. . . . But the law deals in reality, not obscurity—the known rather than the unknown."[45] What Clark considered an abstraction in 1969 had been adopted as the law by the people of numerous states a century before and reiterated in numerous court decisions and statutes by 1969.[46]

All of this led up to Clark's ultimate point: Should abortion laws be reformed or repealed? Should the courts decide the issue? Or should it be left up to the legislatures? In the end—as his daughter-biographer emphasized in 2010—Clark concluded: "It is for the legislature to determine the proper balance. . . ."[47]

Clark's conclusion was conveniently ignored, however, by the lawyers and judges who used it to argue that *Griswold* should be extended to *judicially* create a right to abortion. For example, the federal court that struck down the Wisconsin abortion law in March 1970 cited—in historian David Garrow's words—Clark's "endorsement of applying *Griswold* to abortion."[48]

The only reason that Clark's confused article was noteworthy, apparently, is because he happened to sit on the Supreme Court at the time of *Griswold*. As Roy Lucas put it in a letter to Sarah Weddington after the first oral arguments in December 1971, admonishing her to reference Clark's article more often, "the Court is more likely to read that than any brief from mortals."[49] That Clark's article was used so frequently is evidence of the absence of any real judicial precedent for *Roe*.

The "Rhetorical Bridge" in *Eisenstadt v. Baird*

During the fifteen-week period (September 17, 1971–January 8, 1972) that the Harlan and Black seats were vacant, *Eisenstadt v. Baird*[50] was argued on November 17–18, 1971, a month before *Roe* and *Doe*. *Eisenstadt* dealt with a Massachusetts law that limited the sale (not use) of contraceptives to single (not married) people. After arguments, a majority of the seven Justices voted to invalidate the Massachusetts law.

Justice Douglas, as the senior Justice in the majority, assigned the opinion to Justice Brennan. Four weeks later, on December 13, 1971—the same day that the seven Justices first heard oral arguments in *Roe* and *Doe*—Brennan distributed a draft of his *Eisenstadt* opinion, into which he tucked this broad language:

> If the right of privacy means anything, it is the right of the *individual*, married or single, to be free from unwarranted governmental intrusion into matters so fundamentally affecting a person as the decision whether to bear or beget a child.[51]

There were three problems with this. First, *Eisenstadt* was a case based on the Equal Protection clause of the Fourteenth Amendment, not a privacy case, so Brennan's reference to privacy was "gratuitous dicta," in the words of Edward Lazarus, a former law clerk to Justice Blackmun.[52]

The second is the logical fallacy in the bare assertion "if the right of privacy means anything, it is. . . ."[53] This is a classic *ipse dixit* ("It is true because I say so."). It is simply an assertion of judicial will. Start with the bare assertion, and the sentence can be finished with anything, or at least anything that can be politically sustained.

While he was revising his opinion two weeks later, Brennan wrote a memo to Douglas on December 30, 1971, noting that his draft in *Eisenstadt* would be "useful" for the draft abortion opinion that Douglas was working on in *Roe* and *Doe*.[54] Brennan meant, specifically, that his *ipse dixit* would be useful.

As Lazarus has written, "Brennan knew well the tactic of 'burying bones'—secreting language in one opinion to be dug up and put to use in another down the road."[55] Lazarus continues:

Eisenstadt provided the ideal opportunity to build a rhetorical bridge between the right to use contraception and the abortion issue pending in *Roe*. And taking full advantage, Brennan slipped into *Eisenstadt* the tendentious statement explicitly linking privacy to the decision whether to have an abortion. As one clerk from that term recalled, "We all saw that sentence, and we smiled about it. Everyone understood what that sentence was doing." It was papering over holes in the doctrine.[56]

Brennan's biographers, Stern and Wermiel, put it even more bluntly:

> In the years to come, many of Brennan's colleagues learned to watch for the seemingly innocuous casual statement or footnote—seeds that would be exploited to their logical extreme in a later case.[57]

As another Brennan biographer has written, "Brennan found a way not only to connect the case to the abortion debate but to use it as another strong leg on which a future opinion legalizing abortions could stand."[58]

The third problem is that the *Eisenstadt* opinion was only supported 4–3 by Brennan and three other Justices.[59] Since White and Blackmun concurred separately, and Burger dissented, only three Justices joined Brennan's opinion: Douglas, Stewart, and Marshall. Justices Powell and Rehnquist, not present at the first oral argument, did not participate. The outcome—extending *Griswold*, which was expressly and repeatedly based on marital privacy, to single individuals—was carefully manufactured by a temporary majority of four Justices while the Court was shorthanded.

Nevertheless, Justice Brennan's intent was immediately fulfilled. The *New York Times* used the "bear or beget" phrase to headline an editorial on the Court's decision, and *Eisenstadt*'s gratuitous language that privacy includes "the decision whether to bear or beget a child" was used in an abortion case twenty-six days later. On April 18, 1972, a federal court in Connecticut struck down the Connecticut abortion law, citing the "bear or beget" passage from *Eisenstadt*.[60]

Sarah Weddington quoted Brennan's "bear or beget" passage to the Justices in the second *Roe* argument in October 1972, and Blackmun later quoted the passage in his *Roe* opinion as a "precedent" for what the Court did in *Roe*.

As recently as 2006, however, William Saletan, the liberal, pro–abortion-rights commentator for Slate.com (in reviewing Linda Greenhouse's biography of Justice Blackmun), called *Eisenstadt* a "sham":

> The justices designed the precedent to suit the progeny. Justice William Brennan's draft of *Eisenstadt*, which was circulated months [*sic*] after oral arguments in *Roe*, "was obviously crafted to apply in the abortion context," Greenhouse writes, noting that Brennan made the unnecessary assertion in *Eisenstadt* that the right to privacy entailed a right to choose whether to "bear" a child. Days after the court handed down *Eisenstadt*, Blackmun worked a reference to it into a draft of *Doe*, and later into *Roe*. Meanwhile, a federal court in Connecticut took the cue, declaring that *Eisenstadt* established a right to abortion. Justice Lewis Powell advised Blackmun to follow the Connecticut court's reasoning, and Blackmun ultimately did so, completing the daisy chain.[61]

The First Abortion Case

After the *Griswold* decision in 1965, numerous cases were filed in state and federal courts challenging state abortion laws. The Justices first directly addressed abortion when they reviewed Judge Gerhard Gesell's November 1969 decision to invalidate the District of Columbia's abortion law—a federal law enacted by Congress—in a challenge filed by Maryland abortionist Milan Vuitch. (Fifteen years later, Vuitch was put out of business by an abortion malpractice suit when he injured a woman so badly that she required a hysterectomy.[62])

Historian David Garrow records that Gesell's decision "significantly hastened the litigation plans that had gotten started in a number of states in the nine weeks since [the California Supreme Court's decision in *Belous* striking down the California abortion law in September 1969]."[63]

The *Vuitch* case was appealed to the Supreme Court and postponed by the Justices—including Black and Harlan—during 1970, argued in January 1971, and decided in April 1971. The District of Columbia (D.C.) law prohibited abortion except for "health" reasons that were broadly interpreted. At the oral argument in January, Chief Justice Burger questioned the lack of a factual record. The Court did not create a right to abortion in *Vuitch*, but upheld the D.C. law.[64] *Vuitch*'s lasting significance was that the Justices endorsed a broad, indeed unlimited, interpretation of "health of the mother" as a reason for abortion, which they subsequently adopted in *Doe v. Bolton*.

The day after *Vuitch* was decided, April 22, 1971, the Justices voted to hear *Roe* and *Doe* in the fall.

September 1971

There is a perception that the abortion decisions were inevitable. The available historical evidence, however, shows that a number of factors might have completely shifted the outcome of the decisions.

One of the decisive moments came in September 1971, about three months before the first oral arguments, when Justices Black and Harlan abruptly retired, within a week of each other, due to poor health. Black died a week later, and Harlan died at the end of December.

FIGURE 2. *The Supreme Court before September 1971. Seated, left to right: John Marshall Harlan II, Hugo Black, Warren E. Burger, William O. Douglas, William J. Brennan, Jr. Standing, left to right: Thurgood Marshall, Potter Stewart, Byron R. White, Harry A. Blackmun. Justices Black and Harlan retired before the remaining seven Justices decided to take up* Roe v. Wade *and* Doe v. Bolton. *Collection of the Supreme Court of the United States.*

If Black and Harlan had remained on the Court throughout the deliberations in the abortion cases, there are strong
reasons to believe they would have voted against creating a
constitutional right to abortion, and left the abortion issue to
the democratic process in the states.

Black not only dissented in *Griswold*, but he also expressly rejected a right to abortion during the Justices' discussion of the *Vuitch* case in early 1971. According to Professor Jeffrey Rosen, "Black, who scorned Douglas's whole
idea of penumbras and emanations, had made clear that he
opposed a constitutional right to abortion during discussions
[in *Vuitch*]."[65]

As for Harlan, he noted during the Justices' discussion of
Griswold in April 1965 that "he would feel differently if the
Connecticut law were not a '[marital] use' statute and did
not apply to married couples."[66] Harlan's opinion in *Griswold* pointed to limits on judicial discretion from "respect
for the teachings of history, solid recognition of the basic
values that underlie our society, and wise appreciation of the
great roles that the doctrines of federalism and separation of
powers have played in establishing and preserving American
freedoms."[67]

Harlan's biographer, Tinsley Yarbrough, contends that
Harlan never expressly revealed his views on the constitutionality of abortion laws during the deliberations over
Vuitch, and that "given his flexible approach to due process,
he might well have accepted at least limited restrictions on
governmental authority in that highly sensitive field."[68]

While he may have been flexible, Harlan likely would
have been skeptical of Brennan's *ipse dixit* in *Eisenstadt* and

his attempt to bury a privacy bone in his opinion.[69] Further-more, Harlan's dissents in a series of major Warren Court decisions between 1962 and 1966 suggest he would have been skeptical of the notion that the Court could fix the abortion issue. He likely would have rejected the sweeping scope of the *Roe* decision—creating a right to abortion up to viability and beyond—and of the *Doe* decision, which eliminated the regulations in the new "reform" laws enacted in thirteen states between 1967 and 1970.

Harlan and Black probably would have questioned the lack of an evidentiary record in both *Roe* and *Doe*, recognized that abortions are not done in the privacy of the home, and observed the clear differences between *Griswold* and *Roe*.[70]

That judgment is shared by others. A former Harlan clerk, Charles Fried, a distinguished professor of law at Harvard, concluded that it is "likely—but not certain—that Justice Harlan would have dissented in *Roe*."[71] Fried went further: "The argumentation of Harlan's dissent in [*Poe v. Ullman*] . . . as well as his refusal to condemn laws proscribing adultery, fornication, and homosexuality leave little doubt that he would have held with the dissenters in *Roe*."[72] In addition, Fried noted Harlan's "arduous dedication to analyzing the record in the case, a refusal to twist the historical truth to reach a desired result, a respect for adjacent institutions, and a vision of a judicial opinion as a ruling tailored to address the specific legal issues presented to the Court in a given case."[73] *Roe* would violate all of those principles.

The presence of Justices Black and Harlan at the first argument in December 1971 might have at least narrowed *Roe* to

5–4. Or it might have influenced Blackmun's vote and shifted the decision to 5–4 to uphold the Georgia statute and possibly the Texas statute. It is possible also that Harlan and Black might have influenced Chief Justice Burger's assignment of the opinion to one of them, rather than to Blackmun, who was heavily influenced by Douglas and Brennan.[74]

But history moved differently. On October 21, 1971, President Nixon announced the nominations of Lewis Powell and William Rehnquist to fill the Harlan and Black seats. There is apparently no evidence that the abortion issue had any influence on Nixon's selection of Burger, Blackmun, Powell, or Rehnquist.[75]

By 1970, in anticipation of possible vacancies, Roy Lucas —one of the chief architects of the federal court challenges against the state abortion laws and co-counsel with Sarah Weddington in the Supreme Court in *Roe*—feared that he had to get an abortion case up to the Court quickly, before any Nixon appointees could swing the Supreme Court more conservatively.[76] Historian David Garrow confirms that many believed that, with Black and Harlan gone, the Court could go 4–3 in favor of abortion (Marshall, Brennan, Stewart, Douglas), but that Powell and Rehnquist might join Burger, Blackmun and White to go 5–4 against abortion rights if the cases were argued after Powell and Rehnquist joined the Court.[77] Antiabortion attorneys advising the attorney for Texas also believed this was a possible scenario and urged Texas to seek an extension until the two Nixon nominees could join the Court.[78] This concern was shared by Brennan's clerks, who recorded a summary of the term in June 1972.[79]

A week before the first argument in the abortion cases in December 1971, it was clear that the two new Justices, Powell and Rehnquist, were going to join the Court imminently. Both were confirmed by the Senate just a few days before the first arguments—Powell on December 6, and Rehnquist on December 10. The attorneys for Texas filed a motion to have the arguments delayed until Powell and Rehnquist could take their seats.

Knowing that the Senate had already voted 89–1 to approve Powell, the Justices nevertheless voted on December 7 to *deny* Texas's motion to postpone oral argument until Powell and Rehnquist had been sworn in.[80] That is how only seven Justices sat for the first arguments in the abortion cases on December 13, 1971.

On December 16, 1971, the seven Justices met as a group ("in Conference") to vote in the cases. Bernard Schwartz, a historian of the Warren and Burger Courts, has said that Douglas and Brennan "led the proabortion bloc at the conference."[81] At least Burger, Douglas, and Brennan kept a tally, but the vote tally was unclear to Burger. Blackmun, for example, told the other Justices, referring to the Georgia statute, "Medically, this statute is perfectly workable," that it was "a fine statute" that "strikes a balance that is fair."[82] If Chief Justice Burger voted with the majority, he would assign the opinion. If Burger voted with the minority, the senior Justice in the majority—which, given the vote, would have been William Douglas—would assign the opinion, as he had in *Eisenstadt.*

A major disagreement arose within days over how the seven Justices had voted in the abortion cases.[83] Douglas immediately started to draft an opinion striking down the abortion laws. Burger, however, had already assigned the opinion to Justice Blackmun. One of Douglas's clerks gave him a memo suggesting that Burger had wrongly assigned the opinion to Blackmun.[84] Though Douglas protested in a letter to Burger, Blackmun kept the opinion assignment. Douglas sent his draft opinion to Brennan alone on December 22, 1971.

Douglas and Brennan conversed at length on December 29, 1971, and on the following day Brennan memorialized their conversation in an eleven-page letter to Douglas in which Brennan laid out his views on the right of privacy and his conviction that they could use the cases to decisively set forth "the existence and nature of a right to an abortion."[85] Brennan's biographers, Stern and Wermiel, highlight Brennan's strategy:

> Even more so than in other cases, Brennan worked quietly behind the scenes in *Roe v. Wade*, reluctant to push Blackmun too hard and perhaps a bit reluctant to come out front and center on the issue of abortion. In fact, he worked so quietly that for some time it remained difficult to determine exactly how influential a role he played.[86]

By the end of December 1971, Douglas and Brennan had drafted statements outlining a right to abortion. Knowing that Blackmun was a notoriously slow writer of opinions—Brennan wrote that "some time may pass before we hear from Harry"—they decided to bide their time until Blackmun distributed an opinion.[87]

The June Crisis

The Black and Harlan vacancies gave the four Justices who favored striking down the abortion laws—Brennan, Douglas, Marshall, and Stewart—a great incentive to decide *Roe* and *Doe* without the votes of Powell and Rehnquist.

The four thought that Burger was aiming to sabotage that on January 17, 1972, ten days after Justices Powell and Rehnquist were sworn in, when Burger circulated a memorandum to all the Justices asking them to indicate which cases already argued before seven Justices should be reargued before a full Court. Justice Blackmun replied immediately with a memo to Burger and the Conference on January 18 nominating *Roe* and *Doe* for reargument: "It seems to me that the importance of the issues is such that the cases merit full bench treatment."[88] Apparently no decision was made at that time, because the issue continued to simmer for four months.

The desire of the four to decide the abortion cases without Powell and Rehnquist eventually led to an uproar that "plunged the Court into internal crisis"—in author James Simon's words—behind the scenes in June 1972.[89]

Justice Blackmun distributed his draft opinion in *Roe* on May 18 and then his draft opinion in *Doe* on May 25. Blackmun's draft in *Roe* was relatively narrow, deciding only that the Texas law with its "life of the mother" exception was "unconstitutionally vague."

Stern and Wermiel recorded the dismay of some Justices with Blackmun's drafts:

Brennan did not share with Blackmun his thoughts about how best to approach the abortion cases, at least not di-

rectly. Going out of his way to avoid alienating the justice, he held back his criticism when Blackmun circulated what he considered two disappointing drafts in May
1972.[90]

Despite their doubts, Brennan, Marshall, Stewart, and
Douglas quickly joined the Blackmun opinion, in hopes that
the cases could be decided by the end of June 1972 (before
the summer recess). They also lobbied Blackmun to go further and reach "the core issue": declaring a constitutional
right to abortion.

Brennan sent Blackmun a strong memo on May 18 press-
ing him to decide "the core constitutional question" and
"dispose of both cases on the ground supported by the majority" *with no reargument*:

> My recollection of the voting on this and the Georgia case
> was that a majority of us felt that the Constitution required
> the invalidation of abortion statutes save to the extent they
> required that an abortion be performed by a licensed phy-
> sician within some time limit after conception. I think es-
> sentially this was the view shared by Bill [Douglas], Potter,
> Thurgood and me. My notes also indicate that you might
> support this view at least in the Texas case.[91]

Brennan's essential position in May 1972—"invalidation
of abortion statutes save to the extent they required that an
abortion be performed by a licensed physician within some
time limit after conception"—would, ironically, have resulted in a more limited right to abortion than eventually
transpired, as we will see in chapter 4.

Justice White distributed a brief dissent on Monday, May 29, that effectively demolished Justice Blackmun's May 18 draft opinion that the Texas statute was "unconstitutionally vague." White wrote:

> If a standard which refers to the "health" of the mother, a referent which necessarily entails the resolution of perplexing questions about the interrelationship of physical, emotional, and mental well-being, is not impermissibly vague [as the Court's *Vuitch* decision held], a statutory standard which focuses only on "saving the life" of the mother would appear to be *a fortiori* acceptable. The Court's observation that "whether a particular operation is necessary for a patient's physical or mental health is a judgment that physicians are obviously called upon to make routinely whenever surgery is considered," [*Vuitch*], 402 U.S., at 72 (footnote omitted), is particuarly [*sic*] applicable to medical decisions as to when the life of a mother is endangered, since the relevant factors in the latter situation are less numerous and are primarily physiological.[92]

White's dissent raised key questions that were not covered in the record, and were not explored in the December 1971 arguments—or in the October 1972 rearguments, for that matter.

According to law professor Bernard Schwartz, White's dissent "effectively demonstrated the weakness of the Blackmun vagueness approach in striking down the Texas law."[93] David Garrow called it an "incisive and influential three page dissent. . . . White's trenchant observation was a decisive if nonetheless eventually ironic contribution to the Court's consideration of *Roe* and *Doe*."[94] By this, Garrow meant that White's draft dissent, by effectively rebutting the vagueness rationale, pushed the Court's majority to go beyond vagueness and strike down the abortion laws under the broader ground of the Ninth or Fourteenth Amendments.

Two days after White's dissent was distributed, the crisis that had been simmering below the surface erupted. On May 31, Chief Justice Burger renewed his January motion for reargument with all nine Justices—it was only a motion, not an order—and Blackmun, having previously indicated more than once that he favored reargument, agreed.[95]

The four liberals were enraged; fearful that a 4–3 ruling might become 5–4 against abortion rights, they immediately circulated statements that they opposed reargument.[96] Brennan's willfulness in pushing 4–3 decisions while the Court was shorthanded is reflected in his handwritten note to Douglas at this time.

> I will be God-damned! At lunch today, Potter [Stewart] expressed his outrage at the high handed way things are going, particularly the assumption that a single Justice if CJ [Chief Justice] can order things his own way, and that he can hold up for nine anything he chooses, even if the rest of us are ready to bring down 4–3's for example. He also told me he . . . resents CJ's confidence that he has Powell and Rehnquist in his pocket. Potter wants to make an issue of these things—perhaps fur will fly this afternoon.[97]

On June 1, Powell distributed a memo to the Conference, supporting reargument because Blackmun, the author of the draft opinions, supported it. Powell also indicated that as of that time his views on a right to abortion were undecided.[98] Rehnquist, too, voted for reargument. White added his vote on June 5: "My view has been that these cases should be reargued, and I still think so."

But it was Douglas who pushed the issue to the hilt. On June 1, Douglas delivered a protest letter to Burger. The next day, Douglas sent Brennan the draft of a scorching dissent that he threatened to publish if the majority voted to rehear the abortion cases.[99] Brennan suggested he tone it down. According to James Simon, who interviewed Justice Blackmun in May 1991:

> Douglas refused to withdraw his dissent until Blackmun personally assured him that his position of declaring the abortion statutes unconstitutional was firm, and that he had no intention of reversing that position after reargument. Blackmun gave Douglas that assurance. . . . [A]s it turned out, Justice Douglas was the biggest winner of all. His prolonged tantrum had produced a firm commitment from Justice Blackmun to hold to his original position of voting to strike down the Texas and Georgia statutes.[100]

When the Court issued an order for reargument on June 26, Douglas was listed as the only dissenter to the decision to reargue but published no dissent.[101]

Sometime before the Fourth of July holiday, however,

Douglas's draft dissent got into the hands of the *Washington Post* and the *New York Times*. On July 4, 1972, the *Post* published a front-page story on the abortion cases, entitled "Move by Burger May Shift Court's Stand on Abortion," quoting extensively from Douglas's draft dissent.[102] The *New York Times* followed with a similar story the following day.[103]

Without identifying his source, David Garrow says that Potter Stewart was the source of the leak, because of Stewart's disdain for Burger.[104] Since Stewart was also a significant source for Bob Woodward when he wrote *The Brethren*, this seems plausible. Nevertheless, the crisis passed.

The Opinions Take Shape

The Court recessed for the summer, and some Justices left town before the *Times* and *Post* articles appeared. Justice Blackmun headed back to his Minnesota home and to the Mayo Clinic library, arriving around July 24. On that same day, in *Cheaney v. State*, the Indiana Supreme Court upheld the constitutionality of that state's abortion prohibition and suggested that the unborn child possessed constitutional rights.[105] The judge who wrote the opinion, Donald Hunter, later sent copies of his opinion to the Justices, but not until after the second oral argument in October 1972.[106]

Blackmun had been "resident counsel" of the Mayo Clinic during the 1950s. The day after he was assigned the *Roe* opinion, he wrote Thomas Keys, the Mayo Clinic librarian, and requested research on the history of abortion. Blackmun spent about two weeks there in July, reportedly doing research on the history of abortion and the Hippocratic oath.[107]

Back in Washington, Blackmun's law clerk had substantially revised the draft abortion opinion. He forecast this in an August 4 memo before he finished his clerkship. And then he explained the changes to Blackmun in a memo of August 11, 1972:

> I have written in, essentially, a limitation of the right depending on the time during pregnancy when the abortion is proposed to be performed. I have chosen the point of viability for this "turning point" (when state interests become compelling) for several reasons: (a) it seems to be the line of most significance to the medical professional, for various purposes; (b) it has considerable analytic basis in terms of the state interest as I have articulated it. The alternative, quickening, no longer seems to have much analytic or medical significance, only historical significance; (c) a number of state laws which have a "time cut-off" after which abortion must be more strongly justified by life or health interests use 24 weeks, which is about the "earliest time of viability."[108]

This was perhaps the first introduction of the notion of viability into the *Roe* deliberations, but Blackmun still emphasized the end of the first trimester in his draft opinions until December 1972.

The Expansion to Viability

Roe and *Doe* were reargued, back to back, on Wednesday, October 11, 1972, and the nine Justices met subsequently in conference to vote. Blackmun held to his original position and Powell, for the first time, voiced his support. Until the second argument, Blackmun had considered *Doe* to be more important than *Roe*, but when the Justices met to vote, Justice Powell urged that *Roe* be the lead case, and Blackmun agreed.

Justice Blackmun distributed a second draft opinion on November 21, 1972, which still emphasized the end of the first trimester as the "decisive" limit to the right to abortion:

> You will observe that I have concluded that the end of
> the first trimester is critical. This is arbitrary, but perhaps
> any other selected point, such as quickening or viability,
> is equally arbitrary.[109]

The Justices then began to negotiate over the scope of the abortion right that they were creating. Justices Powell and Marshall played pivotal roles in influencing Blackmun to extend the ostensible limit from the end of the first trimester to viability. (How and why this came about, and its implications, are explained in chapter 4.)

Blackmun adopted the expansion to viability, and in a memo to the Justices of December 15 indicated that he would be revising the draft opinions to shift the decisive point from the end of the first trimester to viability. On December 21, Blackmun circulated his revised third draft in *Roe*, the first to include the trimester framework and the first to identify the right as extending to viability.

At this point, the abortion cases were effectively decided.

The Chaser–*Roe* and *Doe* Together

Very little is ever said about the "companion" case to *Roe*, the case from Georgia, *Doe v. Bolton*. In most collections of the briefs or arguments regarding the abortion cases, the briefs and oral arguments from *Doe* are absent,[110] and the proceedings, unfortunately, have been comparatively ignored. The invaluable volumes on *Roe* by Roy Mersky, for example, do not contain Georgia's briefs or the oral arguments in *Doe*.[111] The book and audio set *May It Please the Court*, published in 1993, does not mention *Doe*. Even the transcripts of the oral arguments in *Doe* were not available at www.oyez.org, a website dedicated to Supreme Court cases, until 2012. The relative disregard of the *Doe* briefs, transcripts, and audio has been a mystery, because the *Doe* case had such a large impact.

The attorney for Georgia, Dorothy Beasley, was a skilled and experienced Supreme Court advocate, and she presented two oral arguments in the abortion cases in December 1971 and October 1972 that were much better than those presented by the two lawyers for Texas. Her arguments have been reputed to be the best.[112] This disregard for *Doe* has hindered public understanding of the significance of the abortion decisions.

Doe was important for several reasons. First, *Doe* invalidated one of the new "reform" laws, rather than a traditional state abortion prohibition like the Texas law. The Georgia law was patterned after a model law written by the American Law Institute (ALI), described by Charles Fried as "a group made up of the recognized leaders of the bench, bar and professoriate."[113] The ALI "model law" allowed abortion for broad reasons and was enacted in thirteen states between 1967 and 1970.

Second, *Doe* invalidated significant health regulations on abortion practice, without any factual record on the impact of or need for the regulations.

But most important, *Roe* states that the two decisions "are to be read together"[114] and *Doe* includes the "health" exception after viability. The Court in *Doe* defined "health" as "all factors—physical, emotional, psychological, familial, and the woman's age—relevant to the well-being of the patient."[115] It is the *Doe* "health" exception that resulted in the Justices legalizing abortion from conception to birth for any reason relating to "emotional well-being."

It was clear to the Justices that the practical effect of their decision would be to eliminate the laws of most states. In his May 25, 1972, memo to the Justices, Blackmun noted:

> I should observe that, according to the information contained in some of the briefs, knocking out the Texas statute in *Roe v. Wade* will invalidate the abortion laws in a *majority* of our States. Most states focus only on the preservation of the life of the mother.[116]

But Blackmun's memo also shows the failure to recognize the impact of *Doe* in eliminating all the other abortion laws. Blackmun clearly underestimated the extent that the decision would unsettle law and policy and public health. In a memo to the Justices on December 21, 1972, Blackmun commented: "*I suspect there will be other aspects of abortion that will have to be dealt with at a future time.*"[117]

Justice Brennan also acknowledged the scope of *Doe* in a memo to Justice Blackmun in December:

> [D]oes not your opinion in the Georgia case [*Doe v. Bolton*] cut the heart out of the Georgia statute? If so, should

we leave other portions of the statute intact, as I think you do? Is this a desirable result, particularly during the interval between our decision and the enactment of a new, constitutionally permissible statute by the Georgia legislature?[118]

Blackmun assumed that the states would be able to immediately respond to the decisions with amendments to their laws, and suggested to the Justices that the abortion decisions should be released "no later than the week of January 15 to tie in with the convening of most state legislatures."[119]

A week before the abortion decisions were released, Blackmun distributed a draft announcement with a number of political considerations that he proposed to read from the bench and distribute to the press:

> Fortunately, the decisions come down at a time when a majority of the legislatures of the states are in session. Presumably where these decisions cast doubt as to the constitutional validity of a state's abortion statute, the legislature of that state may immediately review its statute and amend it to bring it into line with the constitutional requirements we have endeavored to spell out today. *If this is done, there is no need whatsoever for any prolonged period of unregulated abortion practice.*[120]

But Blackmun failed to realize that the vagueness and complexity of the opinions, coupled with the powers of the federal courts to apply *Roe* and *Doe*, would create a public health vacuum that would continue for decades.

That same day, January 16, one of Justice Powell's clerks gave him a memo that noted the "lack of state authority to regulate in the first trimester."[121] Perhaps the Blackmun and Powell chambers had discussed this point. But it was too late; the die was cast.

· CHAPTER TWO ·

The Road to *Roe*

TAKING ABORTION INTO THE COURTS

It will be an unsettled period for a while.

— JUSTICE HARRY BLACKMUN,
WHILE WRITING *DOE V. BOLTON* (OCTOBER 1972)[1]

oe v. Wade was not inevitable. It could have gone the
R other way—the Justices could have left the abortion issue to state legislatures and local public health officials—if a
number of factors had turned out differently.

Still, broad social changes were certainly at work. Professor Joseph Dellapenna, the foremost historian of abortion
law in the Western world, has argued that, by 1960, such
changes shaped the demand for abortion before the cultural
upheaval of the 1960s. These included the impact of the Industrial Revolution on family life and work patterns, the
entrance of more women into the workforce, greater sexual
experimentation, and the desire to limit pregnancy, along
with technology that made abortion—in terms of immedi-

ate risks—more effective and safer for the woman. According to Dellapenna:

> The increasing safety of abortion for the woman at last began to create an opening to criticize the centuries-long traditional prohibition of abortion. . . . Changes in social behavior created a greater demand for abortion services at the very time that abortion was becoming a far less risky choice for a woman. The overall result of these changes was that the arguments against the existing abortion laws began, at first very slowly, to reach a wider audience and to be espoused by others than the professional abortionists. . . .[2]

But while these broad social changes *may* have increased pressure on state legislatures to legalize abortion in the 1960s, they did not make it inevitable that the Justices would legalize abortion themselves rather than leave abortion—like other public health issues—to the states.

What factors uniquely influenced the Justices? Numerous political, legislative, legal, and social currents gained force between the mid-1950s and 1971—when the Justices first voted to eliminate the abortion laws of all fifty states—and motivated legislatures in more than a dozen states, between 1967 and 1970, to legalize abortion in limited circumstances. And they gave momentum to a specific, coordinated court strategy, which had the sweeping aim of eliminating the abortion laws.

The cultural and political intensity of the 1960s—with the sexual revolution, the Vietnam War, and the assassinations of President and Senator Kennedy and Dr. King—

tends to obscure eight major factors—political, social, financial, and legal—that combined to influence some Justices to legalize abortion in January 1973.

The Campaign for Population Control

Agitation to introduce legislative exceptions into the traditional state prohibitions—prohibiting abortion except to save the life of the mother—began to stir in the mid-1950s. The initial push for repealing the abortion laws began as an incremental push for "reform," not by feminist leaders, but by doctors and lawyers affiliated with eugenic and population control organizations in Britain and the United States.[3] The international population control movement proved to be a significant support—in terms of funding, advocacy, and organizational support—for the abortion rights movement in the United States.[4]

Dellapenna marks the Carpentier Lectures by British criminologist Glanville Williams—a fellow of the Eugenics Society in Britain[5]—at Columbia University School of Law in 1956 as the "first real challenge in the United States to the centuries old tradition condemning abortion. . . ."[6] (Williams's lectures were published the following year under the title *The Sanctity of Life and the Criminal Law*.)

By the late 1950s, population control provided an impetus to challenge the abortion laws.[7] Population control groups like the National Committee for Maternal Health and Planned Parenthood provided an existing network of activists and funders.[8] By the late 1960s, claims about a "population crisis" had become an urgent and major theme of national politics. Former Kennedy Administration Defense Secretary Robert McNamara made it a key element in two speeches as president of the World Bank in 1968 and 1969, comparing its urgency to a nuclear holocaust (the "mushrooming cloud of the population explosion").[9]

On July 18, 1969, six months into his first term, President Richard Nixon delivered a "Special Message to the Congress on Problems of Population Growth," in which he named a Presidential Commission to study the issue. The Commission's chairman, John D. Rockefeller III, was a major advocate of abortion and population control, and the Commission's report, "Population Growth and the American Future"—released in March 1972 as Justice Blackmun was working on his draft opinions—was influential in advocating population control and abortion. It added the support of a presidential-appointed body of elites to the need for abortion to alleviate the "population crisis."

The theme of population control was pushed in the federal court cases leading up to *Roe* and was a constant theme in the briefs filed in those courts and in the Supreme Court. Population control heavily influenced federal Judge J. Edward Lumbard, who struck down the original Connecticut abortion law in April 1972.[10] Lumbard cited Paul Ehrlich's book, *The Population Bomb*, and repeatedly cited the report of the Rockefeller Commission released a month before. Lumbard wrote:

> The Malthusian specter, only a dim shadow in the past, has caused grave concern in recent years as the world's population has increased beyond all previous estimates. Unimpeachable studies have indicated the importance of slowing or halting population growth. . . . In short, pop-

ulation growth must be restricted, not enhanced and thus the state interest in pronatalist statutes such as these is limited.[11]

Concern about population directly influenced the Justices. On December 27, 1971, two weeks after the first argument in *Roe* and *Doe*, a psychiatrist from the Cleveland Clinic, Dr. Richard A. Schwartz, wrote a letter to Justice Brennan. Believing that the Court would decide the abortion cases before July 1972, Schwartz enclosed a copy of an article he wrote that was scheduled to be published in the August 1972 issue of the *American Journal of Public Health*, entitled "The Social Effects of Legal Abortion." The abstract read:

> The yearly number of unwanted children born in the United States is 800,000, or 20 percent of all births. Forty percent of all births in poor families are unwanted. Because of the limitations of contraception, the most feasible way of decreasing the incidence of unwanted births is legalization of abortion. If all unwanted births could be prevented, this would lower the birth-rate in the United States by more than 50 percent, substantially lower the incidence of poverty, and lead to a decrease in the number of inadequately reared children potentially destined to become criminals, psychotics, drug addicts, and alcoholics.[12]

Schwartz collaborated with Sarah Weddington's co-counsel, Roy Lucas, and Justice Douglas cited Schwartz in his dissent in *Vuitch*.[13]

Some of the Justices and lower court federal judges, like Lumbard, evidently felt they were leading a cultural wave, as reflected in judicial opinions in some of the abortion cases. One legacy of the Warren Court was the sense that, having been successful in leading civil rights reform in *Brown v. Board of Education*[14] in 1954, the Justices could fix other social problems, too.[15]

Justice Blackmun cited the population control theme in the third paragraph of his opinion in *Roe*: "population growth, pollution, poverty, and racial overtones tend to complicate and not to simplify the problem" of abortion.[16] He returned to it again at the end, implicitly, by referring to "the demands of the profound problems of the present day."[17]

The Marketing of the Pill

The marketing of the Pill in 1961 created an expectation that women should be able to control reproduction, though it was conceded by advocates that contraception use would increase, not decrease, the demand for abortion.[18] By the end of 1963, "[m]ore than 2 million American women were taking oral contraceptives."[19] And the Pill increased political pressure for abortion when nonmarital pregnancies increased.

Justice Tom Clark's influential law review article in 1969 directly connected the sexual revolution and abortion: "Our society is currently in the midst of a sexual revolution which has cast the problem of abortion into the forefront of religious, medical, and legal thought."[20] In 1969 the sexual revolution was mainstreamed, and the Justices gave it a big legal push. In April 1969, the Justices decided *Stanley v. Georgia*,[21] in which they declared Georgia's antipornography law unconstitutional and declared a "right" to possess pornography in the "privacy" of the home. The Court broadly stated that "the mere private possession of obscene matter cannot constitutionally be made a crime"[22] and that the State may not "prohibit mere possession of obscene matter on the ground that it may lead to antisocial conduct."[23] The sexual revolution spurred unwed pregnancy and the pressure for abortion as a backup to failed contraception. A constitutional right to contraception was pushed in the courts for a decade before it succeeded between 1965 and 1972. After the *Griswold* decision in 1965, the drive for a right to contraception then merged with a drive for a right to abortion.[24]

Funding

The eugenics and population control network provided substantial resources. Rockefeller began to fund abortion legalization efforts as early as 1966. In 1967 he stressed the importance of legalized abortion for population control efforts while encouraging his sister to get involved, telling her that "the matter of abortion is the principal remaining area in the population field which has not been given the attention it should."[25] He also encouraged her to fund Robert Hall's Association for the Study of Abortion (ASA). Rockefeller funded both the ASA and Roy Lucas's James Madison Institute, which filed many of the cases against state abortion laws.[26] The ASA sponsored a November 1968 conference on abortion in Hot Springs, Virginia, at which Rockefeller gave the keynote address endorsing the legalization of abortion.[27]

Wealthy benefactors besides Rockefeller also funded abortion rights efforts. Warren Buffett funded the briefs filed in the California Supreme Court in the *Belous* case.[28] Joseph Sunnen, a St. Louis vaginal foam manufacturer, funded a California abortion action organization and Roy Lucas's litigation campaign.[29] Stewart Mott funded Roy Lucas's strategy and the Clergy Consultation Service of New York City headed by Howard Moody, which referred women to abortion providers.[30] Richard Mellon Scaife, who still publishes the *Pittsburgh Tribune-Review*, reportedly funded the litigation efforts. Rockefeller's brother, Nelson, then the governor of New York, supported the legalization of abortion in the 1960s, signed the New York State legalization bill in 1970, and vetoed the bill to repeal legalization in 1971. The Rockefellers' father and grandfather had been members of the American Eugenics Society.[31]

Media Repetition of the Claims about Illegal Abortions and Maternal Deaths

Abortion advocates employed several overlapping themes in the public and legislative debate for legalizing abortion: that the existing laws were being flagrantly violated by millions of illegal abortions; 5,000–10,000 women were dying annually from back-alley abortions; that the original purpose of abortion laws had been to protect women (a need rendered obsolete by medical improvements), not the unborn child; that doctors' hands were tied by unduly restrictive laws; and that the Roman Catholic Church was the only obstacle to reform.

The claims of illegal abortions and maternal deaths drove the impression of ineffective and counterproductive laws. The likely source of the claim of 5,000 maternal deaths was a 1936 book by Frederick Taussig. He repudiated and apologized for his 1936 figures as being too high and inaccurate at a 1955 conference sponsored by the Planned Parenthood Federation of America (PPFA).[32] Abortion advocates continued to use those figures throughout the 1960s despite Taussig's repudiation and their implicit rejection by Dr. Mary

Calderone, the medical director of Planned Parenthood and the editor of the report from the 1955 conference.

In 1960, Calderone published a paper in the *American Journal of Public Health* that concluded:

> Abortion is no longer a dangerous procedure. This applies not just to therapeutic abortions as performed in hospitals but also to so-called illegal abortions as done by physicians. In 1957 there were only 260 deaths in the whole country attributed to abortions of any kind.[33]

Calderone's citation of 260 deaths relied on data from the National Center for Health Statistics (NCHS). Table 1 shows the NCHS data for abortion deaths and total maternal deaths for the thirty-one years stretching from 1942 to 1972;[34] Table 2 shows a detail of the 235 total abortion deaths for the single year of 1965 from the first table.[35]

Besides Mary Calderone's endorsement of the NCHS figures in her 1960 article, there are several factors that support their credibility:

- They are based on many years of repeated analysis.
- Their regularity—they showed a consistent trend of decreasing deaths.
- Unexplained maternal deaths would have been investigated by autopsy, which could uncover pregnancy and sepsis.
- They were endorsed by the American Public Health Association in 1965, which cited 193 deaths in 1965,[36] and by *Williams Obstetrics*, the leading obstetrical text of the day.

TABLE 1. **Total Abortion Deaths and Maternal Deaths
in the United States, 1942–1972**

Year	TOTAL ABORTION DEATHS			OTHER MATERNAL DEATHS			TOTAL MATERNAL DEATHS		
	White	Non-White	Total	White	Non-White	Total	White	Non-White	Total
1942	917	314	1,231	4,598	1,438	6,036	5,515	1,752	7,267
1943	853	312	1,165	4,610	1,422	6,032	5,463	1,734	7,197
1944	695	201	986	3,953	1,421	5,473	4,468	1,622	6,369
1945	602	286	888	3,520	1,260	4,780	4,122	1,546	5,668
1946	535	225	760	3,272	1,121	4,493	3,807	1,346	5,253
1947	385	200	585	3,170	1,223	4,393	3,555	1,423	4,978
1948	321	175	496	2,432	1,194	3,626	2,753	1,369	4,122
1949	236	158	394	1,863	959	2,822	2,099	1,117	3,216
1950	·193	123	316	1,680	964	2,644	1,873	1,087	2,960
1951	170	133	303	1,608	901	2,509	1,778	1,034	2,812
1952	196	124	320	1,428	862	2,290	1,624	986	2,610
1953	162	132	294	1,317	774	2,091	1,479	906	2,385
1954	156	131	287	1,124	694	1,818	1,280	825	2,105
1955	150	116	266	984	651	1,635	1,134	767	1,901
1956	138	83	221	880	601	1,481	1,081	684	1,702
1957	126	134	260	871	615	1,486	997	749	1,746
1958	136	123	259	802	520	1,322	938	643	1,581
1959	138	146	284	789	515	1,304	927	661	1,588
1960			289			1,290			1,579
1961			324			1,249			1,573
1962			305			1,160			1,465
1963			272			1,466			1,738
1964	117	130	247	634	462	1,096	751	592	1,343
1965	106	129	235	550	404	954	656	533	1,189
1966	96	93	189	509	351	860	605	444	1,049
1967	76	84	160	495	332	827	571	416	987
1968			133			726			859
1969			132			669			801
1970			128			675			803
1971			120			610			730
1972			140			640			780

Source: National Center for Health Statistics

TABLE 2. Known Deaths from All Abortions, by State, by Race (1965)

STATE	White	Non-White	Total
Alabama	2	3	5
Alaska	0	0	0
Arizona	1	1	2
Arkansas	0	2	2
California	25	14	39
Colorado	4	0	4
Connecticut	1	1	2
Delaware	0	0	0
District of Columbia	0	2	2
Florida	3	5	8
Georgia	0	6	6
Hawaii	0	0	0
Idaho	0	0	0
Illinois	1	7	8
Indiana	1	0	1
Iowa	1	1	2
Kansas	3	0	3
Kentucky	0	0	0
Louisiana	2	2	4
Maine	0	0	0
Maryland	4	3	7
Massachusetts	1	1	2
Michigan	8	7	15
Minnesota	3	0	3
Mississippi	0	2	2
Missouri	4	2	6
Montana	0	0	0
Nebraska	0	0	0
Nevada	0	0	0
New Hampshire	0	0	0
New Jersey	3	8	11
New Mexico	0	0	0
New York	23	26	49
North Carolina	1	6	7
North Dakota	0	0	0
Ohio	2	2	4
Oklahoma	0	1	1
Oregon	0	0	0
Pennsylvania	4	5	9
Rhode Island	0	0	0
South Carolina	0	4	4
South Dakota	0	0	0
Tennessee	0	3	3
Texas	5	9	14
Utah	0	0	0
Vermont	0	0	0
Virginia	0	4	4
Washington	2	1	3
West Virginia	2	0	2
Wisconsin	0	1	1
Wyoming	0	0	0
	--	--	--
Totals	106	129	235

Source: National Center for Health Statistics

As *Williams Obstetrics* pointed out, 5,000 maternal deaths from abortion annually—as activists commonly claimed in the 1960s—would be five times *the total for maternal deaths from all causes* in 1966 (1,049):

> It is a common fallacy, particularly in lay publications, to exaggerate the number of maternal deaths attributable to abortion each year. For example, [Harriett] Pilpel and Norwick state that "illegal (out-of-hospital) abortions account for as many as 8,000 maternal deaths each year." Although the exact number is unknown, in 1967 there was a total of only 50,683 deaths of women, aged 15 to 44, and only 987 maternal deaths. The often quoted high figure is therefore obviously impossible. The National Center for Health Statistics records 160 abortion deaths in 1967.[37]

Even Christopher Tietze, the statistician for the Population Council, called the claim of 10,000 deaths "unmitigated nonsense."[38] Though Tietze offered an alternative figure for annual abortion deaths of "500–1000," that would still equal the annual number of *all* maternal deaths after 1966, and he had no explanation for his alternative figure.[39]

Robert Hall, the president of the Rockefeller-funded ASA, also repudiated the 5,000 figure in 1967. He disagreed with what he called the "perpetuation of Taussig's thirty-year-old claim that five thousand to ten thousand American women die every year as the result of criminal abortion."[40] Hall elaborated:

> Whether this statistic was valid in 1936 I do not know, but it certainly is not now. There are in fact fewer than

fifteen hundred total pregnancy deaths in this country per annum; very few others could go undetected and of these fifteen hundred probably no more than a third are the result of abortion. Even the "unskilled" abortionist is evidently more skillful and/or more careful these days. Although criminal abortion is of course to be decried, the demand for its abolition cannot reasonably be based upon thirty-year-old mortality statistics.[41]

Despite its repudiation by prominent abortion advocates, the figure of 5,000 women's deaths per year began to be commonly cited by magazines and newspapers, starting with *Newsweek* in 1961, followed by the *Christian Century*, *Time*, and many others.[42] The advocates had, early on, secured the sanction of major media institutions. Roy Lucas thought it so effective that he used the 10,000 deaths figure in the first sentence of his 1968 law review article, one of the first to advocate a constitutional right to abortion.[43]

By 1965, there was a steady stream of magazine and TV coverage critical of abortion laws and favorable toward first "reform" and then "repeal." On April 5, 1965, *CBS Reports* broadcast a documentary on "Abortion and the Law," hosted by Walter Cronkite, which proved influential in making an evocative case for abortion legalization.[44] Cronkite gravely intoned that 5,000 women died annually because of illegal abortions, without any attribution or authority. CBS interviewed alleged abortionists and many advocates for abortion repeal, without any confirmation of their claims. The program framed the Roman Catholic Church as the only opponent of "reform," and the only argument against abortion as an "ethical or religious" one. It repeated all of the advocates' statistics against abortion laws. The CBS documentary was a powerful advertisement for the repeal of abortion laws.

Despite no statistical support for the figure of "1 million illegal abortions and 5,000 deaths," these numbers were repeated so many times that, by 1964, advocates started to refer to the mantra as "general estimates" or "common estimates." Thus, in the *American Bar Association Journal* in 1964, advocates wrote that it is "generally estimated that approximately 1 million or more illegal abortions occur; with 5,000–10,000 deaths as a direct consequence."[45]

This is what Roy Lucas and Sarah Weddington told the Justices in the first papers they filed in the Supreme Court in 1970: "Secret induced abortions are inherently incapable of quantification. Nonetheless, one can be certain that the number is very high. For estimates see Fisher, Calderone, Gebhard [Kinsey], Taussig (1936), Regine (1935) . . ."[46] They repeated the same paragraph verbatim in their brief in the Supreme Court in 1971.[47] All of these "sources" had been discredited fifteen years earlier at the 1955 PPFA conference.

The American Law Institute Model Abortion Law

The abortion rights movement of the 1950s and 1960s made a conscious effort to recruit cultural elites and "experts," including doctors, lawyers, and academics. As early as 1954, Dr. Alan Guttmacher was publishing criticisms of the abortion laws.[48] Between 1959, when the American Law Institute (ALI) wrote a model law, and 1972, when the Rockefeller Commission's report on "Population Growth and the American Future" endorsed the legalization of abortion, the use of doctors and lawyers spurred the abortion rights movement.

Besides Glanville Williams's speech at Columbia Law School in 1956, one of the earliest and most influential examples of elite support is that of the American Law Institute, which wrote a "model" law in May 1959 to legalize abortion in certain circumstances. Even antiabortion legal scholars acknowledged the ALI model as "the first major stimulus toward significant liberalization."[49] After it was published in 1962, it became the model for the thirteen states that passed "reform" bills between 1967 and 1970. These created the impression of widening public support, even when public opinion was mixed.

"Reform" first hit California. Lawyers and activists began to call for "relaxation" of the abortion laws. Legal articles challenging the laws were published in the prestigious *Stanford Law Review* in February 1959, in the *Los Angeles Bar Journal* in October 1959, and in the *Southern California Law Review* in 1962. "Reform" legislation, or "therapeutic reform" legislation, was first introduced in California in April 1961, although the first legislative hearings were not held until May 1963.

Legislative efforts started in a few other states in 1964 and 1965. Drives to "reform" abortion laws by adding exceptions to the traditional statutory prohibition (except to save the life of the mother) eventually reached all fifty states by 1971 or 1972. Virtually every state saw legislative debates before *Roe.*

Mississippi added a rape exception in 1966, but 1967 was the breakthrough year for abortion law reformers. Three states passed "reform" bills. Colorado was the first in the nation, then North Carolina and California.[50]

Historian David Garrow observed how the three 1967

successes were more accidental than the result of public
support:

> [P]olitically the North Carolina victory, like the one in
> Colorado, owed its success to two difficult-to-replicate
> factors. First, proponents in both states had benefitted
> tremendously from very adept and perceptive principal
> [legislative] sponsors. . . . Second, and far more impor-
> tantly, the legislative reform drives in both states had
> emerged from seemingly nowhere with remarkable sud-
> denness and had each been able to prepare and introduce
> a bill before any public attention or threat of controversy
> was drawn to their efforts. . . . [I]t was undeniable that in
> both of abortion reform's first two legislative triumphs,
> swiftness and a large element of surprise had been major
> and probably decisive advantages.[51]

Garrow's observation applied to California as well, where
a legislative hearing was held late into the evening on April
27, 1967, and the opponents of the legalization bill were delayed testifying until 11 p.m. Even then, the bill "was sent
to the senate floor by a razor-thin vote of 7 to 6" "sometime
after two a.m."[52]

Public opinion was in flux during the 1960s, buffeted by
personal stories and incidents, but still tepid at the time of
the abortion decisions. In July 1962, the first significant public controversy over abortion erupted in the media. Sherri
Finkbine was the young hostess of the kids' TV program
Romper Room. Living at the time in Phoenix, she discovered
she was pregnant, but feared the impact of headache pills that
she had taken after her husband brought them back from a

trip to England. Her doctor confirmed that they contained thalidomide, a known cause of birth defects, and she began to seek an abortion. In 1962, nearly all fifty states prohibited abortion except to save the life of the mother. When she could not obtain one in Arizona, she flew to Sweden for an abortion. The media covered her ordeal daily. Her dilemma thrust the issue of "thalidomide babies" and abortion into headlines across the country, including the cover of *Life* magazine on August 10, 1962. Finkbine's dilemma was one of the first publicized stories of the 1960s that caused Americans to think seriously about abortion and abortion laws.[53]

But after Sherri Finkbine's dilemma—thought to be one of the most sympathetic cases—public opinion was still mixed, and women were not heavily in favor of Finkbine's abortion. A September 1962 Gallup Poll found that fewer women than men supported Finkbine. Among women, 50 percent said Finkbine had done the right thing and 33 percent said she had done the wrong thing.[54]

The "rubella scare" of 1965 also affected public opinion and gave more momentum to the drive for "reform." Still, abortion for fetal deformity, on which the public was mixed, was allowed by the thirteen "reform" bills, but was much narrower than the expansive decree in *Roe*.

Public opinion continued to be divided, depending on how the questions were asked. A Field Poll of July 1966 showed that 65 percent of Californians backed "therapeutic liberalization"—whatever that meant.[55]

One very general question, used as a repeated tactic of advocates of legalization, was whether abortion "should be between a woman and her physician."[56] A Gallup Poll in August 1971, four months before the first arguments in *Roe* and *Doe*, found that 64 percent agreed that "the decision to have an abortion should be made solely by a woman and her physician."[57] Perhaps because its wording was vague and equivocal, that proposition garnered majority support in August 1972.[58]

The irony today is that abortion is almost never "between a woman and *her* physician." Fewer than 5 percent of abortions are performed by a woman's regular obstetrician-gynecologist. Almost all are performed by a stranger, whom the woman does not meet until she is gowned and in stirrups. Her regular physician often does not know, and the abortion is not recorded in her medical history, which is important for a woman's long-term health and for public health monitoring.

When specific and practical questions were asked, support for abortion for socioeconomic reasons dropped below 50 percent. A December 1965 National Opinion Research Center poll asked six key reasons for legalizing abortion,[59] and found the following response, as reported by Gallup in January 1966:

"Health seriously endangered":
    71% yes, 26% no
"Rape":
    56% yes, 38% no
"Strong chance of serious defect in baby":
    55% yes, 41% no
"Family has a very low income and
    cannot afford any more children":
    21% yes, 77% no

"Not married and does not want to marry the man":
18% yes, 80% no

"Married and does not want any more children":
15% yes, 83% no

To the media, however, the ASA pushed the 71 percent figure "as showing what a heavy majority backed legal reform."[60]

Compare the polling analysis by Judith Blake, chair of the Department of Demography at the University of California, Berkeley, that was published in the February 12, 1971, issue of *Science*. Blake strongly and openly opposed what she called "pronatalist" policies and was trying to figure out how the abortion laws could be changed in the face of public reluctance. She looked at five Gallup Polls and the National Fertility Study conducted between 1962 and 1969.[61]

Blake grouped the questions into "four reasons for abortion": "mother's health," "child deformed," "money," "no more children." The last two she called "economic and discretionary reasons." Blake—looking at the percentage of those who *disapproved* of abortion in various circumstances—found that:

> As compared with 13 percent for the mother's health, and 25 percent for child deformity, disapproval for economic reasons characterizes about two-thirds of all respondents. Disapproval has declined somewhat during the decade, but it is clear that Americans generally are preponderantly negative toward economically practical reasons for abortion. It is hardly surprising, therefore, that the idea of

purely elective abortion ("where the parents have all the children they want") should elicit disapproval at the end of the decade, from about 80 percent of the white population. . . . *It is worth noting that women are generally more disapproving for all four reasons than men are.*[62]

Howard Moody, the founder of the Clergy Consultation Service in New York City, admitted in 1973 that "our day-to-day work taught us how few women wanted abortions for the reasons most liberals conceded were justifiable."[63]

The first—and only—state legal change by public referendum before *Roe* came in the November 1970 elections, when the voters of Washington State approved a state abortion initiative. But the initiative had a sixteen-week limit and a residency requirement, both of which would be rejected as unconstitutional by the Justices in *Roe* and *Doe*.

If polls and legislative votes are any evidence, the American people and legislatures were not buying *repeal*. In the decade leading up to the abortion decisions, there was never majority support for "abortion on demand"—a term first coined by abortion activists—after the first trimester. In January 1973, the month of the Court's decision, a Gallup Poll showed "when Americans were asked whether an abortion decision during the first three months of pregnancy should simply be left to a woman and her doctor, 46 percent of respondents said 'yes' and 45 percent 'no.' "[64]

After the legislative changes in the four years between 1967 and 1970, no state changed its law by legislation in 1971 or 1972. "At the time *Roe* was decided, thirty States allowed abortion only to save the life of the mother, two states and the District of Columbia allowed abortion to save the life or preserve the health of the mother; one State allowed abortion to save the mother's life or to terminate a pregnancy resulting from rape; thirteen States had adopted [the Model Penal Code] or some variant thereof, allowing abortion under specified circumstances; and four States allowed abortion on demand [Alaska, Hawaii, New York, and Washington], but set limits in terms of the age of the fetus. No State allowed unrestricted abortion throughout pregnancy, as *Roe* effectively does."[65] Washington, for example, had a sixteen-week limit and a residency requirement. Alaska and Hawaii allowed abortion up to viability. New York's was one of the most expansive, legalizing abortion up to twenty-four weeks.

The media played a significant role in pushing abortion on demand beyond the reasons for which most Americans would have allowed abortion. The state legislative debate and the status of the states in 1972 more accurately reflected public opinion than the sweeping decision that the Court issued in January 1973. The decision of the Justices abruptly ended a public debate over abortion laws that had been growing since 1965.

Judicial Endorsement of Abortion "Rights"

After the passage of the first three "reform laws" in Colorado, North Carolina, and California in 1967, a remarkable thing happened. With barely months of experience with these laws, activists decided that the reform laws were not allowing enough abortions and concluded that complete repeal was necessary. Advocates went into the courts because they couldn't get "repeal" laws passed in state legislatures or because the new laws that had passed were not as sweeping as they wanted.

Activists in California had come to that conclusion even

in 1966, and, according to David Garrow, "realized far better than casual observers how very modest an achievement the Beilenson bill [an ALI model bill] would be even if passed into law. . . ."[66] And they were frustrated that even "reform" legislation had failed. Garrow further detailed the activists' worries:

> [National Association for the Repeal of Abortion Laws] executive director Lee Gidding had remarked to Colorado's Dick Lamm . . . that 1971 so far had witnessed only "an impressive series of losses throughout the country" and she added that "those of us on the inside know what a beating the opposition dealt us this year" in state after state. A *New York Times* story reviewing the results of state legislative sessions highlighted how not a single new abortion statute had been approved in 1971, and what a particularly stark contrast that was from the dramatic events of 1970.[67]

There is reason to think that the abortion rights movement was slowing after a four-year run from 1967 to 1970, when they had made the biggest gains in the legislatures. As David Garrow summarized the situation in early 1971, "In virtually every state where a repeal bill had been introduced in the legislature . . . prospects for passage appeared to range from bleak to nonexistent."[68] Repeal bills (in contrast to "reform bills") were voted down in Montana, New Mexico, Iowa, Minnesota, Maryland, Colorado, Massachusetts, Georgia, and Connecticut,[69] and the New York abortion legalization law that went into effect on July 1, 1970, was itself repealed by the New York Senate and by the Assembly, though that repeal was then vetoed by Governor Nelson Rockefeller.

Separate planning for a litigation campaign by the ASA had begun back in July 1968, the month that Roy Lucas published a law review article outlining a litigation strategy against abortion laws.[70] The ASA convened a meeting with Lucas and members of its staff and board to discuss a potential test case. Lucas had prepared a model brief for the ASA based on his article, and they were anticipating the publication of Cyril Means's 1968 article on abortion law. They discussed attacking the statutes on grounds of "vagueness, invasion of privacy of both patient and physician, substantive due process, denial of equal protection, freedom of association, and denial of physician's right to practice medicine according to good professional standards."[71]

If 1967 had been the breakthrough year for legislation, 1970 was the year of the court challenge. Challenges to state laws were filed in many federal courts in 1970. *Roe v. Wade* and *Doe v. Bolton* were two of some twenty cases attempting to strike down state abortion laws filed in federal courts in various states between 1969 and 1972. A woman, "Jane Roe," in 1970 sued Henry Wade, the district attorney of Dallas, Texas, to invalidate the Texas abortion law, which prohibited abortion except to save the life of the mother. In the same year, another woman, "Mary Doe," sued Arthur K. Bolton, the attorney general of Georgia, to invalidate the Georgia abortion law, one of the new and broader laws adopted in 1968, which prohibited abortion except in cases of fetal deformity, rape (including incest), or danger to the woman's life or health.

The first major pro–abortion-rights court decision came

on Friday, September 5, 1969, with the California Supreme Court's narrow 4–3 decision in *People v. Belous*.[72] One Justice, Stanley Mosk, had excused himself from the case. According to David Garrow, the state's Chief Justice, Roger Traynor, "placed the case on his court's Sacramento docket, thus assuring that senior Sacramento-area appellate judge Fred R. Pierce, rather than another jurist, would take Mosk's place and become the seventh member of the *Belous* court."[73] Pierce became the necessary fourth vote to declare the original California abortion law unconstitutional. The impact of the decision was large, despite the narrowness of the vote. Several other courts would cite *Belous* as influential between 1970 and 1973.

Two months after the *Belous* decision, federal judge Gerhard Gesell struck down the District of Columbia abortion law as unconstitutionally vague in *United States v. Vuitch*, which was immediately appealed directly to the Supreme Court. The first *federal* court invalidation of a *state* law came in March 1970 in Wisconsin in *Babbitz v. McCann*.[74] In the next two years, there would be several other decisions, going both ways.

Justice Blackmun's tally in his opinion in *Roe* was six federal decisions to strike state abortion statutes[75] and five to sustain,[76] plus two state court decisions to strike state laws,[77] and three state courts to uphold them.[78] The actual tally was: seven federal court decisions struck down state laws, five federal decisions upheld state laws; five state court decisions struck down state abortion laws, sixteen state courts upheld state laws.[79] A number of other abortion cases in federal court had been thrown out on procedural grounds.[80]

Among the nine courts (seven federal, five state) that held state statutes "unconstitutional," however, there was little consensus in their explanation for why abortion laws were unconstitutional or in their definition of the scope of the abortion right.[81] About the only common theme among the courts was *Griswold*: the courts cited each other for the notion that *Griswold*'s broad phrases meant that abortion laws were unconstitutional. The legal advocates put all their hopes on the Supreme Court's decision in *Griswold*.

The American Medical Association's Endorsement

Dellapenna has documented the strength of public and medical support for abortion laws that existed until the mid-1950s.[82] During the 1950s, a number of "dissident" doctors complained about the restraints of the abortion laws, which in all but a few states prohibited abortion except to save the life of the mother. But Dellapenna found that the concern was "expressed in two contrary directions"—on the one hand, by the creation of "hospital abortion committees" to take the decision (discretion or responsibility) out of the hands of individual doctors, and, on the other hand, through conferences and books in which the doctors "began to question the legitimacy of existing abortion practices and laws."[83]

These early medical proponents could not claim that there was a growing need for so-called therapeutic abortions—those intended to save the life of the mother. It was widely admitted that the reasons for therapeutic abortions were disappearing with medical advances that could better treat rare maternal conditions. And they could not claim that maternal deaths from abortion were increasing when they had, in fact, been declining dramatically since the 1940s due to antibiotics.

The medical reasons for therapeutic abortions—those necessary to save the mother's life—were substantially reduced by the 1950s. Truly therapeutic abortions became rare, and abortion advocates, including leaders like Dr. Alan

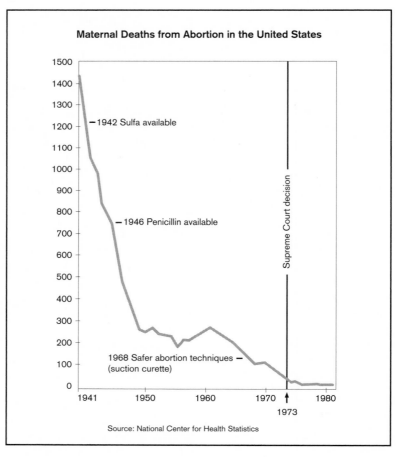

FIGURE 3.

Guttmacher, recognized that.[84] The main reason for doctors' discontent was that they simply did not want to be constrained by the law. They wanted to perform abortions for eugenic, psychiatric, and social reasons.

In 1959, Guttmacher, a leading medical proponent of abortion "reform" who served as vice president of the American Eugenics Society,[85] published *Babies by Chance or by Choice*, in which he wrote: "I am strongly opposed to modifying the law to permit abortion on demand. There must be important medical or sociological necessity. . . ."[86] Until very late in the 1960s, Guttmacher was careful to advocate only "reform," not "repeal."

In a 1967 public policy statement, the American Medical Association (AMA) began to give the first tentative nod to endorsing legalized abortion.[87] But it was not until the AMA's summer meeting in July 1970 that the Association fully adopted legalization in a revised policy statement.[88] Linda Greenhouse reported that "Blackmun had both documents, in manuscript form, in his file when he was working on his opinion in *Roe v. Wade*, with check marks indicating that he read them closely."[89]

While some doctors moved to "reform" abortion laws, there was a technological revolution ongoing in fetal medicine. The *Life* magazine cover of April 30, 1965, featured a famous picture of an unborn child. The September 10, 1965, cover of *Life*, with a picture of the use of ultrasound on a pregnant woman, referred to an "image of baby's head in womb . . . projected onto screen by ultrasonic waves." Some of the earliest medical journal papers on the use of ultrasound for fetal diagnosis were published in 1970 by William Garrett on "prenatal diagnosis of fetal polycystic kidney by ultrasound." But in 1971 and 1972, the dominance of the sexual revolution and population control heavily favored abortion "reform" of some kind, and ultrasound technology did not arrive on the market until three years after *Roe*.[90]

The Powerful Myth of a Long-Dormant "Abortion Right"

That abortion was a common and widely accepted practice throughout history was a constant claim in the 1960s—in the media, the legislatures, and the courts. Ironically, one of the most widely cited articles in support of abortion legalization in the late 1960s shows the lack of evidence for this claim and the contradictory ways in which the claim was used. The article "Abortion" by Christopher Tietze and Sarah Lewit was published in *Scientific American* in January 1969.[91] Tietze was claimed by Mary Doe's attorney Margie Pitts Hames during oral arguments in the Supreme Court to be "the" world expert on abortion statistics.[92]

When Tietze and Lewit wanted to promote the popular acceptance of abortion, they claimed:

> The practice of abortion goes back to human traditions far older than the earliest written history. . . . That induced abortion was probably common among prehistoric peoples is suggested by anthropological studies of primitive tribes still living in isolated parts of the world today. . . . The methods employed by women in primitive societies to terminate unwanted pregnancy vary from hard physical exertion to the application of heat or skin irritants to various parts of the body or the insertion of a variety of instruments into the uterus.[93]

But, on the next page, when Tietze and Lewit wanted to promote the safety of abortion if done by "a competent physician," they wrote: "The methods employed by lay abortionists are generally either ineffective or potentially dangerous to the pregnant woman. Over the centuries many kinds of internal medications have been tried, ranging from the bush tea of preliterate tribes to white phosphorus to hormones; *almost invariably these treatments fail to induce abortion.*"[94]

As Tietze and Lewit revealed, abortion was *not* a common practice, contrary to widespread myths about "folk medicines" that could induce abortion. In fact, abortion was rare "until well into the nineteenth century."[95] This was because all abortion techniques were either ineffective or deadly for the mother—or both. According to Dellapenna, "[A]bortion techniques were so crude before 1800 as virtually to amount to suicide."[96]

Consequently, infanticide, not abortion, was the technique of choice for killing an unwanted infant, which explains why infanticide prosecutions were so much more frequent. As British historian Mary Kenny has written, "The traditional forms of abortion had been infanticide and abandonment."[97]

Why then were "folk medicines" for abortion so widely rumored for so many centuries, if in fact they were ineffective? *Lack of medical knowledge.* Since medicine was so primitive, and the determination of pregnancy was so uncertain, any "remedy" that might be taken could be thought to be connected to the disappearance of virtually any "sign" of pregnancy—at least before quickening (the first feeling by the mother of fetal movement).

The scope and effectiveness of abortion law—like homicide law—was always tied to the current medical understanding. The law could not protect what it did not know existed, so the enforceability of abortion law was always tied to evidence of pregnancy. Until the twentieth century, quickening—which does not typically occur until sixteen to eighteen weeks of pregnancy—was the most reliable evidence. The American colonies adopted the English common law, which prohibited abortion after quickening.[98]

Prosecutions under the English common law go back at least to A.D. 1200. Dellapenna shows that Anglo-American law has always treated abortion as a serious crime and that the reason for the law was to "protect the life of the unborn child."[99] At least by the end of the sixteenth century, abortion was treated as a capital felony under English common law.[100] But the evidentiary hurdles to confirming a pregnancy soon proved formidable, and by 1600 abortion was not treated as a homicide unless the child was born alive and then died. The fact that abortion was not a "felony" at the time of Blackstone's *Commentaries* in 1765—as Justice Blackmun inquired during oral argument[101]—was because of evidentiary hurdles and the leniency of punishment in a context of such uncertainty, not because of any moral doubt about the status of the unborn child.

In the nineteenth century, the American states updated the English common law by passing specific statutes to eliminate the quickening distinction, prompted by developments in medical science that produced a new understanding of fetal development. The AMA strongly endorsed these legal changes in the 1860s.[102] By the 1860s, many states had prohibited abortion after conception except to save the life of the mother, which was called "therapeutic abortion." The uniform practice of virtually all states for the century preceding *Roe* was to target the abortionist and to treat the woman as the second victim of abortion (see chapter 3).

Many lawyers and judges in the 1960s who considered abortion law overlooked the medical context and these evidentiary distinctions. As a result, some concluded that abortion before quickening, if not prohibited, must have been a "right." However, no evidence of such legal or social acceptance exists at any point of Anglo-American legal history. Instead, the distinction only meant that law enforcement depended on the evidence of "quickening"—the best evidence available—to prove that the child was alive.

The advocates offered the Justices a new rationale for the traditional abortion prohibitions: they were intended to protect maternal health, not the life of the unborn child. Abortion advocates cited Cyril Means, the general counsel for the National Association for the Repeal of Abortion Laws (NARAL), in their briefs. Means heavily influenced Judge Jon Newman, who struck down the Connecticut abortion laws in 1972, and Newman heavily influenced the Supreme Court Justices.[103] Means thus enabled the Justices to ignore traditional legal authorities, such as the works of Edward Coke and William Blackstone, in favor of the appearance of a long-dormant "abortion right" that was not so "radical" after all.

Conclusion

The road to *Roe* was designed and built as a detour around public opinion and the democratic process. In 1970 and 1971, when the activists could not win their goal of repeal in the legislatures, they turned to the courts.

There is reason to think that the legislative campaign

had run out of steam by the end of 1970. No state changed its abortion law by legislation in 1971 or 1972, and, in fact, several rejected legalization. No "reform" bills passed in 1971 or 1972, and "repeal" bills were defeated in numerous states between 1970 and 1972. While Justice Blackmun was writing his second draft opinion after the rearguments in November 1972, Michigan (by 61–39 percent) and North Dakota (by 77–23 percent) rejected ballot initiatives to legalize abortion.[104]

The irony is that the Supreme Court took the issue away from the people only a few short years after more people were moving from abstract consideration to practical public policy considerations. No "reform" law was in effect long enough before *Roe* to reliably examine its impact, let alone the short-term or long-term risks to women. The failure of any reform law to pass in 1971–1972, the defeat of virtually all repeal laws, and the defeat of voter initiatives to legalize abortion in Michigan and North Dakota in November 1972 did not seem to give any pause to the Justices about the direction of public opinion.

All of the arguments that were made in the courts could have been made—and were made—to legislators and to the public. That is evident by the blunt sociological sentiments expressed in *Roe* and by other judges in such abortion cases as *Abele v. Markle* in Connecticut.

The fact of the matter is that feminist leaders and organizations were rather late to the battle. Betty Friedan's 1963 best seller, *The Feminine Mystique*, never mentioned abortion. But by 1968 national women's organizations began to advocate for abortion. The endorsement of abortion legalization by the National Organization for Women caused a split in the organization, but lifted the campaign to repeal all abortion laws between 1968 and 1972.[105]

The activists who spurred the abortion cases, and the Justices, were personally affected by the cultural currents. Roy Lucas took his girlfriend to Puerto Rico for an abortion before 1966.[106] Several years before she argued *Roe*, Sarah Weddington reportedly went to Mexico for an abortion.[107] Justice Blackmun's daughter revealed in 2006 that she became pregnant while unmarried in 1966.[108] Justice Powell told journalist Nina Totenberg, in an interview after his retirement, that he had helped a law firm "office boy" avoid prosecution when the man was involved in an illegal abortion that resulted in a woman's death in Richmond, Virginia.[109] And Justice Marshall apparently was also influenced by personal experiences.[110]

As of 1973, the public did not buy repeal—at least in the sense that thirty states still retained their prohibitions on abortion except to save the life of the mother. The reform that changed thirteen state laws over four short years (1967–1970) may have ground to a halt by 1971. However, Roy Lucas and Sarah Weddington filed their appeal to the Supreme Court in October 1970, just *after* the height of the legislative momentum.

If the courts had not stepped in, the issue would have continued to be debated in the states, with an eventual resolution in which most states, perhaps, retained their criminal prohibitions but some experimented with broad exceptions. But the activists for the repeal of abortion laws were not satisfied with their results in the state legislatures and sought to use the courts to get all abortion laws struck down as "unconstitutional" on the same basis on which anti-contraception laws had been struck down by the courts. The activists considered the issues to be the same, though the reasons supporting each, and the state experience with each, were very different.

Women wanted to use their talents and succeed in the marketplace. Women wanted to balance work and family. Americans in the fifty states were actively involved in a debate that only lasted for seven or eight years before *Roe*, hardly enough time for any society to resolve the countervailing currents.

This recounting of the social, legal, and political currents that preceded the abortion decisions tells how the cases got to the Supreme Court with significant momentum behind them, but it is not enough to explain how and why the Justices ultimately decided to legalize abortion, and to such a sweeping extent. That requires a closer examination of the arguments made and the deliberations of the Justices, which is the subject of the next few chapters.

CHAPTER THREE

The Red Flags the Justices Ignored

THE EMBARRASSING ARGUMENTS

IN THE ABORTION CASES

The record that came up to this Court contains the amended petition of Jane Roe, an unsigned alias affidavit, and that is all.

—JAY FLOYD, ATTORNEY FOR TEXAS[1]

And that again is one of the great problems with this case. We know of no facts, there are no facts in this case, no established facts.

—DOROTHY BEASLEY,
ATTORNEY FOR GEORGIA[2]

When Sarah Weddington stood up in the federal courtroom in Dallas on the afternoon of Friday, May 22, 1970 to argue *Roe v. Wade* for the first time, she faced three federal judges, including Sarah Hughes. As Weddington later told a dinner crowd in 1976, "I remember that Sarah Hughes ... was one of the judges. At one point during the hearing, when my nervousness was obviously showing, Sarah winked at me as if to say, 'It's going to be all right.' Sure enough, it was."[3]

Hughes was, in fact, an abortion-rights activist, eager to eliminate the abortion laws. She had lobbied the Texas legislature to repeal the Texas abortion law. Weddington's partner and co-counsel, Linda Coffee, had worked for Hughes the year before as a law clerk. Hughes admitted that she had her mind made up in advance.[4] Hughes's clerk called the leading abortion-rights lawyer Roy Lucas for help.[5] The following year, Hughes sent a "supportive telegram" to an abortion-rights rally in Austin, Texas.[6] When Weddington filed for admission to the Supreme Court bar to enable her to argue the *Roe* case in December 1971, Hughes sponsored her admission.[7]

When Weddington stood up to argue *Roe* before the United States Supreme Court at 10 A.M. on December 13, 1971, she received no winks, but her reception by the Justices was almost as easy and casual. At least four of the seven Justices on the bench were on her side during her thirty-minute argument. Weddington was asked only five minor questions in her first seventeen minutes.[8] In her second argument in October 1972—despite several Justices feeling disappointed with the first argument—Weddington was asked only two minor questions after she had argued for thirteen and a half minutes. Similarly, in the reargument in *Doe* in October 1972, Margie Pitts Hames, the attorney for the Georgia plaintiffs, spoke for thirteen and a half minutes without one question or interruption. The Justices deferred to these attorneys frequently and apologized more than once for interrupting them with questions. It was a reversal of the usual standard of decorum in which counsel immediately pauses when a Justice asks a question.

You can hear the original oral arguments in *Roe v. Wade* and *Doe v. Bolton* at www.oyez.org.

Oral arguments have traditionally been considered an essential part of a Supreme Court case. A lawyer may not win her case solely through the oral argument, but she may lose it. Supreme Court Justice Stephen Breyer, who clerked for Justice Goldberg in 1965 during the deliberations in *Griswold v. Connecticut*, recently said, "You want a conversation between the judges and the lawyers. A conversation is what appellate courts need, because out of that conversation you grow a better decision."[9] Two hundred years ago, oral arguments might consume several days, but by 1970, the Court had reduced the oral argument time to thirty minutes per side.[10]

The oral arguments in both of the abortion cases were burdened from start to finish by two major problems: first, there was no trial record of factual evidence; second, much of the time was spent on procedural and jurisdictional questions, preventing focus on substantive historical, medical, and constitutional questions. These problems plagued both the oral arguments and the Justices' deliberations between December 1971 and January 1973 and thus fundamentally shaped the Justices' decision-making and the opinions in *Roe* and *Doe*.

The Troubling Lack of a Factual Record

Trials and hearings are supposed to thoroughly weigh the evidence and determine the truthfulness and accuracy of the claims of the parties. This is all the more important when a case involves constitutional questions and has sweeping implications for the people and the public health in all fifty states.

In the lower court hearings of *Roe* and *Doe*, however, the parties did not present evidence—there were no trials—and the judges did not look at evidence. The federal court hearings in *Roe* and *Doe* were conducted without examination of medical or other evidence and without hearing witnesses subjected to cross-examination. Instead, both district courts in Texas and Georgia simply decided that "the facts don't matter" (in the words of Georgia's attorney, Dorothy Beasley[11]), and merely held two hour-long oral arguments, in which much of the time was taken up with procedural and jurisdictional questions.[12]

Nor was there any intermediate review by an appeals court in *Roe* and *Doe*. The federal judicial system consists of three tiers: a federal trial court, an appeals (or appellate) court, and the Supreme Court. One of the purposes of this system is to have the facts and legal propositions in cases thoroughly reviewed before the cases get up to the Supreme Court. But in both *Roe* and *Doe* the federal trial court decisions were not considered by intermediate appellate courts. The federal court decisions went directly to the Supreme Court because a federal statute in effect in 1970 allowed for direct appeal to the Supreme Court.[13]

The lack of a factual record posed a major problem of case selection—selecting the best case of several pending that would most clearly define the complex issues at stake, one with a comprehensive factual record, without procedural problems, and with parties with a real and direct interest in the controversy, to sharpen and clarify the unprecedented constitutional and medical issues. Justice Blackmun complained, during the second argument in *Roe* in October 1972, about "the voluminous briefs that we're overwhelmed with here."[14] But he apparently failed to realize that those briefs were the direct result of the Justices taking two cases with no record.

There were numerous abortion cases in the courts in 1970, and more followed in 1971 and 1972; the Justices could have selected other cases with a factual record.[15] At the time the Justices chose *Roe* and *Doe*, at least seven other abortion cases were pending at the Supreme Court. Remarkably, the Justices chose not one but two abortion cases without any factual record. Why?

The Justices agreed to hear the cases in April 1971 not to address abortion but to decide "the *Younger* issue"—whether the plaintiffs in *Roe* and *Doe* could take their case to federal court. The fact that neither case had any trial record lends further credence to Justice Blackmun's story, outlined in chapter 1, that Justice Stewart (or a subcommittee of Justices) decided to hear the cases under the "misapprehension that they involved nothing more than an application of *Younger v. Harris*."[16] Reviewing the application of *Younger* (dealing with the standards for federal court intervention in state criminal proceedings) to *Roe* and *Doe* would not have required an extensive factual record.

The Supreme Court's decisions in *Roe* and *Doe*, however, went well beyond reviewing the application of *Younger*.

Thus the lack of a factual record became quite damaging, as illustrated by three examples of problematic questions.

First, how could the Justices address the issue of fetal viability knowledgably if the cases never addressed the issue? Neither state statute under consideration—of Texas or Georgia—had a time limit for abortion or hinged on viability. What was "viability" and how would it be determined? Did late-term abortions have higher medical risks for women? Would late-term abortions increase the risk of live-birth abortions?

Second, was "Mary Doe" a real person? Chief Justice Warren Burger didn't see the relevance of whether "Mary Doe" was real or fictitious:

CHIEF JUSTICE BURGER: [W]hy do we need to be concerned about whether she [Mary Doe] is a fictitious or a real person?

MRS. BEASLEY: Because it was not a complete divulgence of the facts surrounding her circumstance. For example, we don't know that the hospital abortion committee knew as much about her as in her allegation. We don't know the real reason for which they denied her the abortion. Particularly since she was assertedly granted the approval of another hospital abortion committee, which again makes her situation somewhat moot.[17]

Third, was *Doe* properly a class-action suit? It was never revealed to the Justices that, before the hearing of the case in the district court in Atlanta, Mary Doe (Sandra Cano) voluntarily relented from having an abortion once she felt her baby kick, and she communicated that to her counsel, Margie Pitts Hames.[18] Since the Georgia and Texas cases were "class actions," Mary Doe was supposed to be the "representative" of the "class" of women who wanted an abortion in Georgia. Did Cano accurately represent that class of women? Because there was no trial and no testimony, Hames was able to tell the Justices on December 13, 1971—without fear of contradiction—that Mary Doe "did not obtain her abortion" because of poverty.[19]

Throughout the Court's history, the Justices have frequently remarked on many factors that are essential for good decision-making: a full factual record in the trial court, issues that are fully addressed by the lower courts first, adequate briefing, and thorough oral arguments. Otherwise, the Justices risk poor decision-making.

A few years after *Roe*, a former law clerk for Judge Edward Lumbard (who wrote the first decision in 1972 striking down the Connecticut abortion law[20]) pointed out that the lower court decisions were not thorough and that the Supreme Court was hasty in hearing *Roe* and *Doe* before the issues were fully explored in the lower courts.[21]

In selecting *Roe* and *Doe*, and moving ahead with a decision, the Justices ignored several long-standing principles for good decision-making on constitutional issues:

- Medical and statistical assertions that are not in the trial record but relied on by the judges—what lawyers call "judicial notice"—should be limited to indisputable facts.
- Courts should not decide constitutional questions on an incomplete or inadequate record.
- Courts should not formulate rules of constitutional law broader than required by the facts.
- Courts should not decide constitutional questions unless

the question is presented with the clarity needed for
effective adjudication.

- Courts will not anticipate the decision of a constitutional
  question upon a record that does not appropriately
  present it.

Three years after *Roe*, Justice Thurgood Marshall wrote the
opinion for a unanimous Court noting the impropriety of
deciding constitutional questions "in the absence of 'an adequate and full-bodied record.' "[22] In another case four years
after *Roe*, Justice Blackmun wrote, "The problem is a complex one, about which widely differing views can be held,
and, as such, it would be somewhat precipitate to take judicial notice of one view over another on the basis of a record
as barren as this."[23]

Some of the same Justices who heard and decided *Roe*
and *Doe* had emphasized the importance of a factual record
in prior "privacy" cases. In *Poe v. Ullman* in 1961, Justice
Brennan supported dismissal of the case, in part, because
of the "skimpy record."[24] During the Supreme Court oral
argument in January 1971 in the *Vuitch* case, involving the
District of Columbia abortion law, Samuel Huntington, the
attorney for the United States, pointed out that the record
contained "no development whatever of any of the facts
bearing on the charges contained in the indictment," and
Chief Justice Burger noted that the Court might benefit
from "a record of testimony as to what is the present state of
medical knowledge."[25] And in his opinion in the *Vuitch* case
decided the day before the Justices voted to hear *Roe*, Justice
White emphasized that "this case comes to us unilluminated
by facts or record."[26] If this was true in *Vuitch*—which was

a comparatively limited inquiry into whether the District of Columbia's abortion law was "unconstitutionally vague"—it was even truer in *Roe* and *Doe*, which aimed to sweep away the abortion laws of all fifty states.

It is not as if the Justices were not warned that there was no factual record. In the first *Doe* argument, Georgia's attorney, Dorothy Beasley, made the lack-of-factual-record point no less than five times. Beasley pointed out that there was no record to show how abortions were being done under the new 1968 statute in Georgia. Georgia and thirteen other states had enacted these laws between 1967 and 1970, and the Court did not have any facts about how they operated. How could the Supreme Court decide to legalize abortion on a broader basis, throughout the first and second trimester, when they did not have even a basic understanding, developed through a trial, of how these "reform" statutes had operated in the few months or years since they had been enacted?

These problems suggest that the Court should have reached no decision, or sent the case back for trial, or taken other cases with a trial record, or at least reached a narrow decision. Instead, the Justices issued one of the broadest decisions possible.

Throwing Off Procedural and Jurisdictional Restraints

In addition to the lack of a factual record, the oral arguments were burdened by jurisdictional and procedural issues that consumed a considerable amount of time, leaving little time to focus on the substantive medical, historical, and constitutional questions.

The first twenty minutes of Weddington's first argument in *Roe* in December 1971 was spent on procedure and jurisdiction, and much of the last ten minutes as well. The Court asked questions such as who brought the suit, whether they could sue, whether there was any real controversy between Jane Roe and the public officials named as defendants, whether the Court should even hear the appeal, whether the parties should have gone to the federal appeals court first, whether the case was moot, whether an injunction was appropriate.

A substantial part of the discussion by Jay Floyd, the attorney for Texas in the first *Roe* argument, was also spent on procedure and jurisdiction. In the first *Doe* argument, Margie Pitts Hames addressed some questions on jurisdiction and procedure, and her final question was on jurisdiction. Dorothy Beasley also addressed such questions.

Again, the amount of time spent on these procedural and jurisdictional questions lends considerable credence to Justice Blackmun's story that Justice Stewart urged the subcommittee of Justices to hear *Roe* and *Doe* under the "misapprehension" that they involved "nothing more than an application of *Younger v. Harris.*"

Indeed, the subcommittee could have been easily misled by the first papers filed in the Supreme Court by Roy Lucas and Sarah Weddington on October 6, 1970, asking the Justices to hear the case.[27] The papers (called a "Jurisdictional Statement") consisted of thirty-three pages and presented only two "Questions" for the Justices to address, relating to the propriety of an injunction by the federal court and whether the married couple in the case (not Jane Roe) had "standing" to sue—in other words, procedural issues.[28] Lucas wrote several pages on the lower court proceedings, two and a half pages on the standing issue, and fifteen pages on the injunction issue.

These procedural issues raised many red flags that the Justices ignored. Shouldn't the lower courts have conducted a trial, with witnesses, and evidence, and cross-examination? Did either Jane Roe or Mary Doe accurately represent women who wanted abortions? Some of these "technical" issues dealt with two requirements of any viable constitutional case: "standing" (who can bring a suit to challenge a law?) and "case and controversy" (is there any real conflict between the parties that can clarify the constitutional issues?). These two requirements—"standing" and "case and controversy"—are important for sound judicial decisions because they enable judges to see the practical consequences of legislation.

Georgia's attorney Beasley brought both of these requirements directly to the Justices' attention, but the Justices brushed them aside. The aim of Justices Brennan and Douglas—as evidenced by their phone and written exchanges on December 29 and 30, 1971—was to find the best way to get around them.[29]

Little time was left for the substantive questions in both cases. For example, the question of where the right to "abortion" could be found in the Constitution became virtually a joke at the first argument. Weddington was willing to say it could be found almost anywhere—the "due process clause, equal protection clause, the Ninth Amendment, and a variety of others. . . ." The statement was so weak that Justice Stewart quipped "and anything else that might obtain," provoking laughter from the audience.[30] To which Weddington responded, "yeah, right," and laughed.[31] Another red flag, but again, no Justice challenged Weddington's weak assertions.

So much of the first *Doe* argument in December 1971 was spent on procedural issues that Hames, the attorney for the Georgia plaintiffs, made no statement in her first argument about the constitutional basis of her case or of a right to abortion. And no Justice questioned this. There were virtually no questions on the source of any constitutional right to abortion and almost no questions on the historical basis for such a right. Hames left this fundamental issue to her one-minute rebuttal of Beasley, admitting that "we have not designated a constitutional basis for our case." So Hames gave a one-sentence answer: "I would like to say that it is— we contend that the procedural requirements infringe Due Process and Equal Protection, and that the right of privacy, as enunciated in *Griswold*, of course, is our basic reliance."[32] That was the extent of the constitutional discussion at the first oral argument in *Doe*.

The procedural problems should have cautioned the Justices that the Texas and Georgia cases prevented the evaluation of fundamental questions and were unstable and inadequate bases on which to make a decision. According to various reports, "Burger had complained that part of his problem with the abortion cases resulted from the poor quality of the oral argument. On reargument, he suggested, the Court could appoint 'friends of the court' (*amici curiae*) for both sides, outside counsel who could make better presentations."[33] Blackmun, too, acknowledged that the cases were poorly argued the first time.[34] White probably shared this view. Instead, the bloc of four Justices—Douglas, Brennan, Marshall, and Stewart—heavily pressured Blackmun in May and June 1972 against a second argument.

Seven Major Themes

Besides the record and the jurisdictional hurdles, the Justices and lawyers addressed seven major themes in the arguments—measured by the time spent on them—though they never got the time they deserved:

- Factual and medical assertions about abortion
- The historical purposes for the state abortion laws
- The medical context for the legal protection of life
- Why abortion law treated women as victims and not accomplices
- The legal status and extent of legal protection of the unborn child, including whether the child was a legal or constitutional person
- The difference between abortion laws and laws regulating surgery
- The exceptions for rape, incest, etc., in Georgia's law

Factual and Medical Assertions

Despite the fact that abortion was legal in some other countries and in a few states, there were no reliable, peer-reviewed medical data, and certainly no long-term studies, about it. Nevertheless, Weddington and Hames argued for the elimination of all state abortion laws, relying on unsubstantiated statistics.

For example, in the second argument in *Doe*, Hames

admitted that "there aren't any statistics that are very reliable on this," but then went on to say that "writers in the area estimate several thousand per year in the United States and several thousand deaths have occurred from illegal abortions."[35] Likewise, Hames claimed in the first *Doe* argument that "illegal abortion and the complications therefrom is the largest single cause of maternal mortality in the United States. Therefore, abortion statutes have resulted in one of our nation's largest health problems."[36] This was a large claim for which there was no basis in the record, though this claim was made in several *amicus curiae* ("friend of the court") briefs.[37] No Justice questioned Hames on this or any of her other undocumented sociological claims.

As Figure 3 in chapter 2 showed, *total maternal deaths* per year—from *all causes*—had dropped from 7,267 in 1942 to 780 in 1972. Of the 780 maternal deaths in 1972, 140 (or 18 percent) were attributed to "abortion deaths." But this included *spontaneous miscarriages*, too. The NCHS data were obviously not in the record and were not submitted in any "friend-of-the-court" brief.

Weddington's arguments were filled with sociological claims that had no foundation in the record, including the legal disabilities that pregnant women incurred in Texas, legal problems in Texas for unwed mothers, how many women had abortions, the numbers of illegal abortions, the risks of illegal abortion, the risks of delay in getting a legal abortion, the impact of New York's law that legalized abortion in July 1970, and the impact of laws in other states that had legalized abortion since 1967.

But, whether or not there was any record, Weddington's arguments made a definite impact. After seventeen minutes of the first argument in *Roe*, with only a few minor questions to Weddington, Justice Stewart broke in to ask a question and prefaced it by saying, "so far on the merits, you've told us about the important impact of this law, and you made a very eloquent policy argument against" the Texas law.[38] This may have been the most important moment in the first round of arguments, perhaps in both rounds.

The Historical Purposes behind Abortion Laws

Historical claims also played a key role in the abortion decisions. History was critical for at least two reasons: to show the purpose of the abortion laws and to see whether any right to abortion existed and could be said to be "deeply rooted" in American law and history.

In *Griswold*, Justice Douglas had written for the Court:

> In determining which rights are fundamental, judges are not left at large to decide cases in light of their personal and private notions. Rather, they must look to the "traditions and (collective) conscience of our people" to determine whether a principle is "so rooted (there) . . . as to be ranked as fundamental." The inquiry is whether a right involved "is of such a character that it cannot be denied without violating those 'fundamental principles of liberty and justice which lie at the base of all our civil and political institutions.' "[39]

That standard naturally led to the question of whether abortion qualified. But the Justices failed to apply that test in *Roe* and did not look closely at the relevant history.

Instead, Justice Blackmun ended up relying for most

of his legal history on the novel historical theories of Cyril Means, the general counsel of the National Association for the Repeal of Abortion Laws (NARAL). Weddington and Hames expressly urged the Court, at least three times, to read Means's articles. Weddington subsequently reported that the Justices had copies of Means's articles on the bench during the argument.[40] Beasley specifically denied the accuracy of Means's historical theories, but no Justice questioned them, and they became an essential pillar of Justice Blackmun's opinion in *Roe*.[41]

Means's historical claims—which are explored in greater depth in chapter 6—were completely unprecedented. They were disputed at the time, and legal and historical scholarship has since definitively refuted them, but they had a decisive impact on the Justices' questions, deliberations, and final opinions in the abortion cases.[42]

In the first *Roe* argument, Weddington claimed (citing Means) that "at the time the Constitution was adopted there was no common law prohibition against abortions; that they were available to the women of this country."[43] This was inaccurate on both counts: the English common law's prohibition of abortion after quickening was adopted by the American colonies, and abortion was not available as a practical matter because it was either ineffective or deadly or both.[44]

Means's other claim was that the purpose of abortion laws was only to protect the health of the mother, not the child. If abortion laws were adopted only for the health of the mother, however, there is no adequate explanation for why abortion laws were *criminal* laws. Why was abortion, in contrast to all other surgery, uniquely treated as criminal?

It could not have been because the woman's health was at stake—health is at stake in any surgery.

The Justices did not have to speculate about this question, because, as one legal scholar has summarized the data, there were "thirty-one decisions from seventeen jurisdictions expressly affirming that their nineteenth-century statutes were intended to protect unborn human life, and twenty-seven other decisions from seventeen additional jurisdictions strongly implying the same."[45] Before the nineteenth-century state statutes, the common law prohibiting abortion existed, and the purpose of the common law on abortion was to protect the unborn child.[46] The American colonies adopted the common law prohibition on abortion, and there was a wealth of legal and historical information that the purpose of abortion laws was to protect the lives of unborn children and the health of women. But, again, no Justice questioned the arguments to the contrary.

The Medical Limits to the Legal Protection of Human Life

[T]he State has a greater obligation to protect that fetal life today than it did [when the Georgia abortion statute was enacted] in 1876. And for this reason, it's more protectable now than it ever was before. There are more methods now that can be used to protect it, including blood transfusions and surgery while it's still in the womb. . . . [T]here are more possible ways now—for example, the very growth of the science of fetology, which is, of course, the treatment of the fetus before it's born.

—GEORGIA ATTORNEY DOROTHY BEASLEY,
FIRST ARGUMENT IN *DOE* (DECEMBER 13, 1971)[47]

The law relating to life and death has always been limited and shaped by existing medical knowledge. The law can protect human life only to the extent it can prove that someone is alive. This was important for criminal law (how did the child die?) as well as property law (who is alive to inherit when someone dies?). Evidentiary constraints were severe before the development of modern medicine. After modern medicine eliminated the rationale for the old rules, the historical medical constraints and the evidentiary reasons for the rules were often confused with a lack of concern for the unborn child or a lack of willingness to enforce the old law.

Before modern medicine, proving that a woman was pregnant with a living child was very difficult. The "signs" of pregnancy were equivocal. The common law looked at two markers: "quickening" and "live birth."[48] Neither the quickening nor the born-alive rule was a substantive or moral rule about the "personhood" or the humanity of the unborn child. Rather, they were practical rules of evidence.[49]

The English common law prohibited abortion upon quickening. After 1600, English homicide law said that the killing of an unborn child was not a homicide unless the child was born alive and died thereafter. The quickening and born-alive rules had distinct but related evidentiary purposes. The quickening distinction was necessary because medicine at the time did not have the technology or "tools" to *reliably* determine that the unborn child was alive before the mother first felt fetal movement.

As late as 1937, Dr. Alan Guttmacher—three decades before he became an advocate of abortion legalization—recognized the practical and legal significance of quickening:

Ordinarily between the sixteenth and twenty-second weeks the patient first experiences "quickening," that is, she first perceives the movements of the foetus. . . . Later in pregnancy the movements of the child's arms and legs feel like powerful thrusts from within. . . . As we have seen, the sensation of "quickening" may be brought on by conditions quite other than pregnancy. . . . The English common law has always considered the foetus inanimate, "*portio viscerum matris*" (part of the mother's organs), until it "quickened"—became quick with life and moved. . . . All these evidences of pregnancy noticed by the patient— the absence of menses, morning sickness, aberrations of appetite, urinary frequency, emotional changes, growth of breasts, abdominal enlargement, and quickening—can be simulated by other real or imagined conditions.[50]

The born-alive rule was adopted in a time of high infant mortality and primitive medicine to distinguish between *criminal* and *natural* causes of infant death. That was important because any homicide (the killing of a human being) was a capital offense, and a determination of a criminal cause for a newborn's death (homicide) meant hanging.

Viability (the capacity for the independent survival of the child), which became such a significant part of the abortion decisions, was never a part of the common law, as Cyril Means—on whom Justice Blackmun so heavily relied—acknowledged.[51] It played no role in English law, and it played no role in American law until 1884, when Oliver Wendell Holmes implicitly adopted it in a judicial decision while a Justice on the Massachusetts Supreme Judicial Court.[52]

Quickening—the mother's sense of fetal movement—was the first reliable evidence that the child was alive, and the law depended on it. Why did the English common law prohibit abortion *after* quickening? Because there was no reliable evidence that there was an existing child, or that it was alive, before quickening. When medical science challenged the quickening rule in the 1800s by showing that conception was the beginning of the life of a human being, states quickly moved to repeal the quickening rule and replace it with an abortion prohibition from conception.[53]

This dependence of the law on medical knowledge should have been readily apparent to the Justices. In the first *Doe* argument, for example, Hames said that "it is only about the sixth or eighth week that pregnancy tests actually become accurate. . . ."[54]

Ignoring the evidentiary context of the common law, advocates in the 1960s used the prohibition after quickening to argue that a "right" to abortion existed before quickening. But Joseph Dellapenna sums up the historical data: "Until law professor Cyril Means, Jr. discovered the supposed liberty in 1968 . . . no statement in any legal or other document expressed the claim that anyone had a liberty to abort."[55]

Corresponding to quickening as the first reliable evidence of life, "live birth" was necessary to distinguish natural from criminal causes in the case of an infant's stillbirth. The so-called born-alive rule—which had been a part of the English common law since 1600—proved to be another key point of confusion during the arguments in *Roe* and *Doe*.[56] Like quickening, the born-alive rule was a rule of evidence. The unborn child had to be injured inside the womb, be born alive and die thereafter for the killing to be prosecuted as a homicide. "Born alive" meant alive outside, not birth at term (forty weeks). It was a rule of location, not gestation.

If the child was stillborn, there could be no homicide charge, for at least two very serious practical evidentiary reasons: First, in a time of high infant mortality, infants very often died from natural causes. The only way to *reliably* distinguish natural causes from criminal causes—and thus avoid unjustly executing a mother for infanticide—was to observe the child outside the womb alive before it died. That would enable doctors to determine whether the child had died *in utero* some time ago from natural causes or had died from recently inflicted injuries. Second, homicide was invariably a capital crime in England in the seventeenth and eighteenth centuries, and juries were not willing to convict anyone—especially mothers—on uncertain evidence.[57]

What if a child was stillborn from natural causes, but the mother was suspected of infanticide? In such a case, the born-alive rule would help protect the mother.

This legal history was completely lost on the Justices. They simply misunderstood the practical application of the quickening rule and, instead, assumed a "right" to abortion before quickening. The Justices misunderstood the born-alive rule to signify moral standing rather than evidence. This is reflected in Justice Stewart's comment in the second *Roe* argument that "changing by the act of birth into a human" (in Robert Flowers's words) was "the theory up until now on the lawbooks" (Stewart's conclusion).[58] Likewise, in her argument, Weddington misused "born alive" as a time-based, gestational term to mean birth at term (forty weeks gestation), and asserted that the unborn child had no constitutional protection before that time. The Justices adopted this, despite the fact that "born alive" referred not to gestation (time) but to location (outside the womb).

The Justices' assumption is contradicted by the practical application of the born-alive rule. The "born-alive" rule in the law meant that if the child was injured in the womb and was delivered or expelled from the womb—at any time of pregnancy—and died outside, that was a homicide.[59] Time of gestation of the injury was irrelevant to the operation of the born-alive rule.

There is conclusive evidence that the born-alive rule was not a rule of biological development but a rule of evidence: injuries imposed on the unborn child *in utero* could be prosecuted as a homicide as long as the child was not stillborn but came out alive and died thereafter. If "rights" were truly "contingent" on birth, *then the injury inflicted would have to come only after birth*; if the unborn child was truly a non-entity, the injury could *not* be inflicted while the child was in the womb. This is the principle of *congruence*: the entity that is injured inside and the entity that dies outside is the same entity, the same human being. By granting a remedy for injuries inflicted *in utero*, the law recognized that the child before and after birth was the same human being. Weddington, in fact, in an unreflective moment in the second argument in *Roe*, conceded that "rights" could be "retroactive to the period prior to birth," but completely overlooked the significance of this.[60] No Justice picked up on her concession, or its significance.

Therefore, contrary to Justice Stewart's assumption, the fetus did not "change by the act of birth into a human." The fact that the born-alive rule recognized that the entity injured in the womb was the same entity that died outside the womb, and was the subject of homicide, meant that the entity in the womb was considered a human being inside and outside. If the law did not recognize the child *in utero* as a human being, then the law could only have granted a remedy if the injuries were inflicted *after* birth, but that was never the law.

Neither the briefs filed in the Supreme Court nor the attorneys clarified the evidentiary nature of these two common law rules,[61] except for one brief moment when the attorney for Georgia, Dorothy Beasley, in the first *Doe* argument, clearly explained the definition of "live birth" as expulsion *"at whatever stage it occurs."*[62]

This misunderstanding had an enormous impact: because the Justices misunderstood the born-alive rule as a gestational rule (birth at term or forty weeks), rather than a location rule (outside the womb), the Justices extended the "right" to abortion throughout pregnancy to term (forty weeks gestation).[63]

Women as Victims of Abortion, Not Accomplices

Another key point of confusion in the arguments, and eventually in the *Roe* opinion, was why state abortion laws targeted the practitioner but not the woman. Virtually all the states treated the woman as a victim and never prosecuted the woman as a principal or accomplice to abortion.[64]

Weddington admitted that the abortion laws targeted the practitioner, not women, and that women were treated by Texas law as victims of abortion. Hames likewise acknowledged that women in Georgia were not subject to prosecution.

But why? There were several reasons why the states did

not prosecute women, though these were never discussed in the arguments: Abortions were dangerous, even deadly, until the late nineteenth century. Abortions were often coerced. No one—man or woman—can consent to an illegal act against themselves. The criminal statutes—which judges are to strictly construe—were written in terms that focused on the acts imposed on the woman. And, perhaps most important, effective enforcement of the law required that women not be charged as principals or accomplices.

Treating the woman as the second victim of abortion was the consistent policy of the states for nearly a century before *Roe*. "The attitude that the woman was a victim rather than a criminal, however, continued to be dominant in the twentieth century and remained dominant when *Roe v. Wade* was decided."[65] As Joseph Dellapenna has explained,

> If the woman were a party to the crime of abortion, convictions generally would have been virtually impossible to obtain, even with a grant of immunity from prosecution to the woman to overcome any self-incrimination problems. New York did enact a statutory grant of immunity to aborted women precisely in order to make conviction of the abortionist possible, beginning with the 1869 Abortion Act. The immunity provision was dropped from the 1872 and 1881 acts, but was reenacted in 1942. The statute remained on the books until the 1970 abortion reform.[66]

This easing of procedural and evidentiary rules to promote effective law enforcement did not start with American abortion statutes; it was reflected in the first abortion statute that Parliament enacted to update the common law—Lord Ellenborough's statute of 1803—as historian John Keown has demonstrated.[67]

Ironically, what the Justices also overlooked is that it was abortionists, not prosecutors, who aimed to get women charged as accomplices. If an abortionist charged with the crime could get the woman treated as an accomplice, he could knock out the woman's testimony (under criminal evidence law) and likely get the prosecution's case thrown out. More than anything else, this showed that treating the woman as a victim (and not as a principal or accomplice) contributed to the effective enforcement of abortion laws in the nineteenth and twentieth centuries.

The Legal Status of the Unborn Child

I have a great problem with this human being point. . . .
Do you have to go so far to sustain your position as to say
that the fetus is a human being?

—JUSTICE THURGOOD MARSHALL,
SECOND ARGUMENT IN *DOE V. BOLTON*[68]

The status of the unborn child as a person under the law was affirmatively argued to the Justices by the attorneys for Texas and Georgia in both the first and second arguments. Beasley asserted that the core of the case "is the value which is to be placed on fetal life."[69] To rebut the assertion that the purpose of abortion laws was only to protect the woman's health and not the life of the unborn child, she pointed out that the Georgia statute was placed in the criminal code, where crimes against human life were contained. The original Georgia abortion statute of 1876 was a criminal law, and the new 1968 statute amended the criminal code. The statute also referred to the "unborn child"—a human being—

and not to a "thing" or "organism." Georgia also required a fetal death certificate.

Anglo-American law has called the unborn child an "unborn child" or a "child" from at least the 1200s,[70] a tradition that was inherited from Roman law.[71] The language of "child"—which Justice Marshall questioned at oral argument—was adopted by the English and American courts centuries ago. This includes English courts going back to 1586. English property cases typically used the term "child." The English legal authority Sir Edward Coke used the term "child" in 1648, and William Blackstone used the term "child" in 1776. Oliver Wendell Holmes used the term "child" in an 1884 case.

By the middle of the twentieth century, American courts were making decisions based on the medical understanding that the life of a human being began at conception. As one federal court wrote in 1946, "From the viewpoint of the civil law and the law of property, a child *en ventre sa mere* [in the mother's womb] is not only regarded as a human being but as such from the moment of conception—which it is in fact."[72] And the New Jersey Supreme Court held in 1960, "Medical authorities have long recognized that a child is in existence from the moment of conception."[73] The use of the phrase "with child" to refer to pregnancy, going back thousands of years, shows the breadth and depth of this understanding in world culture.

For these reasons, Beasley disputed the relevance of the *Griswold* contraception case from 1965: "because in that case there was not the introduction of another entity. A person has a right to be let alone, certainly; but not when another person is involved, or another human entity is involved."[74]

Texas's first attorney, Jay Floyd, took the position that a living human being existed with conception and asserted that there could be no "choice" to kill the child after pregnancy began. To which Justice Stewart quipped, "Maybe she makes her choice when she decides to live in Texas."[75] Though the comment sparked laughter, Stewart's quip ignored the fact that Texas was not alone. As of January 1973, thirty states retained their prohibition on abortion except to save the life of the mother.

After judicial prodding, Floyd wrongly agreed that no state "equates abortion with murder."[76] In fact, numerous nineteenth- and twentieth-century statutes equated abortion with homicide (the killing of a human being) if not intentional homicide (murder). As Dellapenna has pointed out,

the nineteenth-century statutes enacted in 17 states (and the District of Columbia) denominated the crime against the unborn child as "manslaughter," "murder" or "assault with intent to murder." Most nineteenth-century statutes referred to the unborn child as a "child," not as a fetus or some other term that might suggest a lesser status, and many states classified abortion with other crimes against persons, usually homicide. After reviewing these statutes, one can only marvel at historians who conclude that "the destruction of the fetus never gained the standing either of infanticide or homicide."[77]

In the second argument in *Roe* in October 1972, Robert Flowers replaced Floyd as the attorney for Texas, but Flowers also affirmed, at the outset, that it was "the position of . . . Texas that, upon conception, we have a human being, a person within the concept of the Constitution of the United States, and that of Texas, too."[78]

Justice Stewart immediately jumped on this. "Now how should that question be decided? Is it a legal question? A constitutional question? A medical question? A philosophical question? Or, a religious question? Or what is it?"[79]

In truth, it was both a legal and a constitutional question. It was a *legal* question because the states had adopted criminal, tort, and property laws to protect the unborn child. It was a *constitutional* question whether the states or the federal government had the authority or power to decide, and whether the framers of the Fourteenth Amendment intended to include the unborn child within the protection of that Amendment. The unborn child could be a person under state law without being specifically brought within the protection of the Fourteenth Amendment by the framers. The laws, in turn, were influenced by medical, philosophical, and religious reasoning.

Floyd was asked whether any court had held that the unborn child was a person within the Fourteenth Amendment, and Floyd wrongly answered "no." In fact, the federal court in Ohio in 1970, in *Steinberg v. Brown*, had concluded that the Fifth and Fourteenth Amendments "impose upon the state the duty of safeguarding" the unborn child.[80] The *Steinberg* case was noted by other federal courts considering state abortion statutes at the time.[81]

Justice Stewart suggested that the Fourteenth Amendment "defines 'person' as somebody who's born, doesn't it?" But he confused the definition of "person," which is undefined, with the description of "citizen" as a person who's been born—"All persons born or naturalized in the United

States . . . are citizens of the United States and of the State wherein they reside"—which Stewart later acknowledged. Thus, the language of the amendment, by saying that citizens are persons who are born, allows, in fact, the possibility that some persons might be unborn.[82]

Flowers quoted Blackstone's *Commentaries on the Law* from 1765—the basic text on the common law which all American lawyers studied until the late nineteenth century—which recognized the unborn child as a person. Justice Blackmun, relying on the articles by Means, noted that abortion was not a "felony" at the time of Blackstone. (Felonies were serious crimes that, under the English common law, incurred the death penalty.)

While Blackmun's statement might have been true as of 1765, that changed under American law in the nineteenth century. Abundant common law authority, state court decisions, and many statutes treated abortion as manslaughter (the killing of a human being). There was the growth of legal protection under state wrongful-death statutes and prenatal injury law. No Justice drew on the specifics of this readily available legal and social history that was set out in the briefs.

Before statutes were gradually enacted in the nineteenth century, the English common law had developed a common law of crimes, which the American colonies adopted. Before the statutory law of crimes, there were "common law crimes," and abortion was one of them. It is surprising that the Justices overlooked this general history of criminal law that applied to all types of crimes, including homicide, robbery, and assault.

Justice Blackmun suggested, relying on Means, that "as

a matter of historical fact . . . most of these abortion statutes came on the books" in "the latter half of the nineteenth century."[83] This was demonstrably wrong. As Dellapenna (and many other scholars) have shown,

- "Abortion statutes were enacted in ten states and one territory by 1841. Maine, in 1840, became the first state to prohibit all abortions by any means at any point of gestation."[84]
- "By 1861, 70 percent of the American states (with 85 percent of the American population) had adopted [abortion] statutes."[85]
- "By 1868, when the 14th Amendment was ratified, thirty of the thirty-seven states had abortion statutes on the books. Just three of these statutes prohibited abortion only after quickening. Twenty states punished all abortion equally regardless the stage of pregnancy."[86]

In the second round of arguments in October 1972, Justice Marshall pushed Robert Flowers to say that if the unborn child was a person, Texas law could not allow abortion even to save the life of the mother. Flowers simply agreed, instead of pointing out the history of the medical exception to save the life of the mother, which was guided by principles of self-defense.[87] Under Justice White's questioning, Flowers stumbled into saying that, if the fetus was not a constitutional person under the Fourteenth Amendment, Texas lost the entire case. That kind of approach was the fastest way for Flowers to lose his case with the Justices.

A better answer by Flowers would have been that the law of Texas was constitutional whether the unborn child was a person under the Fourteenth Amendment or only under state law. The unborn child was treated as a person for many aspects of state law: in criminal law, tort law, and property law. Whether or not it was the specific intent of the framers of the Fourteenth Amendment to include the unborn child as a person within the protection of that particular amendment in 1868, the states had treated the unborn child as a person under state law (property, criminal law, torts, equity) and could constitutionally protect the unborn child as such within their traditional police powers. There was abundant history to support this from colonial times.[88]

The authority of the states to protect the unborn child was not limited by whether it was a *constitutional person* within the Fourteenth Amendment; that is demonstrated by historical protection, as well as the wrongful death laws, the fetal homicide laws, the property laws in virtually all states, and the tort laws that exist today. The Supreme Court has never questioned the constitutionality of these laws.

Beasley, on the other hand, took a balanced approach and wisely refrained from adopting an all-or-nothing position. Beasley pointed out that "the term 'person' is not defined in the constitution," but "the constitution of course is a living document and, today, we know more medically and under science with respect to personhood and what occurs prior to birth and what the movement is and at what stage it's on, what a person is . . . beginning with that . . . [an 1849 Georgia case, *Morrow v. Scott*]. . . . So it was regarded as a protectable right in the very beginning of our state's existence."[89]

In contrast to the Texas attorneys, Beasley argued that whether or not the "fetus is a person under the Fourteenth Amendment, there is a right of the fetus to be let alone that must be balanced with all the other factors involved," and that the state has the authority to prohibit abortion in light of such interests and is not limited to protecting only "those [rights] guaranteed by the federal constitution" because it has the "police power to pass statutes to protect other interests which aren't necessarily constitutional rights."[90]

State Laws Regulating Surgery v. Prohibiting Abortion

Some of the Justices exhibited confusion over the relationship between regulations on surgery and prohibitions of abortion. This confusion was likely sown by Means's spurious theory that abortion was prohibited because all surgery was dangerous.[91]

Justice Marshall, for example, asked why only abortion should be criminalized and not "other operations." In one of Flowers's clearest answers, he forthrightly stated: "because this is the only type of operation that would take another human life."[92] When Chief Justice Burger asked Beasley whether the state could enact "a statute that would forbid tonsillectomies," Beasley rightly pointed out that "the great distinction is that there is not another entity—human entity involved . . . and that's the source of the protection here."[93] And when Burger persisted that sometimes people die in surgery, she pointed out that the state could regulate surgery for safety purposes, "but that has little to do with the purpose of the state in prohibiting abortion."[94]

Burger asked Beasley whether Georgia could ban open-heart surgery based on evidence that there were "50% fatalities." Beasley responded, "It might be under a health measure, a policy to protect health, but that's not what's involved here. This is not to protect the health of the person who wants the operation which is what you would have in the open heart surgery . . . but that's not the purpose of the Georgia abortion statute. . . . The underlying assumption and basic foundation was we are not going to destroy fetal health or fetal life except in very unusual and exceptional extreme circumstances."[95]

Abortion was uniquely covered by the criminal code because abortion directly intends to take the life of the child. Other surgery is intended to preserve life, even if it has risks. And abortion was typically included not just in a criminal code—criminal laws address life, limb, and property—but in the section of the code *protecting persons*, as it was in Blackstone.

The Exceptions Allowed by
Georgia's 1968 Abortion Law

If the unborn child was a person protected by state law, could a state allow any exceptions for abortion in the law? While Texas allowed abortion only to save the life of the mother, Georgia had enacted a new statute in March 1968 that followed the American Law Institute (ALI) model bill (the Model Penal Code) and allowed abortion for three reasons (in addition to saving the life of the mother): rape (incest), serious and permanent injury to the mother's health, and severe genetic deformity of the unborn child.[96]

One of Hames's main points was to charge that Georgia was "inconsistent" by claiming that a human being existed from conception despite allowing abortion for rape, fetal deformity, and mental health. Hames took a damned-if-you-do-damned-if-you-don't approach to the Georgia exceptions: If Georgia was "really" interested in protecting fetal life from conception, Hames seemed to say, Georgia couldn't "abandon" those that fell within the exceptions. While Weddington challenged the Texas prohibition (except to save the life of the mother) as too strict, Hames challenged the less strict Georgia exceptions as "inconsistent."

Since Beasley could not change the fact that the Georgia statute contained certain exceptions, she defended them as "a balancing of competing interests."[97] The state "recognizes the competing interest of self-preservation that the mother has in extreme circumstances . . . the exceptions are not broad. The exceptions are very narrow. The health must be very seriously impaired."[98] She argued that "underlying the exceptions, the reason for the exceptions in the statute is the broad principle of self-preservation" which she asserted was involved in the "very special circumstances" reflected in the exceptions.[99]

Thus, the role of the medical committee in the Georgia statute was not to "make a medical judgment about the operation itself," Beasley said, but only to decide

> is this an extreme instance in which we should allow the fetus to be destroyed? That's all, and that shows that the purpose is the fetus' protection. . . . [T]he exceptions are only when extreme circumstances of self-preservation or self-defense . . . not things that have to do with her health. So the statute itself shows that the underlying purpose is the protection of fetal life.[100]

Justice Marshall readily adopted Hames's damned-if-you-do-damned-if-you-don't approach to abortion laws:

either the exceptions established inconsistencies in the law or the laws were unconstitutionally strict if they lacked exceptions. Justice Brennan, as evidenced by his December 30, 1971, memo to Justice Douglas, seems to have been sympathetic to this, too. And Justice Blackmun adopted this criticism in his final opinion.[101]

Conclusion

The oral arguments in December 1971 and October 1972, consuming no more than four and a half hours, ended with many critical questions left unasked and unanswered:

- What are the long-term risks to women from abortion?
- How did so-called abortion reform laws enacted in thirteen states between 1967 and 1970 operate?
- Who would end up performing abortions? Would regular ob-gyns, with long-term relationships with their patients?
- Could local or state public health officials regulate facilities?
- What would happen to all those back-alley abortionists?
- Who would track deaths and injuries and short-term and long-term risks from legal abortions for the future of women's health?
- Would women be fully informed before undergoing the procedure?
- If the Court struck down the existing laws, what would fill the public health vacuum and who would monitor the safety of abortion practice?
- What evidence was there that abortion had ever been considered to be a right in history?

- How had states enforced their laws historically, and more specifically over the past two decades with advancing medical technology?
- What efforts had states made to make abortion law enforcement more effective?
- Did the legal barriers for pregnant women cited by Weddington really exist in Texas, or other states? Was state or federal legislation redressing those barriers?
- Could and would the states increase legal protection for the unborn child in the case of third-party assailants, outside the context of abortion? What about wrongful death law, or prenatal injury law, or criminal law?
- What would be the impact of advancing fetal medicine and therapy?
- What would be the social impact from excluding men, including husbands, from the abortion decision?

The failure to ask and answer these questions, among many others, sowed the seeds for the political, legislative, and public health problems that we have had for nearly forty years.

One of the most significant oversights was the Justices' unilateral move, after the second argument, to expand the abortion right to viability, despite the fact that viability was never discussed—*the word was never mentioned once*—in the four hours of oral arguments in December 1971 and October 1972. Why they took that monumental step is addressed in the next chapter.

CHAPTER FOUR

The Abrupt Expansion to Viability (and Beyond)

*Before [Glanville] Williams' Carpentier Lectures
[in 1956], viability had played no significant role in the
common law or statute law on abortion, nor had it played
a role in medical or popular discourse on the subject in
the United States. Professional and popular opinion had
focused instead either on "quickening" or on "conception"
as the critical events in establishing the legal and moral
status of the fetus.*

— JOSEPH DELLAPENNA, *DISPELLING THE MYTHS OF ABORTION HISTORY*[1]

*By that time [viability] the state's interest has grown
large indeed.*

— JUSTICE HARRY BLACKMUN, LETTER TO JUSTICE POWELL[2]

[These killings of infants born alive after abortion]
were so routine that no one could put an exact number
on them. They were considered "standard procedure."
Yet some of the slaughtered were so fully formed, so much
like babies that should be dressed and taken home, that
even clinic employees who were accustomed to the practice
were shocked.

—PHILADELPHIA GRAND JURY REPORT ABOUT
KERMIT GOSNELL'S CLINIC, JANUARY 2011[3]

The United States is an outlier when it comes to the scope of the abortion "right." The United States is one of approximately ten nations (of 195) that allow abortion *after* fourteen weeks of gestation. The others are: Canada, China, Great Britain, North Korea, the Netherlands, Singapore, Sweden, Western Australia, and Vietnam.[4] When it comes to allowing abortion for any reason after viability, however, the United States is joined only by Canada, North Korea, and China.[5]

The United States got into this situation because after the second round of arguments in *Roe* and *Doe*, the Justices abruptly decided to expand the abortion right they were creating to fetal viability—and then beyond. For forty years, this abrupt decision has had profound implications for late-term abortions, live-birth abortions, and women's health. Why and how did the Justices make that decision?[6]

The Non-Issue

Viability is the stage in development when the unborn child can survive outside the womb, independent from its mother.

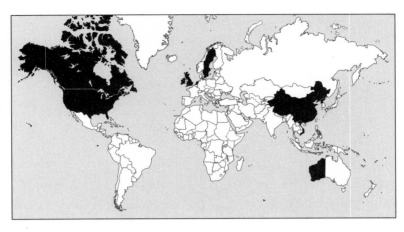

FIGURE 4. *Only ten countries or states allow abortion after fourteen weeks:*
Canada, China, Great Britain, North Korea, the Netherlands, Singapore, Sweden,
the United States, Vietnam, and Western Australia (which allows abortion up to
20 weeks). Source: Center for Reproductive Rights, http://www.reproductiverights.org.

In 1973, it was thought to occur, typically, at twenty-eight
weeks of pregnancy.[7]

Viability was not an issue in the lower courts in the abortion cases. It was not an issue in the Supreme Court, either.
The parties did not discuss viability in their briefs or urge the
Justices to adopt viability as a standard. There was no mention of viability in the arguments, and it was not mentioned
during the first conference of the Justices in December 1971.[8]

Justice Blackmun's first draft opinions in *Roe* and *Doe* in
May 1972 did not mention viability.[9] The first draft merely
declared the Texas statute "unconstitutionally vague."[10] But
Justices Douglas, Brennan, and Marshall, at least, pushed
Blackmun to go beyond vagueness and expressly declare a
right to abortion. Negotiations between the Justices at this
time centered around the notion that there was "a majority" who, in Justice Brennan's words, "felt that the Consti-

tution required the invalidation of abortion statutes save to the extent they required that an abortion be performed by a licensed physician within some limited time after conception."[11]

That is how Brennan phrased it in his May 18, 1972, letter to Blackmun regarding Blackmun's May 18 draft opinion in *Roe*. Brennan pressed Blackmun to decide "the core constitutional question" and "dispose of both cases on the ground supported by the majority" (meaning Brennan, Douglas, Marshall, and Stewart) with no reargument.[12] Douglas expressed the same sentiment in a letter to Blackmun the following day: "my notes confirm what Bill Brennan wrote yesterday in his memo to you—that abortion statutes were invalid save as they required that an abortion be performed by a licensed physician within a limited time after conception."[13] Still, there was no mention of viability.

The earliest reference to viability in the Justices' records seems to be a memo by Blackmun's clerk on August 11, 1972, during the summer recess, about revisions he was making to Blackmun's draft opinion:

> I have written in, essentially, a limitation of the right depending on the time during pregnancy when the abortion is proposed to be performed. I have chosen the point of viability for this "turning point" (when state interests become compelling) for several reasons: (a) it seems to be the line of most significance to the medical professional, for various purposes; (b) it has considerable analytic basis in terms of the state interest as I have articulated it. The alternative, quickening [the first fetal movements], no longer seems to have much analytic or medical significance,

only historical significance; (c) a number of state laws which have a "time cut-off" after which abortion must be more strongly justified by life or health interests use 24 weeks, which is about the "earliest time of viability."[14]

The clerk's proposal of viability did not make it into Blackmun's second draft of November 21, 1972,[15] but it was raised, at least within the Blackmun chambers, before Judge Jon Newman's opinion in the Connecticut abortion case *Abele v. Markle* in September 1972.

The Strange Influence of *Abele v. Markle*

The Justices' papers show that Judge Newman's opinion in *Abele*, which mentioned viability in passing, had a significant influence on the Justices' decision in *Roe* and *Doe*. *Abele* involved a challenge to the Connecticut abortion law, one of the court challenges to abortion laws in twenty states.[16] *Abele* resulted in two opinions. The first opinion by Judge Edward Lumbard in April 1972 (in which Newman joined) invalidated Connecticut's 1860 abortion law, which prohibited abortion except to save the life of the mother. The Connecticut legislature and governor quickly responded in May 1972 by passing another prohibition of abortion, with new legislative findings, expressing the state's commitment to protect the life of the unborn child from conception. The new statute went back before the same judges.

Judge Newman wrote the decision, released on September 20, 1972, striking down the new Connecticut abortion law.[17] After addressing many other issues, Newman suggested in one paragraph that the state might have a greater interest in protecting the unborn child after viability than before.

For unknown reasons, Justices Stewart, Powell, and Brennan were particularly influenced by Newman's opinion.[18] There are numerous instances in the historical record where the Justices raise Newman's name, including an October 6 memo from Powell to his clerk a week before the second *Roe* argument, in which Powell writes: "When we come to decision time in the pending abortion cases, keep in mind that we may wish to take a look at the Lumbard/Newman opinions."[19] Weddington raised Newman's name at the second oral argument on October 11, but could not remember it, and Justice Stewart readily supplied the name from the bench. Stewart also cited the Newman opinion in the Justices' conference after the rearguments.

Why was Newman so influential? He was not a great federal judge of long standing; rather, he was a brand-new judge, sworn into office just one month before the first hearing in the Connecticut abortion case on February 18, 1972.[20]

Further, Newman's opinion was not particularly insightful or well researched. His mention of viability was a gratuitous dictum because the Connecticut statute—like those in Texas and Georgia—did not hinge on viability, and his discussion of viability in his opinion was cursory, a mere one paragraph:[21]

> If a statute sought to protect the lives of all fetuses which could survive outside the uterus, such a statute would be a legislative acceptance of the concept of viability. While authorities may differ on the precise time, there is no doubt that at some point during pregnancy a fetus is capable of surviving outside the uterus. And it is equally clear that there is a minimum point before which survival outside the uterus is not possible. . . . A statute designed

to prevent the destruction of fetuses after viability has been reached would be subject to these considerations. Like the present statute, it would be conferring statutory rights on a fetus which does not have constitutional rights. However, the state interest in protecting the life of a fetus capable of living outside the uterus could be shown to be more generally accepted and, therefore, of more weight in the constitutional sense than the interest in preventing the abortion of a fetus that is not viable. The issue might well turn on whether the time period selected could be shown to permit survival of the fetus in a generally accepted sense, rather than for the brief span of hours and under the abnormal conditions illustrated by some of the state's evidence. As to the latter situations, the nature of the state interest might well not be generally accepted. Finally, and most important, such a statute would not be a direct abridgement of the woman's constitutional right, but at most a limitation on the time when her right could be exercised. The present statute, however, does not present any of the considerations favorable to the state that might be found in either type of statute of more limited scope.[22]

That is the extent of Newman's comment on viability that, for some unknown reason, so impressed the Justices.

Like other judges, Newman completely misunderstood the born-alive rule to mean birth at term and misunderstood the congruence that the born-alive rule established between the unborn child and the born infant.[23] The "brief span of hours and under the abnormal conditions illustrated by some of the state's evidence" that Newman so casually dismissed actually satisfied the born-alive rule for a charge of homicide under the common law going back centuries. After concluding that only "fetuses born alive" have constitutional rights, Newman made perhaps his main point:

> the state interest in protecting the life of a fetus capable of living outside the uterus could be shown to be more generally accepted, and, therefore, of more weight in the constitutional sense than the interest in preventing the abortion of a fetus that is not viable.[24]

This was simply a personal theory of Judge Newman. No law was cited. The year before (1971), the leading authority of tort law in the country, Dean William Prosser, had written:

> Viability of course does not affect the question of the legal existence of the foetus, and therefore of the defendant's duty; and it is a most unsatisfactory criterion, since it is a relative matter, depending on the health of mother and child and many other matters in addition to the stage of development. Certainly the infant may be no less injured; and all logic is in favor of ignoring the stage at which it occurs. But with our knowledge of embryology what it is, as we approach the beginning of pregnancy[,] medical knowledge, and therefore medical testimony and medical proof of causes, becomes increasingly unreliable and unsatisfactory, so that there is good reason for caution. This, however, goes to proof rather than principle; and if, as is undoubtedly the case[,] there are injuries as to which reliable medical proof is possible, it makes no sense to deny recovery on any such arbitrary basis.[25]

Newman's theory was dead wrong, whether tested by the common law, public opinion, or the state of law in 1972, and his speculation about what the public would "accept" has been rejected over the past forty years by the growth of legal protection for the unborn child, without regard to the time of gestation, in state tort and criminal law.[26]

In the first *Abele* case in April 1972, Judge Newman wrote a concurring opinion that "relied heavily upon the work of Cyril Means," as David Garrow observed.[27] Newman read Means's theories into the background of the Connecticut abortion statute, and then concluded that the purpose of the Connecticut statute was what Means suggested as the sole purpose for all the abortion laws—to protect women's health—even though Means's article, which has since been repudiated, had only looked at New York history.[28] And Newman overlooked Means's admission that viability played no role in the common law's protection of the unborn child.

The Abrupt Shift to Viability as the "Critical Moment"

Three weeks after Newman's opinion was issued, *Roe* and *Doe* were reargued before the Justices on Wednesday, October 11, 1972. Given Blackmun's clerk's memo and Newman's opinion, it is surprising that viability was never mentioned during the rearguments or even during the second conference of the Justices on the abortion cases on October 13, 1972.[29]

Five weeks later, on November 21, 1972, Justice Blackmun distributed his second draft opinion to the Justices. The cover memo stated: "You will observe that I have concluded that the end of the first trimester is critical. This is arbitrary, but perhaps any other selected point, such as quickening or viability, is equally arbitrary."[30] Blackmun had settled on the end of the first trimester (twelve weeks gestation) as the "critical" dividing line, before which the states would have little "interest" in regulating abortions, but after which the states could regulate abortion.[31]

Up to this point, Justice Blackmun's draft opinion said that the states, throughout the first trimester, "must do no more than to leave the abortion decision to the best medical judgment of the pregnant woman's attending physician."[32] And that "[f]or the stage subsequent to the first trimester, the State may, if it chooses, determine a point beyond which it restricts legal abortions to stated reasonable therapeutic categories. . . ."[33]

Justice Powell may have had the biggest influence on shifting Blackmun from the end of the first trimester to viability. And Powell, in turn, was heavily influenced by his clerk and by Judge Newman.[34] On November 27, Powell's clerk gave a six-page memo to Powell, criticizing the end of the first trimester and "emphasizing the practical effects of a shift to viability."[35] The clerk recognized that "fixing" such a line was a dictum—unnecessary to the decision of the case—stating, "I would have the Court await that event and not anticipate it in advance."[36] (By December 11, Powell's clerk had come to call the issue "the line-drawing problem in the abortion cases."[37]) Nevertheless, he wrote to Powell:

In this case, since the statutory prohibition was total, it is unnecessary to the result that we draw the line. If a line ultimately must be drawn, it seems that "viability" provides a better point. This is where Judge Newman would have drawn the line. *It is consistent with common law history.*[38]

Here is where the empty record and the faulty arguments in the abortion cases had a real impact: *the clerk's last statement was completely wrong.* As even Means acknowledged, the common law disregarded viability.

Relying on his clerk's memo of November 27, Powell delivered a letter to Blackmun on November 29, 1972:

> I have wondered whether drawing the line at "viability" —if we conclude to designate a particular point in time— would not be more defensible in logic and biologically than perhaps any other single time. [Quoting Newman's opinion in *Abele v. Markle*] I rather agree with the view that the interest of the state is clearly identifiable, in a manner which would be generally understood, when the fetus becomes viable. At any point in time prior thereto, it is more difficult to justify a cutoff date. . . . Of course, it is not essential that we express an opinion as to such a date. Judge Newman did not do this explicitly. In holding the Connecticut statute unconstitutional, he pointed the way generally toward "viability" without making this an explicit ruling.[39]

This was "self-conscious dicta," as one scholar has pointed out—Powell knew that the Court was drawing a line ("a cutoff date") that was unnecessary to the Court's decision.[40]

Another federal judge, Pierre Leval, has highlighted one

of the problems with judges adopting and imposing dictum—propositions unnecessary to the decision—with an observation that is directly relevant to *Roe*:

> When courts declare rules that have no consequence for the case, their cautionary mechanism is often not engaged. They are far more likely in these circumstances to fashion defective rules, and to assert misguided propositions, which have not been fully thought through.[41]

Even as late as December 4, in his response to Powell, Justice Blackmun's views were unformed and equivocal:

> I have *no particular commitment* to the point marking the end of the first trimester as contrasted with some other point, such as quickening or viability. I selected the earliest of the three because medical statistics and the statistical writings *seemed* to focus on it and to draw their contrasts between the first three months and the remainder of the pregnancy. In addition, I *thought* it might be easier for some of the Justices than a designated later point.
>
> I could go along with viability if it could command a court. By that time the state's interest has grown large indeed. I *suspect* that my preference, however, is to stay with the end of the first trimester for the following reasons: (1) It is more likely to command a court. (2) A state is still free to make its decision on the liberal side and fix a later point in the abortion statutes it enacts. (3) I may be wrong, but I have the *impression* that many physicians are concerned about facilities and, for example, the need for hospitalization.[42]

This last statement—among others—was a hunch that had no basis in the record, or in the briefs, or in the two sets of arguments. Nevertheless, according to David Garrow, Powell's memo significantly influenced Blackmun and induced him to expand the right to abortion from the first trimester to viability.[43]

After fifteen months of consideration of the cases, Blackmun distributed a memo on December 11 to the other Justices, asking about viability:

> I selected the earlier point because I felt that it would be more easily accepted (by us as well as others) and because *most medical statistics and statistical studies* appear to me to be centered there. Viability, however, has it[s] own strong points. It has logical and biological justifications. There is a practical aspect, too, for I am sure that there are many pregnant women, particularly young girls, who may refuse to face the fact of pregnancy and who, for one reason or another, do not get around to medical consultation until the end of the first trimester is upon them, or, indeed, has passed.[44]

Here, Blackmun had put his finger on the rationale that finally motivated the Justices to expand the right to viability.

The shift to viability was a practical consideration for Powell and Marshall—they simply wanted to expand the window for access to abortion. In a December 13 draft letter to Blackmun, Powell wrote:

> My guess is that older women, married women and others who are experienced or sophisticated will know when

they are pregnant and be willing to acknowledge it. They also will know where abortions can be obtained (e.g., in New York), and how to go about arranging for them. But the women who most need the benefit of liberalized abortion laws are likely to be young, inexperienced, unsure, frightened and perhaps unmarried. It may well be that many in this category either would not know enough to be sure of pregnancy in the early weeks, or be too embarrassed to seek medical advice prior to the expiration of the first trimester. If there is a constitutional right to an abortion, there is much to be said for making it effective where and when it may well be needed most.[45]

A handwritten note at the top of this letter in the Powell Papers states: "We are not certain the original of this letter was even sent to J. Blackmun or circulated to the Conference."[46] It is likely due to this notation that David Garrow concluded that this remained "unsent."[47] However, Garrow pointed out that Powell "scrawled a bold, dark 'yes' in the margin" of his law clerk's memo next to the passage about girls not seeking help "during the first 12 weeks."[48]

Whether or not the particular memo was sent, Marshall's and Powell's lobbying led to Blackmun's key Memo to the Conference on December 11, 1972, proposing viability, in which he asked the Justices, *"May I have your reactions to this suggestion?"*

This casual inquiry failed to express the large medical window that was being opened. The difference between the end of the first trimester and viability was sixteen weeks—four entire months—between twelve weeks and twenty-eight weeks, with largely unknown medical risks.

Justice Douglas responded on December 11 that he "favor[ed] the first trimester, rather than viability" and eventually mentioned quickening in his concurring opinion in *Doe*.[49] Justice Brennan too questioned viability, but eventually went along with it.[50] Justice Marshall responded to Blackmun on December 12, saying that he supported viability, a letter that James Simon and David Garrow say was written by Marshall's clerk, Mark Tushnet.[51] In a December 12 memo, Powell's clerk wrote to Powell:

> I am shocked at Justice Douglas' note. The Justice, who more than anyone else on this Court stakes his judicial reputation on protecting the poor and the black . . . cannot fail to recognize that a first trimester rule falls most heavily on those classes. . . . I will find time to devote a day to seeing what empriical [*sic*] research is available on the question of how long it takes women—especially the yound [*sic*], the poor, and the minorities—to recognize their predicament.[52]

After the responses, Blackmun finally responded with another Memo to the Conference dated December 15, 1972, which indicated that he would change the draft to adopt viability:

> I have in mind associating the end of first trimester with an emphasis on health, and associating viability with an emphasis on the State's interest in potential life. The period between the two points would be treated with flexibility. I shall try to do this revision next week and circulate another draft before the end of the year. It is my

earnest hope, as you know, that on this sensitive issue we may avoid excessive fractionation of the Court, and that the cases may come down no later than the week of January 15 to tie in with the convening of most state legislatures.[53]

Powell recognized the large role played by his clerk. In a December 27 memo, Powell wrote: "[Blackmun] has made some improvements, which resulted—in significant degree—from the suggestions you made to me."[54] And then in a January 3, 1973, memo to his clerk, Powell wrote: "Although he [Blackmun] gives credit in his memo of December 1 [*sic*] to others, I suggest that you are entitled—particularly in view of your education of me on the viability issue—to credit that is nonetheless substantial because it will never be recognized. I think I was perhaps the first to press for viability change."[55]

Countervailing Considerations That Were Overlooked

If the viability line was not supported by the record, or by the argument, what was the support for viability outside the record? What rationale could the Court have for arbitrarily moving the "critical moment" four entire months—from the end of the first trimester to viability?

In the end, it was not law or medicine or safety that affected the Justices' adoption of viability; it was the pragmatic motivation of expanding the time allowance in pregnancy for abortions.[56] That was expressed by Justice Marshall in his memo of December 12 to Blackmun:

I am inclined to agree that drawing the line at viability accommodates the interests at stake better than drawing it at the end of the first trimester. Given the difficulties which many women may have in believing that they are pregnant and in deciding to seek an abortion, I fear that the earlier date may not in practice serve the interests of those women, which your opinion does seek to serve.[57]

The same motive was expressed by Blackmun in his December 11 memo and by Powell's clerk in his influential December 11 and 12 memos to Powell, and by Powell himself in his December 13 draft letter to Blackmun.

The unilateral shift to viability in November–December 1972 was careless. Several countervailing considerations should have weighed against viability—even assuming there was otherwise a majority to create a "right" to abortion—including the simple fact that viability, and its implications, were never argued in the lower courts, never briefed in the Supreme Court, and never mentioned, even once, during the four hours of oral arguments in December 1971 and October 1972.[58]

The creation of the trimester system and the designation of the first trimester was dictum. Neither the Texas nor the Georgia statute mentioned or hinged upon viability. There was no time limit in the Texas or the Georgia statute. In a December 14, 1972, letter to Blackmun and the Conference, Stewart specifically objected to "the specificity of its dictum—particularly in its fixing of the end of the first trimester as the critical point for valid state action. I appreciate the inevitability and indeed wisdom of dicta in the Court's opinion, but I wonder about the desirability of the dicta being quite so inflexibly 'legislative.' "[59]

The Justices knew that no time limit was before them. This is clear from an exchange with Margie Pitts Hames in the second *Doe* argument:

[JUSTICE]: Mrs. Hames, have you studied the 1970 draft of the Uniform Abortion Act recommended by the Uniform Commission as enough to have an opinion as to its constitutionality?

MRS. HAMES: To my recollection, it does have a time limitation on it. Is that correct? I think that it's my recollection that there are no consultants required, no committee, no limitation on facility, but a 20-week limitation with some exceptions as I recall. I would think it's constitutional.

Q: You mean the state is free to protect the life of the fetus by saying that no abortions after 20 weeks with some exceptions?

MRS. HAMES: I'm not prepared to say 20 weeks, but I am prepared to say that the reason for enacting abortion laws in the very beginning was to protect the health of the woman.

Q: Yes. . . . but

MRS. HAMES: And that reason may come back into existence at some period during the pregnancy. So that, it could be—

Q: You're saying that the state may put a limit on abortions time-wise in the period of pregnancy.

MRS. HAMES: Yes, Your Honor. I think that's possible.

> That's not involved in the Georgia case. There's no
> time limitation in our statute at all.
> Q: I understand.[60]

Over four hours of oral argument in December 1971 and October 1972, this is the closest that the Justices ever came to discussing any time limit. Note that this exchange only vaguely touched on the potential of maternal health risks.

Chief Justice Burger in the *Doe* arguments asked Dorothy Beasley about the theoretical possibility of "one set of standards for the first trimester or the first 140 days under a more rigorous standard after that period."[61] Beasley, in response, emphasized that such a distinction should be left to legislative judgment. In the four hours of argument, these were the only two brief and cursory instances in which a time limit of any kind was mentioned.

Even if a majority of Justices in October 1972 was committed to overturning the abortion laws, the Justices could have, in the alternative, struck the Texas (or Georgia) law as too restrictive and allowed state legislatures to consider time limits, which would have "set up" the issue more precisely and thoughtfully, with the possibility of a factual record.

Contrary to Newman's and Powell's assumption, viability was not and is not more definite than quickening. It is not, like quickening, something that a mother senses. That is more significant to women than viability, which has become increasingly a technical assessment of survivability. Viability is today a matter of survival rates, and those are largely determined by medical technology, which has changed over the years.

This is one of the great ironies of the abortion decisions. The plaintiff in the Georgia case, Mary Doe (Sandra Cano), never had an abortion because of quickening—she felt her baby kick and decided to give birth.[62] The Justices were not informed of this.

The seven medical sources that Blackmun relied upon did no more than suggest that abortion might be safe in the first trimester. The Justices had absolutely no data that suggested that abortion was safe *after* the first trimester.

In fact, extending the abortion "right" to viability contradicted the arguments of the abortion attorneys who said that the risk to women rose significantly after the first trimester. The little medical data that were contained in the briefs and the arguments contradicted any expansion beyond twelve weeks. In the first *Doe* argument, Hames told the Justices that "mortality and complications for late abortions are three times greater, after 12 weeks."[63] In the second argument, Hames reiterated that "first trimester abortions are safer than a lot of late abortions. Complications are three to four times higher in the second trimester."[64] And it conflicted with Blackmun's own acknowledgment in *Roe*: "Because medical advances have lessened this concern [protecting the woman], *at least with respect to abortion in early pregnancy. . . .*"[65]

Safety concerns should have been a very large caution, since there was nothing in the record or in the arguments to suggest that abortions between twelve and twenty-eight weeks were safe. Blackmun's clerk saw the safety issue, and apparently urged Blackmun, unsuccessfully, to "stand by your original position."[66]

The Justices never grasped the safety problem, or, if they

did, they only saw it in one narrow dimension—the immediate safety of the procedure—without consideration for long-term risks. The shift to viability ignored the medical statistics that the Justices had, indicating that the immediate medical risks to women grew considerably after the first trimester.

Given all of the countervailing considerations that were overlooked, it should have been no surprise that the Justices' adoption of viability was immediately and heavily criticized.[67] The renowned law professor John Hart Ely (who had clerked for Chief Justice Earl Warren at the time of *Griswold* in 1965) criticized the Court for failing to explain "exactly why that [viability] is the magic moment. . . . [T]he Court's defense seems to mistake a definition for a syllogism."[68]

No Legal Justification

Aside from the complete lack of medical support, there were also several legal problems with Justice Blackmun's adoption of viability. Viability was irrelevant to "common law history," as many scholars have shown.[69] It was never a part of property law. And it was never a part of homicide law or abortion law. Homicide law looked to quickening and live birth as evidentiary markers, never to viability.[70] As Dellapenna has noted:

> The concept of "viability" in any event could not have had a very long history—it would have been meaningless before the time when medical intervention before full-term birth could have a significant effect. That point came only in the second half of the nineteenth century.[71]

Modern tort law, as developed by judges, was the one legal area that put any significance on viability. That trend began in the late nineteenth century and then waned in the 1960s. Wrongful death actions in tort law did not exist at common law; they were a product of statute or judicial development in the nineteenth century. Some commentators think that viability first came into American law in 1884, when Oliver Wendell Holmes, Jr.—then a Justice on the Massachusetts Supreme Judicial Court—wrote it into that court's decision in the *Dietrich v. Inhabitants of Northampton*[72] case, which rejected a suit for prenatal injury. But, if so, it was only by implication: the child who died was only three or four months along, and Holmes never used the word "viability." Holmes mentioned a notion of "independent existence" and said that the "child" (his word) was "part of the mother" at the time of the injury.[73] (Holmes's opinion and the viability rule were eventually overturned six years before *Roe* by the Massachusetts Supreme Judicial Court.[74]) As of 1974, as one reviewer pointed out, "[o]nly in one narrow area of tort law do courts today generally attach significance to viability and deny recovery—where the fetus is not viable when injured, and is subsequently stillborn."[75]

Viability Rejected in Tort Law

As medical science developed in the twentieth century, there was considerable movement in favor of broadening legal protection in tort and criminal law for the unborn child. Prenatal injury protection grew considerably after 1946, when a federal court first recognized a suit for prenatal injuries in the *Bonbrest* case. A legal study in 1962 showed the progress in allowing prenatal injury actions up to 1962.[76] Between the *Dietrich* decision in 1884 and 1946, twelve state courts had denied a suit for prenatal injuries. The *Bonbrest* case in 1946 was "the turning point in allowing recovery for prenatal injuries in this country."[77] After *Bonbrest*, six of the twelve courts reversed course and allowed a suit for prenatal injuries. In addition, eleven more states after *Bonbrest* allowed a suit between 1949 and 1960.

Tort liability was limited to a viable infant until 1953, when a New York court first allowed a suit for prenatal injury for a "nonviable infant." Five more states allowed a suit for a nonviable infant between 1953 and 1962, with the New Jersey Supreme Court in 1960 concluding that the child was "in existence [as a human being] from the moment of conception."[78] A law review writer noted that "the exact point of time at which the child becomes viable is practically impossible to determine in a border-line case unless the child is born immediately after the injury, so it would seem that the 'viability theory' would therefore lack practical application as a test of liability."[79]

A number of legal scholars have noted that Justice Blackmun misstated the extent to which the law protected the unborn child as of 1972.[80]

[I]n a trend *Roe* missed . . . a majority of state courts (twenty-eight) have expressly or impliedly rejected viability as an appropriate cutoff point for determining liability for nonfatal prenatal injuries and allow actions to be brought for such injuries without regard to the stage of pregnancy when they were inflicted. Many of these decisions were handed down before *Roe*. A minority of jurisdictions (twelve States and the District of Columbia)

recognize a cause of action for prenatal injuries sustained
after viability but have not yet decided whether the action will lie for injuries suffered before viability. An even
smaller minority of States (ten) have not yet been asked to
recognize a cause of action for prenatal injuries. No state
court has rejected a cause of action for prenatal injuries
in twenty-five years. And where prenatal injuries result
in death after live birth the modern cases appear to reject
any requirement of viability as a condition of recovery
under wrongful death statutes.[81]

The viability distinction was questioned or rejected by
numerous courts between the 1920s and 1973, including
the Supreme Courts of Alabama, Georgia, Louisiana, New
Hampshire, New Jersey, Pennsylvania, Rhode Island, Texas,
and Wisconsin.[82] As of 1992, one scholar noted:

> The overwhelming majority of jurisdictions (thirty-six
> states and the District of Columbia) now allow recovery
> under wrongful death statutes for prenatal injuries that
> result in stillbirth where the injury causing death (or at
> least the death itself) occurs after viability. (Few of those
> jurisdictions, however, have allowed recovery where
> both the injury and the death occur before viability.) A
> minority of States (ten) have denied wrongful death ac-
> tions for prenatal injuries unless the death followed a live
> birth. And a handful of States (four) have not yet decided
> whether a wrongful death action will lie for prenatal in-
> juries resulting in stillbirth.
>
> Both the common law action for prenatal injuries and
> the statutory action for the wrongful death of an unborn

child recognize a duty of care that is owed *to the unborn child*. Duties, of course, are owed only to *persons*. Neither *Roe* nor *Casey* [the Court's 1992 decision] displayed any familiarity with the sustained critique of viability in the reported cases on prenatal injuries and wrongful death. As early as the 1920's, courts began to question its relevance in civil cases.[83]

The Supreme Court has frozen viability into American abortion law by edict. But it has had a declining relevance in other areas of law. *Roe* has failed to be influential, and states have moved ahead in increasing legal protection for the unborn child without regard to the stage of gestation at which the injury occurred:

- Forty-seven states allow a cause of action for prenatal injury, thirty before viability.
- Forty states allow a cause of action for wrongful death, thirty-one before viability.
- Thirty-eight states allow a prosecution for fetal homicide, twenty-eight from conception.

Tort and criminal law have increasingly ignored *Roe*, as the Alabama Supreme Court pointed out in an opinion in 2012, which rejected the viability rule and extended legal protection from conception under the state's wrongful death law.[84]

A Medical Rationale?

Some would like to think that the Justices' rationale for viability was medical—that they merely followed the medical data of the time. But almost nothing in the historical record would support that rationale, and much more in the historical record shows that broadening "access" to more abortions was the real reason.

- None of the parties in *Roe* or *Doe* argued viability.
- No amicus brief argued viability, not even a medical brief. The brief filed by the American College of Obstetricians and Gynecologists (ACOG) in August 1971 never mentioned viability.[85]
- No position statement of the AMA, the ACOG, or the American Psychiatric Association before 1972 mentioned viability.[86]
- The Model Penal Code disavowed an abortion right beyond the "fourth month of pregnancy" (i.e., quickening).[87]
- Of the state abortion statutes enacted between 1967 and 1970, only three or four states allowed abortion as late as twenty-four weeks.[88]

Expanding the "Right" beyond Viability

This was not the end of the problem, however. The Justices went even further.

Justice Blackmun wrote in *Roe* that the two decisions are to be "read together."[89] His opinion in *Doe* then defined "health" in abortion law as *"all factors—physical, emotional, psychological, familial, and the woman's age—relevant to the wellbeing of the patient. All these factors may relate to health."*[90] So, whenever and wherever used in abortion law, "health" means "emotional well-being."

As Harvard Law Professor and comparative law expert Mary Ann Glendon has noted:

Doe's broad definition of "health" spelled the doom of statutes designed to prevent the abortion late in pregnancy of children capable of surviving outside the mother's body unless the mother's health was in danger. By defining health as "well-being," *Doe* established a regime of abortion-on-demand for the entire nine months of pregnancy, something that American public opinion has never approved in any state, let alone nationally.[91]

The Justices mandated that there could be no prohibition of any abortion after viability if the abortion provider decided that the "health" of the mother was at issue. If the provider could say that the pregnancy affected the woman's emotional well-being after viability, no prohibition could be enforced and an abortion for any reason could be performed. It was up to the provider, and has been for forty years. The post-viability prohibitions on the books in thirty-eight states have been unenforceable for years.[92]

This has been the law across the fifty states since January 1973. There may be prohibitions after viability on the books, but they are unenforceable, and any time limits that abortion providers observe are only *voluntary*. This is how the Court legalized abortion throughout pregnancy and handed off the whole issue of the safety of post-first-trimester abortions to the discretion of the individual operator.

Due to the ambiguity of the abortion decisions, it became clear only over time that a prohibition of any abortion even after viability was impossible. Because of the *Doe* "health" exception, the United States stands out from the rest of the world—except for Canada, North Korea, and China—with a national policy of abortion on demand from conception to birth—at any time, for any reason.

Some federal courts have gone further and applied the *Doe* health exception to negate any state *regulation* of abortion—parental notice or consent laws, informed consent laws, clinic safety regulations, and so on.[93] Whereas the original context in *Doe* suggested that the "health exception" might apply only to *prohibitions* of abortion *after viability*, some federal courts extended the "health" definition to apply at *any time* of pregnancy and to invalidate *any state regulation*.[94]

The "health" definition is a trap door for any legal prohibition or regulation of abortion. A regulation cannot be enforced if the "emotional well-being" of the patient—including any minor—might be affected by the regulation. And the Justices gave the abortion provider complete discretion to decide whether the patient's "emotional well-being" was impacted by a regulation. The federal courts soon required that the *Doe* health exception be written into the text of any state abortion law, and if a law was written without that language, it was utterly invalid. That's the significance of the "health exception" in abortion law.[95]

There are additional problems with the *Doe* "health" definition. It focuses exclusively on potential risks to "emotional well-being" from *delaying* abortion, and *excludes* any recognition of the risks—short-term or long-term—to women *from abortion*. The *Doe* "health" exception is a one-way ratchet, and thus a big part of the public health vacuum that the Justices created in January 1973.

Conclusion

There was really only one reason why the Justices expanded abortion to fetal viability in November–December 1972: the pragmatic consideration that a broader "right" to abortion would mean more access for more abortions. This reason is expressed in the correspondence of Justices Blackmun, Marshall, and Powell.

Since 1973, the Justices have stuck to viability without a coherent reason.[96] In 1992, a plurality of Justices argued that the Court's adoption and explanation of viability in *Roe* was "a reasoned statement, elaborated with great care."[97] Both parts of that claim are contradicted by the wealth of evidence that we have today.

· CHAPTER FIVE ·

The Medical Myth That Drove the Outcome in *Roe* (and Its Continuing Impact)

Regardless of indications or the methods and procedures, the physical and psychologic risks are real, even under the most careful scrutiny and medical supervision, and the long-term effects are not entirely clear.

—DUNCAN E. REID, *PRINCIPLES & MANAGEMENT OF HUMAN REPRODUCTION*[1]

The brief of Certain Members of the American College of Obstetricians and Gynecology "contains a fairly extensive survey of the medical hazards attendant to legally induced abortions."

—MEMO TO JUSTICE DOUGLAS FROM HIS LAW CLERK[2]

In 2001, nineteen-year-old Stacy Zallie became pregnant while attending college in New Jersey. When she found out, she hoped to marry her boyfriend. But he had other ideas. He made an appointment for an abortion and took

Stacy to a clinic operated by Stephen Chase Brigham. (Nine years later, the *Philadelphia Inquirer* of July 21, 2010 reported that Brigham's license "has been revoked, relinquished, or temporarily suspended in five states," though he still operated a chain of fifteen abortion clinics in New Jersey and Pennsylvania.[3])

According to court papers in a wrongful death case filed by Stacy's father, the "counselor" at Brigham's clinic was not qualified or educated, had no training, and did not provide adequate information on the risks of abortion. She just read from a "Fact Sheet" that included the statement that a woman was "10 times more likely to die from childbirth than from an abortion." That "got Stacy's attention," and she had an abortion on July 6, 2001.[4] Stacy became melancholy and continued to be depressed for several weeks. When she saw a psychiatrist in September, she admitted that she had twice tried to kill herself since August 1. Three days later, she attempted suicide a third time, and the psychiatrist diagnosed Stacy as having major depression. Ten days later, on October 1, 2001, in the middle of the night, Stacy hung herself from the ceiling fan in her bedroom.

The Supreme Court's abortion decisions have been subject to numerous criticisms over the past forty years.[5] But one major factor that has been almost completely overlooked is the medical assumption that led the Justices to decide these two landmark cases without any trial record in either case: At the very heart of the deliberations and decision in the abortion cases was the assumption that "abortion is safer than childbirth."[6]

This notion drove the outcome in the abortion cases perhaps more than any other factor. It was key to the Court's historical rationale for a right to abortion. It was the one reason the Justices used to prohibit health and safety regulations in the first trimester.[7] Because of this notion, the Justices gave abortion providers complete discretion to manage any issues of health and safety and prohibited public health officials from regulating abortion in the first trimester. Because of this medical assumption, the Justices extended the right to abortion throughout pregnancy.

But, perhaps more important, the claim—backed by Supreme Court endorsement—directly influenced the information that women seeking abortion have gotten. Thus, it is important to understand how the notion came to dominate the Justices' decision-making in *Roe* despite the complete absence of reliable medical data to support it.

The Risks of Abortion

The danger of abortion has a long history, which was directly shaped by the growth of medical knowledge and technology. Abortion, like any medical surgery, was unsafe until probably the middle of the nineteenth century. As Georgia's attorney, Dorothy Beasley, told the Justices, the primary purpose of abortion laws was to protect the unborn child, but protecting maternal health was at least a secondary purpose.

Professor Joseph Dellapenna has identified a three-fold typology for primitive abortion practices: injury techniques, ingestion techniques, and intrusion techniques.[8] They were as bad as they sound. All were clearly unsafe—in fact typically ineffective and dangerous, if not fatal. Dellapenna points out that, owing to the ineffectiveness and danger of these techniques, the method of choice for killing an unwanted baby until the nineteenth century was in fact infanticide, not abortion. Trying to end a pregnancy inside the womb was so dangerous and ineffective that it was "better" to wait until the child was outside (born), and then suffocate or kill it by other means. This is confirmed by the infanticide laws and prosecutions in England and, later, in the colonies and states in America.[9]

As medical technology developed, abortion gradually became safer, but it was a relative progress until the "breakthrough" technology of devices like the cannula or the dilator in the late nineteenth century.[10] As Dellapenna has written, "The increasing safety of abortion for the woman at last began to create an opening to criticize the centuries-long traditional prohibition of abortion. . . . Changes in social behavior created a greater demand for abortion services at the very time that abortion was becoming a far less risky choice for a woman."[11] Less risky than before, perhaps, but not without significant risks.

Abortion has short-term risks and long-term risks. Short-term risks, such as lacerations, hemorrhage, or infection, appear within forty-nine days after the procedure. Long-term risks were not adequately studied until after *Roe*, but today there are at least six documented long-term risks:

- Increased risk of preterm birth (or premature delivery) in future pregnancies[12]
- Increased risk of placenta previa in future pregnancies[13]
- Increased incidence of drug and alcohol abuse[14]
- Increased risk of suicide and psychiatric admission after abortion[15]
- Loss of the protective effect against breast cancer of a first full-term pregnancy[16]
- Increased risk of violence and assault after abortion[17]

These may not be the only long-term risks of abortion, and causation may not yet be proved, but they are the best documented in the medical literature today. (A more complete review of current medical studies is addressed in chapter 8.)

Where Did the Mantra Come From?

Sometime in the 1960s, the claim began to be made that abortion was actually safer than childbirth. Up through the 1950s, neither leading abortion advocates nor Planned Parenthood made any claims that abortion was safer than childbirth. Furthermore, until at least 1970, the major British and American medical institutions warned about the dangers of abortion, especially after the first trimester. Between 1968 and 1970, analyses by the American College of Obstetricians and Gynecologists (ACOG),[18] the Royal College of Obstetricians and Gynaecologists (RCOG),[19] and the Medical Society of the State of New York[20] all raised concerns about the risks of abortion.

The source of the claim that abortion is safer than childbirth was apparently an April 1961 report by abortion advocate Christopher Tietze in the *Journal of the American Medical Association*.[21] From then on, attorneys for abortion advocates made the claim in numerous cases in the 1960s in an attempt to influence the courts to legalize abortion.[22] Before long, Tietze's claim began to make its way into court decisions.

The California Supreme Court's decision in the *Belous* case in September 1969, the first state court decision to invalidate a state abortion law, was the first to make the claim.[23] That decision actually cited three of the medical sources that the Supreme Court later cited in *Roe*.[24] By the end of the 1960s, the claim that "abortion is safer than childbirth" was so frequently repeated that it had become a mantra.

No Factual Record in the Abortion Cases

As outlined in chapter 3, the factual records in *Roe* and *Doe* were virtually nonexistent—consisting merely of a complaint, an affidavit, and motions to dismiss that addressed legal, not factual, issues. No factual hearings. No witnesses. No testimony. No cross-examination. Just two hour-long hearings, in which the judges addressed procedural and jurisdictional issues more than substantive questions. And then a direct appeal to the Supreme Court was made, without any intermediate appellate review.

Realizing that *"Doe*'s lack of any evidentiary record" was a problem, Sarah Weddington's co-counsel in the Supreme Court, Roy Lucas, stressed the need to fill that vacuum at a strategy meeting of attorneys in Manhattan in July 1971, as historian David Garrow recounts.[25] Lucas sought to rectify the lack of a factual, medical record by filing "a supplemental appendix of more than four dozen prior court rulings and medical journal papers that all-told came to an imposing 477 pages, far larger than the brief itself."[26] He filled the "supplemental appendix" with sixty papers, fifteen of which dealt with "medical" and "sociological" issues. The Appendix contained nine medical articles or essays.[27] *But none of these nine articles claimed that abortion was safer than childbirth.* And none of these was among the seven that the Court eventually cited. Many of the articles were not peer-reviewed; some were not even published; and none was part of the record.[28] So the mantra was first presented in the briefs filed in the Supreme Court in the summer of 1971 before the first oral arguments on December 13, 1971.

There are passing references to medical statistics and the

supposed safety of abortion in the Justices' papers. The first reference—after the first oral argument on December 13, 1971—is in Justice Brennan's eleven-page letter responding to Justice Douglas's December 22 draft opinion in *Doe*. Brennan suggested that "statistics apparently indicate that abortions in the early part of the term are safe, even when performed in clinics rather than hospitals."[29]

This causal uncertainty—"apparently indicate"—aptly characterizes the Justices' tentative understanding of the medical data. In the end, with no evidentiary record, the Justices had no basis to evaluate the medical claims that were raised in oral argument, and they had an exaggerated belief that they had a command of the medical issues that they clearly did not have, due to the poor record in the cases.

The Oral Arguments

Despite the centrality of the mantra that abortion was safer than childbirth to the abortion decisions, it was mentioned only in passing in the first and second round of oral arguments in *Roe* and *Doe*. The Justices never questioned the truthfulness of the mantra or of the proffered medical data, though it was disputed by the attorneys for Texas and Georgia.

The arguments in the abortion cases hardly touched on medical statistics or the risks of abortion. In the first *Roe* argument, on December 13, 1971, Sarah Weddington asserted the mantra, but it was denied twice by Jay Floyd, the attorney for Texas.[30]

During the first *Doe* argument, that same day, the mantra was not asserted by Margie Pitts Hames, the attorney for the Georgia plaintiffs, but Beasley, the attorney for Georgia, emphatically pointed out that the data were not part of the record in the case:

> And all these statistics and what the doctors think on one side or on the other, and whether abortions are safer than childbirth, and so on, are not really before the Court because they were not introduced into evidence in the court below. So they are not part of the record.[31]

In the second *Roe* argument, on Wednesday, October 11, 1972, Weddington reasserted the mantra, and cited Planned Parenthood data and New York City data that covered only the ten months after New York had legalized abortion. The second attorney for Texas, Robert Flowers, did not address it.

Only in the second *Doe* argument that day did one Justice mention the data. Hames cited "last Sunday's *New York Times*" and "the New York experience statistics" in arguing that clinics instead of hospitals could do abortions safely. But, at the mention of the *New York Times*, Justice Rehnquist—who was not on the Court for the first round of arguments in December 1971—asked: "Mrs. Hames, is there any limit to the judicial notice which we can take? I mean, is last Sunday's newspaper a perfectly permissible thing for us to rely on in deciding a case like this?"[32]

"Judicial notice" is the discretion that judges have to take note of assertions of fact that are not part of the case record.[33] But it is supposed to have some limit. Justice Rehnquist alone had the good sense to mention that there were important reasons for the limits on judicial notice in deciding constitutional cases.

But Rehnquist's question addressed more than just the assumption that abortion was safer than childbirth; it applied to *all* of the factual assumptions that the Justices relied on in drafting the opinions in *Roe* and *Doe*. None of those assumptions was based in the case record or tested by the advocacy process. The four hours of oral arguments in 1971 and 1972 ended without any specific focus on the truth of the data. Throughout these four hours of argument and reargument, not one Justice asked about the data or the medical substance of the proposition that "abortion was safer than childbirth."

The Data the Justices Relied On

After a long and spurious discussion of history taking up the better part of twenty-five pages of Justice Blackmun's opinion in *Roe v. Wade*, the mantra takes center stage. Blackmun asserts that abortion is safer than childbirth and then cites only five medical sources.[34] (He repeats the mantra in his opinion in *Doe*: "advances in medicine and medical techniques have made it safer for a woman to have a medically induced abortion than for her to bear a child."[35]) He never analyzes or discusses the data; he simply cites the articles.

What data did the Court look at? Between them, Justice Blackmun and Justice Douglas (in his separate, concurring opinion) relied on seven articles for the proposition that abortion is safer than childbirth.[36]

It seems clear that the medical articles got into Blackmun's opinion from Douglas's draft opinion. They were possibly the product of independent research by Douglas's clerks, since only two—a 1969 article by Christopher Tietze and the New York City data—were cited in the friend-of-the-court (*amicus curiae*) briefs.[37] Five of the seven medical articles that eventually appear in the opinions in *Roe* first appear, two months after the first argument, in Justice Douglas's draft opinion of January 24, 1972.[38] Douglas's draft opinion states: "Many studies show that it is safer for a woman to have a medically induced abortion than to bear a child."[39] This became a footnote in Douglas's future drafts throughout 1972, and eventually becomes footnote 5 of Douglas's concurrence in *Doe v. Bolton*.[40] Blackmun thanked Douglas in May 1972 for allowing him to review Douglas's draft opinion, and a memo from Blackmun's clerk refers to the articles cited in Douglas's draft.[41] The articles do not appear in Blackmun's opinion until the "2nd Draft" of November 21–22, 1972.[42]

Justice Blackmun makes two statements in his final opinion regarding the safety of abortion. After contending (erroneously) that state abortion statutes were passed solely to protect the health of the woman (and not the unborn child), he says that the situation has changed:

> [A]bortion in early pregnancy, that is, prior to the end of the first trimester, although not without its risk, is now relatively safe. Mortality rates for women undergoing early abortions, where the procedure is legal, *appear to be* as low as or lower than the rates for normal childbirth. [Footnote 44 cites medical articles.] Consequently, any interest of the State in protecting the woman from an inherently hazardous procedure, except when it would be equally dangerous for her to forgo it, has largely disappeared.[43]

This extremely significant claim about the limitations on the state's "interest" in protecting the health of women—the foundation for the Court's decisions in *Roe* and *Doe*—was hardly touched on in the four hours of oral arguments in *Roe* and *Doe*. It was asserted in the Planned Parenthood briefs but was vigorously and thoroughly rebutted in competing briefs filed in the case.

Later in his opinion, Justice Blackmun makes the significant conclusion that "the State's important and legitimate interest in the health of the mother" becomes "compelling . . . in the light of present medical knowledge . . . at approximately the end of the first trimester."[44] He continues:

> This is so because of the *now-established medical fact*, referred to above at 149, that, until the end of the first trimester mortality in abortion *may be less* than mortality in normal childbirth. It follows that, from and after this point, a State may regulate the abortion procedure to the extent that the regulation reasonably relates to the preservation and protection of maternal health.[45]

The "appear to be" on page 149 suddenly becomes an "established medical fact" on page 163, but Justice Blackmun then immediately qualifies the "established medical fact" with "may be less." So, despite the contradiction in this paragraph, the mantra was taken to be fact by the Justices.

How reliable are the seven sources cited by Justices Blackmun and Douglas?

The first, the April 1961 article in the *Journal of the American Medical Association* (*JAMA*) by Christopher Tietze and Hans Lehfeldt, is merely a self-styled "report" of a so-called

International Conference on Abortion Problems and Abortion Control that was held in May 1960 in then-Communist East Germany.[46] Tietze evidently attended. It is not an analysis of data, much less a peer-reviewed study, but a "report" on conference papers addressing 1950s statistics from Eastern European countries. Moreover, much of the Tietze and Lehfeldt "report" is based on nothing more than personal communications with the conference speakers—particularly with a Dr. Herschler on Hungarian data—rather than published data. No evidence is given that any of the asserted numbers are peer-reviewed or reliable.[47]

Given the number of times that this 1961 *JAMA* article was cited in the 1960s, it can justifiably be said that the mantra that crept into so many federal court decisions on abortion before *Roe* was based on Tietze's conversations with Herschler about the Hungarian experience with legalized abortion, and not much more.

The second source cited by the Justices (and by other state and federal courts before *Roe*[48]) was also a Tietze paper. Entitled "Mortality with Contraception and Induced Abortion," it was less than two pages long. In it, Tietze claims to compare the risk of mortality from contraception and abortion.[49] He starts by imagining a "statistical model," with an express assumption of a mortality rate from childbirth of 20 per 100,000 as "a reasonable approximation."[50] He then assumes an *illegal* abortion mortality rate of 100 per 100,000 pregnancies. He calls this a "very rough estimate and almost certainly conservative" but gives no basis for this claim. The paper does not claim to compare mortality from childbirth and *legal* abortion, and there is no data in the paper that would enable one to make such a comparison.[51] His methodology—which involves mixing and matching numbers from different countries and from different time periods—suffers from fundamental problems.

The third paper, yet another by Tietze, on "therapeutic abortions" from 1970 is a brief, three-page report.[52] This report did not claim to be a study of maternal mortality from abortion compared to childbirth. Very little is said about maternal mortality; only bare numbers of deaths are reported. The category of "therapeutic abortion" is undefined, and there is no consistent measure in the paper that limits his commentary to "therapeutic" abortions. The data in this article came from the Professional Activities Survey (PAS) "conducted by the Commission on Professional and Hospital Activities," which involved the *voluntary* participation of hospitals. Tietze makes at least four devastating concessions that leave the reliability of the data in tatters:

- The hospitals participating in the PAS survey were "not a random sample of all American hospitals."
- "[R]eliable statistical information on the incidence of *therapeutic* abortion in American hospitals is difficult to obtain because the data are scattered over thousands of hospitals with their individual records and record-keeping systems. To date, most states have no effective centralized agency for the compilation of this information, and none exists on the federal level."
- "The data presented here may be used to arrive at *rough estimates* of the numbers of therapeutic abortions performed in all hospitals in the U.S. during the period 1963–1968."
- "[T]he true number of therapeutic abortions in any particular year *may well have been 10 per cent smaller or 20 per cent larger* than the estimate shown in Table 4."[53]

Given these concessions about the poor quality of the data, this report is virtually worthless in providing any comparison of mortality from childbirth and abortion, and the so-called data are worthless for drawing any other reliable conclusions.

The fourth source was a 1970 paper by Malcolm Potts from "the International Planned Parenthood Federation of London, England."[54] It seems, on its face, to be the most substantial of the seven sources, with thirteen pages and twenty-eight references. But that is misleading. Potts first addresses the incidence of abortion in various countries and then points to Eastern European data but cannot cite one published study with such data, let alone a peer-reviewed one. He makes broad statements, claiming, for example, that abortion deaths fell when "liberalized" laws were enacted, without the data to support that claim. Virtually all assertions on data are undocumented and have no citations whatsoever.[55]

The fifth source was a June 1971 report on data from New York City supposedly documenting the city's experience since New York legalized abortion on July 1, 1970. The June date shows that it is based on barely the first ten to eleven months of legalization in New York. Critics at the time pointed out that more than 50 percent of New York City patients were lost to follow-up: many flew in and out of the city for their abortion, so their health status after the abortion could not be verified.[56]

The sixth source was a 1966 "article" by a Czech doctor, Vera Kolblova. But it was really a *six-paragraph letter to the editor*. Kolblova comments on Czech law since 1957 with the purpose of showing that the law "has great advantages and ameliorates health problems."[57] Kolblova describes the law, includes some statistics from 1957 to 1964 on complications and deaths, and asserts that the law accomplished its purpose "to limit the number of criminal abortions and reduce the number of consequent complications and deaths."[58] The purpose of this letter to the editor was not to contend that abortion is safer than childbirth, and, in any case, there are no data in the letter to support that proposition.

Finally, the seventh source was an article from the 1966 *World Medical Journal*. The author, K. H. Mehland, is identified as a professor at the University of Rostock in East Germany. Mehland surveys the social indications for which abortions are allowed in several Soviet Bloc countries. No graph, figure, or table shows maternal mortality rates from abortion (legal or illegal) or childbirth. Mehland asserts that "the number of deaths due to abortion decreased in the period 1959–1965 in Poland from 76 to 26, Bulgaria 47 to 16, CSSR 53 to 11 (1962), Hungary 83 to 24 (1964)." He claims that "there has also been a clear decline in deaths due to abortion, the rate now standing at 6 deaths per 100,000 operations performed in hospitals by specialists. The numbers of complications and late sequelae have also been reduced significantly." Mehland cites no other publications and has no bibliography.

None of the articles offers a real analysis of the data; none is peer-reviewed. None of the articles cited by Justices Blackmun or Douglas provides any information that would allow the data to be verified.[59] These seven sources provide no reliable data for which to confidently compare maternal mortality from abortion and childbirth as of 1972. And there is no consideration whatsoever of long-term risks. The seven sources deal only with immediate risks.

Instead of these articles, the Justices might have looked

at existing obstetrical-gynecological textbooks, which commonly cull published articles for the best data. Presumably, Justice Blackmun did something like this during his two weeks researching at the Mayo Clinic in July 1972. But no textbooks are cited in *Roe* to support the mantra because the existing obstetrical textbooks published before 1972 never made the claim that abortion was safer than childbirth.[60]

In the end, only Chief Justice Burger publicly voiced unease about the Court's reliance on the medical statistics. When the abortion decisions were released on January 22, 1973, Burger made the vague statement in his separate, concurring opinion in *Doe* that he was "troubled that the Court has taken notice of various scientific and medical data in reaching its conclusion."[61] But he then dismissed these concerns. If nothing else, this showed his misunderstanding of the significance of the mantra and its central role in *Roe v. Wade*.

The Contrary Data Ignored

In addition to relying on unreliable data, the Justices disregarded contrary data. One of Justice Douglas's law clerks wrote a memo to Douglas on October 27, 1971, before the first oral arguments, noting that a brief filed by "Certain Members of the American College of Obstetricians and Gynecology" on October 15 "contains a fairly extensive survey of the medical hazards attendant to legally induced abortions."[62]

The assertion that abortion was safer than childbirth—and the data from the Soviet Bloc countries and from New York City—was challenged as unreliable many times in the years leading up to *Roe*. Friend-of-the-court briefs filed in

Roe and *Doe* challenged the Soviet Bloc data, and pointed out that, although Denmark and Sweden had allowed legal abortion ten to fifteen years longer than any Soviet Bloc country, they had abortion mortality rates that exceeded mortality rates from childbirth.

Furthermore, briefs filed argued that the New York City data were unreliable: 55.5 percent of the abortions (in the first ten to eleven months) were performed on out-of-state residents, making it difficult if not impossible to monitor their condition, and a report confirmed that 53.5 percent of the out-of-state residents were lost to follow-up. There were reports in 1970 and 1971 of injuries to out-of-state residents at airports or upon their return to their home state. New York officials excluded some abortion deaths from the New York calculations because they were, allegedly, not the result of "legal" abortions. But distinguishing between "legal" and "illegal" abortions is an extremely complicated and subjective measure for at least three reasons: first, the categorization of an abortion as "illegal" may rest on some very technical judgment of regulations; second, the "illegal" abortion might be performed by a more highly skilled operator than the "legal" abortion, and under similar medical conditions; and, third, the reason for these subtle distinctions were likely never recorded by the officials.

The unreliability of the New York data was brought directly to Justice Blackmun's attention by a law clerk. An undated, unsigned, one-page memo in Justice Blackmun's papers shows that his clerk pointed out the "devastating" criticism of the New York City data that had been made by one medical brief, showing that more than 50 percent of the women who underwent abortions in New York City were lost to subsequent follow-up, so their health outcome could not be determined. The clerk wrote, sometime after May 22, 1972:

> The New York City abortion data, referred to in Mr. Justice Douglas' opinion, is devastatingly criticized by one of the amicus briefs. It is there pointed out that 55.5% of the 150,629 abortions legally performed in New York City between July 1, 1970, and May 31, 1971, were on out-of-state residents and another 3.3% on out-of-city residents of New York State. . . . These away-from-home patients obviously presented follow-up difficulties of greater magnitude than local residents. In the May 22, 1972, issue of U.S. News and World Report, . . . the statement is made that "in New York City alone, more than 278,000 legal abortions were performed in the first 18 months the new law was in effect—almost two-thirds of them involving women from outside the city."[63]

Justice Blackmun edited the clerk's grammar in his recognizable handwriting—as he was famously prone to do[64] —changing the clerk's "is devastatingly criticized" to "receives devastating criticism from," but otherwise apparently ignored the point of the memo and nevertheless cited the New York report in his final opinion.[65] The Justices did not analyze—let alone refute—the contrary data; they simply ignored them.[66]

Why Maternal Mortality and Abortion Mortality Rates Cannot Be Compared

Today, the mantra that abortion is safer than childbirth is based on a mechanical comparison of the published abortion

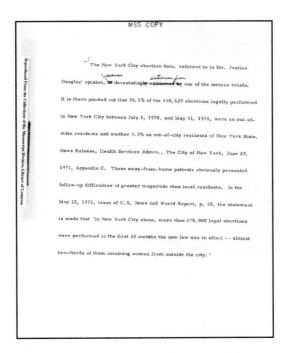

FIGURE 5. *One-page memo on New York City abortion data, Harry A. Blackmun Papers, Library of Congress, Box 151, Folder 8. Reproduced from the Collections of the Manuscript Division, Library of Congress.*

mortality rate—sometimes cited as "0.6 per 100,000 abortions"—and the maternal (childbirth) mortality rate—sometimes cited as "6.7 per 100,000 deliveries."[67] These two rates cannot be compared, however, and do not give an accurate picture of the risks of abortion.[68]

The first problem is that the accuracy of the rate is completely dependent on an accurate number of deaths—the numerator. But there are serious reasons to doubt the accuracy of published figures on abortion deaths in the United States: there is no uniform, mandatory tracking and reporting system in the United States to give any confidence that abortion deaths are accurately tracked and reported. Neither the federal nor the state governments maintain any system of uniform, mandatory reporting of abortion deaths (mortality) or injuries (morbidity). The federal Centers for Disease Control and Prevention (CDC) depends on *voluntary* reporting systems and has estimated that maternal deaths are underreported by 30 to 150 percent.[69] A death certificate may or may not tell if the death was maternal or abortion-related. In contrast, the childbirth mortality numbers have been scrupulously collected for years by state and national agencies.

In addition, the two rates are inherently noncomparable because their denominators are completely different. They might be comparable if both rates were deaths (from abortion or childbirth) per 1,000 pregnancies, but that is not the case.

The maternal mortality rate is defined by the CDC as all maternal deaths per 100,000 live births, rather than pregnancies:[70]

$$\frac{\text{maternal deaths}}{100,000 \text{ live births}}$$

Using live births rather than pregnancies shrinks the denominator (since pregnancies are a larger group, and some end in miscarriage or stillbirth) and thereby inflates the mortality rate.[71] The use of live births as the denominator is actually dictated by the World Health Organization (WHO), for purposes of enhancing international comparability.

By contrast, the abortion mortality rate is defined by the CDC as "known legal induced abortion-related" deaths per 100,000 legal abortions.

$$\frac{\text{known legal induced abortion-related deaths}}{\text{100,000 legal abortions}}$$

The identification of a "legal" abortion—when one considers all the potential regulations at the local, state, or federal level that could theoretically apply—is prone to being highly subjective and manipulated. In addition, both the numerator and denominator in this rate are also based on *voluntary* reporting systems.

So, the abortion mortality rate includes only "legal" abortion deaths, while the childbirth mortality rate includes all maternal deaths (including deaths from abortions, ectopic pregnancies, accidents, and homicides). Accidents and homicides—which have nothing to do with the biological risks of pregnancy—are also included in maternal death figures. The maternal death numbers are likely inflated, while the abortion death figures are likely undercounted. The childbirth mortality rate and the abortion mortality rate are simply apples and oranges.

Beyond the inherent difference in what these rates measure, there are additional problems. The maternal mortality figures do not take account of the stage of gestation. A genuine comparison would assess only the prospective risk of continuing the pregnancy from the time in gestation that abortion is considered—e.g., what's the risk for this particular woman at eight weeks—rather than the mathematical risk throughout pregnancy. This is not done—adjustment is not made—because it is not statistically feasible; those data are not available because death certificates do not provide data on gestational age.

In 2004, Dr. Julie Gerberding, then director of the CDC,

Why the Mortality Rates for Abortion and Childbirth Are Not Comparable

THE TWO RATES

ABORTION MORTALITY RATE =

$$\frac{\text{LEGAL INDUCED ABORTION DEATHS}}{100,000 \text{ LEGAL ABORTIONS}}$$

CHILDBIRTH MORTALITY RATE =

$$\frac{\text{MATERNAL DEATHS}}{100,000 \text{ LIVE BIRTHS}}$$

How These Rates Are Both Relatively Inaccurate and Measure Different Things

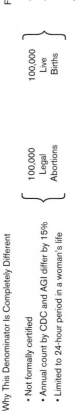

Number of Legal Induced Abortion Deaths

Number of Maternal Deaths

100,000 Legal Abortions

100,000 Live Births

Why These Numbers Are Undercounted

- No formal ascertainment
- Societal bias against self-report
- Intimate partner and family may be unaware
- Only direct deaths included

Why This Denominator Is Completely Different

- Not formally certified
- Annual count by CDC and AGI differ by 15%
- Limited to 24-hour period in a woman's life

Why These Numbers Are More Reliable

- Most states link birth and death certificates
- Includes direct and indirect deaths like homicides and suicides

From This Denominator

- All states have birth certificates
- Excludes all pregnancies that end by miscarriages, ectopic, and stillbirths
- Time period covers pregnancy and 1 year after birth

FIGURE 6.

discouraged the mechanical comparison of the two rates and warned that they are two different measures. She emphasized that the two rates "are conceptually different and are used by CDC for different public health purposes."[72] Despite this warning, abortion providers and medical organizations regularly cite this comparison of abortion mortality rates and childbirth mortality rates to claim that abortion is safer than childbirth.[73]

Only a Snapshot

The comparison of maternal and abortion mortality rates is a snapshot approach that really needs a video to look at the broader context. A snapshot of a man pointing a gun, for example, does not tell us much. Context makes all the difference.

Abortion mortality is inherently limited to immediate causes—what happens to the woman in the first forty-nine days after the procedure. "Safety" is defined very narrowly and exclusively in terms of death, that is, by comparative mortality rates; other complications short of death (morbidity) are not taken into consideration.

As Dellapenna describes the comparison:

> The studies compare a procedure that usually takes a few minutes and rarely more than a day (with any long-term complications rarely being traced back to the abortion) to a process that lasts nine months. The studies often compare complication and fatality rates to statistics drawn from all births within the general population of the region, state, or nation rather than to birthing-samples matched for maternal age, health, and similar variables

that could well affect the relative safety of the two procedures. The studies usually did not consider maternal
morbidity, an effect that is more difficult to measure.[74]

In effect, the comparison of abortion and childbirth
mortality rates narrowly focuses on who walks out of the
clinic or hospital alive. But even that analogy is not accurate,
because the health of a woman who walks out of an abortion
clinic is monitored less than a woman who walks out of a
hospital after childbirth.

How Recent Research on Long-Term Risks
Further Undercuts the Mantra

Emphasizing the mechanical comparison of mortality rates
also disregards the growing data on possible long-term risks:
the increased risk of preterm birth, increased risk of placenta
previa, the increased incidence of drug and alcohol abuse,
the increased incidence of suicide and psychiatric admission,
the loss of the protective effect of a first full-term pregnancy
against breast cancer, and the increased risk of death and
injury from violent assault. These risks have been studied
in medical journals internationally for several decades, but
the studies, reviewed in chapter 8, have been increasing in
number and sophistication in the last decade.

These data on the long-term risks directly affect the relative risks between childbirth and abortion and how women
should be informed. If a pregnant patient comes to an ob-
gyn and says she is considering abortion, the doctor might
lay out the relative risk of childbirth and abortion, but this
information only considers the short-term. The doctor
should also lay out the long-term risks for her patient, and
the data is fuller today than it was a decade ago. If the doctor

wants to consider the impact on the woman's psychological comfort one or two years after the abortion, or her risks of preterm birth in future pregnancies, then the woman needs to consider the growing number of recent studies that have found an increased risk of long-term consequences.[75]

Does Anyone Believe the Mantra?

There's good reason to believe that, aside from abortion providers, obstetricians and gynecologists do not believe that abortion is safer than childbirth.

If the comparison were valid, a doctor would likely commit malpractice unless she informed *every* pregnant woman of the mechanical comparison and counseled every pregnant woman to consider abortion—if childbirth is really "10 times more dangerous than abortion." But regular obstetrician-gynecologists do not do that because they apparently don't believe the comparison is valid. Only women considering abortion are given the mantra.

Conclusion

The medical mantra that abortion is safer than childbirth was false in 1972. It was based on seven medical articles with no reliable medical data. The Justices took "judicial notice" of a highly contested medical claim for which there was no record. There were contrary data in the briefs filed in the Supreme Court, and the claim was directly contradicted at oral argument. Any one of these signs should have cautioned the Justices against ruling without a trial record, or cautioned them in favor of the narrowest ruling possible. Instead, the Justices issued a more sweeping ruling than any participant imagined possible.

Unfortunately, the influence of the mantra did not stop

with the Justices' decisions. Because the Justices proclaimed
it to be true, the mantra has shaped abortion practice and
popular culture for forty years. Dellapenna has noted that
Guidelines for Women's Health Care published by the American College of Obstetricians and Gynecologists (ACOG)
in 1996—twenty-three years after *Roe* and *Doe*—claimed
"that maternal deaths from pregnancy and birth are 25 times
higher than maternal deaths during abortions, but without
reference to any research or other sources."[76] As the case of
Stacy Zallie shows, the mantra directly affects the medical
information that women seeking abortion get—or do not
get—about abortion.[77] And the consequences of such misinformation being passed off as fact can have serious consequences for women's health.

· CHAPTER SIX ·

The American Experience the Justices Overlooked

Abortion is no longer a dangerous procedure. This applies not just to therapeutic abortions as performed in hospitals but also to so-called illegal abortions as done by physicians. In 1957 there were only 260 deaths in the whole country attributed to abortions of any kind. . . .

—DR. MARY CALDERONE,
MEDICAL DIRECTOR OF PLANNED PARENTHOOD[1]

[T]he data suggest that there have been as many maternal deaths in the United States annually from legal abortions (estimates range from 15 to 35 per year) as there were maternal deaths from illegal abortions in the years immediately before Roe v. Wade *was decided.*

—JOSEPH DELLAPENNA,
DISPELLING THE MYTHS OF ABORTION HISTORY[2]

Where the important thing is to win the case no matter how, however, I suppose I agree with [Cyril] Means's technique: begin with a scholarly attempt at historical research; if it doesn't work, fudge it as necessary; write a piece so long that others will read only your introduction and conclusion; then keep citing it until courts begin picking it up. This preserves the guise of impartial scholarship while advancing the proper ideological goals.

—DAVID TUNDERMANN TO ROY LUCAS,
CO-COUNSEL WITH SARAH WEDDINGTON[3]

The Justices' consideration of the abortion cases in 1971 and 1972 was overshadowed by numerous assumptions about the history, purpose, and *ineffectiveness* of abortion laws—assumptions never tested at trial or reviewed by any intermediate appellate court. But their powerful impact was evident.

Justice Stewart told Sarah Weddington during oral argument that her opinion of the negative impact of the Texas abortion law was a "very eloquent" statement. Justice Blackmun referred to "[t]he prevalence of high mortality rates at illegal 'abortion mills'" in his final opinion.[4] And while the "effectiveness" of the existing antiabortion laws was never expressly mentioned, claims were made about the public health impact of illegal abortions and of women injured by illegal abortions. The image of the "back alley" served to make a mockery of the laws.

But the Justices never confronted whether the assumptions or the images were fact or fiction. When the issue is returned to the states, what states might do and the range of policies that they might consider should be evaluated with an understanding of the American experience that preceded *Roe*.

The Medical Context and Limits

The past four decades have been an age of ultrasonography, *in utero* surgery and transfusions, and fetal medicine and therapy.[5] Medicine can identify and treat the health problems of the unborn child in the womb earlier in gestation.[6] It is not often recognized how new this technology is, nor how radically it has changed and enhanced society's understanding of life in the womb.

Knowledge about pregnancy—its onset, determination, progress, and the causes of its failure or termination—has always been limited by contemporary medical science.[7] In Anglo-American culture, laws against abortion have been enforced since at least the thirteenth century,[8] but the language and enforcement of abortion laws have been necessarily tied to the contemporary state of medical science. The text and scope of abortion statutes, the mechanisms of enforcement, and the protection for mothers and their children have changed over the past eight centuries as medical science has improved.

A key medical factor in abortion law enforcement has always been determining pregnancy. Urine tests for pregnancy, for example, were developed only fifty years ago and were not completely reliable during the 1960s.[9] In fact, Margie Pitts Hames told the Justices in the first *Doe* argument in December 1971 that "it is only about the sixth or the eighth week that pregnancy tests actually become accurate, or the degree of accuracy is such that can reasonably predict whether one is pregnant or not."[10] Hames's statement inadvertently showed why quickening was important in the centuries before pregnancy tests, and also why talk about "knowing" about pregnancy before quickening was largely speculation.

It is clear that the mere detection of pregnancy early in gestation was quite difficult from the fourteenth to the nineteenth century.[11] Early treatises on midwifery devoted entire chapters to determining the signs of pregnancy. The English common law developed at a time of both primitive medical conditions and high infant mortality. If a child was stillborn, or if an infant's body was discovered, was it due to criminal or natural causes?

Consequently, the common law fixed upon the mother's first sensation of fetal movement—quickening—as the first true sign of pregnancy for purposes of legal proof. Before then, all other signs or symptoms of pregnancy were considered ambiguous and uncertain. Since quickening does not usually occur until sixteen to eighteen weeks of pregnancy, it was therefore very difficult, if not impossible, for medicine to prove a live pregnancy before sixteen weeks of gestation, and it was thus impossible for the law to apply the homicide law before that time.[12] Quickening was an evidentiary distinction, not a moral one.

Besides quickening, the other medical criterion that the common law focused on was "live birth." At quickening, a woman might have a sensation of having felt the child move within. But someone might assault the mother, and it was necessary for the law to prove that the child was alive at the time of the assault and that death was caused by the assault, and not by natural means. As a result, the common law created the "born-alive rule" as an evidentiary buffer against false charges and ambiguous medical evidence.[13]

> The term "born alive" means expulsion from the womb
> alive; it does not mean term birth; it does not relate to
> any particular time of gestation.[14]

It was virtually impossible for the law to prove a homicide (the killing of a human being) unless the child was expelled alive (born alive), observed outside the womb, and died thereafter. A child could die in the womb or shortly after birth for myriad reasons. These could not be easily identified, and natural causes could not be readily separated from criminal causes. Since homicide at common law was invariably a capital crime, judges and juries were reluctant to convict on uncertain evidence.[15]

There is an important distinction between the recognition of legal rights and their enforcement. Declaring a principle and proving its violation are two very different things. Thus, William Blackstone, the foremost common law historian, could declare the unborn child to be a person at the earliest moment that it could be determined to be alive, but enforcement of the law protecting the child's life, which depended on evidence, was another matter.[16] The law was constantly constrained by problems of evidence.

Because of these evidentiary problems, the law of abortion developed independently of the law of homicide, at least after the born-alive rule was adopted in 1600. Abortion law applied to the unborn child, homicide law applied to the born infant. Since the abortion law could only be applied when there was knowledge of life, the law could not be enforced until quickening. There was, therefore, never a "right" to abortion before quickening, but that distinction was lost on the Justices. The medical limitations on the law should not be misunderstood as legal tolerance for abortion, but that is exactly what the Justices assumed.

It is often falsely assumed that because the English common law did not treat abortion before quickening as homicide, it did not prohibit abortion before quickening as any crime.[17] In Joseph Dellapenna's 2006 groundbreaking treatise, *Dispelling the Myths of Abortion History*, however, he makes it clear beyond any doubt that the common law prohibited abortion in order to protect the life of the unborn child to the greatest extent possible given contemporary medical science.

> [B]y the close of the seventeenth century, the criminality of abortion under the common law was well established. Courts had rendered clear holdings that abortion was a crime, no decision indicated that any form of abortion was lawful, and secondary authorities similarly uniformly supported the criminality of abortion. The only differences among these authorities had been about the severity of the crime (misdemeanor or felony), an uncertainty that, under [Edward] Coke's influence, began to settle into the pattern of holding abortion to be a misdemeanor unless the child were born alive and then died from the injuries or potions that lead to its premature birth.[18]

The Justices' Misplaced Reliance on Cyril Means's Spurious History

Instead of relying on the English common law (which the American colonies adopted) and numerous state court decisions confirming the purpose of the nineteenth-century state statutes to protect the unborn child as a human being, the Justices relied almost exclusively on the historical revisionism in two articles by Professor Cyril Means, published in 1968 and 1971.[19] Means was general counsel to the National Association for the Repeal of Abortion laws (NARAL) when he filed briefs in the courts containing his historical theories, and his articles were funded by the Association for the Study of Abortion (ASA), which was funded by John D. Rockefeller III.

Means pushed two unprecedented theories on the courts: that abortion was not a crime (even after quickening) before the nineteenth-century statutes, and that the original purpose of the nineteenth-century statutes was not to protect the unborn child but only the mother from dangerous abortions.[20]

Relying entirely on two English cases from the fourteenth century, Means argued that abortion was a common law liberty.[21] But Means mischaracterized those cases.[22] His reading of them was unprecedented, and he overlooked many other common law cases penalizing abortionists.[23] As historian Shelley Gavigan points out, Means's starting premise was the most incomprehensible: there is a "contradiction inherent in attempting to defend women's right to abortion . . . by relying on a fourteenth century case in which a woman was beaten and her unborn infants killed as a result."[24] In light of the interpretation given those two fourteenth-century cases by English legal authorities and subsequent scholars—that they simply were not precedents that correctly stated the law—it is incredible that the Justices relied on Means for two critical conclusions in *Roe*: (1) "it now appear[s] doubtful that abortion was ever firmly established as a common law crime,"[25] and (2) "at common law, at the time of the adoption of our Constitution and throughout the major portion of the 19th century, abortion was viewed with less disfavor than under most American statutes currently in effect."[26]

Nevertheless, Means's theories were used by Roy Lucas and other attorneys who challenged the state abortion laws, and they were cited by a number of courts in the cases that led up to *Roe*. Because of Means, federal judges such as Jon O. Newman looked at the common law of the sixteenth and seventeenth centuries through the lens of modern medical knowledge instead of understanding it through the contemporary medical constraints that had actually shaped the law and its application. Newman cited Means several times in his opinion in the second Connecticut abortion case that was issued in September 1972, three weeks before the second round of arguments in the Supreme Court, and the Justices were influenced by Newman. Means influenced California Chief Justice Roger Traynor and the California Supreme Court's 1969 decision in *People v. Belous*.[27] Justice Blackmun cited Means seven times in his opinion in *Roe*.

Means's theories were critical for three reasons: first, he gave novel reasons to doubt previously unquestioned English and American legal authorities in their affirmation that the abortion laws were meant to protect the unborn child; second, he gave the Justices the notion that the historical reason for the abortion laws was not protection of the unborn child but only protection of women's health (once technology produced the means to do abortions with relative safety, according to Means's theory, the historical reasons for abortion laws became obsolete); and, third, Means allowed the

Justices to think that they were not making a radical decision because a "right" to abortion (at least before quickening and into the second trimester) preceded the nineteenth-century state statutes, which had eclipsed that "right." Means's writings allowed the Justices to escape several centuries of Anglo-American legal history and practice that treated abortion as a serious crime against human life.

Means's "history" was challenged at the time, although it was not until 2006 that Dellapenna, with the benefit of further research on the English common law, exhaustively refuted Means's spurious history.[28] One example of Means's distortions is his use of a 1787 medical treatise. According to Justin Dyer,

> [t]he chief evidence Means cited in support of his view that the American Founders considered the unborn to be non-persons was Samuel Farr's 1787 *Elements of Medical Jurisprudence*, which was published the same year as the Constitution. But Farr's medical treatise directly contradicted Means' theory. In unambiguous language, Dr. Farr maintained that human life began "immediately after conception" and that "nothing but the arbitrary forms of human institutions can make it otherwise."[29]

Legal history as known in 1973, and reinforced by recent historical research, has eclipsed the myths about the history of abortion law that Means put forward and that the Justices adopted in *Roe*.[30] But it is upon Means's theories—as an attempt to tie a right to abortion to American legal principles—that *Roe*'s foundation rests.[31]

Enforcement against Practitioners, Not Women

One of the most interesting ironies of the abortion decisions is the notion that women who had abortions were the target of abortion laws before *Roe*. There are three interrelated angles to this myth.

First, although women were prosecuted for participation in abortion under the English common law,[32] the common law was replaced in America in the nineteenth century by the pragmatic judgment that the abortionist was the most significant culprit, that the woman was a second victim of abortion, and that criminalizing women's participation undermined effective law enforcement.

Most states expressly treated women as the second victim of abortion.[33] This was so even for self-abortion. Dellapenna provides evidence that treating the woman as a second victim was "based on both the rarity in practice of voluntary, elective abortion and the danger of the procedure when it did occur."[34]

Second, the woman's personal guilt was not the issue in abortion prosecutions, but rather whether she should be considered an "accomplice" as a matter of legal doctrine. If the court concluded that she was, legally, an accomplice, that would prevent—under the then-applicable rules of evidence—the introduction of evidence against the abortionist without corroboration (a large hurdle for the prosecution against the abortionist). Approximately thirty-nine of the forty state courts that considered whether aborted women were accomplices concluded that women were not.[35]

Third, women were not charged by police or prosecuted by district attorneys for abortion. In fact, it was *abortionists* who raised the issue during the prosecutions and claimed that women were "accomplices" as a ploy to get the evidence against the practitioner thrown out under the applicable rules of evidence. As one commentator has aptly summarized the law:

> The primary issue in the complicity cases was not the guilt of the woman but of her abortionist. The defense— not the prosecution—sought to have such women named as accomplices because they often were the only eyewitnesses to their abortions. Since most states required that the testimony of an accomplice be corroborated before being admitted into evidence, the abortionist would typically allege that the woman was his accomplice in the performance of the abortion. The defense hoped thereby to make the woman's testimony inadmissible and thus, in the absence of corroborating evidence, to win acquittal.[36]

If the abortionist could convince the court to treat the woman as an accomplice, and her testimony could not be corroborated by another person, her testimony would not be admitted, and the case would likely dissolve.[37] As late as 1968, Ruth Barnett—the Portland abortionist cast as heroine in a 1994 book, *The Abortionist*—used this tactic unsuccessfully in her appeal from her conviction.[38]

Although some state laws in the nineteenth century allowed the prosecution of the woman who had an abortion, there is apparently no reported appellate decision in the twentieth century upholding the conviction of a woman for self-induced abortion or for submitting to an abortion. The last two cases that involved such a conviction were in 1911 and 1922, and they show exactly the dilemma the prosecution was pushed into if the woman was treated as an accomplice.[39] This policy of treating the woman as the second victim of abortion controlled the enforcement of abortion law throughout the twentieth century.

In sum, the most that the states did in the way of penalizing women for abortion in the twentieth century was to prohibit both men and women from *soliciting* abortion. At the time of *Roe*, seventeen states still had anti-solicitation laws on the books that applied to abortion.[40] Anti-solicitation laws apply to a whole range of crimes, from prostitution to murder.[41] These laws were applied even-handedly in the abortion context against men and women.[42]

Active Enforcement Until *Roe*

Though marked by lapses and marred by corruption like other areas of law enforcement, abortion laws were actively enforced. While there is some evidence that police and prosecutors were lax in their enforcement in some cities, vigorous and successful prosecutions were undertaken in major metropolitan areas in every decade throughout the last half of the nineteenth century,[43] and prosecutors in all parts of the country enforced abortion laws in the early decades of the twentieth century.[44] In the 1940s and 1950s, prosecutions for abortion were brought in many states, including New York.[45]

There are a few points in history where sustained, coordinated efforts to improve the enforcement of criminal abortion laws were undertaken. One example of such a campaign was that conducted by New York State Assistant Attorney General John Harlan Amen. In the 1930s and 1940s, Amen—a crime-busting district attorney—contributed to, and improved, abortion prosecutions. At the appointment of New York's governor, Amen conducted a three-year probe into municipal corruption in Kings County (Brooklyn) New York.[46] Part of the corruption he unearthed included the bribery of assistant district attorneys to obstruct the prosecution of abortionists.[47] Amen's professional campaign in New York was cut short at the end of World War II, when he went to Nuremburg as part of the prosecution team, but in the mid-1950s, a decade after Amen's historic investigation, the Kings County (Brooklyn) district attorney renewed a vigorous prosecution of abortionists.[48]

This background casts a revealing light on an exchange at the 1955 Planned Parenthood conference between Edwin Schur, a Yale law student and advocate for the repeal of abortion laws, Dr. Sophia Kleegman, clinical professor of obstetrics and gynecology at the New York University College of Medicine, and Dr. Milton Helpern, the Chief Medical Examiner of New York City (whose office was responsible for "the investigation and post-mortem examination of all deaths from abortion").[49] After Schur criticized law enforcement, Kleegman asked Helpern:

DR. KLEEGMAN: Dr. Helpern, are you aware of the fact that there are far fewer criminal abortionists practicing in New York City now than there used to be, say, fifteen years ago?

DR. HELPERN: Yes, I think that is correct.

DR. KLEEGMAN: To what do you attribute this?

DR. HELPERN: In spite of Mr. Schur's observations I think there has been a tremendous improvement in the way in which these cases are being prosecuted.[50]

Indeed, authorities in virtually all states regularly enforced the abortion laws until the Supreme Court's decision in *Roe v. Wade*.[51] This is evident in reported appellate cases involving abortion in the 1950s, 1960s and early 1970s.[52] Even New York City, a leading center of abortion-rights agitation, and California prosecuted abortionists in the 1960s.

The regularity of enforcement is also seen in passing references in histories of abortion. For example, in a 1993 book intended to support legalized abortion, Patricia Miller notes that of the "former abortionists" she interviewed, "almost all of them had at least one brush with the law."[53] She also cites a Baltimore doctor in the 1940s and 1950s who refused to perform abortions "because the personal risk to me was too great. There was no way in the world I was going to jeopardize my entire family and risk going to jail."[54]

Enforcement of the laws was actively conducted in virtually all the states in the 1960s. In state constitutional challenges to state abortion laws before *Roe v. Wade*, 75 percent of the state courts upheld their abortion laws.[55] Two states— Michigan (with a vote of 62–28 percent) and North Dakota (with a vote of 79–21 percent) rejected modifications of their laws by state referenda in the November 1972 elections, on the eve of the *Roe* decision. The Supreme Court shut down prosecutions in January 1973; they were not voluntarily suspended.[56]

The Effects of Enforcement

The movement to repeal abortion laws in the 1960s focused its attack on the effects of enforcement. Opponents contended that the laws resulted in negative effects and that these outweighed the utility of enforcement. They focused their arguments on two claims: the number of illegal abortions and the number of women killed or injured by illegal abortion.

Usually, the incidence of crime provokes calls for more effective law enforcement, not for the abolition of the law itself. For example, during the 1980s an average of more than 20,000 persons were murdered annually in the United States, yet there was a conviction in slightly less than half of those cases.[57] There are tens of thousands of vehicular homicides, rapes, robberies, and burglaries each year.[58] It is never suggested that any of these crimes should be legalized because the law is broken or because so many crimes go unpunished.

> During the 1980s an average of more than 20,000 persons were murdered annually in the United States, yet there was a conviction in slightly less than half of those cases.

In the legal challenges to abortion law in the 1960s, however, these enforcement questions were not neutrally applied to abortion law. Advocates for the reform and repeal of abortion laws required that abortion law justify its utility by demonstrating its general prevention effect to a *higher* degree than that required for any other area of criminal law, or by requiring the complete *elimination* of the crime.[59]

In other words, it was claimed that abortion laws were ineffective because they were broken. This type of reasoning, of course, is rarely applied to other areas of law enforcement, and for good reason. According to former U.S. Assistant Attorney General Jeffrey Sedgwick:

> Some may argue that the only appropriate level of crime is no crime at all. But while it may be technically possible to eradicate crime, the cost of such a policy would most likely be exorbitant, especially in view of the multitude of other demands on public coffers. If there is not an unending supply of public funds and if there are more demands on public coffers than there are funds to satisfy these demands, then the public sector is faced with economic problems of choice and scarcity.[60]

Certain areas of criminal law—like laws against rape—continue to operate without regard to proof of general prevention and despite claims that the incidence of the crime is increasing undeterred. As another criminologist has observed:

> The disagreement over the importance of general prevention is of course largely due to the fact that its effectiveness cannot be measured. We do not know the true extent of crime. In certain areas of crime there is reason to believe that the figures available for offenses which are prosecuted and punished correspond roughly to the true incidence of crime. In other areas recorded crimes represent only a small fraction of the true incidence. We know still less about how many people *would* have committed crimes if there had been no threat of punishment.[61]

Nevertheless, it was rarely recognized that general deterrence of abortion could be accomplished by one successful,

well-publicized prosecution. Leslie Reagan, author of *When Abortion Was a Crime*, recorded that persistent police investigations even without prosecutions served as an effective deterrent.[62]

Estimates of Illegal Abortions

Reliable data on abortion before *Roe* were difficult to compile because abortion was a crime in most states.[63] Judith Leavitt makes the point through comparable problems with statistics on childbirth before the twentieth century:

> [W]e simply do not know how often women in the past found themselves pregnant or even how frequently women labored to give birth. It is only in the twentieth century that the recording of births (live and still) began to be noted reliably by local and state health departments, and even today we cannot calculate precisely the risks women face each time they become pregnant. Because we can not be sure about the number of labors or pregnancies, our statistical conclusions have limited meaning.[64]

Throughout the twentieth century, social scientists made widely varying estimates of the number of illegal abortions.[65] In the early part of the century, rough estimates of the number of abortions were cited by physicians and medical societies in their efforts to suppress illegal abortion. It was frequently stated that illegal abortion was widespread. But there were no data available, and no scientific efforts were made to estimate the numbers. Furthermore, anecdotal evidence was not evaluated for its representativeness—it was presumed to stand on its own. Even the anecdotal evidence was largely confined to cases in large cities, and thus it was most unrepresentative.[66]

At a 1942 conference on abortion, sponsored by the National Committee on Maternal Health, a number of physicians and statisticians admitted that it was not possible to estimate reliably the number of abortions, and, worse, no distinctions were made between spontaneous, therapeutic, or illegal abortions. They acknowledged that "reliable figures are not available."[67]

Most estimates of illegal abortion begin with Frederick Taussig, the leading medical proponent of legalized abortion in the 1930s.[68] Taussig's 1936 book on abortion, sponsored by the National Committee on Maternal Health, first suggested a figure of 681,600 illegal abortions annually in the United States, and—because his estimate was novel and had the appearance of scientific objectivity—it was widely cited and relied upon for decades.[69] Taussig's figures, however, were extrapolations based on speculations based on isolated figures that could not be demonstrated to be representative. As historian Marvin Olasky explained:

> Basing his calculations on the records of a New York City birth control clinic, Taussig decided that one abortion took place for every 2.5 confinements [for delivery] in urban areas; he did not note that visits to still-controversial birth control clinics were hardly typical jaunts. He also postulated a rural total of one abortion for every five confinements throughout the United States; his evidence for that were estimates by some physicians in "the ru-

ral districts of Iowa." Dubious techniques yielded totals of 403,200 abortions in urban areas and 278,400 in rural areas, for a nationwide annual total of 681,600.[70]

So spurious were Taussig's claims that many abortion advocates—such as Dr. Alan F. Guttmacher—questioned the numbers.[71]

Taussig himself subsequently repudiated his 1935 figures on abortions and abortion deaths and adopted a lower estimate at a 1942 conference:

> I would like . . . to apologize for the very meager information contained in my book, which was published in 1935 [sic], on the actual number of abortions and abortion deaths. We had, at that time, the wildest estimates as to the number of abortions and the number of abortion deaths both in Europe and in this country, and I thought the numbers were conservative. . . . Since 1936, I have reviewed the figures carefully. . . . They were trimmed down considerably, particularly as to the number of abortion deaths. . . . I think we can positively say there do not occur over 5,000 abortion deaths annually in this country, no matter how we try to cull the various brackets in the mortality statistics.[72]

Taussig reduced his estimates of abortion deaths, but he still gave no reasoning for the figure of 5,000. At the same time, the National Center for Health Statistics (NCHS) recorded 1,313 abortion deaths from all causes.

Taussig's 5,000 estimate was derived from the large estimates of the 1930s that preceded the medical developments that brought about the dramatic decrease in general maternal mortality and abortion mortality in the decades after World War II.[73] Even though maternal mortality fell considerably after World War II, and NCHS data consistently showed a downward trend from 1940, Taussig's revised 1942 estimate of abortion deaths became the basis for the regular claim of 5,000 deaths annually in the 1960s.

Other Estimates

Three other studies—by Marie Kopp, Regine Stix, and Alfred Kinsey—were also often cited in the 1960s. Taussig relied on Kopp, but recognized that Kopp's study was unrepresentative. At the 1942 conference, Dr. Halbert L. Dunn, chief statistician for Vital Statistics of the Bureau of the Census, was critical of the estimates given by both Kopp and Taussig.[74] Stix acknowledged her own earlier sample to be unrepresentative.[75]

Kinsey's estimate of illegal abortions is important because it served as the only basis for the "upper limit" of 1,200,000 illegal abortions suggested by the 1955 Planned Parenthood Conference. The Kinsey study was based on a sample that was projected for the entire country, but the statistical committee for the 1955 Conference doubted the representativeness of the study.[76]

The widely quoted 1955 Planned Parenthood Conference estimate of "200,000–1,200,000" illegal abortions annually was substantially contradicted by the conference participants themselves. The figure is taken from the Statistics Committee for the Conference, which, in arriving at the figure, significantly qualified its factual basis: "There is no objective basis for the selection of a particular figure between these two estimates as an approximation of the actual frequency."[77] Indeed, the Committee provided no "objective basis" for any figure lower or higher than those estimates. Individual conference participants also noted that there were no reliable figures on abortions.[78]

Despite the lack of any reliable basis for the enormous estimates, they were adopted as common wisdom without verification in the 1960s. For example, a widely cited 1962 law review article by Zad Leavy and Jerome Kummer cited a figure of "more than 1 million" illegal abortions annually based on "the mounting evidence that one out of every five pregnancies in this country terminates in illegal abortion."[79] There was no such "evidence": just Taussig's "confinement" estimate from 1935. Leavy and Kummer cited Taussig's book, Kopp, Stix, and Kinsey, without apparently realizing that all these sources were challenged as unreliable at the 1955 Planned Parenthood Conference. For their claim of 5,000 deaths annually, they cited Russell Fisher's 1951 article, which cited Taussig's total.[80]

As late as 1964, sociologists Jerome Bates and Edward Zawadzki cited a figure of 1,000,000 abortions annually, referencing the same four sources: Taussig, Kopp,[81] Stix's 1935 figures,[82] and Kinsey.[83] So the daisy chain led to the same pre–World War II estimates that had been challenged at the 1955 Planned Parenthood conference as unreliable.

Furthermore, the claims of advocates were contradictory. Leavy and Kummer contended that "an extremely small number of physicians are believed to be engaged in the performance of illegal abortions" and they cited the 1955 conference for the proposition that "most of them [physicians] scrupulously refuse even to discuss abortion with their patients."[84] At the same time, Dr. Mary Calderone, the medical director of Planned Parenthood who edited the papers of that conference, stated that "90 per cent of all illegal abortions are presently being done by physicians."[85] Dr. Alan Guttmacher reiterated this in 1967 when he estimated that 80 percent of illegal abortions were done by physicians.[86] These two claims together would make it impossible for there to be hundreds of thousands of illegal abortions annually, because it would be impossible for that "extremely small number of physicians" to perform such large numbers of procedures. High volume has only prospered since the states began to legalize abortion in the late 1960s.

In addition to the inherent problem of the reliability of the original estimates, there are significant reasons now to believe—forty years later—that the claims of even hundreds of thousands of illegal abortions annually in the United States before *Roe v. Wade* were much exaggerated. This necessarily calls into question the "replacement" argument: that *Roe v. Wade* did not significantly increase the number of abortions because a high percentage would have occurred anyway.[87] A 1974 study suggested that "well over half—most likely between two-thirds and three-fourths—of all legal abortions in the United States in 1971 were replacements for illegal abortions."[88] The replacement argument, of course, assumes accurate statistics for pre-*Roe* abortions.

The great rise in the number of abortions *after Roe* was real, and it is confirmed by the rise in the *repeat* abortion rate after legalization. The percentage of repeat abortions (the second or third abortion for the woman aborting) has more than tripled since 1973. The abortion decisions dramatically changed the availability of abortion.

The Large Drop in Maternal Mortality between World War II and 1970

While maternal mortality from illegal abortion was one of the most significant public arguments for the legalization of abortion before *Roe*, maternal mortality actually dropped significantly between 1940 and 1970—long before the national legalization of abortion—due to medical developments and antibiotics.[89] Candace Crandall, a former Adjunct Fellow at the National Center for Public Policy Research in Washington, D.C., summarizes the trend:

> In 1940, the National Center for Health Statistics confirmed just 1,313 deaths as a result of illegal abortions, most of them due to infection. As antibiotics became available and surgical techniques improved generally, abortion-related deaths fell sharply; from 159 deaths in 1966, to 41 in 1972, the year before *Roe*.[90]

Three key medical developments in the decades before *Roe* made significant improvements to women's health. First, due to advances in medicine, cases of maternal mortality from all causes declined dramatically throughout the first half of the twentieth century.[91] The medical "need" for therapeutic abortions was declining. The foreword to psychiatrist Harold Rosen's 1954 book on *Therapeutic Abortion* stated:

> The progress of medicine is rendering therapeutic abortion less and less important, and less and less frequent. The rachitic pelvis is disappearing. The safety of Caesarian section has been immeasurably increased. Tuberculosis is a vanishing disease; and we are by no means so positive as

we once were that the offspring of the mentally-deficient woman will be similarly afflicted.[92]

Doctors were increasingly able to treat pregnant mothers and sustain the pregnancy, and the medical reasons for therapeutic abortion were consistently decreasing.[93] Doctors acknowledged that some so-called therapeutic abortions that were performed were unnecessary.[94] Even as early as 1954, Alan Guttmacher said that "the truly legal abortions, in which the procedure is absolutely essential to preserve the mother's life, are relatively few."[95]

Calderone reached the same conclusion in 1960: "Medically speaking, that is, from the point of view of diseases of the various systems, cardiac, genitourinary, and so on, it is hardly ever necessary today to consider the life of the mother as threatened by a pregnancy."[96]

Second, due to the same advances in medicine and the use of antibiotics occurring after World War II, deaths from illegal abortion (the primary cause being infection) were declining.[97] Most of the pre-*Roe* maternal deaths—from all causes—were due to infection, and when antibiotics were introduced widely in the 1940s, maternal deaths declined precipitously. As Dr. Robert Nelson, the medical director of Planned Parenthood of Washington, D.C., reporting on septic abortions in the District of Columbia at the 1955 Conference, stated: "I have the figures from 1940 to 1943, and since that time the deaths from septic abortions have ranged between five and none."[98] At the same conference, Milton Helpern reported that "in 1918, I found that we used to have about 140 such cases [fatal abortion] a year, and most of them were criminal abortions. But, since 1940, the fatal cases of abortion have dropped to about 25 a year, and you don't see as many infected abortions in the hospital, for modern therapy has led to a great many more recoveries than formerly." Later at the conference, Helpern reported the following figures for abortion deaths in New York City since 1921, showing a progressive drop: 1921 (144), 1931 (140), 1936 (92), 1940 (70), 1941 (48), 1944 (25), 1951 (15).[99]

Third, obstetric technology improved up to the time of *Roe v. Wade*. These three aspects mean that maternal mortality, both generally and from abortion, declined dramatically in the years *preceding Roe v. Wade*.

Calderone endorsed the NCHS statistics before the campaign for abortion rights got under way. In 1960 she wrote:

> Abortion is no longer a dangerous procedure. This applies not just to therapeutic abortions as performed in hospitals but also to so-called illegal abortions as done by physicians. In 1957 there were only 260 deaths in the whole country attributed to abortions of any kind. . . . Two corollary factors must be mentioned here: first, chemotherapy and antibiotics have come in, benefiting all surgical procedures as well as abortion. Second, and even more important, the [1955 Planned Parenthood] conference estimated that 90 percent of all illegal abortions are presently done by physicians. Call them what you will, abortionists or anything else, they are still physicians, trained as such; and many of them are in good standing in their communities. *They must do a pretty good job if the death rate is as low as it is.* Whatever trouble arises usually comes after self-induced abortions, which comprise approximately 8 per cent, or with the very small percentage

that go to some kind of nonmedical abortionist. Another corollary fact: physicians of impeccable standing are referring their patients for these illegal abortions to the colleagues whom they know are willing to perform them, or they are sending their patients to certain sources outside of this country where abortion is performed. . . . So remember fact number three: abortion, whether therapeutic or illegal, is in the main no longer dangerous, because it is being done well by physicians.[100]

This general point had been made the year before by Guttmacher in his 1959 book, *Babies by Choice or by Chance*.[101]

Despite the unreliability of pre–World War II figures and the 1957 figure of 260 maternal deaths from abortions of all kinds, the common claim in the 1960s was that 5,000 to 10,000 women died every year from illegal abortion.[102] As one scholar observed, "By 1967, the year the [*New York Times*] was declaring 4,000 women dead annually from abortion, there were 133 such deaths on record. The *New York Times* had allowed itself an editorial adjustment of slightly more than 3,000 percent."[103]

Dr. Bernard Nathanson, a founder of NARAL and an abortionist who managed a clinic performing tens of thousands of abortions in Manhattan in the early 1970s, wrote in retrospect:

How many deaths were we talking about when abortion was illegal? In N.A.R.A.L. we generally emphasized the drama of the individual case, not the mass statistics, but when we spoke of the latter it was always "5,000 to 10,000 deaths a year." I confess that I knew the figures were totally false, and I suppose the others did too if they stopped to think of it. But in the "morality" of our revolution, it was a useful figure, widely accepted, so why go out of our way to correct it with honest statistics? The overriding concern was to get the laws eliminated, and anything within reason that had to be done was permissible.[104]

Conclusion

The American experience is that:

1. Abortion laws were uniformly enforced against physicians and virtually never against women, who were considered second victims of abortion.
2. The medical reason for therapeutic abortions (to save the life of the mother) steadily declined by 1960 due to advances in medical care.
3. The number of women who died by illegal abortion steadily declined after World War II due to advances in antibiotics.
4. By 1970, women did not die by illegal, "back-alley" abortions to a significantly greater extent than women die today from legal abortion.
5. Abortion laws effectively inhibited the performance of abortions.
6. Generally, abortion laws were regularly enforced before *Roe v. Wade*.

The best evidence indicates that the effectiveness of the criminal law in inhibiting abortion and protecting men, women, and children from abortion has gone through an ebb and flow over the decades. It has not been entirely successful in stopping abortion. Supplementary enforcement schemes and nonlegal mechanisms are needed to bolster the effectiveness of the law. If the courts got out of the way and the issue was returned to state and local public health officials, officials might seek to discourage abortion through other legal means. They might creatively focus on ways to reduce demand.

Reducing nonmarital pregnancies and the pressure that induces women to consider abortion; encouraging men to assume responsibility, concern, and support for women they have impregnated; and offering realistic alternatives for women in crisis pregnancies—all of these are needed to relieve the burden from the law and thereby make the law more effective in protecting human life. But this is asking no more than we ask of any other aspect of criminal law, which depends on general deterrents and general habits and character throughout the population.

When states were just beginning to consider different approaches in the early 1970s, the Supreme Court imposed a rigid, one-size-fits-all edict. The freedom to implement different policies and observe their effectiveness is why the American system of federalism holds more promise than the one-size-fits-all straitjacket that has fostered such turmoil over the past forty years.

PART II

UNINTENDED CONSEQUENCES

· CHAPTER SEVEN ·

The Public Health Vacuum
the Justices Created

The legislature can make choices among these variants,
observe the results, and act again as observation may
dictate. Experience in one state may benefit others. . . .
In contrast a court can only strike down a law, leaving a
vacuum in its place.[1]

—FEDERAL JUDGE HENRY J. FRIENDLY,
UNPUBLISHED 1970 OPINION IN AN ABORTION CASE

The Courts very effectively knocked the Department of
Health out of the picture. We're not even entitled to cross
the threshold of these clinics.[2]

—EDWARD F. KING, DEPUTY DIRECTOR OF THE
CHICAGO MEDICAL SOCIETY IN 1978

When the police raided the doctor's office, they found "deplorable and unsanitary" conditions, and numerous health and safety violations, including blood on the floor and parts of aborted infants in jars. The one doctor, who only worked evenings, was the only employee who had a medical license. Doubling as a pain-management clinic, the doctor also did abortions, especially on college coeds from the local university. Another employee, who was not a doctor, conducted gynecological examinations and administered painkillers. This was not the first time this doctor had had a run-in with authorities, but the authorities had been alerted when a patient died after being given two separate doses of painkillers plus anesthesia before an abortion. The state board of medicine suspended the doctor's license. A grand jury released a report a year later and charged the doctor with multiple counts of homicide.[3]

This was not the "back alley" of the 1960s. These were the findings of a Philadelphia grand jury investigating the clinic of Dr. Kermit Gosnell in November 2009. The conditions in the Philadelphia clinic are the direct result of the Supreme Court's abortion decisions. By striking down the abortion laws of all fifty states, the Justices created a public health vacuum that they can not fill.

Clinic Scandals 1973–2012

Since *Roe*, there have been repeated problems with abortion clinics and providers in New York, Chicago, Philadelphia, Phoenix, Los Angeles, and many other cities.

1978 A twelve-part series by the *Chicago Sun-Times* documented terrible conditions in Chicago clinics.[4]

1981 Dr. James Franklin of Denver was convicted of manslaughter on October 18, 1981, for the 1980 death of Betty Jane Zellers Damato and sentenced to three years in prison.[5]

1983 Six years after the fact, the *Miami Herald* reported that four women died in 1983 in a Miami abortion clinic.[6]

1983 At least five women died from abortion-related causes in California in 1983 and 1984. Yet California reported no maternal abortion deaths for either year.[7]

1984 The court of appeals of the District of Columbia allowed the medical malpractice suit of a woman to proceed against Dr. Milan Vuitch after a January 1981 abortion resulted in serious internal injuries to her, requiring a total hysterectomy.[8]

1989 In Illinois, regulators suspended the license of Dr. Inno Obasi after three botched abortions, including one death and two women who suffered perforated uteruses.[9]

1989 At least three women died due to complications arising from legal abortion in Maryland, but the state's Department of Health and Mental Hygiene reported no abortion deaths for that year.[10]

1990 Abortion clinics in Louisville were shut down by public health officials.[11]

1993 Dr. Abu Hayat in Manhattan was convicted after performing a late-term abortion in which he severed the arm of a baby who survived.[12]

1994 Legislative testimony in South Carolina exposed dangerous clinic conditions.[13]

1995 Michigan state officials investigated the clinic of Jose Gilberto Higuera, who had a history of abortion malpractice claims, for aborting a twenty-eight-week-old infant.[14]

1998 The July death of Louann Herron, after an abortion at the clinic of Dr. John Biskind in Phoenix, sparked

new legislative regulations, against which a federal
court quickly slapped an injunction. Biskind was later
convicted of manslaughter.[15]

1999 After the Biskind indictment in Phoenix, the *Arizona
Republic* published a report on Sunday, January 17,
entitled "History of Trouble at Clinic."[16]

2000 California abortion provider Bruce Steir pled guilty
to killing Sharon Hamptlon during an abortion on
December 13, 1996, at a Moreno Valley, California,
clinic.[17]

2002 On January 29, police arrested Planned Parenthood
abortion provider Brian Finkel in Phoenix on charges
that he sexually molested many abortion patients.
Finkel was later convicted of twenty-two counts of
sexually abusing patients, incidents that occurred
between 1993 and 2001, and sentenced to thirty-five
years in prison.[18]

2002 In January, a Delaware Superior Court found an
abortion provider negligent in the death of a patient
and ordered the payment of $2.2 million in damages.[19]

2003 Kansas City police investigated the abortion clinic of
Krishna Rajanna on September 18, and later testified
to unsanitary conditions in the clinic. Two years later,
Rajanna was fined $1,000 by the Kansas state medical
board.[20]

2004 Florida officials revoked the license of Dr. Roberto A.
Osborne for malpractice in the injury of an abortion
patient.[21]

2005 Kansas state officials investigated Dr. George Tiller
when a nineteen-year-old patient died after a third-
trimester abortion at his clinic.[22]

2006   Florida closed two Orlando abortion clinics operated
       by James Pendergraft.[23]

2006   California abortion practitioner Laurence Reich
       sexually assaulted women during abortions, which led
       to his second sex crimes conviction and the surrender
       of his license in 2006.[24]

2006   The notorious Clinica Medica Para la Mujer de Hoy
       clinic in Santa Ana, California, was the scene of
       multiple investigations involving numerous abortion
       providers.

2007   Laura Hope Smith died after an abortion in
       Massachusetts in September. Abortion provider
       Rapin Osathanondh was convicted of manslaughter
       three years later.[25]

2007   The family of Edrica Goode filed a wrongful death
       suit against a Planned Parenthood clinic in Riverside,
       California.[26]

2008   Caitlin Bruce filed suit against Michigan abortion
       provider Alberto Hodari and his assistant for allegedly
       holding her down and forcing an abortion on her at his
       Flint, Michigan, abortion clinic in April 2008. Hodari
       is also alleged to have done abortions that resulted in
       the deaths of Tamia Russell and Regina Johnson.[27]

2009   Abortion practitioner Feliciano Rios was indicted by
       a San Diego County Grand Jury on five felony counts
       of grand theft and Medi-Cal fraud, and pled guilty in
       July to perjury and insurance fraud, both felonies.[28]

2009   The death of Ying Chen in July after an abortion by
       Dr. Andrew Rutland at a San Gabriel, California,
       clinic eventually led to a wrongful death suit in
       August 2010.[29]

2009 Pennsylvania officials uncovered the conditions in the clinic of Dr. Kermit Gosnell in November.[30]

2010 In January, the *New York Daily News* reported the abortion death of Alexandra Nunez after an abortion at the A-1 Women's Care center in Jackson Heights in Queens, New York.[31]

2010 The Maryland Board of Physicians in September suspended the medical license of Maryland-based abortion practitioner Romeo A. Ferrer after a woman allegedly died after a failed abortion at his clinic.[32]

2010 The New Jersey Board of Medical Examiners in October suspended the medical license of abortion practitioner and business owner Steven Chase Brigham, concluding that he presented "a clear and imminent danger to the public health and safety." According to the *Philadelphia Inquirer* of July 21, 2010, Brigham's license "has been revoked, relinquished, or temporarily suspended in five states," though he still operated a chain of fifteen abortion clinics in New Jersey and Pennsylvania.[33] Brigham had been previously disciplined in 1994.[34]

2011 In April, abortion practitioner Nicola Irene Riley surrendered her Wyoming medical license after officials with the Wyoming Board of Medicine caught her lying about her criminal background on her license application. Riley's medical license had previously been suspended in Maryland (2010) and Virginia.[35]

2011 In July, a jury in Orlando, Florida, awarded $36.7 million in damages against abortion provider James Pendergraft for severe and permanent injuries to a ten-year-old girl who had been aborted alive by Pendergraft in the fall of 2001.[36]

2011 In July, the Pennsylvania Attorney General's office charged employees at the Allegheny Women's Center in Pittsburgh with violations of prescription drug laws over a several-year period.[37]

2012 In January, a district attorney in Maryland charged two reportedly unlicensed abortion providers, Stephen Chase Brigham and Nicola Riley, with homicide, after investigators found "nearly three dozen late-term fetuses in a freezer at the clinic," but later dropped the charges when he could not prove whether the infants had died in Maryland or Pennsylvania.[38]

2012 A healthy young woman, Tonya Reaves, a mother of one, died on July 20 after a late-term abortion at a Planned Parenthood clinic in downtown Chicago.[39] The local CBS radio station, WBBM, reported that documents indicated that she bled in the clinic for five hours before she was transported to a local hospital.[40]

Clinic scandals are rarely published in major radio, TV, or newspapers. They have to be uncovered through Google. As the Gosnell case exemplifies, the media rarely report problems at abortion clinics unless a woman dies or felony charges are filed.

How the Justices Created the Vacuum

The decisions in *Roe* and *Doe*, together, created the public health vacuum. The Justices declared a right to abortion at any time before fetal viability and at any time after viability if the woman's emotional "well-being"—as the Justices broadly defined "health"—was, in the discretion of the abortion provider, at issue.[41]

In January 1973, thirty-one states did not regulate abortion because it was a prohibited crime. These laws were knocked out by *Roe*. The other nineteen states allowed abortion to some degree, though none allowed it as broadly as the Court. Those laws were knocked out by *Doe*. The Justices also eliminated three key elements of Georgia's regulations of clinics: the requirements that abortions be performed in hospitals, that two other doctors agree to the need for the abortion (a two-physician concurrence), and that abortions be limited to state residents.

Even if five Justices were committed to creating a right to abortion, the Justices could have written a more narrow decision that struck down the Texas statute but left the Georgia regulations in effect. That would have been safer, especially when the Justices had no facts about the impact of the Georgia regulations, *and knew they had no facts*.[42] Justices Douglas and Blackmun considered sending the Georgia case back to the lower court for fact-finding on the impact of the Georgia law.[43] Instead, the Justices threw caution to the winds and issued a sweeping decision.

One of the major themes of the abortion decisions was freeing up doctors and deferring to their discretion and self-regulation. In effect, the Justices wrote a national abortion statute that gave enormous discretion to abortion providers —they thought of it as deferring to "medical judgment"— and prohibited clinic regulations in the first trimester, when 90 percent of abortions are done. They authorized abortion providers to go into federal court and speak for their patients *against* safety regulations.[44] They empowered federal judges in every state to implement their decision by issuing injunctions against regulations.

The Justices went back and forth, with contradictory rulings about what regulations were permissible, throughout the 1970s and 1980s. It took nearly twenty years—until the Court's *Planned Parenthood v. Casey*[45] decision in 1992—for the Justices to clarify that some regulations were permissible. But that was again cast into doubt by the Court's 2000 decision in *Stenberg v. Carhart*,[46] until the possibility of regulation was restored in 2007 by the Court's decision in *Gonzales v. Carhart*.[47] As of 2011, twenty-eight states had some form of abortion clinic regulations on the books, but they have only partially filled the public health vacuum; in others, it remains wide open.

The Justices' Ill-Considered Assumptions

At the end of the Justices' first meeting, or Conference, on the abortion cases on Thursday, December 16, 1971, after the first oral arguments, nothing was clear about how the Court would deal with the new "abortion practice" if the Texas and Georgia statutes were eliminated. The issue had not even been discussed, for even a minute, in the first two hours of oral argument. Justice Brennan was all set to strike down "the three doctor thing" in Georgia's law (the two-physician concurrence), as was Justice Stewart.[48] But Justice Blackmun originally pronounced the Georgia statute as having struck a fine "balance."[49]

The Justices asked almost no questions about abortion practice and made numerous assumptions. There was no evidence in the lower court record about these issues, so all the

Justices' assumptions were based on the medical and sociological advocacy briefs filed by interest organizations in the Supreme Court.[50]

The Justices eventually became aware that their decision would eliminate the abortion laws. In a May 25, 1972, memo to the other Justices with a copy of his first draft opinion in *Doe v. Bolton*, Justice Blackmun noted, "I should observe that, according to information contained in some of the briefs, knocking out the Texas statute in *Roe v. Wade* will invalidate the abortion laws in a *majority* of our States. Most States focus only on the preservation of the life of the mother."[51] But it is not clear that the Justices realized that their decisions would, in fact, invalidate *all* of the abortion laws in all fifty states, and they apparently gave little thought to how abortion would be regulated if they declared abortion to be a "constitutional right." What would it mean for public health if the Justices declared abortion to be the only medical procedure that is a "constitutional right"? This question was never asked during the four hours of arguments.

When Justice Blackmun thought of abortion providers, he thought of his friends and colleagues back at the Mayo Clinic in Rochester, Minnesota, where he had been resident counsel in the 1950s. He assumed that doctors just like them would step in to do abortions if it were legalized. As historian David Garrow told a reporter in 2005, "[Justice Blackmun] was thinking of this in the medical framework of Rochester, Minnesota. He imagined abortions would be performed by a family physician or in a hospital."[52]

In fact, Mayo doctors—including "David Decker, chairman of the Mayo Clinic's Department of Obstetrics and Gynecology, and Joseph Pratt, Mayo's director of gynecological surgery"—filed an advocacy brief in the Supreme Court in *Roe* and *Doe* in an attempt to influence the Justices to legalize abortion.[53] They argued that abortion laws were "an unconstitutional interference with the right to practice their profession" and that the abortion law "unfairly discriminates against" physicians and "denies these physicians equal protection of the laws."[54] Blackmun's first draft opinion, distributed inside the Court in May 1972, adopted the Mayo doctors' argument that the laws were unconstitutionally "vague."

The sweeping scope of the Court's abortion decisions was unclear to Justice Blackmun himself, as seen in a letter he wrote to Justice Powell twenty-one months after the abortion decisions. In 1975, the Justices decided the case of *Connecticut v. Menillo*[55] and held that *non-physicians* could still be criminally prosecuted for doing abortions. Justice Powell's draft opinion of October 15, 1975, contained the sentence: "*Roe* teaches that a State cannot restrict *a woman's decision to terminate her pregnancy....*"[56] Justice Blackmun asked Powell to change that sentence to read "a woman's *and her physician's....*" Blackmun explained the reason for his request:

> We are constantly accused of permitting "abortion upon demand." *Roe* and *Doe* certainly did not go that far, and I would prefer to avoid any intimation that it did.[57]

Blackmun was suggesting that the woman's desire for an abortion was subject to the judgment of the doctor. Powell made the requested change in his second draft of October

16, 1975: "*Roe* teaches that a State cannot restrict a decision by a woman, *with the advice of her physician*, to terminate her pregnancy...."[58]

Justice Blackmun's letter suggests that he thought that a physician's involvement in an abortion actually involved a medical judgment, seemingly oblivious to the fact that 99 percent of abortions are for social reasons alone. His letter suggests that he believed that the Court had not really legalized "abortion on demand" for the technical reason that the physician's medical judgment could be a veto on the woman's "request" for abortion. Blackmun still had this image that doctors were actively making *medical decisions* in "allowing" women to have abortions.

In addition, the Justices' notion that regular ob-gyns would fill the gap was a key assumption for which there was little evidence. It is likely that the Justices were influenced by the statement of Sarah Weddington in the first *Roe* argument:

> We have affidavits in the back of our brief from each of the heads of public—of heads of obstetrics and gynecology departments from each of our public medical schools in Texas. And each of them points out that they were willing and interested to immediately begin to formulate methods of providing care and services for women who are pregnant and do not desire to continue the pregnancy.[59]

The Justices were likely influenced by the fact that the American College of Obstetricians and Gynecologists (ACOG) filed a brief in the Supreme Court that endorsed abortion on demand and self-regulation by abortion providers. But the brief was not approved by the board of directors of the ACOG or by ACOG's membership.[60]

The Justices had no evidence before them as to what the vast majority of ob-gyns would do; nor did they take into account the impact of ultrasound and the quickly developing practice of maternal-fetal medicine. These questions were not asked by the lower court federal judges in Texas and Georgia in 1970, and they were not asked by the Justices in December 1971 or October 1972.

With perhaps one exception. When the attorney for the Georgia plaintiffs, Margie Pitts Hames, insisted in the second *Doe* argument that abortion providers should be allowed to self-regulate, Justice Rehnquist pointed out that states have regulated the professions, including the medical profession, since the 1700s.[61]

The courts can strike down laws; they cannot draft new regulations. When the Court struck down all existing laws, it left nothing in place. It is not clear why the Justices did not recognize this, as Judge Henry Friendly did. Friendly sat on the U.S. Court of Appeals for the Second Circuit, which includes New York, and was considered by many, including former Justice John Paul Stevens, to be "one of the greatest federal judges."[62] Friendly was one of three judges in 1969–1970 who heard the federal challenge to the original New York State abortion prohibition filed by Roy Lucas. Friendly's draft opinion concluded that eliminating the abortion laws would "leav[e] a vacuum in its place."[63] Unfortunately, Judge Friendly's opinion was not made public for three decades because the case was dismissed as "moot" when New York legalized abortion in July 1970.

The Justices expressly endorsed the trend toward clinic abortions by striking down Georgia's hospital requirement. They were undoubtedly influenced by the contention that the New York City clinic experience since legalization on July 1, 1970, had been completely safe, though no reliable, peer-reviewed data confirming safety existed. Data contradicting the supposed record of safety in New York were brought to the personal attention of, at least, Justices Douglas and Blackmun.[64]

Justice Douglas had dissented when the Court upheld the District of Columbia abortion law in *United States v. Vuitch* in April 1971. He cited an article authored in early 1971 by Dr. Robert Hall, president of the abortion advocacy group Association for the Study of Abortion (ASA),[65] that endorsed a hospital requirement and a residency requirement for abortions in New York. Hall frankly noted the maternal deaths and injuries that had occurred in New York abortion clinics after legalization in July 1970, and advocated such requirements to prevent more deaths and injuries.[66] The article was noticably absent from Douglas's concurring opinion in *Doe* when the Justices struck down those requirements in the Georgia law.

The one safety requirement that the Court has consistently upheld has been the requirement that abortion be performed by a licensed physician. That was noted by Justice Brennan in May 1972 in a memo telling Justice Blackmun that the view of the majority of the seven Justices was that abortion was a right except for the requirement that abortion be done by a licensed physician.[67]

The stark image of the "back alley" presumably drove the assumption that eliminating abortion laws would immediately eliminate unsafe abortions. Experience in other countries contradicted that notion at the time,[68] as has our own experience in the United States since 1973. If abortion cannot be regulated, what prevents the "back alley" abortionist from continuing in business? What distinguishes "back alley abortionists" from safe providers? As long as they had an M.D., those who practiced in the "back alley" before January 1973 were able to set up shop on Park Avenue after January 22, 1973. And no expertise in obstetrics and gynecology has ever been required.[69]

There were several reasons to doubt the Justices' assumption and to think that regular ob-gyns would not do abortions. The first was the strength of the Hippocratic oath, which forbade doctors to do abortions. Blackmun himself described it in powerful terms in October 1972, referring to the oath, in the reargument in *Roe*, as "*the only definitive statement of ethics of the medical profession.*"[70] And, in the reargument in *Doe*, he called the oath "*the definitive statement of medical ethics for centuries.*"[71]

The second was that some doctors filed extensive briefs in *Roe* and *Doe* that opposed elective abortion and emphasized both the biological development of the unborn child and the health risks to women from abortion.[72]

A week *before* the first arguments in December 1971, a renowned British medical journal, *The Lancet*, referred to the "high incidence of post-abortion complications" in a lead editorial.[73] Six weeks *after* the abortion decisions, in March 1973, an editorial in the *British Medical Journal*, addressing the "long-term effects of abortion," reported:

> A previous abortion increases the chances of a subsequent perinatal death by 50%, according to the British Perinatal Mortality Survey, and the experience of some other

countries suggests that even this figure is an underesti-
mate. In addition, there may be a 40% increase in premature births, and these are known often to be associated
with impaired mental and physical development.[74]

The third reason was that some discussion of conscientious objection arose; Sarah Weddington argued—and the
Justices apparently readily assumed—that any doctor had a
right to, and could, refuse to be involved in abortion. Within
two years after *Roe*, forty to forty-five states had passed legislation granting to doctors a conscientious right of objection.[75]

The Justices assumed that abortion would be mainstreamed, but, due to medical, cultural, and legal factors,
it never has been.[76] A common target of abortion providers were the requirements that the abortion provider have
privileges at a hospital with obstetrical and gynecological
services. Such privileges are necessary for a doctor to ad-
mit any patient who suffers complications. By invalidating
these requirements, it meant that abortion providers could
live outside a state and just fly in for a day or two of abortions
and fly out. The notion that abortion was between a woman
and "her" physician became a fiction. Regular ob-gyns did
not do the procedure.

The Immediate Aftermath of *Roe*

When the abortion decisions were released on January 22,
1973, public health officials and their lawyers in cities across
the country attempted to decipher the opinions and their
impact on the regulation of abortion clinics in their town.
With abortion clinics sprouting up, local officials had to
know how they could ensure public health safety.

The breadth and vagueness of the legislative character of the Justices' abortion decisions plunged the law into uncertainty. Justice Rehnquist's prediction in dissent was immediately apparent: "[T]he Court's opinion will accomplish the seemingly impossible feat of leaving this area of the law more confused than it found it."[77] The Justices swept away existing abortion regulations but did not give clear guidance as to what regulations would be acceptable.

In an October 9, 1973, letter, Edward Press, state public health officer of the Oregon Department of Health, wrote to Justice Blackmun, asking him a basic question that he could not decipher from the Court's opinion: whether an abortion by a non-doctor was "unconstitutional" or whether the state could prohibit an abortion by a non-doctor. Blackmun wrote back on October 16, saying that, as a federal judge, he could not "practice law" or advise the director, and suggested he seek the advice of a state government lawyer.[78]

Judicial Hostility to New Regulations

In Chicago, abortion clinics opened in February 1973. Within months of the abortion decisions, the federal courts were asked to invalidate health and safety regulations and immediately obeyed the decisions. Efforts by state and local boards of health to fill the vacuum were quickly blocked by litigation.[79]

Despite public debate during the 1960s about the "back alley" where illegal abortions were performed in dirty conditions, the Justices gave "back alley abortionists"—as long as they had an M.D.—as much right as any other doctor to go into court and challenge medical regulations. Abortion providers and their attorneys intimidated public health officials and legislatures from filling that vacuum. By treating abortion as the only medical procedure that is a constitutional right, the Justices made abortion—at least in the first trimester when 90 percent of abortions are done—virtually immune from public health (i.e., government) oversight.

A former "back alley" abortionist who operated the Friendship Medical Center immediately sued the Chicago Board of Health in federal court to keep regulations from going into effect. That case took more than two years, and the city public health officials eventually lost, despite the fact that, within two months of the *Roe* decision, several women had to endure hysterectomies after botched abortions at the Center.[80]

Four years after the federal appeals court in Chicago threw out the city's regulations, a five-month undercover investigation of numerous clinics was conducted by the Better Government Association and the *Chicago Sun Times*, in which they exposed widespread corrupt, unsafe, and abusive abortion practices in a series of articles in November 1978. The deputy director of the Chicago Medical Society, Edward F. King, told the *Chicago Tribune*: "The Courts very effectively knocked the Department of Health out of the picture. We're not even entitled to cross the threshold of these clinics."[81]

One reporter, Pam Zekman, who wrote a series of exposés on the problems in Chicago abortion clinics, told *Time* magazine, "In 1973, the Supreme Court legalized abortion. As it turns out, what they legalized in some clinics in Chicago is a highly profitable and very dangerous back-room abortion."[82]

The Justices were given at least three opportunities to

approve health and safety regulations in the first three years after *Roe*. They declined to hear a Florida regulation in 1974.[83] The Justices refused to hear the appeal brought by the Chicago Board of Health on March 24, 1975, with Justice White dissenting, leaving in place the federal court's invalidation.[84] Another opportunity came eighteen months later, when Indiana appealed its clinic regulations in *Sendak v. Arnold*. The Indiana statute required that abortions be performed in "a licensed health facility... which offers the basic safeguards as provided by a hospital admission, and has immediate hospital backup...." The majority of Justices not only refused to hear the case on November 29, 1976, but *summarily affirmed* the invalidation of the statute—the equivalent of a judicial brushoff—sparking a strong dissent by Justices White, Burger, and Rehnquist.[85] Despite the Justices' supposed concern for safety, they never examined public health regulations or gave their stamp of approval. The decisions in *Friendship Medical Center* and *Sendak v. Arnold* sent exactly the opposite message to federal courts and public health officials and legislators across the country.[86]

What happened in Chicago between 1973 and 1975 spread across the country within two or three years. The United States is divided into federal circuits, and a federal circuit (appellate) court has legal authority over several states. A decision by a federal circuit court invalidating one state's law applies to all the states in that circuit. Suits were filed in different federal circuits to eliminate the clinic regulations in all the states in those circuits. The federal courts quickly applied *Roe* and *Doe* to eliminate clinic regulations.[87] Between 1973 and 1984, courts in virtually all of the federal circuits struck down clinic regulations (see Table 3).[88]

TABLE 3. Federal Cases Invalidating State and Local Abortion Clinic Regulations

Circuit	Case	Result
1st	*Women's Medical Center of Providence v. Cannon*, 463 F.Supp. 531 (1st Cir. 1978)	Invalidated first-trimester clinic regulations
	Baird v. Department of Public Health of the Commonwealth of Massachusetts, 599 F.2d 1098 (1st Cir. 1979)	Invalidated first-trimester clinic regulations when not applied to both abortion and non-abortion clinics
3rd	*Pilgrim Medical Group v. New Jersey State Board of Medical Examiners*, 613 F.Supp. 837 (D.N.J. 1985)	Invalidated second-trimester hospitalization requirement
4th	*Hallmark Clinic v. North Carolina Department of Human Services*, 380 F.Supp. 1153 (Feb. 19, 1974)	Invalidated first-trimester clinic regulations
5th	*Mobile Women's Medical Clinic v. Board of Commissioners of Mobile*, 426 F.Supp. 331 (D.C.Ala. 1977)	Invalidated requirement that physician have admitting privileges or an agreement with a physician with such privileges
	Emma v. Edwards, 434 F.Supp. 1048 (E.D. La. 1977)	Invalidated requirement that abortions be performed in a hospital

Circuit	Case	Result
	Margaret S. v. Edwards, 488 F.Supp. 181 (E.D. La. 1980)	Invalidated requirement that abortions be performed in a hospital
6th	*Wolfe v. Schroering*, 541 F.2d 523 (6th Cir. 1976)	Invalidated explanatory, written consent, and twenty-four-hour waiting period
	Mahoning Women's Center v. Hunter, 610 F.2d 456, 460 (6th Cir. 1979), vacated and remanded on other grounds, 477 U.S. 918 (1980)	Invalidated licensing and facility design requirements for first-trimester abortions, along with informed consent and recordkeeping requirements
	Wolfe v. Stumbo, 519 F.Supp. 22 (W.D. Ken. 1980)	Invalidated second-trimester hospitalization requirements
	Birth Control Center v. Reizen, 743 F.2d 352 (6th Cir. 1984)	Invalidated first-trimester clinic regulations
7th	*Friendship Medical Center v. Chicago Board of Health*, 357 F.Supp. 594 (N.D. Ill. 1973), rev'd 505 F.2d 1141 (7th Cir. 1974), cert. denied, 420 U.S. 997 (1975)	Invalidated first- and second-trimester clinic regulations
	Arnold v. Sendak, 416 F.Supp. 22 (D.C. Ind. 1976), aff'd summarily, *Sendak v. Arnold*, 429 U.S. 968 (1976)	Invalidated first-trimester clinic regulations

TABLE 3 (cont.)

Circuit	Case	Result
	Fox Valley Reproductive Health Care Center v. Arft, 446 F.Supp. 1072 (E.D. Wis. 1978)	Invalidated first-trimester clinic regulations
	Christensen v. Wisconsin Medical Board, 551 F.Supp. 565 (W.D. Wis. 1982)	Invalidated second-trimester hospitalization requirement
	Ragsdale v. Turnock, 841 F.2d 1358 (7th Cir. 1988), appeal dismissed, 503 U.S. 916 (1992)	Invalidated first-trimester clinic regulations
8th	*Hodgson v. Anderson*, 378 F.Supp. 1008 (D. Minn. 1974)	Invalidated first- and second-trimester clinic regulations
	Word v. Poelker, 495 F.2d 1349 (8th Cir. 1974)	Invalidated first- and second-trimester clinic regulations
11th	*Coe v. Gerstein*, 376 F.Supp. 695 (S.D. Fla. 1974)	Invalidated first- and second-trimester clinic regulations
	Florida Women's Medical Clinic v. Smith, 478 F.Supp. 233 (S.D. Fla. 1979)	Invalidated first-trimester clinic regulations
	Florida Women's Clinic v. Smith, 536 F.Supp. 1048 (S.D. Fla. 1982)	Invalidated first-trimester clinic regulations

Perhaps the nail in the coffin for clinic regulations in the 1970s came when federal courts said that the Civil Rights Attorney's Fees Awards Act of 1976[89] applied to cases challenging abortion regulations.[90] That meant that if a state or local government enacted clinic regulations and lost in court, they would pay the attorney's fees of the abortion providers—usually hundreds of thousands of dollars. After numerous federal courts eliminated state regulations in the 1970s and 1980s, many states and cities simply stopped trying, due to the enormous time and expense involved in enacting and defending health and safety regulations.

Not until ten years after *Roe* did the Justices hear a case with clinic regulations, but only of *second-trimester* abortions. In a masterful understatement, Justice Powell observed that "not all abortion clinics, particularly inadequately regulated clinics, conform to ethical or generally accepted medical standards."[91] Citing the *Chicago Sun-Times* series, the Court upheld Missouri regulations requiring that *second-trimester* abortions be performed in an outpatient surgical hospital, noting that the standards of medical practice in many clinics "may not be the highest,"[92] and that a state could "conclude reasonably" that women seeking abortions in the least expensive clinics would be most in need of regulatory protection. But that 1983 decision gave no green light to regulations in the *first trimester*, and, in fact, demonstrated renewed hostility to first-trimester regulations.

Unfortunately, Justices Powell, Brennan, and Blackmun demonstrated their inability to be frank about the impact of the abortion decisions. While writing his opinion for the majority in *City of Akron v. Akron Center for Reproduc-*

tive Health,[93] Justice Powell wrote to Justice Brennan: "I had thought from the discussion at Conference that we were of one mind, namely, that abortion mills do exist, and are operated to the great profit of unethical physicians who care little about their patients."[94] Powell had included such an acknowledgment in a draft of his opinion in *Akron,* but Justices Blackmun and Brennan persuaded him that such a public acknowledgment would, as Justice Brennan put it in his letter to Powell, give "aid and comfort to those who would justify burdensome regulation."[95] Justice Blackmun dismissed the entire issue with a casual aside in a letter to Powell: "we all know that there are rascals in the medical profession as there are in the legal profession,"[96] virtually the same casual language that Justice Blackmun had used in his opinion in *Doe* in 1973.[97] Far from imposing stronger restrictions, or allowing even minimal clinic regulations in the first trimester, Justices Powell, Brennan, and Blackmun could not even acknowledge what they knew to be true, and proceeded to strike down a regulation that second-trimester abortions up to sixteen weeks be conducted in a hospital setting.[98]

Not until 2000, twenty-seven years after *Roe,* did a federal appeals court uphold South Carolina's regulations for clinics performing five or more first-trimester abortions per month. But the uncertainties continued in other federal circuits, since the Justices have yet to give their imprimatur to clinic regulations. After Louann Herron died in a Phoenix abortion clinic in 1998 (the operator was convicted of manslaughter), Arizona enacted new regulations and they were challenged and bottled up in federal court for an entire decade, until the fall of 2010.[99]

In effect, state and local governments can investigate after the fact: if a woman is rushed to the emergency room, they can investigate. But their authority to take preventive action through regulation is unclear and can readily be challenged through a federal lawsuit. *Since the state and local governments have been disabled by the federal courts, and Congress does not have the constitutional authority to fill the gap, no level of government has clear authority to take action.*[100]

How Abortion Injuries and Deaths Are Laundered Out of the U.S. Public Health System

Short-term complications—those that appear within forty-nine days after the procedure—include hemorrhage, infection, embolism, uterine perforations, and anesthetic complications. These result from practitioner negligence or lack of skill and the inherent danger of the procedure. The United Kingdom's Royal College of Obstetrics and Gynecology concluded in a 2000 report "that the immediate physical complication rate of induced abortion is at least eleven per cent."[101] Short-term injuries occur every day, but they are often not tracked and connected to the abortion, except in cases of death.

There are several reasons why legal does not necessarily mean safe. The safety of abortion is determined less by legality than by a number of other, more subtle factors, including technology, length of pregnancy, and the skill of the practitioner. Legality does not directly correlate with these. The safety of women undergoing abortion depends on a functioning public health system that monitors the safety of abortion, objectively studies risks and their causes, tracks data about injuries and deaths, thoroughly reports the data to the public, and intervenes to protect the health of patients. The dysfunctional state and federal abortion-monitoring system that resulted from the abortion decisions performs none of these tasks.[102]

Abortion injuries and deaths are washed out of the U.S. public health system through a series of filters. The first filter is the clinics. Clinics do not take responsibility for injuries if they can avoid it. Standard procedure is for clinics to tell a patient who suffers pain or bleeding to go to the nearest emergency room, not back to the clinic. Only twenty-two states—less than half—require reporting of complications, but, if they do, neither the clinic nor the ER is inclined to keep records and do so. If clinics urge women to go to the nearest ER, the clinics will not see the injury to report it.

The second filter is the ER. The ER doctor may have no reason to suspect abortion or may simply report the presenting symptoms rather than the underlying cause. A 1992 medical journal study found that 50 percent of abortion patients conceal their abortion from the medical personnel who interview them about their medical history.[103]

Payment mechanisms are the third filter. Most abortions performed in the United States are currently paid for in cash.[104] There is no submission of the procedure to a third-party payer and no financial record of the transaction.

Coding procedures are the fourth filter. Even if an ER doctor suspects an induced abortion, coding procedures actually give an ER doctor a financial incentive to report the woman's condition as caused by something else, such as embolism, sepsis, or cardiomyopathy. The ER doctor will be paid more if the ER doctor submits the billing as "treatment for septic shock" rather than "abortion." Or, given the emotional discomfort associated with abortion, medical personnel might choose an alternative cause to protect the privacy of an abortion patient.

The ER doctor will most likely use codes for fever, abdominal pain, and sepsis to report to the patient's insurance company, because they do not want to risk the claim being denied because it was related to complications of an elective abortion. The surgeon treating the patient has the choice of several codes with which to bill the surgery:

- 59812: Treatment of Incomplete Abortion, any trimester, completed surgically
- 59830: Treatment of Septic Abortion, completed surgically
- 59160: Postpartum Curettage

The procedure code is linked to a Relative Value Unit (RVU) code.

- 59812: RVU = 7.79
- 59830: RVU = 11.66
- 59160: RVU = 5.02

The surgeon would be paid the most money if the 59830 code, treatment of septic abortion, is used for billing, rather than a code for abortion. And the coding does not distinguish between legal, illegal, spontaneous, or elective.

Abortions billed to insurance companies in the United States are billed according to coding requirements (current procedural technology or CPT codes). The CPT codes are created and controlled (by patent) by the American Medical Association. The CPT codes must be linked with an International Classification of Disease (ICD) Code. The ICD codes are controlled by the World Health Organization (WHO).

Here are the ICD-9 codes for abortion:

ICD-9: Abortion: 634–639

- 634.XX   Spontaneous Abortion
- 635.XX   Legally Induced Abortion
- 636.XX   Illegally Induced Abortion
- 637.XX   Legally Unspecified Abortion
- 638.XX   Failed Attempted Abortion
- 639.XX   Complications Following Abortion or Ectopic and Molar Pregnancies

Here are the ICD-9 codes for complications following abortion:

ICD-9: Complications: 639

- 639.1   Delayed or excessive hemorrhage *following abortion or ectopic and molar pregnancies*
- 639.2   Damage to pelvic organs and tissues *following abortion or ectopic and molar pregnancies*
- 639.3   Renal failure *following abortion or ectopic and molar pregnancies*
- 639.4   Metabolic disorder *following abortion or ectopic and molar pregnancies*
- 639.5   Shock *following abortion or ectopic and molar pregnancies*
- 639.6   Embolism *following abortion or ectopic and molar pregnancies*

- 639.8   Other specified complication *following abortion or ectopic and molar pregnancies*
- 639.9   Unspecified complication *following abortion or ectopic and molar pregnancies*

The ICD-9 codes (the current version used in the United States) lump four different events together: spontaneous abortion, elective abortion, ectopic pregnancy, and molar pregnancy. The ICD-9 codes make it impossible to specifically link a complication to elective abortion.

The fifth filter is unreliable death certificates.[105] The federal Bureau of Vital Statistics (BVS) formulates a national *death* certificate form, which serves as a template for states in creating their own form. The national form omits any history of prior spontaneous abortion (miscarriage) or elective induced abortions. Yet this would be important information to gather in order to analyze data on prior pregnancy history and pregnancy outcome. In addition, the doctor who might certify an abortion death is typically not the one who originally treated the woman. Death certificates are often inaccurate by as much as 30–40 percent. Abortion statistician Willard Cates, Jr., and his colleagues found that "inadequate physician documentation on the death certificate" occurs in about 40 percent of abortion-related deaths.[106]

The sixth filter is birth certificates. The BVS is also complicit in avoiding any data collection that could link maternal abortion history to adverse pregnancy outcome. During the 1990s, a federal representative from the BVS met with an ACOG committee to review the recommended national *birth* certificate forms, which served as a template by which states could create their own birth certificates. Notably absent from the form was any history of the mother's prior spontaneous or elective abortions, and the committee immediately recognized this omission and recommended that this information be included, since it is important information to gather in order to analyze data on prior pregnancy history and subsequent pregnancy outcome and assess women's health. But the representative from the BVS stated that the federal government did not want to collect any data that might link abortion history to adverse pregnancy outcome, and that there was pressure from Congress to not collect this data; hence, it would not be included on the birth certificate data form. The BVS birth certificate recommendations have excluded any reference to prior abortions.[107]

All of the prior filters may make it clear why the seventh filter is haphazard data collection. The federal Centers for Disease Control and Prevention (CDC) in Atlanta has been charged by federal law since 1969 with keeping track of the annual number of abortions and keeping track of abortion mortality and morbidity.

The CDC does this through its Abortion Surveillance program; these data are published in the *Morbidity and Mortality Weekly Report* (*MMWR*), which covers reasons for death and disease, including abortion.[108] The abortion data that are reported to the CDC come not from clinics or practitioners but from the states, and the states give the data to the CDC *voluntarily*. Not all states give their data to the CDC: for example, California—which accounts for one-quarter to one-third of all abortions in the United States—has not reported data to the CDC for several years.

The CDC has the responsibility by federal law to track abortions and deaths but not the mechanism to do it accurately. There is no national law that requires either practitioners or the states to report their data to the CDC. No federal law requires reporting of such injuries or deaths. Given the fact that several states do not report abortions to the CDC, neither the total number of annual abortions nor the number of deaths can be accurate. All collection is voluntary, and state laws are haphazardly enforced. The national figures on deaths are kept by the CDC and reported about four years late (e.g., 2006 data is reported in 2010).

The Achilles heel of the CDC system is that it is completely dependent on an initial report of a death from abortion. Induced abortion must be identified in the report as the *immediate* cause of death or the CDC will not investigate the death. The accuracy of the CDC data is highly dependent on the accuracy of data voluntarily provided by the states, and inconsistent methods are used by the states.[109]

State collection of data is hit or miss. In June 2011, the *Chicago Tribune* reported that "state abortion records [were] full of gaps" and that "thousands of procedures" and six deaths were not reported to the state health department.[110] It is not surprising that the CDC conceded in 1992 that "data of the AGI [Alan Guttmacher Institute] demonstrated significantly more abortions each year" than the CDC reported.[111]

That is why a CDC official in the 1970s said that more accurate data on the annual numbers of abortion were kept by the Alan Guttmacher Institute (AGI), a private organization that used to be the research arm—and remains a "special affiliate"—of Planned Parenthood, the largest abortion provider in the United States.[112] AGI gets its data from practitioners, not the states. Since AGI works for unregulated abortion on demand, abortion providers have an incentive to give their data on annual numbers to the AGI, but they still do so *voluntarily*. To keep the abortion mortality figure low, providers have an incentive to report the number of abortions but not the deaths.

For these reasons, any estimate of complications, injuries, and deaths in the United States is unreliable.[113] And it shows why the mechanical comparison of the abortion mortality and childbirth mortality rates is comparing apples and oranges.

Conclusion

The medical mantra that "abortion is safer than childbirth" had an immediate impact in invalidating public health regulation of abortion clinics. The Justices relied on this mantra and assumed that abortion was safer than childbirth in the first trimester and therefore gave complete discretion to providers and excluded public health officials from the picture.

The Court assumed the role of national public health administrator over abortion, but it cannot function as a public health expert in this area because it lacks the wherewithal and the means to oversee this important medical issue. Public health officials need authority to act quickly in medical emergencies to protect public health. The Justices cannot determine unsafe conditions. They cannot move quickly. They cannot close unsafe clinics.

Perhaps the most serious problem is that the Justices cannot do anything about it. The Court is a passive institution. The Court works only through cases appealed to it, usually after years of litigation in the lower courts. The Court cannot regulate; it cannot intervene in a public health problem;

it cannot step in to legislate or set safety regulations; it cannot monitor the effectiveness or safety of new procedures or "innovations." For example, part of the campaign for the legalization of abortion in the 1960s was the complaint that illegal abortionists "sent the women away to abort elsewhere," but the protocol for RU-486 (mifepristone) today involves just that—sending women elsewhere to complete their abortion.[114]

The continuing impact of *Roe* in creating and perpetuating this public health vacuum was once again demonstrated in September 2010 when the Center for Reproductive Rights (CRR) filed suit in federal court against a new Louisiana clinic regulations law.[115] The suit challenged Louisiana House Bill 1370, enacted as Act 490. It amends an existing health licensure law to add that health officials can deny, refuse to renew, or revoke an existing license if an investigation determines that the clinic is in violation of any provision of the health law, or licensing rules, or any other federal or state law or regulation. This law apparently equally applies to *any* licensed health facility, but since it does not exempt abortion clinics, the abortion providers filed suit, which *Roe* and subsequent decisions empowered them to do.

The public health vacuum still threatens women's health and safety forty years after *Roe*. The gap has not been filled —despite the mounting evidence of clinic abuses and the mounting medical data about the risks to women—leaving women vulnerable to the physical and psychological risks of abortion, the hazards of some abortion providers, unsafe and unsanitary clinics, and poor information about the long-term risks of abortion.

The Justices created a vacuum that they cannot fill and prevented others from filling it. There is no way for the Court to fix the problem it created unless it gets out of the way and returns the issue to public health officials at the state and local level.

· CHAPTER EIGHT ·

Detrimental Reliance

THE INTERNATIONAL DATA

ON THE RISKS TO WOMEN

*I am mindful of what was brought out by our psychologists
. . . that in almost every case, abortion, whether legal
or illegal, is a traumatic experience that may have severe
consequences later on.*

—DR. MARY CALDERONE, MEDICAL DIRECTOR
OF PLANNED PARENTHOOD[1]

*A 1994 study conducted by the Fred Hutchinson Cancer
Research Center . . . , supported by the National Cancer
Institute, showed that an induced abortion more than
doubles a woman's breast cancer risk, which becomes
greater the younger the woman and the later the stage
of pregnancy at the time of the abortion. . . . These
observations must be pursued to see if the link bears out.
Some 1.5 million women undergo abortion in this country
each year; if the breast cancer connection is valid, we will
be seeing a continuous rise in breast cancer in this country
for many years into the future.*

—DR. BERNADINE HEALY, FORMER DIRECTOR
OF THE NATIONAL INSTITUTES OF HEALTH[2]

[W]omen contemplating their first induced abortion early in their reproductive life should be informed of two major long-term health consequences. First, their risk of subsequent preterm birth, particularly of a very low birth weight infant, will be elevated above their baseline risk in the current pregnancy. Second, they will lose the protective effect of a full-term delivery on their lifetime risk of breast carcinoma. This loss of protection will be in proportion to the length of time that elapses before they experience their first delivery. Increased rates of placenta previa and the disputed independent risk of induced abortion on breast cancer risk warrant mention as well.

—STUDY IN THE *OBSTETRICAL AND GYNECOLOGICAL SURVEY (OGS)*, JANUARY 2003[3]

The Justices did not have the whole story. There was no evidentiary record in the abortion cases, and the data that were available in 1971 and 1972 could not have told the whole story. Neither the United States nor most other countries had any experience with abortion on demand in the first trimester, let alone for any reason, at any time of pregnancy, as *Roe* would decree.[4] After forty years and 54 million abortions, there is now much more data with which to evaluate abortion's impact on women's health.[5]

In 1972, some numbers on short-term risks and complications from the Soviet Union, Scandinavia, Eastern Europe, and Japan existed, but they were not widely accessible or published in reliable studies. Some studies reported on short-term complications from Denmark, Poland, Czechoslovakia, Sweden, Great Britain, and Japan; there were also reports on complications in the United States from California, New York City, and Rochester, New York.[6] As for long-term risks, few long-term studies had been conducted.[7] Those that existed looked at premature labor and delivery, ectopic pregnancies, and spontaneous miscarriage. Few, if any, were peer-reviewed.

The little public discussion of abortion risks that transpired in the 1960s focused on the risk of psychiatric trauma. For example, Dr. Harold Rosen was a leading activist during the 1950s and 1960s pushing for the legalization of abortion on psychiatric grounds. He pressed for it in the early 1950s with a book, *Therapeutic Abortion*.[8] But his most famous essay in the late 1960s was a stream of political consciousness rather than a careful review of data. In this essay of thirty-four pages, entitled "Psychiatric Implications of Abortion: A Case Study in Social Hypocrisy," Rosen's discussion of "psychiatric indications" took just three pages.[9] He admitted that the suicide rate for pregnant women was actually less than the rate for the general population, and that suicide by pregnant women "is extremely rare." His main complaint seemed to be that "emotionally sick" patients came to psychiatrists asking for an abortion, and that was really stressful for the psychiatrist.

Rosen's most disturbing admission was that "a fairly large number of psychiatrists" believed that abortion "for psychiatric reasons is indicated" for immature women who "cannot be trusted with the responsibilities of an adult."[10] And it ended with the concession that psychiatric indications for abortion were not based on medicine but were really needed to induce officials to approve an abortion:

> [Psychiatric indications] are the ones stressed on certificates forwarded by physicians to hospital abortion boards. Nevertheless, in most cases these are mere rationalizations. The medical, including the psychiatric, indications must be utilized if the abortion is to have legal justification. However, in most cases, the socioeconomic factors are pronounced; and whether the interruption of the pregnancy is legal or extra-legal, the actual indications are, for the most part, socioeconomic.[11]

Rosen's essay was cited in three of the briefs filed in support of Jane Roe, telling the Justices that abortion had no psychological risk.[12]

Roy Lucas and Sarah Weddington cited a handful of medical journal articles.[13] The joint brief of the American College of Obstetricians and Gynecologists (ACOG) and the American Psychiatric Association cited just two.[14]

In contrast, the brief by Certain Physicians, Professors and Fellows of the American College of Obstetricians and Gynecologists (ACOG), filed in support of Texas and Georgia, contained a medical bibliography of at least 145 medical articles and books on various aspects of abortion and maternal–fetal medicine.[15]

At the time of the arguments, several studies existed that suggested significant psychological risks of abortion to women.[16] These studies certainly did not settle the question then, one way or another, but the existing medical literature—including medical texts, statements from international medical societies, and studies—gave a hint of problems ahead. At the very least, they gave reason for caution in overturning the laws of the fifty states.

Reading the Data

Much has changed, both in the amount of data and in the quality of studies, over the past forty years, yet one thing has remained the same: *the data need to be handled with care.*

A billboard by a local hospital in Chicago in the fall of 2011 said, "*You don't choose cancer. You can choose your team.*" Induced abortion, unlike disease, is chosen. Induced abortion does not occur randomly. That reduces the ability of researchers to objectively study abortion and its effects. Abortion is elective and not medically indicated in 99 percent of the cases. Therefore, the study of abortion necessarily depends on retrospective, observational studies. Prospective, randomized studies are difficult, if not impossible, to do with induced abortion.[17]

Women are interested in whether abortion *causes* any particular medical or psychological outcome. No *one* study will definitively answer that question. The question of causation depends not on any one study but on a number of studies, each conducted according to reliable methods. Association should not be confused with causation, and the data should be accurately described and not exaggerated. One study does not settle an issue, and more are needed. A number of studies have found no increased risks after abortion, and these need to be taken into consideration and evaluated for their quality. Nevertheless, dozens of peer-reviewed, international studies currently exist that find, with statistical significance, increased risks after abortion.[18]

One leading researcher in the field has cautioned about the need for studies to follow well-established guidelines for reliable research:

> Because the causal question is at the heart of any review addressing the psychological and behavioral ramifications of abortion, the evaluation of research must be framed around the extent to which the available literature meets the conditions for causality. Each individual study should be examined to assess the quality of evidence suggestive of a causal link (time precedence, covariation, and control of third variables) between abortion and negative outcomes. After evaluating individual studies for causal evidence, the consistency (people, places, and time) and magnitude of associations between abortion and particular mental health outcomes must be evaluated across all available studies. Strong associations detected in many studies are more likely causal than slight or modest associations.[19]

Despite the need to understand the medical and psychological consequences of abortion, public information in the United States has been fragmentary, due, at least in part, to the public health vacuum that the Justices created. Ironically, many other countries collect and maintain better data than the United States on abortion and its health impact because they have centralized health care systems.

Comprehensive morbidity (complications) data in the United States are not collected. But the extent of injuries may be suggested by a 2000 report from the Royal College of Obstetricians and Gynaecologists (RCOG) in the United

Kingdom, which concluded that the *immediate physical complication rate* of induced abortion was at least 11 percent.[20]

A 2003 Assessment

A landmark article in the January 2003 issue of the *Obstetrical and Gynecological Survey (OGS)*—one of the three leading obstetrical journals in the United States—examined medical studies of abortion going back to the 1960s to assess the long-term physical and psychological health consequences for women from induced abortion.[21]

The authors of the *OGS* study reviewed existing studies on the risks of abortion and pointed out that previous researchers "lament the lack of long-term follow-up and call for detailed study of the health effects of this common procedure."[22] But "[d]espite strong recommendations for substantive research, and the clear need for women to have accurate information . . . current data remain sparse, studies are small and methodologically flawed. . . ."[23] For example, the authors could find no "studies of *medical* abortions with long-term follow-up."[24]

Nevertheless, the authors of the *OGS* study reached several significant conclusions:

> Given the central role that abortion has played in the life of women over the past thirty years, we are distressed by the lack of [long]-term, well-done research designed to understand the sequelae. A clear and overwhelming need exists for a large epidemiologic, cohort [group] study of women with an unintended or crisis pregnancy. Follow-up across participants' lifetimes with careful measurement

of other pertinent exposures would dramatically advance knowledge. Until such an investigation is invested in, women are making important health decisions with incomplete information.[25]

The high prevalence of a history of induced abortion means that even small positive or negative effects on long-term health could influence the lives of many women and their families.[26]

[W]omen contemplating their first induced abortion early in their reproductive life should be informed of two major long-term health consequences. First, their risk of subsequent preterm birth, particularly of a very low birth weight infant, will be elevated above their baseline risk in the current pregnancy. Second, they will lose the protective effect of a full-term delivery on their lifetime risk of breast carcinoma. This loss of protection will be in proportion to the length of time that elapses before they experience their first delivery. Increased rates of placenta previa and the disputed independent risk of induced abortion on breast cancer risk warrant mention as well.[27]

Preterm delivery and depression are important conditions in women's health and avoidance of induced abortion has potential as a strategy to reduce their prevalence.[28]

Together with the *OGS* study, other international studies have begun to provide evidence of at least six long-term physical and psychological risks from abortion that need to be seriously considered:

- Increased risk of preterm (premature) birth in future pregnancies[29]
- Increased risk of placenta previa in future pregnancies[30]
- Increased incidence of drug and alcohol abuse[31]
- Increased incidence of suicide and psychiatric admission after abortion[32]
- Loss of the protective effect against breast cancer of a first full-term pregnancy[33]
- Increased incidence of violence and assault associated with abortion[34]

These may not be *all* of the potential long-term risks from abortion, but they seem to be the best documented in the medical literature in 2012.[35]

What's impressive about the data on the long-term risks of abortion to women is the growth of the number of studies over several decades from numerous countries. The published studies grow year by year. These studies need to be carefully read and considered, especially by doctors. But women also need to begin a dialogue with their doctors about the risks.

Preterm Births and Low-Birth-Weight Infants

Preterm birth means birth before thirty-seven weeks gestation. (Very preterm birth means birth at less than twenty-eight weeks.) "Preterm birth is . . . the leading cause of infant morbidity and mortality,"[36] and very preterm birth is associated with cerebral palsy. The *OGS* authors observed that "[d]espite substantial investigative effort, primary preventive measures to lower the rate of preterm births have proven futile and rates have been steady or increased over the past two decades."[37]

The *OGS* study examined several international studies that consistently found an association between induced abortion and subsequent preterm births and low birth weight infants. Some studies found an almost two-fold increased risk of very early deliveries (twenty to thirty weeks gestation) after an induced abortion.[38]

Studies found that the risk increases when the woman had more induced abortions.[39] These studies contradict previous studies that purported to show that abortion "improves infant outcomes by reducing the number of low birthweight babies and neonatal mortality."[40]

> The World Health Organization (WHO) reported in May 2012 that the rate of premature birth in the United States has increased 30% since 1981.[41]

- A 2006 Institute of Medicine (IOM) report acknowledged that induced abortion is a risk factor for preterm birth.[42]
- A 2007 study in the *Journal of Reproductive Medicine* listed sixty studies finding a statistically significant increased risk in preterm birth or low birth weight after an induced abortion.[43]
- 2009 saw the publication of three studies (systematic evidence reviews) that all found a increased risk of preterm birth after abortion.[44]
- A 2010 study in *Human Reproduction* concluded that "prior pregnancy termination is a major risk factor for cervical insufficiency,"[45] and black women have an increased risk of cervical insufficiency—and the more prior abortions, the greater the increased risk.

- A December 2011 study from the Italian Preterm Network Study Group found that prior induced abortions almost double the risk of premature birth.[46]
- A January 2013 review in *Scientifica* cited over 130 published studies showing "an association between TOP [termination of pregnancy] and either preterm birth or its surrogate, low birthweight."[47]

> The complications of pre-term birth for mother and child after induced abortion cost an estimated $1.2 billion annually.[48]

Placenta Previa

Placenta previa occurs when the placenta covers all or part of the cervix during pregnancy. While the placenta normally attaches at the top of the uterus, scarring from the curette scraping from a prior induced abortion can prevent proper implantation of the placenta or increase the risk of abnormal implantation in future pregnancies. The formation of the placenta over the cervical opening, if it persists until the onset of labor, carries substantial risk to the mother (including life-threatening hemorrhage, increased risk of postpartum hemorrhage, and increased incidence of cesarean delivery) and to the unborn child (including preterm birth, low birth weight, and perinatal death).[49] In labor, it creates a medical emergency, making a cesarean section medically necessary to deliver the child, with obvious risks to mother and child.

The OGS authors noted that "placenta previa . . . is the leading cause of uterine bleeding in the third trimester and of medically-indicated preterm birth," and that "pregnancies complicated by placenta previa result in higher rates of pre-term birth, low birth weight, and perinatal death."[50]

The *OGS* study found that induced abortion increases the risk of placenta previa in subsequent pregnancies, with one study finding a 30 percent increased risk.[51] Three studies before 2003 showed an increased risk of placenta previa of 50 percent after abortion. A more recent study found there is *more than twice* the risk of placenta previa when there are two prior induced abortions.[52] This is what researchers call a "dose effect"—the stronger the dose (or exposure), the stronger the effect that can be seen.

Psychological Risks

Since *Roe*, more than 50 million abortions have been induced in the United States. In January 1989, then–U.S. Surgeon General Dr. C. Everett Koop published a brief report that concluded that the existing data on the psychological outcome of abortion were inconclusive because of the methodological flaws in the published research.

Since then, a number of rigorous studies have been published that have found an association between abortion and:

- Emotional distress[53]
- Depression[54]
- Substance abuse[55]
- Suicide or suicidal ideation[56]
- Attempts at self-harm[57]
- Anxiety[58]
- Violence and assault[59]
- Frayed relationships[60]
- Coercion[61]

There have been more than one hundred peer-reviewed studies published in international medical journals that suggest an association between abortion and adverse mental health outcomes.[62] These were published in Australian, Scandinavian, Canadian, British, American, and European journals. These look at drug and substance use, anxiety and depression, partner relationships, sexual problems, and risk of violence after abortion.

Some studies come down on both sides of the question—some find an increased risk of mental health trauma, some do not—and certainly there is a need for additional, extensive research in the years ahead. Some researchers dismiss the data and contend that the vast majority of women feel relief, not regret, and that those women who suffer had preexisting psychological problems that are the cause of their suffering and not the abortion. But many studies—and recent, well-done ones—controlled for such preexisting conditions and found a negative mental health impact from abortion.

Though it might be supposed that any outcome with an unintended pregnancy will not be good, in fact, when abortion is compared with carrying an unintended pregnancy to term, some studies find that abortion is associated with a higher risk for negative psychological outcomes compared with giving birth. It might also be assumed that abortion is no different from other forms of child loss, and that women might suffer after abortion just as women suffer after miscarriage or adoption. But some studies find that women suffer more after abortion than after miscarriage or adoption. Studies that have examined women over a longer period of time have found that feelings of depression increased as time went on and feelings of satisfaction with the abortion decreased over time.[63]

Risk of Alcohol and Drug Abuse

Since the 1970s, numerous studies have been published finding an association between abortion and increased use of alcohol and drugs. Joseph Dellapenna has observed that "[t]here is considerable evidence that having an abortion is a significant predictor of later drug and alcohol abuse and dependence."[64] The studies suggest an association between a history of induced abortion and substance abuse.[65] And the number of studies continues to grow.

- A 2000 study in the *American Journal of Drug and Alcohol Abuse* found a "five-fold increased incidence of abuse of alcohol and drugs in those who had aborted compared with those who carried to term."[66]
- A 2004 study in the *American Journal of Drug and Alcohol Abuse* looked at data from the National Longitudinal Study of Youth and found that women who had abortions had a higher rate of subsequent substance abuse than women who had never been pregnant or women who gave birth after unexpected pregnancies.[67]

Certainly continued research on alcohol and drug use after abortion is needed.

Increased Risk of Suicide

Legal abortion in the United States has clearly not been associated with an increase in psychological health for young women. Generally, the suicide rate for females age fifteen to nineteen increased between 1970 and 1990 and then dropped, but as of 2010 remained above the rate in 1970.[68] While it is not possible today to tie that increase directly to the availability of abortion, legalized abortion has obviously not been associated with any decrease in the suicide rate, and there is growing evidence that the risk of suicide for women rises after abortion.

- The 2003 *OGS* study identified a number of sound studies that found that "induced abortion increased . . . [the incidence of] mood disorders substantial enough to provoke attempts of self-harm."[69]
- A 1996 study by Mika Gissler in Finland found a more than three-fold increase in the risk of suicide after induced abortion.[70]
- A 2002 study in the *American Journal of Orthopsychiatry* compared the use of mental health services by women after giving birth with the use of services by women after an abortion, and found that the rate of mental health claims was 17 percent higher for women after abortion than after childbirth.[71]
- An American study in 2002 found a more than twofold higher risk of suicide after elective abortion.[72]
- A study reported in the *Medical Science Monitor* examined data from the National Longitudinal Study of Youth and found that women with a history of abortion have a significantly higher risk of experiencing clinical depression than women who carry their children to term.[73] This is reinforced by a 2005 study in the *Journal of Anxiety Disorders*.[74]
- A study by Gissler in 2005 in the *European Journal of Public Health* found an elevated risk of suicide and

homicide after abortion in a fifteen- to twenty-four-year age group in Finland.

- A 2006 study in the *Journal of Child Psychology and Psychiatry* looked at a group of women fifteen to twenty-five years old over the course of twenty-five years and concluded that "young women who aborted were at a higher risk for various mental health problems compared to women who carried to term or who were never pregnant."[75] By age twenty-five, 42 percent reported major depression, 39 percent suffered from anxiety disorders, 27 percent reported experiencing suicidal ideation, and 6.8 percent reported alcohol dependence.[76]

- A July 2006 study in the *Journal of Youth and Adolescence* examined data from the National Longitudinal Study of Adolescent Health and found that "adolescents who aborted an unwanted pregnancy were more inclined than adolescents who delivered to seek psychological counseling and they reported more frequent problems sleeping and more frequent marijuana use."[77]

- A study published in 2010 in the *Canadian Journal of Psychiatry* found that "abortion was associated with an increased likelihood of several mental disorders—mood disorders . . . substance use disorders . . . as well as suicidal ideation and suicide attempts."[78]

The trauma that some women feel after an abortion is a factor that needs to be taken more seriously than it has been in the past.[79] Even some Justices recognized this as a risk in their 1992 *Casey* opinion, though the Court has done nothing—and can do nothing—to ensure comprehensive informed consent:

> In attempting to ensure that a woman apprehends the
> full consequences of her decision, the State furthers the
> legitimate purpose of reducing the risk that a woman may
> elect an abortion, only to discover later, with devastat-
> ing psychological consequences, that her decision was not
> fully informed.[80]

This research needs to be more widely known and discussed
by doctors with their patients.

The 2008 American Psychological
Association Report

A report by the American Psychological Association published
in August 2008 dismissed all existing data showing negative
psychological outcomes to women, even if the studies were
well done. The task force that produced the report was supposed to collect, examine, and summarize peer-reviewed
research published over the prior seventeen years relating to
psychological outcomes after abortion. Instead, the report
excluded a third of the published studies and relied primarily
on a single study that found no negative effect. The report
also disregarded important studies from outside the United
States. Studies showing no negative outcome after abortion
were less thoroughly examined than studies showing a negative outcome. The American Psychological Association dismissed data showing negative outcomes to women as simply
the result of a cultural stigma against abortion in the United
States. The Association did not seriously examine the most
thorough studies that had been done up to that time. A 2003
study by Bradshaw and Slade, for example, concluded that
"the proportion of women with high levels of anxiety in
the month following abortion ranged from 19–27%, with

3–9% reporting high levels of depression. The better quality studies suggested that 8–32% of women were experiencing high levels of distress."[81] The American Psychological Association's August 2008 Report should be viewed with some skepticism as a reliable guide to the published data on the psychological outcome of abortion for women.

The 2011 *British Journal of Psychiatry* Study

A landmark study on the effects of abortion on mental health—perhaps the most important since *Roe*—was published in September 2011 in the *British Journal of Psychiatry* (*BJP*), a journal published by Britain's Royal College of Psychiatrists.[82]

The study critically reviewed the results of twenty-two previous studies on abortion and mental health published between 1995 and 2009. These twenty-two studies included data on 877,181 women from six countries, 163,831 of whom had experienced an abortion. The study used a standard method for combining the results of multiple studies and examined the twenty-two studies for the strength of their analysis and significance of their findings. Only studies that met stringent criteria were included in the *BJP* study (including a sample size of 100 or more participants, use of a comparison group, and use of controls for variables that could confound the effects, such as demographics, exposure to violence, or prior history of mental health problems).

The results revealed a moderate to high increased risk of mental health problems after abortion. Women with a history of abortion had an 81 percent increased risk of subsequent mental health problems. More specifically, the study found that women with a history of abortion had an increased risk of anxiety (34 percent higher), depression (37 percent higher), alcohol use (110 percent higher), marijuana use (220 percent higher), and suicidal behavior (155 percent higher).

These results have sparked a lively debate and they challenge the August 2008 Report of the American Psychological Association, which dismissed studies finding mental health problems after abortion.[83]

Loss of Protective Effect Against Breast Cancer from a Full-Term Pregnancy

It is well-recognized that age at first pregnancy is a risk factor for breast cancer, and that a full-term pregnancy provides some protection against breast cancer.[84]

The biological plausibility of an association between abortion and breast cancer is based on the physiology of the breast and, in particular, the interaction between hormones and the differentiation of breast tissue cells during pregnancy.[85] It is relatively undisputed that the effects of hormones on the differentiation of breast tissue in the course of a full-term pregnancy lowers a woman's long-term risk of breast cancer, and that this protective effect is lost when a pregnancy (especially a first pregnancy) is artificially terminated by induced abortion. This is why it makes sense to think that the artificial termination of a viable pregnancy would increase the risk of breast cancer.

Medical studies concluding that an association between induced abortion and breast cancer exists are not new; nor are they limited to the United States. A 2005 Nigerian medical journal article recognized that "epidemiological evidence of a positive association between induced abortion and the incidence of breast cancer was first presented by Segi in 1957 [a Japanese study] based on cases diagnosed between 1948 and 1952."[86]

The 2003 OGS study concluded that "clinicians are obligated to inform pregnant women that a decision to abort her first pregnancy may almost double her lifetime risk of breast cancer through loss of the protective effect of a completed full-term pregnancy earlier in life."[87] This loss of protection is "most pronounced in women under 20 years of age who elect to undergo abortion rather than continue a pregnancy."[88]

The OGS researchers added an enhanced perspective on the association between abortion and breast cancer through their use of the Gail Model, a familiar scale for assessing breast cancer risk. The OGS authors, utilizing the Gail Model, concluded that, if an eighteen-year-old finds herself pregnant for the first time, her decision to abort almost doubles her lifetime risk of breast cancer. Accordingly, the 2003 OGS study urged, as a matter of professional ethics, that women be informed of the loss of this protective effect through induced abortion.[89]

Induced Abortion as an Independent Risk for Breast Cancer

A second, separate claim about the association between induced abortion and breast cancer is that induced abortion is an "independent risk" for breast cancer—in other words, that induced abortion directly causes breast cancer.[90] This purported association between induced abortion and higher risk of breast cancer is one of the most hotly disputed issues in American medicine today.

But that does not mean the issue is new. Since 1957,

there have been numerous epidemiological studies that have addressed a possible association.[91] As of 2012, eighteen of twenty-four studies on American women found an increased risk of breast cancer after having an induced abortion.[92] Worldwide, at least thirty-one studies have found an elevated risk with statistical significance.[93]

The controversy first received wide national attention in the United States in 1994, when Janet Daling and her colleagues published an important study in the *Journal of the National Cancer Institute*.[94] Daling's study found an increased risk of breast cancer after abortion. Daling told the *Los Angeles Daily News* in September 1997:

> If politics gets involved in science . . . it will really hold back the progress that we make. I have three sisters with breast cancer and I resent people messing with the scientific data to further their own agenda, be they pro-choice or pro-life. I would have loved to have found no association between breast cancer and abortion, but our research is rock solid, and our data is accurate. It's not a matter of believing, it's a matter of what is.[95]

Two years later, a scientific study published in the October 1996 issue of the *British Journal of Epidemiology and Community Health* concluded that an induced abortion increases a woman's risk of developing breast cancer by 30 percent. In 2000, Britain's RCOG reviewed that study and a second one finding an increased risk of breast cancer after abortion and concluded: "These two meta-analyses were independently assessed for the RCOG Group. The assessor concluded that both were carefully conducted reviews."[96]

Two studies are held out as having refuted the epidemiological data suggesting an association, but these contained serious methodological flaws.[97] The first, by Mads Melbye and colleagues, was published in 1997.[98] The second, published in *The Lancet*, a British medical journal,[99] purported to analyze fifty-three epidemiological studies, including a total of 83,000 breast cancer patients from sixteen countries. While that study did not dispute the biological conclusion that a full-term pregnancy lowers a woman's long-term risk of breast cancer, and that this protection is not afforded by a pregnancy that ends in induced abortion, it argued that there was insufficient evidence to support the abortion– breast cancer link. The *Lancet* study has been criticized for its methodology, however.[100]

Further analyses of the existing epidemiological data and new epidemiological studies are needed to resolve the dispute among researchers and analysts over induced abortion as an independent risk. Nevertheless, taken together, the weight of the data supports the creation of at least some legal duty for abortion practitioners to inform women about the possibility of the link.[101]

The authors of the 2003 *OGS* study reached a sensible and conservative conclusion regarding an association between abortion and breast cancer based on the existing data:

> Whatever the effect of induced abortion on breast cancer risk, a young woman with an unintended pregnancy clearly sacrifices the protective effect of a term delivery should she decide to abort and delay childbearing. . . . [W]e conclude that informed consent before induced

abortion should include information about the subsequent risk of preterm delivery and depression. Although it remains uncertain whether elective abortion increases subsequent breast cancer, it is clear that a decision to abort and delay pregnancy culminates in a loss of protection with the net effect being an increased risk.[102]

Conclusion

Central to *Roe* was the assumption that "abortion is safer than childbirth." Since 1973, a growing body of international data suggests a negative impact of abortion on women's health and relationships. These data are significant but largely unknown to American women.

Both the original Jane Roe of *Roe v. Wade* (Norma McCorvey) and Mary Doe of *Doe v. Bolton* (Sandra Cano) have publicly expressed regret for their role in the original lawsuits, and each filed lawsuits to reopen those decisions. The federal courts dismissed the cases, and the Supreme Court refused to hear them in 2005 and 2006.[103]

But one federal judge explored the Supreme Court's record in light of the evidence presented in McCorvey's suit. Judge Edith Jones of the U.S. Court of Appeals for the 5th Circuit in Dallas, in reviewing McCorvey's claim, examined the Supreme Court's record on abortion.[104] Judge Jones surveyed the "thousand affidavits of women who have had abortions and claim to have suffered long-term emotional damage and impaired relationships from their decision," as well as the medical studies submitted "suggest[ing] that women may be affected emotionally and physically for years afterward and may be more prone to engage in high-risk, self-destructive conduct as a result of having had abortions," and affidavits by abortion clinic personnel testifying that "women are often herded through their procedures with little or no medical or emotional counseling."[105]

Judge Jones wrote that "if courts were to delve into the facts underlying *Roe*'s balancing scheme with present-day knowledge, they might conclude that the woman's 'choice' is far more risky and less beneficial . . . than the *Roe* Court knew." She observed that the Court's abortion jurisprudence has made the Court impervious to any new medical, scientific, or factual understanding:

> The perverse result of the Court's having determined [this social policy] . . . is that the facts no longer matter. . . . Hard and social science will of course progress even though the Supreme Court averts its eyes. It takes no expert prognosticator to know that research on women's mental and physical health following abortion will yield an eventual medical consensus. . . . That the Court's constitutional decision-making leaves our nation in a position of willful blindness to evolving knowledge should trouble any dispassionate observer not only about the abortion decisions, but about a number of other areas in which the Court unhesitatingly steps into the realm of social policy under the guise of constitutional adjudication.[106]

CHAPTER NINE

The Costs of Schizophrenia

[M]edical authority has recognized long since that the child is in existence from the moment of conception, and for many purposes its existence is recognized by the law. The criminal law regards it as a separate entity, and the law of property considers it in being for all purposes which are to its benefit, such as taking by will or descent. . . . All writers who have discussed the problem have joined in condemning the old rule, in maintaining that the unborn child in the path of an automobile is as much a person in the street as the mother . . .

—PROFESSOR WILLIAM PROSSER,
LAW OF TORTS[1]

Introduction

During the spring of 2011, Pampers and Apple partnered on an iPad app to track "your baby's development before birth." The app—called "Hello Baby!"—allows you to download the free app onto your iPad and track your baby's development "from four weeks to forty." The YouTube video tells viewers: "from the very first moment your baby starts growing, a bond begins to form between your little one—when it's really, really little—and you."[2]

Six months before, an October 2010 issue of *Time* featured a pregnant woman on the cover. Inside, there was a lengthy excerpt from Annie Murphy Paul's book *Origins: How the Nine Months before Birth Shape the Rest of Our Lives*.[3] Paul's book is an up-to-date report on the medical knowledge that has grown over the past four decades about fetal development.

Four hundred years ago, when the English common law was shaping the legal rules for protecting human life, none of this science or technology was even imagined, let alone possible. Technology, in hand with medical knowledge, has long spurred our understanding of prenatal development. Earlier forms of technology helped doctors in the 1800s to conclude that the life of the individual human being began at conception.[4]

Medical understanding has influenced legal protection of the unborn child for centuries. Indeed, the law's protection has been utterly dependent on the extent of medical knowledge. The law cannot protect what it does not know exists. As medical knowledge has grown, so has the law's protection.

Legal protection for the unborn child had been growing since the 1700s, and it continued to grow in tort and criminal law in the decades leading up to *Roe*. But *Roe* did not eclipse those areas of law. Legal protection has grown considerably—outside the area of abortion—since *Roe*. The public supports these laws, prosecutors are using them, and juries are convicting under the criminal laws. How and why that legal protection has grown is the subject of this chapter.

Legal Protection of the
Unborn Child at the Time of *Roe*

When the Justices first heard oral argument in the abortion cases on Monday, December 13, 1971, Bill Maledon was in his last year at Notre Dame Law School, where he was editor-in-chief of the *Notre Dame Law Review*.[5] Months before, the law review had published an article by Maledon titled *The Law and the Unborn Child: The Legal and Logical Inconsistencies*.[6]

Maledon's impressive record as a student (he eventually graduated *summa cum laude*), his stint as editor-in-chief of the law review, and a recommendation from a professor landed him some interviews for a Supreme Court clerkship. He interviewed with Justice Brennan and Justice White and accepted a clerkship with Justice Brennan.

Maledon arrived at the Court in July 1972 to begin his year as a law clerk for Justice Brennan, just a few weeks after the May–June 1972 crisis in the Court and the coverage in the *New York Times* and *Washington Post* of Justice Douglas's memo against Chief Justice Burger. The Court had recessed for the summer; Justice Blackmun headed to the Mayo Clinic library for two weeks of research on the history of abortion and the Hippocratic oath; and the Justices were anticipating a second argument in the early fall.

By the time he arrived, Maledon recalled, "it was clear that there were six or seven votes to legalize abortion and that the only question was how the opinion was going to be written."[7] Maledon's law review article was noticed by the clerks and Justices, and it was eventually cited by Justice Blackmun in his opinion in *Roe*.[8] Maledon was assigned the abortion cases in a meeting with his fellow clerks during which they divvied up the pending cases. He had many discussions with Justice Brennan about the cases, as well as many discussions with Justice Blackmun's clerks. But when Maledon listened to the second oral argument in the abortion cases on Wednesday, October 11, 1972, he was listening for points that might shape the writing of the opinion, because the outcome, it was clear, was foreordained.

Over two hundred law review articles were published on abortion in the 1960s, but Maledon's twenty-four-page-article was unique in its insight. He summarized well all of the legal material, including statutes and court decisions on abortion and the law protecting human life. He surveyed the existing legal protection of the unborn child in criminal law, property law, tort law, and equity. In Maledon's view, the thirteen to fourteen states that had legalized abortion in some circumstances since 1967 introduced confusion into an area of law that already had inconsistencies. How those contradictions would be resolved was completely uncertain. His conclusions forecast that the nationwide legalization of abortion by the Justices would only enlarge the contradictions.

One significant issue that Maledon's article did not cover was the relationship between medicine and law that formed the backdrop for the English common law. The English common law, and its need to prove life and death, was limited by medical and technological constraints in 1600. Imagine a world with no modern medical technology—no electronic monitors, no ultrasound, and no stethoscopes. (The stethoscope was not invented by René-Théophile-Hyacinthe Laennec until 1816.) Those medical constraints resulted in the quickening and born-alive rules outlined in earlier chapters.

Property Law

Protection of the rights of the unborn child in property law goes back centuries. How did these property questions about the unborn child's life even arise? They began when British courts were first called upon to interpret language in wills, such as "children living at my death." Maledon pointed out in 1971 that "the property rights of the unborn child are as old as the common law itself," and cited cases from the eighteenth century that protected the property rights of the unborn child.[9]

For example, in 1798 in *Thellusson v. Woodford*, an English court declared, "They ['children *en ventre sa mère*'] are entitled to all the privileges of other persons."[10] (The term *en ventre sa mère*, "in its mother's womb," was adopted from French civil law.[11]) In response to the claim that a child *en ventre sa mère* was a "non-entity," the judge responded with a summary of the conclusions of prior courts:

> Let us see what this non-entity can do. He may be vouched in a recovery, though it is for the purpose of making him answer over in value. He may be an executor. He may take under the Statute of Distributions. . . . He may take by devise. He may be entitled under a charge for raising portions. He may have an injunction; and he may have a guardian.[12]

American courts adopted the property rules of the English common law. As a practical matter, the effective protection of these property rights sometimes required a guardian, as is true with infants and adolescents even today. So, in 1941, a New York court stated:

> It has been the uniform and unvarying decision of all common law courts in respect of estate matters for at least the past two hundred years that a child *en ventre sa mere* is "born" and "alive" for all purposes for his benefit.[13]

But property law had easier proof problems than criminal or tort law. If a father died while the mother was pregnant and the child was *en ventre sa mère*, courts held that the child had rights that vested upon the date of the father's death, even if the child was *en ventre sa mère* on the date of death. The courts held that the *rights vested while the child was unborn.* Property law did not need the quickening or born-alive rules because it did not have the problems of proof that the criminal law had. From his review of the law in 1971, Maledon concluded that "the legal life of a human being begins at conception for purposes of the law of property."[14]

Tort Law (Prenatal Injury and Wrongful Death)

Tort law developed later than property law. Judicial recognition of the rights of the unborn child in wrongful death and prenatal injury law began to grow in the middle of the twentieth century. In his 1971 article, Maledon counted twenty-nine states and the District of Columbia that allowed suits for prenatal injuries.[15] Maledon noted that "the trend at the present time is to allow recovery without regard to whether or not the child was viable at the time the injury was inflicted."[16]

A New York state appellate court in 1953 seems to have been the first to reject, on medical grounds, viability as a legal limitation:

> While the point at which the foetus becomes viable has been of usefulness in drawing some legal distinctions, the underlying problem that has usually troubled the Judges who have written on the subject of recovery for prenatal injuries, has been in fixing the point of legal separability from the mother. We ought to be safe in this respect in saying that legal separability should begin where there is biological separability. We know something more of the actual process of conception and foetal development now than when some of the common law cases were decided; and what we know makes it possible to demonstrate clearly that separability begins at conception.[17]

Maledon counted nine states in 1971 that had "rejected the viability distinction in allowing recovery for prenatal injuries."[18] Texas first allowed a suit for prenatal injury when the unborn child was viable in 1967,[19] and extended that ruling to the pre-viable child two months before the oral argument in *Roe*—apparently becoming the tenth state by Maledon's count.[20]

The rationale for rejecting viability was also stated by the Pennsylvania Supreme Court in 1960:

> As for the notion that the child must have been viable when the injuries were received, which has claimed the attention of several of the states, we regard it as having

little to do with the basic right to recover, when the foetus is regarded as having existence as a separate creature from the moment of conception.[21]

Courts recognized that problems of proof might be more difficult the earlier in gestation the injury to the child occurred, but that proof problems should not cancel the claim entirely.[22]

Wrongful Death

It was traditionally understood that a suit for wrongful death did not exist under the common law—for anyone, born or unborn. William Prosser wrote in 1971 that "under the common law, death gave rise to no causes of action, and terminated all those for personal torts; and that . . . statutes now have altered the common law rule to a greater or less extent to authorize recovery."[23] Wrongful death statutes were enacted by the states "in the late 1880's."[24] In 1971, Maledon counted twenty-eight to twenty-nine states as allowing a suit for wrongful death *if the child was born alive* and died afterward.[25]

The prenatal injury and wrongful death cases proved two things: that the born-alive rule was a rule of location, not gestational development, and that the child in and out of the womb was the same human being (the doctrine of congruence).

First, born-alive meant expulsion from the womb (location) at any time of gestation; it did not mean birth at term. That meant as a practical matter that if the child was injured in the womb and was miscarried and died after birth, at any time of pregnancy, recovery could be made, even if the child was injured and died at one or two months gestation.[26]

Second, if the unborn child really was a non-entity until birth and the "rights" of the child were really "contingent" on birth—as Justice Stewart assumed at oral argument and the Justices asserted in the opinion in *Roe*—then there could be no recover for any injury *inflicted before birth*. Only injuries inflicted after birth could be actionable. But the courts in the prenatal injury and wrongful death areas never questioned that there was congruence—that the child before birth was the same entity as the child after birth. And this congruence confirms that the born-alive rule was an evidentiary, not a substantive, rule.

Criminal Law

These questions arose in criminal law whenever a pregnant mother might miscarry from an injury, or the child died *in utero* or shortly after birth. Homicide—the killing of a human being—was invariably a capital offense that carried the death penalty in the English common law of the seventeenth and eighteenth centuries. Because of such serious penalties, the common law of crimes developed evidentiary rules to prevent convictions on uncertain evidence.

The quickening distinction was dropped by doctors and state legislatures by the 1860s, as medical science showed that the unborn child was alive from conception, long before the mother felt fetal movements. And the born-alive rule, by the twentieth century, was no longer needed for medical science to distinguish natural from criminal causes. But some courts and legislatures hung on to the common law born-alive rule despite its medical obsolescence.[27]

When, for example, the California Supreme Court in 1970 adopted the born-alive rule in *People v. Keeler*,[28] it meant that the killing of a nearly full-term unborn child could not be charged as a homicide if it was stillborn, even if the prosecutor could prove beyond a reasonable doubt that the child was alive and killed by the assailant while unborn.

Inside the Court

In the briefs in the abortion cases (more than in the oral arguments), the Justices got a full medical description of prenatal development. Pictures of the unborn child at various stages of development were included in the brief from Texas and in a brief filed on behalf of Certain Physicians, Professors, and Fellows of the American College of Obstetricians and Gynecologists (ACOG). (The facts of fetal development had been previously presented to the Justices in the briefs in the District of Columbia abortion case, *United States v. Vuitch*.[29]) Dorothy Beasley, Georgia's attorney, argued that the unborn child was a person from conception and that greater knowledge of fetal development imposed on the states a greater responsibility to protect human life.

But basic questions about the common law of homicide and abortion were not asked or answered in the oral arguments, and the extent of legal protection for the unborn child in the law of prenatal injury and wrongful death was not explained. The Justices did not seem to realize that other states could or would move ahead with legislation updating the law and increasing legal protection. They overlooked the trends in prenatal injury, wrongful death law, and fetal homicide law.

For example, the Justices cited the *Keeler* decision (in which California judges held that there could be no homicide of an unborn child by adopting a strict application of the born-alive rule) and accepted it at face value as a correct statement of the common law.[30] But they ignored the fact that the California legislature quickly overturned the *Keeler* decision in September 1970.

The Justices also overlooked (or ignored) the extent of legal protection in 1971, as scholars have noted. "The discussion [by the Justices in *Roe*] was perfunctory, and unfortunately largely inaccurate and should not be relied upon as the correct view of the law [on wrongful death] at the time of *Roe v. Wade.*"[31] At the time of the first argument in *Roe* in December 1971, the division of case authority was 14–11 favoring recovery for the wrongful death of a stillborn child, and the Justices failed to see that "between 1971 and 1973, courts in five additional jurisdictions had considered the question, four more allowing recovery. . . ."[32]

Elimination of the quickening distinction in tort law meant that lawsuits for injuring a child in the womb could be filed even if the child was injured before quickening. Elimination of the born-alive rule meant that a violent offender could be prosecuted for homicide even if the child was stillborn. It also meant that wrongful death suits in tort law could be filed even if the child was stillborn and even if the child died in the womb at any time after conception.

These developments did not eliminate the need to prove who caused the death or injury, but such proof problems are common in criminal and tort law, even in cases of born children or adults. As chapter 4 shows, the Justices latched on to viability even though the preceding centuries of legal protection of the unborn child considered viability irrelevant.

The extent to which the Justices overlooked these developments is seen in the fact that the opinions in the abortion cases did not attempt to explain away prenatal injury law.

Instead, they ignored or minimized these developments. If the Justices had understood the implications of the wrongful death, prenatal injury, and fetal homicide law, they might have understood the confusion they were sowing by legalizing abortion nationwide in so sweeping a manner.

Because of medicine, technology, and past legal precedents in tort and criminal law, there was an inexorable trend toward greater legal protection. Today we have ultrasound pictures that everyone can put on their refrigerator—a powerful reminder of reality. These images have brought the wonder of prenatal development into millions of homes. Parents want to protect children, and medical developments enable them to do so to a greater and greater degree, a degree that was not possible in earlier centuries. The Justices failed to see that the trend toward greater protection that Prosser identified in 1971 would grow.

How the *Roe* Opinion Left Open the Door for Schizophrenia

The Justices in *Roe* eliminated the abortion laws of the fifty states but left in place the existing law of prenatal injury, wrongful death, and fetal homicide. How could this schizophrenia—as some have called it—come about?

One of the least-understood aspects of the abortion decisions is how the Justices created a nationwide right to abortion at any time of pregnancy for any reason, but allowed the states, through property, tort, and criminal law, to protect the unborn child from other violence throughout pregnancy.

The irony in the eventual opinion in *Roe* was Justice Blackmun's dismissive attitude about the "well-known facts of fetal development."[33] The Justices claimed to understand the "facts" but failed to understand the *significance* of the facts.

In the wake of *Roe*, some advocates would broadly claim that the Court's decision meant that the states were barred from protecting unborn human life in any circumstance. But the Court's decision did not go that far. A few courts adopted that interpretation in the 1970s, but that interpretation was abandoned by the early 1980s.

There are a couple of reasons for the schizophrenia in the law today. Blackmun's opinion left open the door for the state legislatures or state courts to move ahead with legal protection *in the non-abortion context*. The signs were there—such as California's quick passage of its fetal homicide law in September 1970—that the states could increase legal protection.[34] The legal doctrine, going back centuries, was there in court decisions and legislation. The decision in *Roe* allowed it to move forward.

By its own terms, *Roe* was limited to abortion, and only the woman had a "right" to abortion, and no one else. This left open the possibility for tort law and criminal law to prosecute *third parties* who injured or killed women or their unborn children. If the woman is pregnant and wants the pregnancy, the state can fully protect the unborn child from *third parties*—strangers, husbands, or boyfriends who might injure or kill it. The states can act as long as they do not interfere with the woman's right. That "right" belongs to the woman, and subsequent decisions by the Court made clear that that right is the woman's alone and not the doctor's or the husband's or parents' or any "third party." Another way of saying it is that only the woman has a Fourteenth-Amendment "liberty" to abort; no third party has that Fourteenth-Amendment right, and thus they can be prosecuted for killing an unborn child.

This also means that *Roe*'s limitations on state regulation in the abortion area (like the viability doctrine) do not apply to prenatal injury, or wrongful death, or fetal homicide law, which can extend protection from conception.

The best evidence seems to indicate that the Justices were so focused on legalizing abortion, and so caught up in dismissing abortion law's historic protection of the unborn child, that they never focused on the law's ability to protect the unborn child *in situations other than abortion*. In the immediate aftermath of the social turmoil of the 1960s, they were so caught up by advocates and interest groups arguing that women needed abortion, that they did not see the legal and medical and technological currents that were coming together to support stronger legal protection, and they did not recognize how strongly public opinion would support such protection.

Since the Justices defined the abortion right as the right to "terminate pregnancy," there are two areas in which the states' ability to protect the unborn child or developing human being is very broad: first, when the woman is pregnant and wants the pregnancy, and, second, when the human life is developing outside a woman's womb and there is no "pregnancy" in the traditional sense. In these areas, the states can rely on the historic powers that the states have to protect human life, including police power and tort and criminal law.

The Growth of Legal Protection Despite *Roe*

Roe did not stop the growth that was evident at the time of *Roe* and reflected in Professor Prosser's famous statement. Courts soon realized that *Roe* was limited to abortion and did not limit state protection of the unborn as long as that legal protection did not impede abortion.

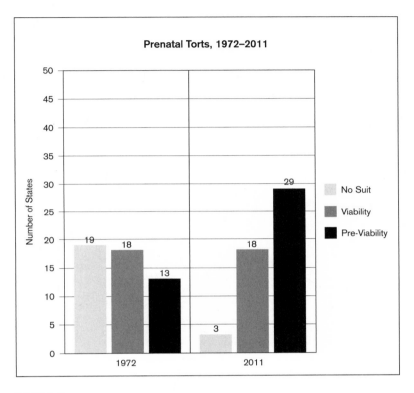

FIGURE 7.

Figures 7, 8, and 9 show the progress in legal protection in the areas of prenatal tort law, wrongful death, and fetal homicide since 1972 and the significant movement away from gestational markers to legal protection at any stage of gestational development.

In prenatal tort law, the states generally allow a suit for prenatal injuries at any time of pregnancy.

In wrongful death law, thirty-eight states allow a wrongful death suit for the killing of an unborn child. Ten states allow a wrongful death suit at any time of pregnancy. Since

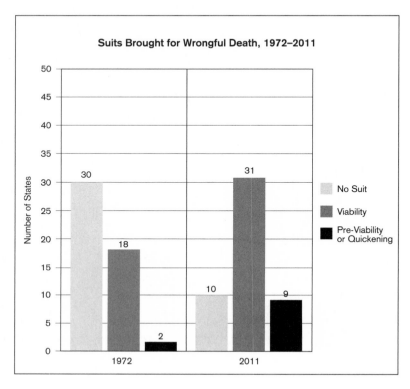

FIGURE 8.

2004, Texas and Nebraska have extended protection by statute.

Fetal homicide law has shown the most significant shift against a viability limitation, with most states (twenty-seven to twenty-eight as of 2011) allowing prosecution at any time of pregnancy.

Today, thirty-eight states have abolished the born-alive rule and allow a prosecution for fetal homicide, a few by court decision but the vast majority by legislation. That

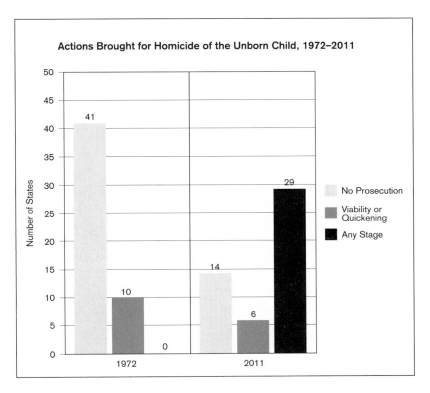

Actions Brought for Homicide of the Unborn Child, 1972–2011

FIGURE 9.

means that prosecution can go forward even if the child is stillborn.

In 2011, both North Carolina and Tennessee enacted such laws. Twenty-eight states now recognize a child as a human being subject to homicide *from conception*. In addition, twenty-one states, as of 2010, treat nonfatal assaults against an unborn child as a criminal offense. These statutes are actively enforced, and juries regularly convict third-party assailants.

The Court's adoption of viability in *Roe* has not been

influential, and states have increasingly moved away from it, especially in prenatal injury and fetal homicide law. Nevertheless, the Court has repeatedly refused to review constitutional challenges to state protection in the tort and fetal homicide areas.[35]

Conclusion

One critical difference between abortion law and these other areas in tort and criminal law is that fetal homicide, wrongful death, and prenatal injury laws are all areas of the law that have been decided by representative bodies that have been accountable to the people over the past forty years. Numerous state courts have allowed prenatal injury and wrongful death suits, and these could be reversed by legislatures accountable to the people. But no legislature has done so in the years since *Roe*.

These laws are effectively enforced and supported by popular opinion. Juries could nullify fetal homicide laws or wrongful death verdicts, but such nullification is virtually unheard of. Juries routinely convict in criminal cases and routinely award damages in tort cases involving unborn children.

Abortion law as enforced by the Supreme Court is neither accountable to the people nor supported in popular opinion. As historian Joseph Dellapenna has written:

> In *Roe* and since, the Court has never actually considered the values and perceived facts underlying the prohibition of abortion. All we have in *Roe* is a falsified argument that abortion was "contested" throughout history, a matter of taste rather than an expression of mores basic to our

culture. It is time that the Court took seriously its own premise that the constitutional status of a claimed right to abort is to be tested against the history and traditions of this nation. The accumulated wisdom relating to abortion teaches us that the prohibition of abortion was always viewed as the protection of emerging, yet real, human life—a concern only . . . made more certain by the continual growth of medical knowledge of gestation during the last two centuries.[36]

Though Georgia's attorney Dorothy Beasley stressed the importance of fetology in the oral arguments, she could not have shown the Justices an ultrasound machine. But given the single-minded focus on abolishing the abortion laws that Justices Douglas and Brennan (and perhaps Marshall and Stewart to a lesser extent) showed between December 1971 and May 1972, it is doubtful that any ultrasound machine would have influenced their strong desire to eliminate the abortion laws.

CHAPTER TEN

The Public Is Not "Polarized" Over Abortion

WHAT MOST AMERICANS CAN AGREE ON

As late as 1972, elective abortion was disapproved by approximately two-thirds of American adults.

—JUDITH BLAKE, DEMOGRAPHER, UNIVERSITY OF CALIFORNIA, BERKELEY 1973[1]

By contrast, 31% want abortion legal in all or most circumstances.

—GALLUP ORGANIZATION (MAY 2011)[2]

Americans decide a lot of public health issues through elected representatives at the local, state, and federal level—such as AIDS policy, health care reform, and the security of the public water supply—and a lot of controversial issues, such as gay marriage, food stamps, taxation, deficit spending, and immigration.

One of the reasons that these issues seem less controversial than abortion is because the public decides these issues through elected representatives. The public can lobby their representatives, in person or via phone calls or letters, in the state capitol or at their district offices, or at public meetings.

The public can re-elect them or throw them out. And the public can continue to lobby and get involved in campaigns. In these actions, there is a sense that facts can be persuasive, that reason can prevail, and that change can happen.

Why is abortion different? Why should nine judges in Washington, D.C. decide the issue? Is the public too divided to decide anything about abortion? What might the public do if abortion were again decided at the state and local level? What would the public support?

The Court's Conflict with Public Opinion Since 1973

The conventional wisdom is that the Court "led public opinion" in 1973—that the country was moving inescapably toward legalizing abortion, and that the Court was just ahead of public opinion. While there were certainly polling data in the 1960s that suggested that a majority of Americans thought abortion "should be between a woman and her doctor," anyone could read practically anything into that vague statement, and the Justices probably did.

But even support for that question changed in the two years before *Roe*:

- In August 1971—four months before the first arguments in *Roe* and *Doe*—a Gallup Poll found that 64 percent of Americans agreed that "the decision to have an abortion should be made solely by a woman and her physician."[3]
- In January 1973—the month of the Court's decision— a Gallup Poll found "when Americans were asked whether an abortion decision during the first three

months of pregnancy should simply be left to a woman and her doctor, 46 percent of respondents said 'yes' and 45 percent 'no.'"[4]

In fact, *Roe* and *Doe* were controversial from the start. Even if the Justices assumed that the abortion decisions would be controversial, they seriously underestimated the scope of the negative public reaction. As Bernard Schwartz has pointed out, "Blackmun understated the outcry. The scare headlines and controversy were far greater than any-thing anticipated by the Court."[5] The Justices were deluged with hundreds of thousands of critical letters, asking the Court to overturn *Roe*, and letters continued at least into the 1980s.[6]

There are several reasons why *Roe* remains controversial:

- *Roe* was imposed by the Justices, not by Congress or state legislatures.
- *Roe* is more expansive than the law of almost all other nations in allowing abortion.
- Majority support for abortion only in "certain circumstances" has continued since 1973.
- *Roe* is constantly mischaracterized as allowing abortion in the "first three months."[7]
- Support for abortion for any reason, at any time of pregnancy, fell to 7 percent by 2009.
- The viability doctrine was abruptly adopted without benefit of record, briefs, or argument.
- Outside of abortion law, where the public can act, the public supports protection for the unborn child in tort and criminal law, and from conception.

There are additional reasons, but these are probably the best explanation.

Roe conflicted with what states were actively doing. Until 1967, virtually no state allowed abortion except to save the life of the mother. Laws were actively enforced. And they were enforced against practitioners, not women.

Efforts to enact broad exceptions to criminal prohibitions of abortion started in 1967. After Mississippi added a rape exception in 1966, thirteen states passed "reform" measures in 1967, 1968, 1969, and 1970—California, Colorado, and North Carolina in 1967; Georgia in 1968; Arkansas, Delaware, Kansas, Maryland, New Mexico, and Oregon in 1969; and Alaska, Hawaii, New York, South Carolina, and Washington in 1970 (Washington by ballot initiative). But none of these laws was as broad as *Roe* and *Doe*.

It is possible that the Justices looked at the political reform up to 1971 as exemplifying public opinion, or looked at what happened in 1971 and 1972 as "too little, too late," or simply did not pay attention to legislative developments or electoral results in 1971 and 1972.

But what happened in 1971 and 1972 was significant. In the two years before *Roe*, no state enacted a reform measure through the legislature. In 1971, "repeal" measures—which were closest to what *Roe* did—were rejected in at least thirteen states: Colorado, Connecticut, Georgia, Illinois, Iowa, Maine, Maryland, Massachusetts, Minnesota, Montana, New Mexico, North Dakota, and Ohio.

Between 1967 and 1972, virtually all the states had considered reform or repeal. The issue was thoroughly debated. Referenda are typically considered more reliable than transient polling, and the people in various states rejected legalization by referenda on several occasions. In 1972, some polls showed that 59 percent of the people in Michigan favored repeal, but in November 61 percent of the voters rejected repeal.[8] And thirty states still had prohibitions on January 22, 1973.

The critical point, however, is that *Roe* and *Doe* together invalidated the laws of all fifty states: *Roe* invalidated the thirty prohibitions, while *Doe* invalidated the "reform" measures that had already existed or had been approved by state legislatures in the preceding five years. Even in New York State, considered by many to be the most liberal, an abortion legalization bill was passed very narrowly. The 1970 bill was repealed on May 10, 1972, by an Assembly vote of 79–68 and on May 11, 1972, by a Senate vote of 30–27, but it was vetoed by Governor Nelson Rockefeller.[9]

In 1970, the cases in *Roe* and *Doe* were filed because it was believed by abortion advocates that they could not succeed in the legislatures. They were filed to ask the courts to do what the legislative representatives of the people would not do.

In November 1972, while Justice Blackmun was working on his second draft in *Roe* and *Doe*, voters rejected repeal by ballot initiative by 61 percent in Michigan and by 77 percent in North Dakota. Two months later, the Court in *Roe* dictated nationwide what voters in North Dakota and Michigan had just rejected.

It was obvious at the time of *Roe*, as Judith Blake's polling data shows, that the public did not support the result in *Roe*,[10] but the decision was publicly reported as allowing abortion only in the first three months of pregnancy.

The 1990 Gallup Poll—the largest and most in-depth survey of American attitudes toward abortion ever undertaken—showed that Middle America—the 60 percent in the middle who are neither consistently pro-life nor consistently pro-choice—are deeply troubled by abortion. Gallup found that 77 percent of Americans consider abortion to be the taking of human life (28 percent) or murder (49 percent). Clearly, Americans consider abortion troubling because it takes a human life. *Roe* is uniquely controversial because most Americans support some legal protection for the unborn child. That is seen in support for fetal homicide and wrongful death laws, and in public support for abortion only in "certain circumstances."

The fact of the matter is that a majority of Americans do not favor the status quo and would support significant restrictions on abortion. That was clear in 1975. It was clear in the mid-1980s.[11] It was confirmed by the 1990 Gallup Poll. And it has been confirmed by succeeding polls.[12] It is confirmed by state polls as well. As historian Joseph Dellapenna observed in 2006:

> While the percentages approving or disapproving of abortion under particular circumstances vary widely from state to state, in every state only a minority favors abortion on demand. The range of support for abortion on demand ranges from a high of 48 percent in Colorado to a low of 12 percent in Kentucky.[13]

A May 2011 Gallup Poll showed once again that the majority of Americans supported abortion only in certain circumstances.[14]

The 7 Percent

A poll by the Pew Research Center for the People and the Press, conducted from March 31 to April 21, 2009, found that only 18 percent thought abortion should be legal in "all cases."

What Pew and many other polls do not specifically ask, however, is the percentage of Americans who support what *Roe* has imposed in every state—*abortion for any reason, at any time of pregnancy.*

A May 17–18, 2009, poll conducted by the Polling Company found that a mere 7 percent of Americans think abortion should be allowed at any time of pregnancy for any reason. That poll found a five-point drop in the percentage of Americans favoring legal abortion "any time, any reason" (from 12 percent to 7 percent) between 2006 and 2009.[15]

What makes abortion uniquely controversial is that the Justices sided with a small sect—7 percent of Americans— who support abortion for any reason at any time. And the Justices have for forty years prevented the 60–70 percent of Americans in the middle from deciding differently. That conflict between public opinion and the Supreme Court's nationwide policy is one key reason why *Roe* is uniquely controversial.

The Paradigm of "Polarization"

Nevertheless, political commentators and reporters often refer to Americans as "polarized" on the issue of abortion. This suggests "polar opposites"—that half the people are on one side of a political spectrum while the other half are all the way on the other side of the political spectrum. This paradigm implies that the public is evenly divided between abortion on demand and a total prohibition.

This paradigm is useful for advocates: it implies that there is no majority position, that the public could not make a decision, and that there is no alternative to control by the Justices. Some Justices also believe the polarization theme and seem to think it justifies their continued control of the issue.[16] The paradigm feeds the notion that nothing can be done about the issue one way or another, and that the American people could not "handle" the issue if the issue were returned to them.

Consequently, the strategy of some advocates has been to persuade the public that there is no alternative but the status quo. As the legal scholar Michael McConnell observed two decades ago:

> The threat to the current regime of abortion on demand . . . comes, instead, from the fact that a clear majority of the American people support significant restrictions on the abortion right. . . . If the American people were persuaded (contrary to their own sense of the matter) that there are no plausible, intermediate positions between the status quo and the uncompromising pro-life position, they would choose the status quo. There is little doubt about that. The solution to the political problem, then, is to do one's utmost to avoid serious, substantive discussion of the law and morality of abortion, for this discussion would reveal that intermediate solutions are possible. It is to condemn all thought of compromise, since compromise would constitute a retreat from *Roe*.[17]

The paradigm of polarization is useful for some but completely wrong. The facts are quite different. There certainly exist political activists who are on one side of the political spectrum—supporting abortion on demand for any reason from conception to birth—and there are political activists on the opposite side of the political spectrum, believing abortion should be prohibited except to save the life of the mother. But there is a real majority between the theoretical opposites, as Gallup's annual polling since 1975 shows (see Table 4).

A Better Understanding of What *Roe* Means

Part of the challenge to seeing democracy work is achieving a greater public understanding of what *Roe* dictates—what our national abortion policy is today.

Like the repeated polling question in the 1960s—whether "abortion should be between a woman and her physician"—there is a repeated polling question today—whether the public "supports *Roe v. Wade.*"

The 1990 Gallup Poll showed that many Americans were confused about the meaning of *Roe* and what the decision did, and they remain confused today.[18]

Roe established the United States as one of a handful of nations that allows abortion after fourteen weeks and one of only four nations, besides Canada, North Korea, and China, that allows abortion for any reason after fetal viability. Forty years after *Roe*, any prohibitions after viability are still unenforceable because the courts have required a "health" exception, which means "emotional well-being."[19]

TABLE 4. Annual Gallup Poll of Opinions about Abortion, 1975–2011

Year	Any Circ.	Certain Circ.	Illegal	No Opinion	Year	Any Circ.	Certain Circ.	Illegal	No Opinion
1975	21%	54%	22%	3%	1999	27%	55%	16%	2%
1977	22%	55%	19%	4%	2000	26%	56%	15%	3%
1978	22%	55%	19%	4%	2000	28%	51%	19%	2%
1979	22%	54%	19%	5%	2001	26%	51%	18%	5%
1980	25%	53%	18%	4%	2001	26%	58%	15%	1%
1981	23%	52%	21%	4%	2001	26%	56%	17%	1%
1983	23%	58%	16%	3%	2002	26%	54%	18%	2%
1988	24%	57%	17%	2%	2002	27%	53%	19%	1%
1989	27%	50%	18%	5%	2002	25%	51%	22%	2%
1989	29%	51%	17%	3%	2003	24%	57%	18%	1%
1990	31%	53%	12%	4%	2003	23%	57%	19%	1%
1991	32%	50%	17%	1%	2003	26%	55%	17%	2%
1991	33%	49%	14%	4%	2004	24%	56%	19%	1%
1992	31%	53%	14%	2%	2005	23%	55%	20%	2%
1992	34%	48%	13%	5%	2005	23%	53%	22%	2%
1993	32%	51%	13%	4%	2005	24%	55%	20%	1%
1994	31%	51%	15%	3%	2005	26%	56%	16%	2%
1994	33%	52%	13%	2%	2006	30%	53%	15%	2%
1995	33%	50%	15%	2%	2007	26%	55%	18%	1%
1995	31%	54%	12%	3%	2008	28%	54%	17%	2%
1996	25%	58%	15%	2%	2009	22%	53%	23%	2%
1996	24%	52%	17%	7%	2009	21%	57%	18%	4%
1997	22%	61%	15%	2%	2010	24%	54%	19%	3%
1997	26%	55%	17%	2%	2011	27%	50%	22%	2%
1998	23%	59%	17%	1%					

- As Justice Ginsburg observed before she became a member of the Supreme Court, the Court in *Roe* "fashion[ed] a regime blanketing the subject, a set of rules that displaced virtually every state law then in force . . . *Roe v. Wade*, in contrast, invited no dialogue with legislators. Instead, it seemed entirely to remove the ball from the legislators' court. . . . No measured motion, the *Roe* decision left virtually no state with laws fully conforming to the Court's delineation of abortion regulation still permissible."[20]

- As Harvard Law Professor Mary Ann Glendon has observed, "The United States is alone . . . in forbidding any state regulation of abortion for the sake of preserving the fetus until viability. . . . It is alone, too, in that even after viability, it does not require regulation to protect the fetus. If a state does choose to try to preserve the life of the fetus after viability, it must observe the ruling in *Roe v. Wade* that state regulation may not interfere with abortions which are 'necessary to preserve the life or health of the mother.' 'Health,' in *Roe*'s companion case of *Doe v. Bolton*, is broadly understood as related to 'all factors . . . relevant to the well-being of the patient.' "[21]

- As Professor Michael McConnell noted twenty years ago, "The *Roe* opinion holds that states may not interfere with abortions after viability if the abortion is 'necessary, in appropriate medical judgment, for the preservation of the life or health of the mother.' . . . In the companion case, *Doe v. Bolton* . . . the Court interpreted 'health' to include 'all factors—medical, emotional, psychological, familial, and the woman's age—relevant to the well-being of the patient.' Under this interpretation, the only genuine restraint on post-viability abortions is medical, not legal."[22]

Since *Roe* is one of the most controversial Supreme Court decisions in American history, many might expect that its content and meaning have become clear. But there are several factors that work against public understanding.

The Court's opinion in *Roe* is nearly sixty pages long and the opinion in *Doe* is another thirty pages. *Roe* has been called vague and ponderous and confused, not something that non-lawyers would read.

The sweeping scope of *Roe* has repeatedly been cloaked by repeated public statements—by reporters, commentators, and major newspapers—that the Court "merely" created a right to abortion in the first trimester (twelve weeks) or the "first three months."[23]

This, unfortunately, includes Justice Sandra Day O'Connor and Justice Stephen Breyer. This is how Justice O'Connor described *Roe* in her 2003 book, *The Majesty of the Law: Reflections of a Supreme Court Justice*: "Since the Court struck down as unconstitutional limitations by states on abortions in the first three months of pregnancy, large numbers of people have taken regularly to the streets to demonstrate either their support of or their opposition to the decision."[24] A second time, she described *Roe* as: "When in the 1970s the Court struck down as unconstitutional limitations by states on abortions in the first three months of pregnancy, a new body of protestors took to the streets in opposition."[25]

This mischaracterization was brought to public attention

by the abortion-rights historian David Garrow, author of
Liberty and Sexuality. In a review of Justice O'Connor's book,
Garrow expressed confusion and surprise at O'Connor's
erroneous description of the scope of the abortion license.
"Most puzzling of all," Garrow wrote, "is how 'The Majesty of the Law' twice misstates the full import of the court's
1973 decision in *Roe v. Wade*. In identical language in two
separate chapters, the book states that *Roe* 'struck down as
unconstitutional limitations by states on abortions in the first
three months of pregnancy.' Actually, *Roe* not only legalized
women's access to safe abortions right up to the time of fetal
viability . . . but also precluded the states from prohibiting
post-viability abortions if a pregnancy in any way threatens
a woman's health."[26]

Justice O'Connor's book was published three years after
the Supreme Court's 2000 decision in *Stenberg v. Carhart*, in
which O'Connor, in her own concurring opinion, rejected
the Nebraska statute as unconstitutional because its prohibition on abortion when the fetus is viable lacked a "health"
exception for the mother.[27]

In 2010, Justice Stephen Breyer published *Making Our
Democracy Work: A Judge's View*, in which he refers to "the
decisions protecting a woman's decision to have an abortion
in the early months of pregnancy."[28] This could not have
been an oversight. In 1998, the Supreme Court denied review in an Ohio case where the Sixth Circuit struck down
Ohio's post-viability prohibition because it lacked a sufficiently broad exception for the mother's "health." Justice
Thomas, joined by Scalia and Rehnquist, dissented from the
denial of review and argued that a "health" exception was
not required post-viability. Justice Breyer did not join the

dissent.[29] And Justice Breyer wrote the majority opinion for the Court in 2000 in *Stenberg v. Carhart*,[30] which reaffirmed the *Doe* "health exception" after viability. The Justices' inability to be frank about the practical outcome of the abortion decisions suggests that something is seriously wrong with the results.

Another factor contributing to public confusion is the perverse and lengthy cycle by which state legislatures pass and federal courts enjoin abortion laws under *Roe*. Majority public opinion supports common-sense regulations like parental notice and informed consent. The legislatures pass laws. The media reports. The federal courts issue injunctions. The cases drag on for several years. A final judgment is issued. The public does not hear of the final outcome until years later.

These are at least some of the reasons why the public remains confused about the sweep and meaning of *Roe* forty years later.

How *Roe* Prevents Common Ground

Many Americans would like to see some sort of common ground on abortion. But what might "common ground" on abortion look like, and how could it be practically achieved?

In the Gallup polling data since 1975, there is common ground: *a majority of Americans have agreed that abortion should only be legal under certain circumstances early in pregnancy.* That majority could likely agree on a public policy that could be called "common ground."

This is so for almost all social issues. The majority, through elected officials accountable to the people on a regular basis, decide public policy on reproductive technology, cloning, embryo research, surrogate motherhood, and stem-cell research. It is through the democratic process that public passions are expressed, deliberated, and moderated on all these issues—but not on abortion, which the Justices took away from the American people.

It should be clear by now that the single biggest obstacle to "common ground" on abortion in America is the Supreme Court. "Common ground" is achieved in a democracy not just by talking about an issue but by deciding it through representatives elected by and accountable to the people. Activists can appeal to the public and elected officials, but the majority will ultimately decide, through elections and through legislative outcomes, and settle the issue publicly. At the end of the debate, Americans may not agree with what the majority decided, but they are free to keep trying to persuade.

This is how representative government moderates public divisions on a host of issues. As with other controversial issues, the single most effective way to promote "common ground" on abortion is to return the issue to the normal democratic processes, and let the majority decide.

How Judges Exacerbate the Conflict

Future presidents and the judges they nominate to the Supreme Court and lower federal courts are going to determine whether there is any common ground on the issue of abortion. Judges who will reinforce *Roe v. Wade* will reinforce *Roe*'s edict of abortion for any reason at any time. Treating abortion as a "fundamental right" or as being protected under the Equal Protection Clause of the Constitution are additional ways of reinforcing the broadest interpretation of

Roe and of the right to abortion for any reason, at any time of pregnancy. That means striking down the common-sense limits on abortion supported by 70–80 percent of the public —like parental notice laws, limits on taxpayer funding for abortion, clinic regulations, requirements for informed consent, and prohibitions on partial-birth abortion. Such judges will vote to entrench the view held by 7 percent of Americans that abortion at any time for any reason is a "right." That will prevent resolution of the issue and postpone the day when the American people might achieve common ground.

Instead of siding with the 7 percent, the Supreme Court should get out of the way and return the issue to the people to allow the majority of Americans to agree on common ground, instead of abortion at any time for any reason.

By deferring more to the people and their elected representatives, the Court could avoid the wholly unnecessary political turmoil that has been caused by the Court deciding the abortion issue for the entire country without regard to majority opinion.

If one really wants common ground, it is wholly contradictory to nominate or support a Justice who will reinforce a nationwide "right" to abortion for any reason at any time of pregnancy, which is supported by only 7 percent of Americans. That is the most obvious way to prevent any common ground on abortion for the foreseeable future.

An Abortion Policy That a Majority Can Support

What do Americans support?

Most Americans believe that abortion is the taking of human life. The 1990 Gallup survey found that 77 percent of Americans consider abortion to be the taking of human life (28 percent) if not murder itself (49 percent).

Most Americans would like to see fewer abortions. An August 2010 Rasmussen poll found that:

> Nearly half (48%) of U.S. voters continue to believe that an abortion is too easy to obtain in this country. . . . Fifteen percent (15%) say it's too hard to get an abortion in America, and 23% think the level of difficulty is about right. Fourteen percent (14%) are not sure. This is in line with findings on this question in surveys for over four years now.[31]

And women are more pro-life than men; men are more supportive of abortion than women.

> Women (53%) feel more strongly than men (42%) that abortions are too easy to get. Unchanged over the years is the belief held by 54% that abortion is morally wrong most of the time. Thirty-two percent (32%) disagree, and 14% more are undecided. Again, 58% of women believe that abortion is morally wrong in most cases, compared to 49% of men.
>
> Forty-nine percent (49%) of all voters describe themselves as pro-choice, while 43% say they are pro-life. Ninety-one percent (91%) of pro-life voters say abortion is morally wrong most of the time, but 61% of those who are pro-choice do not share that view.[32]

Most Americans oppose most abortions that are done. But there is a divergence between opposition to abortion and the role of law and policy: while most Americans oppose most abortions, many are skeptical about whether a legal prohibition can be effective and make a positive difference.

And yet most Americans support a wide array of legal limits. What Americans support can also be seen in the abortion regulations that many states have passed, supported by majority opinion.

It has been clear for more than two decades that most Americans support common-sense limits on abortion. The 1990 Gallup Poll showed that more than 80 percent of Americans supported requirements that a woman receive information about abortion and more than 80 percent supported setting health and safety standards for abortion clinics.[33]

But do they support prohibitions? Americans do support a prohibition on partial-birth abortion, and that support continues five years after the Supreme Court upheld the federal prohibition in 2007.[34]

But what Americans support today and what they might support in the wake of an overturning of *Roe* is difficult to imagine. The consistency of the Gallup data between 1975 and 2010—showing majority support for abortion in "certain circumstances"—is probably the best evidence. It should always be open to Americans to change majority opinion and lobby the public to support different policies, but those consistent data are a good indicator of where the states might go.

Conclusion

There is more agreement among the public on abortion than most people realize. The clash between public opinion and the Court's nationwide edict for forty years has been a source of continual political frustration. And the repeated rejection by the federal courts of limits passed by the people through their elected representatives aggravates the situation.

The American people support legal protection for the unborn child. Thirty-seven states have enacted fetal homicide laws. Thirty-eight states have wrongful death laws that protect the unborn child. Juries have consistently enforced these and convicted perpetrators. The people have no trouble supporting such legislation—whether through their representatives or through the local work of juries.

If the American people could vote on the issue, they might approve abortion in the first trimester to some extent but most likely not beyond twelve weeks, except for serious medical situations.

The clash that makes the abortion issue so divisive will continue as long as the Court continues to enforce its national edict. Public deliberation and decision naturally dissipate political tensions. Public issues arise, the media reports, public debate ensues, the people's representatives decide, and the sense is created that a fair and open debate was had. This process of self-governance can occur on most other controversial issues, except abortion. The lack of public support for the Court's nationally imposed policy is the main reason why the abortion issue continues to simmer with no end in sight.

· CHAPTER ELEVEN ·

Has *Roe* Solved the Problems It Was Supposed to Solve for Women?

With highly effective contraception, backed up by safe and legal abortion, it has now become possible for a woman to make and carry out firm plans for her life in a way that was never possible before. Now that effective planning of fertility can be counted on, education and career planning can proceed with more confidence. More women are looking ahead, and in doing so, they are planning for fewer children than might have been born without plans.

—BARBARA BERGMANN, *THE ECONOMIC EMERGENCE OF WOMEN*[1]

If legal abortion has given women more choice, it has also given men more choices as well. They now have a potent new weapon in the old business of manipulating and abandoning women.

—DANIEL CALLAHAN, "AN ETHICAL CHALLENGE TO PROCHOICE ADVOCATES"[2]

Mary Smith was a successful young lawyer when she sought medical advice in 2010. After several years of legal practice, she wanted to get pregnant but was concerned that the medication that she had taken for years for her chronic anxiety would not be safe for her baby. She was hoping a doctor could advise her on alternative medications that could safely address her anxiety.

Dr. Jones sat down with her and began to discuss her medical history. Eventually he asked about her anxiety. "Tell me about your feelings of anxiety. Have you always lived with this?" Could she recall when it started? "Oh, no," she replied. "I know the day it started." About a week before she was to begin law school, she found out she was pregnant. And the day before she started law school, she had an abortion. "The anxiety started with my abortion."

Roe v. Wade was believed by many in January 1973 to be a liberating decision that would enhance women's lives. *Roe* was supposed to solve a host of social and personal problems for women. *Roe* was supposed to be for the Mary Smiths.

In December 1971, Sarah Weddington told the Justices about the disruptive nature of unwanted pregnancy and that pregnant women suffered from legal disabilities in Texas that prevented a pregnant woman from continuing her schooling or holding a job. Legalized abortion would enable the Mary Smiths to avoid a disruption and continue their education. That—along with "abortion is safer than childbirth"—were Weddington's leading themes.

That snapshot does not capture the broader context or the long-term impact. The experience of the past forty years and the testimony of numerous women, confirmed in some cases by a growing body of sociological and medical data, indicate that many gains have been ephemeral or have been offset by countervailing problems. Forty years of experience have given Americans a larger understanding of the impact of *Roe*.

Has *Roe* Solved the Problems It Was Supposed to Solve for Women?

The Justices' opinion in *Roe* outlined some of the problems they expected to solve by legalizing abortion:

> The detriment that the State would impose upon the pregnant woman by denying this choice altogether is apparent. Specific and direct harm medically diagnosable even in early pregnancy may be involved. Maternity, or additional offspring, may force upon the woman a distressful life and future. Psychological harm may be imminent. Mental and physical health may be taxed by child care. There is also the distress, for all concerned, associated with the unwanted child, and there is the problem of bringing a child into a family already unable, psychologically and otherwise, to care for it. In other cases, as in this one, the additional difficulties and continuing stigma of unwed motherhood may be involved.[3]

The Justices also assumed that the adverse consequences of "population growth, pollution, poverty, and racial overtones" would be relieved by legalized abortion.[4] Concerns about population growth, for example, are evident in Justice Douglas's drafts of his opinion in *Griswold v. Connecticut*[5] and in his concurring opinion in *Doe*.[6] Bob Woodward, in *The*

Brethren, reported that, "as [Justice Potter] Stewart saw it, abortion was becoming one reasonable solution to population control."[7] Maybe legalized abortion would not solve all these problems, but it would alleviate them.

What has happened over the past forty years? Have the claims for abortion been realized?

Reduce maternal mortality? The great reduction in maternal mortality preceded *Roe* by twenty to twenty-five years. It came after World War II, and it was due to antibiotics and other medical advancements, not abortion. "[T]he data suggest that there have been as many maternal deaths in the United States annually from legal abortion (estimates range from 15 to 35 per year) as there were maternal deaths from illegal abortions in the years immediately before *Roe v. Wade* was decided."[8] The percentage reduction since *Roe* has been negligible compared to the reduction between 1945 and 1970.[9]

There are five leading causes of maternal mortality in the United States today: hemorrhage, pre-eclampsia, heart disease, sepsis, and ectopic pregnancy. Even without data, advocates would still claim that early termination of the pregnancy avoids *any possible* later risks. This, of course, is a very speculative claim for which there can be no comparative data. There is no evidence that *Roe* has improved women's health in these areas.[10] Any further decline in pregnancy-related deaths since *Roe* cannot be assumed to be due to legal abortion. Northern Ireland and the Irish Republic, for example—where abortion is illegal—have lower maternal mortality rates than Scotland and England, where abortion is broadly legal.[11]

Death after abortion is uncommon but does occur. The

Centers for Disease Control's (CDC) Abortion Surveillance Report of November 2004 cites 470 abortion-related deaths between 1972 and 2000 (362 "legal," 93 "illegal," 15 "unknown").[12] This total is supported by a medical journal survey from 1994 that showed at least 15 deaths per year from legal abortion—which would suggest a total of approximately 600 deaths from legal abortion over the past forty years.[13] However, the CDC admits that information about deaths to women from legal abortion comes from formal and informal sources, and that documentation is always a work in progress.[14]

For each anecdote of a maternal death before *Roe*, there is an incident of maternal death from legal abortion since *Roe*. Take the case of thirteen-year-old Dawn Ravenell, who died after an abortion in New York City in January 1985;[15] or twenty-one-year-old Angelica Duarte, who bled to death from a perforated uterus after an abortion at the Women's Place Clinic in Las Vegas in October 1991; or seventeen-year-old Latachie Veal, who died in Houston in November 1991, after an abortion at the West Loop Clinic; or thirteen-year-old Deanna Bell, who died in Chicago in September 1992 after an abortion at the Albany Medical Surgical Center; or Guadalupe Negron, the thirty-three-year-old mother of four, who died in July 1993 in New York City from a punctured uterus and resulting blood loss; or Pamela Colson, who died from a perforated uterus, lacerated uterine artery, and loss of blood after an abortion in June 1994 at Women's Medical Services in Pensacola, Florida;[16] or Magdalena Ortega Rodriguez, a twenty-three-year-old who died from a perforated uterus on December 8, 1994, after an abortion in San Ysidro, California.[17] Each account of a fearful woman suffering before *Roe* can be compared with another fearful woman since *Roe*.

Erase fear and danger of the "back alley"? The 2010 prosecution of Dr. Kermit Gosnell in Philadelphia, and the evidence laid out in chapter 7, make clear that women today run the gauntlet of fear and substandard conditions in abortion clinics.[18]

Reduce child abuse? Child abuse has increased, not decreased, since 1973. "In this country nearly three million cases of child abuse and neglect are reported each year, up from an estimated 167,000 in 1973, the year *Roe v. Wade* was decided."[19] Rates of infanticide also increased after *Roe* rather than decreased.

> The rate of killing for infants before their first birth[day] rose from 7.2/100,000 to 8.7/100,000 over the period from 1983 to 1991. It continued to rise thereafter, reaching 9.1/100,000 in 2000. In fact, homicide was the only leading cause of childhood death in the United States that increased during this period. . . . The resurgence in infanticide was not limited to particular classes or racial or ethnic groups, but appears to have occurred across the board in American society.[20]

As a result of this increased incidence in infanticide, a movement began in Alabama in 1998 to provide "safe havens" for infants, and at least 32 states have enacted safe-haven laws since 1999.[21] One of the reasons that legalized abortion may be associated with the rise in child abuse is that abortion undermines relationships, and "[c]hildren in single-parent families are . . . more likely to become a victim of domestic violence"—by unattached men.[22]

Reduce illegitimacy? Perhaps the number-one assumption in 1973 was that legalized abortion would reduce the number of "unwanted children." The reality is that between 1972 and 1990, teen pregnancy rates increased from 55 per 1,000 teenagers to nearly 100 per 1,000 teenagers, birth rates for teenagers increased from 22 per 1,000 to 42 per 1,000, and abortion rates increased from 20 per 1,000 to 43 per 1,000. In sum, "the number of unmarried teenagers getting pregnant nearly doubled in those two decades."[23]

> The abortion rate and the unwed pregnancy rate for teenagers in the United States are much higher than in Europe or other industrialized countries—even for industrialized countries with similar rates of premarital sexual activity among teenagers.[24]

The National Center for Health Statistics points out that "[b]etween 1994 and 1996 the percent of births to unmarried mothers remained essentially level at about 32–33 percent following a threefold increase between 1970 and 1994."[25] A 1996 study by George Akerlof and Janet Yellen—appointed by President Obama in 2010 to be vice chairman of the Federal Reserve—found that "the legalization of abortion and the increased availability of contraception to unmarried women increased the number of out-of-wedlock first births."[26]

Writer Candace Crandall summarized the trend:

> [I]llegitimacy, far from disappearing, has become a serious social problem. In 1970, the dawning of the age of abortion, just 10.7 percent of all births were to unmarried

mothers. By 1975, after *Roe*, the illegitimacy rate in the United States had jumped to 14.3 percent. . . . 33 percent of all children are born out of wedlock today.[27]

Reduce divorce? The divorce rate increased considerably from 1965 to 1980, when it peaked, and fell from 1980 to 2009, but the rate in 2009 was still 60 percent higher than it was in 1965. The divorce rate in 2003 was twice the rate in 1960.[28] Cohabiting also increased, from fewer than 500,000 couples in 1970 to nearly 8 million couples between 1970 and 2010, but "divorce rates are 48% higher for those who have lived together previously. . . ."[29] Abortion on demand has not been associated with more stable marriages in American society.

Reduce poverty? The poverty rate in families with married couples is about five times lower than the poverty rate in female-headed families with children, and the percentage of American children living with married parents dropped from 85.2 percent in 1970 to 66 percent in 2010.[30]

Roe has not reduced, let alone solved, these problems.

Equal Opportunity from Other Legislative and Judicial Developments

Sarah Weddington told the Justices in *Roe* that pregnant women suffered from legal disabilities in Texas that prevented a pregnant woman from continuing her schooling or from holding a job.[31] Weddington cited a number of legal disabilities placed on pregnant women in Texas in the 1970s as justification for repealing the abortion laws. These included education discrimination, hiring discrimination, loss of job security or chance of rehire, and lack of provision for maternity leave, unemployment compensation, or welfare.[32]

Since 1970, these disabilities have been lifted, in large part, but not by *Roe*. It is important to realize how narrow the *Roe* decision is: *Roe* dealt with abortion specifically and not with women's equal rights more generally. Other state and federal laws have created equal rights in employment and education for women, not *Roe*. The advance of women in the legal profession, for example, is due to the elimination of overt legal barriers to legal practice that existed before the 1960s, not to *Roe*.[33] As was observed twenty years ago,

> *Roe* is rarely cited as a precedent for women's rights in any area other than abortion. Virtually all progress in women's legal, social and employment rights over the past 30 years has come about through federal or state legislation and judicial interpretation wholly unrelated to and not derived from *Roe v. Wade*.[34]

As another legal scholar has pointed out,

> Whatever progress has been made in the law in combating sex discrimination is attributable to other, independent constitutional doctrines or to Congressional or state action, rather than to any particular reliance on *Roe*.[35]

If *Roe* did not exist, other Supreme Court decisions, supported by public opinion, would remain. Other state and federal laws, supported by public opinion, would protect equal opportunity in education and employment. Progress in equal opportunity for women over the past forty years has come from a national commitment to equal rights, not to *Roe* or abortion, and that national commitment would remain even if *Roe* were changed. In an August 2010 analysis, David Leonhardt in the *New York Times* wrote:

> Women and men with similar qualifications—age, education, experience—are much more likely to be treated similarly than in the past. The pay gap between them, while still not zero, has shrunk to just a few percentage points.[36]

Some of these developments were not caused by *Roe* because they in fact preceded *Roe*.[37] But since 1972, federal and state legislation—sometimes motivated, sometimes bolstered by judicial opinions—has eased or erased women's legal disabilities in areas of job discrimination, pregnancy discrimination, equal pay, educational equity, sexual harassment, maternity coverage and maternity leave, medical leave, domestic violence, and sexual assault. These changes in the law have occurred almost entirely independent of *Roe v. Wade*.

But if so much has changed since *Roe*, is the connection between abortion and equal opportunity for women more than an assumption? And even if there is a connection, has abortion's impact on women's happiness overshadowed, for many women, their progress in education or career?

The Paradigm of Liberty and Control

Today, the leading claim by abortion advocates is that *Roe* has been liberating. To some, it seems to solve the short-term problem: it alleviates the risks and burden of pregnancy, it avoids the fears and risks of the "back alley," it alleviates the burdens of "forced pregnancy" and the burdens of "forced motherhood." Some women feel relief and get on with life. But forty years of experience—with practitioners and clinics, with relationships, with the physical and psychological impact of abortion—has turned out differently than expected.

The notion of *Roe* as liberation is offset by the long-term risks outlined in chapter 8, the increased rate of repeat abortion, the burden of male pressure, abandonment, and coercion, the feeling some women sense of having no other options, the struggle with STDs, and the long-standing regret that many women feel. It is women who have to cope with the heightened medical screening that will be required for long-term risks.

The abstract assumption of autonomy may not jibe with the broader, longer impact of abortion on women's lives, health, and relationships. The impression that the short-term solution avoids "disruption" in education or career does not take into account the risks and complications that result in long-lasting disruption for years after the abortion is over. Abortion is not "liberating" if the short-term relief that is so widely claimed obscures lingering problems—subtle or obvious—that will not go away over the long term.

The image of control through abortion overlooks several surrounding problems, in particular the repeat abortion rate, the increased rate of out-of-wedlock births among twenty- to twenty-four-year-olds, problems caused by uncommitted men, the increase in STDs, the risks and persistent substandard care that women must endure, and the disorienting impact of abortion on women's lives—physically, psychologically, and relationally.

The Repeat Abortion Rate

One worrisome development over the past four decades is that abortion is not something that women experience only rarely. Twenty years after *Roe*, at the time of President Clinton's first inauguration, journalist Fawn Vrazo with the *Philadelphia Inquirer* concluded that "of all the predictions made about the effect of *Roe* when it was decided . . . the only prediction that came true was that 'some women would rely on the procedure almost as a form of birth control.'" Frazo reported then that "Today, 27 percent of women undergoing abortions have had one before; 10 percent have had two.[38] The repeat abortion rate—the percentage of abortions that are the second or third abortion for the same woman—has more than tripled, from 15 percent in 1974 to more than 50 percent by 2000. In some metropolitan areas, the repeat abortion rate exceeds 50 percent.[39] This means that nearly half of all abortions in any given year are performed on women who have previously had one or more.[40]

The rise of the repeat abortion rate confirms that many women are increasingly *relying* on abortion as birth control. That, in turn, means they have less control of their reproductive lives. Multiple abortions for more women mean more women need heightened medical screening to monitor the long-term risks, such as preterm birth in future pregnancies.

The repeat abortion rate—the second, third or fourth abortion for the same woman—more than tripled between 1973 and 2000—from 15 percent to almost 50 percent.

Magnifying the Power of Uncommitted Men

Sarah Weddington's argument to the Justices in December 1971 framed pregnancy as though it happened accidentally, like a Texas tornado, to solitary, individual women. This snapshot left out many aspects, including the responsibility and impact of men.

A key assumption of *Roe* was that the sexual and social equality of women would be promoted by the availability of abortion as a remedy for failed contraception. Lucas and Weddington made exactly that argument in their Supreme Court brief.[41] And several Justices explicitly adopted that notion in 1992 in the *Casey* decision.

The cliché of the 1960s that men wanted to keep women "barefoot and pregnant" was a useful political slogan. But at least by 1968, when Roy Lucas sought funding from the Playboy Foundation for his abortion litigation campaign, it should have been obvious that men would find abortion useful.[42] No one should have been surprised to find that it has long been the case—if not widely reported—that men favor legalized abortion more than women.[43] Polls consistently show that men are more for abortion—more "pro-choice"—than women.[44] Easy access to abortion serves some men's interests.

The broader social impact of *Roe* can be seen in the way the abortion license has leveraged male influence over women and damaged male-female relationships over the past four decades.[45] Researchers George Akerlof and Janet Yellen concluded that "the legalization of abortion reduced women's ability to withhold premarital sexual favors from men."[46] Another scholar has observed, "[g]iving women the option of abortion weakens social pressure on men to take emotional and financial responsibility for the reproductive consequences of sex."[47]

The availability of abortion has often isolated women in their pregnancies and made them more vulnerable to domestic abuse from uncommitted men. Far from a free, independent, autonomous choice, the decisions women make to terminate pregnancies are influenced by male abandonment, pressure, or outright coercion.[48] One study noted that 51 percent of the women who had abortions said they were doing so because of "problems with relationships or wants to avoid single parenthood" and 23 percent noted that their husbands or partners wanted them to abort.[49] Several studies have documented how abortion "choice" is negatively influenced by relationship problems.[50] Abortion has coarsened the relationship between men and women.[51] Far from restoring male-female relationships, the relationships *invariably* end after the abortion.[52]

With the comparatively low cost of abortion, men are able to pressure women to abort; men thus escape both the financial and emotional responsibilities of child support and they are able to remain almost superficially detached from the physical and psychological consequences of abortion. While some men may grieve deeply and are profoundly affected by abortion, they do seem to be a minority. Unfortunately, these costs seem either to have been brushed aside or perhaps accepted as an inevitable feature of male and female relationships in modern society.[53]

Beyond damaged relationships, *Roe* has had a still more negative impact. By stripping men—both husbands and unmarried partners—of any right to *notice of or consent to* the abortion decision, the Justices' abortion policy has *discouraged responsibility* on the part of men. The irony here is that this separation of men from the abortion decision—on the unfounded supposition that they might be strongly opposed to it—may well encourage violence of a different sort. Already prone to shirk responsibility for the child, many men have been culturally taught that—since abortion is cheap, easy, safe, and quick—any woman who does not have an abortion is behaving *unreasonably* by refusing to exercise her "right." Small wonder, then, that some men—emotionally and physically detached from the pregnancy—have reacted with rage and violence when women—prompted and offered financial assistance—still refuse abortions. However irrational, some men may wonder how they can be held responsible for simply trying to get women to do what they have a right to do.

Whatever the risk of spousal abuse in 1973, the risk for women has been replaced by increasing rates of *domestic* abuse of women—by uncommitted men. A series of articles in the *Washington Post* in December 2004, based on a year-long investigation, highlighted this subtle dynamic.[54] The *Post* quoted one criminal investigator: "If the woman doesn't want the baby, she can get an abortion. If the guy doesn't want it, he can't do a damn thing about it. He is stuck with a child for the rest of his life, he is stuck with child support for the rest of his life, and he's stuck with that woman for the rest of his life. If she goes away, the problem goes away."[55] The *Post* cited several specific cases where this dynamic resulted in the murder of the pregnant woman. There is evidence that homicide is now the leading cause of death in pregnant women, as the federal CDC suggested in February 2005.[56]

Numerous incidents have been publicized where men assault women for not having an abortion; and data suggest that these incidents are not rare.[57] Rather than stemming *spousal* violence, it seems clear that abortion has increased *domestic* violence. It often comes from men who do not understand why a woman would not exercise her "right" to abort when it would be so much easier and less costly. As another legal scholar has put it:

> This transfer of casual responsibility from sex act to choice act does more than increase pressure on women to give in to male desires for irresponsible sex. . . . It also adds loneliness and guilt to the choice of birth, and abandonment after birth, since women are now solely to blame for any burdens (to themselves and to others) that are incurred with the arrival of a child.[58]

The guy is not responsible for the baby, according to this logic, only the mother is, because she could have decided to terminate—easily and inexpensively—and did not.

Coerced abortion is an old problem, with records of numerous examples in English legal history.[59] But there is reason to think that it has been aggravated and magnified by legalized abortion.[60]

- New York pharmacist Orbin Eeli Tercero was arrested in April 2010 and then convicted in 2011 of doctoring his "girlfriend's" drink with an abortion drug to force her to have an abortion.[61]
- In June 2010, a Connecticut man, Arturo Rojas, was arrested for assaulting his "girlfriend" because she would not get an abortion.[62]
- In August 2010, Thomas O. Hill was arrested in

Pennsylvania for "allegedly sexually assaulting his partner in front of their children after she refused his demand to get an abortion."[63]

- In October 2010, a Columbus, Ohio, man, Dominic L. Holt-Reid, was arrested and then indicted after he "allegedly tried to force his pregnant girlfriend, Yolanda Burgess, at gunpoint to have an abortion after she refused to keep an abortion appointment."[64]

- In September 2010, in West Pottsgrove, Pennsylvania, Roderick Douglas Gaines was arrested and charged with several felonies after he violently injured a woman when she "refused his demands that she have an abortion" when she was five months pregnant.[65]

- In 2009, Daniel Thomas Hicks was arrested in Washington State and charged with murder for killing twenty-eight-year-old Jennifer "J" Morgan and three-month-old Emma Morgan because Jennifer had refused his demand to get an abortion.[66]

- In August 2011, Houston police charged Joseph Mike Delvia with the death of Omoyeme Obehi Erazua, who was pregnant with a baby boy, after he pressured Erazua to have an abortion after a paternity test proved Delvia to be the father.[67]

- In November 2011, the Los Angeles County Sheriff's Department charged Derek Smyer with the September 25, 2001, murder of Crystal Taylor. "Smyer allegedly hired 30-year-old Skyler Jefferson Moore to shoot Taylor after she refused to abort her pregnancy."[68]

The creation of the unlimited abortion license—at any time, for any reason—works to isolate women in their decision about abortion. Choice is the public mantra, autonomy is supposedly the principle, but the dark side of autonomy is isolation and loneliness.

The right to choose is not purely autonomous but burdened and influenced by all kinds of outside pressures. Abortion fosters an attitude and a culture of male sexual irresponsibility by promising no consequences.

Abortion significantly changes the dynamic between men and women and clearly gives greater power to men. The dynamics change in subtle ways. Though the violence may be sharp and clear, recognizing that it traces back to abortion may be difficult.

This dynamic was completely lost on the nine men who decided *Roe*; at least nothing in the decision or the historical record indicates that they perceived the changed dynamic that they were introducing. As the feminist philosopher Catherine MacKinnon noted in 1987, "Virtually every ounce of control that women won out of this legislation [the *Roe* decision] has gone directly into the hands of men."[69]

Roe does not protect women from the prospect of government-imposed forced abortion: *State-imposed abortion before* Roe *would have been a homicide of the child; today, state-imposed abortion would be merely an assault on the mother.* This diminishes the severity of coerced abortion in legal terms, but the impact is seen in women's emotional health.[70] Abortion on demand eliminates the detectability of coerced abortion and the motivation to detect it. It becomes merely "he said, she said," and abortion clinics prefer to ignore or overlook it. Reflecting the problem, the Michigan House of Representatives in March 2012 passed a prohibition on coerced abortion.

Daniel Callahan was a leading 1960s abortion rights advocate who published a book in 1970 arguing for legalized abortion. But later in the 1980s, he noticed:

> If legal abortion has given women more choice, it has also given men more choices as well. They now have a potent new weapon in the old business of manipulating and abandoning women.[71]

One of the most vivid accounts comes from Sue Nathanson, in her 1989 book, *Soul Crisis: One Woman's Journey through Abortion to Renewal.* Coercion by her husband played a determinative role in her abortion of what she refers to as her "fourth child." "I am absolutely clear that I do not want a fourth child under any circumstances," he said. "If you don't choose to abort this child, I will push you to do it."

Nathanson felt she had little alternative. "It is at this moment," she says, "that I know that I will take responsibility for the decision that must be made and that I will have an abortion, even though Michael and I will repeat this discussion over the next few days with no variation in our positions."

What is perhaps most remarkable about this account is that Nathanson is a trained psychologist and that it happened within an apparently healthy marriage—under ideal economic, social, and emotional conditions to support mother and child. If the abortion liberty can prompt such coercion within an intact marriage, its impact outside of marriage can only be more pervasive and more devastating.

The Struggle with STDs

About 3 million teenagers each year will contract a sexually transmitted disease. To give one example, human papillomavirus—HPV—is directly related to the increase in cervical cancer. HPV is one of the most common sexually transmitted diseases. The National Cancer Institute has estimated that as many as 24 million Americans are infected with HPV. There are about 5,000 deaths in the United States from cervical cancer each year, and over 90 percent of these cancers are HPV-related. That's why sexual behavior has been identified as the major risk factor for cervical cancer.

Sexual promiscuity, encouraged by the availability of abortion as a contraceptive technique, has been identified as a major risk factor for cervical cancer.[72] And STDs, in turn, are a major cause of infertility. Women disproportionately feel the impact of sexually transmitted diseases.

Abortion fosters all of this by promising to be the "failsafe contraceptive"—by promising to be safe, easy, and cheap, by promising no mess, no fuss, by promising to "solve the problem" quickly, by promising no consequences.

The medical and econometric data reinforce this broader impact of indirect harm on women's health.

- A 2001 study by John Donohue and Steven Levitt found that abortion legalization led to an increase in promiscuous and unprotected sexual activity.[73]
- A 2003 study by Jonathan Klick and Thomas Stratmann found that the legalization of abortion has fostered sexually transmitted diseases (STDs).[74]

Philip Levine and others use the metaphor of "insurance" to explain why the availability of abortion leads to promiscuous sexual behavior.[75] The availability of abortion fosters an attitude and a culture of sexual irresponsibility by furthering the view that sex can be engaged in without adverse consequences.[76]

The Major Studies of Women's Success Never Mention Abortion

If *Roe* was truly essential to women's education and career, we would expect to see that documented over the past forty years in studies of women's professional development, but few mention abortion as a part of a woman's career path. None contains any evidence that abortion is essential for educational or career progress.

Barbara Bergmann's *The Economic Emergence of Women* (1986) claims that abortion has fostered women's advancement in education and career. "Now that effective planning of fertility can be counted on, education and career planning can proceed with more confidence."[77] But Bergman provides no empirical evidence for the claim.

Rita J. Simon and Gloria Danziger, in *Women's Movements in America* (1991), make no argument for abortion as necessary for women's educational or professional advancement; nor do they suggest that abortion rights have facilitated women's educational or professional advancement.

Arlie Hochschild does not mention abortion in *The Second Shift: Working Parents and the Revolution at Home* (1989); instead, she focuses on how to manage the two-working-parent home.

Joan Williams, in *Unbending Gender: Why Family and Work Conflict and What to Do about It* (2000), mentions abortion in passing but never argues its connection to women's educational or career progress.

Sylvia Hewlett's *Creating a Life: Professional Women and the Quest for Children* (2002) does not suggest that abortion is necessary for women's educational and professional advancement; instead workplace policies are essential.

Hewlett's subsequent book, *Off-Ramps and On-Ramps: Keeping Talented Women on the Road to Success* (2007), does not mention abortion; instead, she argues that the old "white male competitive model" does not work for women and seeks ways to enable women to balance career and family. She argues for a new model of "nonlinear careers" that offers women "flexibility to move in and out of their careers as childcare and eldercare responsibilities require."

Cathie Black, in *Basic Black: The Essential Guide for Getting Ahead at Work (and in Life)* (2007), never once mentions abortion as playing any role for her or for other women.

Joanna Barsh and Susie Cranston never mention abortion in *How Remarkable Women Lead* (2010).

A consistent theme through these books is not abortion but helping women to balance career and family. The only exception may be Rosalind Petchesky's book *Abortion and Woman's Choice: The State, Sexuality, and Reproductive Freedom*. But hers is a philosophical book, not an empirical one, and she does not show that abortion has enabled women to achieve more in education or employment.

On the other hand, some feminist scholars think that *Roe* has, in fact, seriously impeded women's equal opportunity in American society by impeding social changes in employment that would allow women to more flexibly balance work and family. *Roe* told women (and employers) that abortion was up to them: the flip side of all the talk of autonomy is that "it's your problem." It's all up to women. That put the nation on notice that women had what they needed—abortion—to be equal to men in education and career, and there was no need for employers to adopt changes to allow women to more flexibly balance work and family. That has impeded greater changes since 1973.[78] As legal scholar Erika Bachiochi has written:

> Abortion works to perpetuate both the cultural devaluation of motherhood (and parenting generally) and the social conditions that . . . are inhospitable to childrearing. Abortion eliminates the incentive to make institutional change.[79]

Or, as Professor Sidney Callahan has noted:

> Since attitudes, the law, and behavior interact . . . unless there is enforced limitation of abortion, which currently confirms the sexual and social status quo, alternatives will never be developed. For women to get what they need to combine childbearing, education, and careers, society has to recognize that female bodies come with wombs.[80]

And law professor Helen Alvare has observed:

> Denying that women are drawn to their unborn child, as well as to spending considerable time and effort rearing born children, only results in policies reinforcing an outdated and largely male model of social life and employment—a model in which no institution need "flex" or change to allow women and men to meet chil-

dren's needs. On the other hand, recognizing that both men and women feel keen obligations to meet is both more realistic and a more likely premise for a successful argument in favor of family-friendly work and education policies.[81]

Do Women Consider Abortion to Be "the First Right"?

However women may have felt about abortion in the 1960s or 1970s, women seem to be growing skeptical about abortion today. Women themselves do not consider abortion "the first right."

The benefits claimed from legalizing abortion in the 1960s were made in the abstract. No one could point to any Western society in which abortion had been legalized for any significant period of time. Claims based on the Soviet Union or Eastern Europe were very sketchy, because solid, objective data from those countries were not available. And the trend of thirteen states legalizing abortion in the United States between 1967 and 1972 was not sufficiently developed to allow solid conclusions about such a public health experiment.

- In 1989, around the time of the Supreme Court's decision in *Webster v. Reproductive Health Services*, which was publicized as a "threat" to "abortion rights," a poll found that "only 2 percent of women considered abortion to be the most important issue for women's organizations, compared to 27 percent who listed job equity and 5 percent who listed childcare. . . ."[82]

- "[R]eliable opinion survey results demonstrate consistently that women as a group remain more opposed to unlimited choice regarding abortion than men—who as a group are (and have been) more supportive when compared to women."[83]
- In June 2000, an analysis of polling results by Alissa Rubin of the *Los Angeles Times* concluded that "72% of women support a ban on all abortions after the first trimester of pregnancy, compared to only 58% of men."[84]

At least since the 1990s, abortion advocates have been concerned about the attitudes of young women toward abortion.

- A 2007 study from Overbrook Research "found that the share of Missouri women identifying themselves as 'strongly pro-life' rose from 28 percent in 1992 to 37 percent in 2006, with the ranks of the 'strongly pro-choice' shrinking from about a third to a quarter of Missouri women. The shift was even more pronounced among young women, whose 'strongly pro-life' ranks jumped to 40 percent from 24 percent during that time period."[85]
- In 2009, Gallup found a significant change in "pro-life" sentiment among woman over 2008. While 50 percent of women called themselves "pro-choice" versus 43 percent who called themselves "pro-life" in 2008, a year later, 49 percent called themselves "pro-life" and 44 percent called themselves "pro-choice."

As Erika Bachiochi has written:

[E]ven after forty years of feminist gains for professional women, most women would elect to work part-time when their children are young, if it were economically feasible, and would especially appreciate the ability to enter and exit the labor market more flexibly without losing gains they had made professionally.[86]

The polling and sociological data seem to indicate that women would prefer to balance work and family. The zealous focus on abortion is not responsive to women's expressed needs and desires.

Sex Selection and Gendercide

The irony of advocacy for abortion as a necessity for equal opportunity for women is that women have borne the brunt of it. That is no more starkly demonstrated than in the tendency toward sex-selective abortion in the United States and around the world. Abortion actually has global negative effects on women in the form of sex-selective abortion.

In March 2010, the *Economist* magazine coined a new word, "gendercide," for the fact that 100 million girls have been intentionally aborted—because they are girls—around the world. "Women are missing in the millions—aborted, killed, neglected to death. In 1990 an Indian economist, Amartya Sen, put the number at 100m; the toll is higher now." The editors admitted that "the cumulative consequence for societies of such individual actions is catastrophic." The editors called on China to "scrap the one-child policy."

A book published in 2011, *Unnatural Selection: Choosing*

Boys over Girls and the Consequences of a World Full of Men, by Mara Hvistendahl, shows that since the 1970s, 163 million female babies have been aborted across the world.

There are several major consequences of sex selection abortion for women. It is not just the immediate loss of female babies. There are also the long-term consequences of unnaturally skewing the male-female proportion, the "sex ratio," in society. As Jonathan Last describes the phenomenon, "In nature, 105 boys are born for every 100 girls. This ratio is biologically ironclad. Between 104 and 106 is the normal range, and that's as far as the natural window goes. Any other number is the result of unnatural events. . . . If the male number in the sex ratio is above 106, it means that couples are having abortions when they find out the mother is carrying a girl."[87]

High sex ratios (with the male number above 106) mean that a society is going to have "surplus" men. And that will have serious, and possibly violent, social consequences for men and women. It means, among other things, that an increasing number of men will not be able to marry because there are not enough women.[88] According to Columbia economics professor Lena Edlund, "the greatest danger associated with prenatal sex determination is the propagation of a female underclass," with the result that some women will be "stolen or sold from their homes and forced into prostitution or marriage."[89]

This is happening abroad now, and may not happen in the United States if the sex ratio remains within the normal range, but sex selection does happen here,[90] and *Roe* has led the way, here and internationally, by legalizing abortion for any reason, at any time of pregnancy.

Roe and *Doe* gave us sex-selective abortion in the United States because of the Justices' abrupt expansion of the abortion "right" to viability in *Roe* and because of the breadth of the "health" exception in *Doe*. The health exception applies even in the third trimester and it applies in all fifty states. This, again, is an example of how the breadth of the Justices' edict goes far beyond public opinion in the United States. A large majority of Americans oppose sex-selective abortion.

Even today, it is still not possible to catalogue the full personal or social impact of *Roe*, because its full implications have yet to be felt by Americans. Because there is no uniform, national system of abortion data collection and analysis, we cannot accurately determine the number of abortions annually or assess the medical impact on women.[91] We are only beginning to see the impact on the workforce and Social Security and other "entitlement programs" from the "graying of America" by the fall of the birthrate.[92] In the future, we may begin to see the impact on society from the disparity between male and female births through sex-selective abortion, which other countries like India and China are beginning to see.[93]

Conclusion

Roe is a powerful symbol of autonomy that obscures its practical impact on women's lives. With the rhetoric of abortion as a "fundamental right," *Roe* proclaimed a national policy based on the assumption that abortion leads to freedom. But thinking of abortion as "liberty" is like looking at a badly cropped snapshot that captures only part of the picture.

There is growing evidence that the national policy of abortion for any reason at any time of pregnancy—never yet approved by the people through popular referenda—has brought a load of physical, emotional, and social problems that in fact burden women and impede their happiness.

When you get beyond the snapshot—that abortion "solves" an immediate problem—there is considerable evidence that legalized abortion has undermined women's ability to control their reproductive lives. Real "control" that contributes to women's independence, maturity, flourishing, and happiness does not result from abortion, but from avoiding premature emotional and sexual ties and out-of-wedlock pregnancy altogether. The focus needs to be there, rather than on abortion.

All of this is apparent from the testimony of women themselves, backed up by public health data. Relationships with men do not survive abortion. Or there is coercion. Women have to deal with long-term risks and the heightened medical screening involved. Abortion encourages more casual sex and greater coercion from men, resulting in an increase in STDs. Women's psychological health and happiness have been diminished. The gains seem ephemeral, and any gains have been discounted by countervailing problems.

· CONCLUSION ·

What Will Happen
on the Day After *Roe*?

*[W]hen we are concerned with extremely sensitive issues,
such as the one involved here [abortion], "the appropriate
forum for their resolution in a democracy is the legislature."*

—JUSTICE SANDRA DAY O'CONNOR[1]

Roe was the perfect storm—a unique combination of impulses, errors, and miscalculations that came together, at a unique point in American history and at a unique point in Supreme Court history, after a decade of unusual political and cultural turmoil. The Justices seriously underestimated the storm they were heading into, and the conditions that caused it.

One of the great urban legends about the abortion decisions has been that they were considered with "great care." That defense was raised by some Justices in the 1980s and 1990s.[2] That notion cannot be squared with the record we now have.

Roe was heavily influenced by short-term legal, political and social calculations, including heated population crisis predictions that were eventually proven false.[3] Numerous assumptions—about the risks of abortion and future abortion practice—were based on little more than a hunch.

The Justices abruptly intervened at exactly the wrong time, when a significant public debate was ongoing across the fifty states in legislatures and public referenda. The Justices imposed a one-size-fits-all approach when the states were considering different approaches to abortion, and when the results of those new policies had not even begun to be understood.

At the end of the 1960s, the Justices thought they were riding a wave of cultural sentiment in favor of abortion. But the Justices seriously misread public opinion, and their expansion of the decision over several months, pressured by the 4–3 bloc of Justices, gradually produced a decision that went far beyond what the public supported.[4] By so doing, the Court isolated the United States as one of only four nations out of 195—with China, North Korea, and Canada—that allow abortion for any reason after fetal viability.

The conflict with public opinion has been real and sustained. The Justices likely gave too much credence to the vague polling question that "abortion should be between a woman and her physician."[5] Annual polling data since 1975 show that a majority of Americans consistently support abortion only in "certain circumstances" early in pregnancy. The majority of Americans have never supported the result of *Roe*—abortion for any reason, at any time of pregnancy. A CNN poll in September 2011 found, for example, that 62 percent of Americans favored making all or most abortions illegal.[6]

Of all the bioethical issues and public health issues that concern Americans, the Supreme Court took abortion alone away from the American people. The Justices made the issue more divisive and irresolvable by taking it out of the democratic process where even the most controversial political issues are moderated by political and legislative debate.

However controversial abortion might have been in 1972, the Justices aggravated rather than settled the issue, and did so by coming down on one side—and not just one side, but that of a tiny minority. As of 2009, only 7 percent of Americans supported legal abortion for any reason, at any time of pregnancy. By siding with a decreasing minority, the Justices ensured that a large percentage of Americans would disagree with the decisions. The Court's edict cannot be changed by regulations or legislation that better reflect public opinion.

By 2009, public support for abortion for any reason, at any time of pregnancy—the practical impact of the abortion decisions—had fallen from 12 percent to 7 percent.[7]

Despite the fact that there was a Court majority in 1973 bent on legalizing abortion, there were still numerous alternatives to the Justices' sweeping edict. They could have taken other cases with a trial record of facts, or they could have sent the Texas and Georgia cases back for a trial.[8] Or, the Justices could have struck down the stricter Texas law but not the broader Georgia law, leaving in place the laws in the thirteen states that had legalized abortion (in more limited circumstances) between 1967 and 1970, and waited to see what the public health experience would be in those thirteen states. The impact on women's health could have been compared with the experience in those thirty states that had debated the issue but decided to retain their prohibitions on abortion except to save the life of the mother.

The Supreme Court's abortion decisions were tragic mistakes that happened at a unique moment in the Supreme Court's history and at a unique moment in American history. They were an unfortunate and short-sighted attempt by the Justices to "solve" the issue and settle the countervailing currents in American law and society. A judicial edict could not resolve such deep-seated sentiments and cultural practices. It could and should have been settled by the American people, as they have settled—through private initiative, legislative responses, and political activity—the labor versus corporate conflict of the 1910s, the Depression, the civil rights struggle, and many other areas of social ferment over the past two centuries.

The abortion issue is unresolved because the American people cannot resolve it in any meaningful way. They can talk about it. But—subject to federal court oversight—Americans can enact regulations only around the margins of an abortion right that extends for any reason throughout pregnancy. That fact alone explains why *Roe* (and *Doe*) have been so controversial.

Would *Roe* Happen Today?

While it might be too much to say that *Roe could not* happen today, there are several reasons why *Roe* most likely *would not* happen today. The cultural, medical, and legal assumptions about abortion that influenced the Justices in 1971 and 1972 have been challenged by the experience of the past forty years.

The key to the future of *Roe v. Wade* is not history or philosophy or personhood or fetal development or judicial nominations or presidential elections. The key to *Roe* is pragmatic results. The Justices in their 1992 decision in *Planned Parenthood v. Casey* called it the "reliance interests" of women. The Justices concluded that women have come to rely upon abortion as a backup to failed contraception for equal opportunity in American society. "Has *Roe* been good for women?" is the ultimate question for the future of *Roe*.

Roe did not solve the problems it was supposed to. The claims for legal abortion seem exaggerated today, but in the heyday of the 1960s they were believed by many. Instead, child abuse and infanticide have increased. Domestic abuse of pregnant women who will not abort is an increasing risk.[9] The percentage of single women between twenty and twenty-four giving birth to babies has risen. There is growing evidence that abortion on demand has contributed to the incidence of STDs, as well as to the number of nonmarital pregnancies.

Some will counter that abortion promoted public health by reducing maternal mortality. But these claims are unscientific and not based on reliable data. And they do not consider the growing international data on various long-term risks.[10] There is no peer-reviewed data to show a reduction in maternal mortality. The claim is based on assumptions of pre-*Roe* numbers that cannot be verified, or on nothing more than "estimated" numbers of abortions and deaths today. Data from countries like Ireland and Chile, with laws limiting abortion, show that maternal health is better there than in neighboring countries with legalized abortion.[11] The claim that *Roe* has reduced maternal mortality is a house of cards.

We also know more about the facts of the development of the unborn child. The notion that the fetus was just part of the mother, as some Justices believed in 1972, has been exploded by medical developments, legislation, and judicial decisions. Dorothy Beasley, Georgia's attorney, told the Justices about fetal medicine, but the Justices did not have knowledge of ultrasound and other technology that was on the verge of hitting the commercial market in 1973.[12] Such technology and surgery in the womb have revolutionized the way Americans see the unborn child. That technology was brought home to kitchen refrigerators just a few years after *Roe* and has influenced medicine, public attitudes, and public policy.

Ultrasound eventually had two additional effects: informing women and informing abortion clinic personnel about what they were doing. The late Dr. Bernard Nathanson, a leader in the abortion reform movement in New York City who did thousands of abortions, recounted "the effect of ultrasounds on others working in abortion clinics":

> [I]n 1984 I said to a friend of mine, who was doing fifteen or maybe twenty abortions a day, "Look, do me a favor, Jay. Next Saturday, when you are doing all these abortions, put an ultrasound device on the mother and tape it for me." He did, and when he looked at the tapes with me in an editing studio, he was so affected that he never did another abortion.[13]

Ultrasound graphically brought the the humanity of the fetus to the eyes of abortion doctors and nurses. Two abortion providers, Warren Hern and Billie Corrigan, concluded a 1978 essay by acknowledging that a dilation and evacuation (D&E) abortion leaves "no possibility of denying an act of destruction." As they wrote, "It is before one's eyes. The sensations of dismemberment run through the forceps like an electric current."[14]

The partial-birth abortion debate that began around 1995—now more than fifteen years ago—changed the way the public thinks about abortion. The partial-birth abortion debate moved public attitudes generally against abortion, perhaps as much as 10 percent.[15]

The "population crisis" predictions of Paul Ehrlich failed. Population grew, but so did rising standards of living—in the United States and in Africa and Asia.[16] In 2011, William McGurn reviewed the record:

In the two centuries since [Thomas] Malthus first predicted the apocalypse, the world population has risen sixfold—from one billion to more than six billion. Over the same time, average life expectancy has more than doubled—and average real income has risen ninefold.

In the four decades since Paul Ehrlich declared the battle to feed humanity over, a Chinese people who saw millions of their fellow citizens perish from famine as recently as the early 1960s are now better fed than ever in memory.

And in the years since Mr. McNamara predicted we could not sustain existing population levels, we have seen

the greatest economic takeoff in East Asia—among nations with almost no natural resources and some of the
largest and most crowded populations in the world.[17]

The refutation of the overwrought predictions came too
late, unfortunately, to influence the Justices' deliberations.

The Justices in *Roe* assumed that doctors like those at
the Mayo Clinic would do abortions; that abortion would
be mainstreamed in obstetrical-gynecological practice in
America. But it never happened.[18] Within five years of the
Roe decision, it became clear that the social stigma against
performing elective abortions was not going to disappear
with the *Roe* decision. Abortions were not going to be performed generally by physicians throughout the medical profession. Nor were hospitals going to get into the business of
providing a high volume of elective abortions.

The notion that abortion was "between a woman and
her physician" quickly became a myth. Few women sought
abortions from their family or personal physician and most
sought abortions from high-volume abortion providers
whom they had never seen before. These factors have fundamentally shaped abortion practice and the rushed, substandard care that women receive in abortion clinics.

That abortion practice has never been mainstreamed was
confirmed in 2010 by Emily Bazelon in the *New York Times
Sunday Magazine*.[19] She wrote that abortion providers "had
become increasingly isolated from mainstream medicine."
Bazelon's attempt to cheerlead "a deliberate and concerted
counteroffensive" to "mainstream" abortion reflects just
how marginal abortion providers remained in 2010.

Although the Justices were given reason to believe, by some of the briefs filed in 1971 and 1972, that abortion might carry significant long-term risks, we now have numerous international studies that provide a growing body of data suggesting significant long-term risks. More than 130 published studies find an increased risk of preterm birth,[20] and more than 100 studies suggest an increased risk of negative impact on mental health.[21] The international data have grown considerably. More studies will be published year by year.

The shame associated with an out-of-wedlock pregnancy in the 1950s or 1960s has dissipated over the years, in part due to a national network of pregnancy care centers for women that did not exist in the 1960s. There are now more than 2,300 such centers across the country. They are required to maintain high professional standards. They offer a large number of free, charitable services, including free pregnancy tests, counseling, material assistance, medical referrals, childbirth and parenting classes, and education and employment counseling.

Protection for the unborn child in criminal and tort law has grown, state by state, year by year. In 2011, North Carolina became the thirty-seventh state to pass fetal homicide ("unborn victims of violence") laws. Twenty-eight have extended protection from conception, meaning that *more than half the states now protect the unborn child, from conception, through fetal homicide laws.* In September 2011, the Alabama Supreme Court unanimously held—following the state's fetal homicide law that protects the unborn child from conception— that Alabama's wrongful death law should also allow a civil suit for damages for killing an unborn child *at any time of pregnancy.*[22] In December 2011, the Utah Supreme Court held that a wrongful death action can be brought for the killing of an unborn child at any time after conception.[23]

Roe was no compromise, no incremental step, but instead a sweeping decision—abortion for any reason, at any time of pregnancy. This fact—a sweeping decision despite the serious problems in the case—sowed the seeds of the national controversy that has continued for forty years.

The Day after *Roe*

Is there an alternative to *Roe*?

Legal abortion will not end if *Roe* (or *Casey*) ends. The widely held assumption that abortion will be immediately re-criminalized if *Roe* is overturned is simply wrong. There will be no abrupt or dramatic change the day after *Roe* is overturned.

If Roe were overturned today, abortion would be legal in at least forty-one states tomorrow, perhaps all fifty. That is because no enforceable prohibitions exist in those forty-one states. Either there are no prohibitions on the books or state court decisions (state versions of *Roe*) would block enforcement of any prohibitions, or both. Returning the issue to the people would result in virtually no immediate change because fewer than ten states have any enforceable prohibition on the books.[24]

It is unreasonable for the Justices to continue to impose one sweeping, nationwide, one-size-fits-all rule on the assumption that dramatic change will immediately occur if the Justices relinquish their control, when that assumption is false. The public authority of *Roe* rests, in large part, on

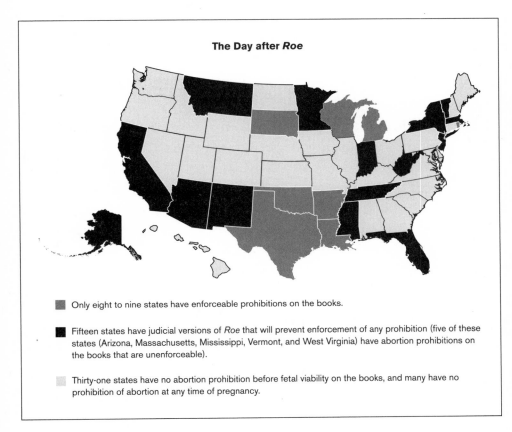

The Day after *Roe*

■ Only eight to nine states have enforceable prohibitions on the books.

■ Fifteen states have judicial versions of *Roe* that will prevent enforcement of any prohibition (five of these states (Arizona, Massachusetts, Mississippi, Vermont, and West Virginia) have abortion prohibitions on the books that are unenforceable).

░ Thirty-one states have no abortion prohibition before fetal viability on the books, and many have no prohibition of abortion at any time of pregnancy.

FIGURE 10. *This map shows, state by state, the current legal and judicial status of the availability of abortion if* Roe v. Wade *were overturned.*

the mistaken belief that overturning *Roe* means immediate change and social disruption.

Overturning *Roe* means that the issue will return to the democratic process. The media will cover the debate intensely, of course. There will be confusion in many states about what the law is. In some states, legislatures may not do anything. In others, state legislatures may act to pass restrictions. Different states may try different approaches. Congress might try to pass a national law.[25] The American people will ultimately decide the issue—over time—through elected representatives that are accountable to them through regular elections.

Perhaps the most likely outcome is that over a period of two to three legislative sessions, the state legislatures might enact a bill that more accurately reflects public opinion than *Roe* does. As public policy on abortion more accurately reflects public opinion, the controversy and the tension will diminish. For example, ten to twelve states might maintain abortion on demand as under *Roe*, ten states might prohibit abortion except to save the life of the mother, and thirty states might move toward a more restrictive policy than that allowed under *Roe*. A majority of states would likely continue to enforce existing parental notice and consent law, regulations requiring fully informed consent, and rigorous standards to protect the health of women. Many states might move to hold abortion clinics to the same standards as other outpatient surgery centers. That is not a "settlement" that would satisfy activists on either side of the spectrum, but it would be more in accord with public opinion.

This legislative debate would not be completely new. Debate over abortion and the passage of marginal regulations is going on now in the states. Since 2010, several states have enacted prohibitions on abortion after twenty weeks of pregnancy. One or more of these is now being challenged in the courts for "violating *Roe*."

Returning the issue to the people, through their elected representatives, would enable public health officials to deal effectively with the public health vacuum and address the threats to women's health from the Kermit Gosnells, Brian Finkels, James Pendergrafts, LeRoy Carharts, and Steven Chase Brighams in America. And it would limit and reduce abortions in ways that would better align with public opinion. The long-term legality of abortion depends on public opinion.

Legislatures afford the prospect of open, even-handed debate, public evaluation of the results, and of regular accountability to the people. Congress and the state legislatures have a higher percentage of female legislators than in 1973. Some are leaders in sponsoring laws to limit abortion. If it is so obvious that *Roe* was right, or that abortion should be unlimited, or that providers should be completely self-regulated, that will be obvious to the public and to the legislators that represent millions of Americans.

At the core of *Roe* is not the Constitution, nor values deeply rooted in American history and culture, but a short-sighted view of America and of human liberty. It is captured in Justice Blackmun's closing reference to "the demands of the profound problems of the present day" that guided the Court's "holding."[26] The Justices were plainly in the grip of the scare of the population crisis that subsided within a decade. Their answer was abortion on demand.

Despite the heavy imposition of a nationwide judicial edict proclaiming abortion to be a "fundamental right" for forty years, Americans have, thankfully, proved remarkably resilient. Millions of Americans have turned aside that blighted view of the human spirit by supporting adoption, by reaching out as foster parents, by marshalling the personal resources to reach out to women through thousands of centers across the nation that did not exist in the 1960s. That view of the human spirit and of human potential provides a more solid foundation for equal dignity and human flourishing in our democratic republic than the transient impulses reflected by the Justices in *Roe v. Wade*.

· ACKNOWLEDGMENTS ·

This book is based on a quarter century of research, culminating in intense focus over the past four years, and I am indebted to many for their assistance over those years.

The papers of several of the Justices released since 1993 have added new data. The papers of Justice Black, Justice Douglas (released upon his death in 1980), Justice Marshall (opened upon his death on January 24, 1993), Justice Brennan (some released in 1997, some released in 2012), and Justice Blackmun (opened March 4, 2004) are available at the Library of Congress. Those of Justice Powell, opened in 1994, are at Washington and Lee University. The Supreme Court papers of Justice Stewart, released in 2010, are at Yale University. Justice White's papers were first opened at the Library of Congress in April 2012. Chief Justice Rehnquist's are located at the Hoover Institution at Stanford University. Those of Chief Justice Burger are still unavailable to the public. I have examined all but Chief Justice Burger's.

Additional answers have come with the public release of the audio and transcripts of the oral arguments. The transcripts are public documents, but the originals in the Supreme Court Library are available only to lawyer-members of the Supreme Court Bar. The transcript of *Roe* was privately published in booklet form in the 1970s, but not widely disseminated. A helpful website, www.oyez.org, has been established in the last few years. (Oyez is pronounced *oh-yay*, and is part of the formal, public announcement that the Clerk of the Supreme Court repeats before the opening of each of the Court's public sessions.) Not until 2009–2010 was the audio of *Roe* and *Doe* posted. The transcripts in *Roe v. Wade* have been available for years; the transcripts in *Doe v. Bolton* only became available in 2012. I have made the transcripts in *Roe* and *Doe* available on the website of Americans United for Life, at www.aul.org.

The pioneering work of the following scholars and historians has uncovered original sources and eased my research: David Garrow, Joseph Dellapenna, Bernard Schwartz, James Simon, and Mary Meehan.

I am grateful to the following institutions and individuals, which have allowed me to republish some of the material in this book: *The Villanova Law Review*; *The Texas Review of Law and Politics*; and Brad Stetson, for permission to republish material from Clarke D. Forsythe, "The Effective Enforcement of Abortion Law before *Roe v. Wade*," chapter 12 in *The Silent Subject: Reflections on the Unborn in American Culture*, edited by Brad Stetson (Praeger, 1996).

I want to thank Charmaine Yoest, Yuval Levin, Jeanneane Maxon, and the board of directors of Americans United for Life for supporting this project. I also want to express my admiration to all my colleagues at Americans United for Life who inspire me, day by day, week by week, with their commitment and extraordinary work. I am grateful to my former assistant, Peg Kucharz, for her spirit, character, and dedication over many years, and for numerous projects related to the completion of this book. The opinions expressed herein are mine and not necessarily those of Americans United for Life.

I want to especially thank Phil King and Ken Chastain, and my parents, Richard and Imogene Forsythe, and my father-in-law and late mother-in-law, Lee and Sally Meyers, for their support and encouragement in innumerable ways during work on both my first and second books.

I am grateful to Robert Gallagher, Conor Gallagher, Rick Rotondi, and Christian Tappe (my first editor) of St. Benedict Press for their gracious generosity and support and encouragement at a critical stage of my work. And I want to thank my agent, John Eames, for his counsel, patience, and perseverance.

I am grateful to the following, who read all or part of the manuscript and gave me critical feedback: Erika Bachiochi, Randy Beck, Watson Bowes, Steve Calvin, Steve Chapman, Bill Forsythe, Mike Lawrence, Paul Linton, Brad Meeder, Eric Meeder, Mike Moses, Allan Sawyer, Patricia Wirtz (graphic design), and Jack Yoest.

A number of lawyers, law students, and college students helped with research: Keith Arago, John Blazek, Will Brewer, Yvonne Chapman, Jed Conrad, Mike Duffy, Sally Forsythe, Catherine Foster, Royce Hood, Brad Kehr, Mary Kerner, Hon-Man Lee, Tyson Marx, Patrick Sciacca, Linda B. Selover, Courtney Thiele, Renee Trotter, Fran Lebajo Wu (for medical journal research), and Emily Younger. Thank you!

Michael Ash, Dorothy Toth Beasley, William Maledon, Michael McCann, and John Spindler have helped through interviews.

I am grateful to the following institutions and their

staff for granting me access to various collections of papers: Jeffrey M. Flannery and the staff of the Manuscript Division and Reading Room, Madison Building, Library of Congress, Washington, D.C.; John N. Jacob, Archivist, Washington and Lee University School of Law, Lexington, Virginia; William R. Massa, Jr., Archivist and Head of Collection Development, Manuscripts and Archives, Yale University, Sterling Memorial Library; Suzy Taraba and the staff of the Archives and Special Collections Division of the Olin Memorial Library at Wesleyan University, for access to the Roy Lucas Litigation Papers; Sister Maria and the staff of the Dr. Joseph R. Stanton Human Life Issues Library and Resource Center; and the staff of the Hoover Institution at Stanford University.

I also want to thank the staffs of the Homewood Public Library and of the Flossmoor Public Library for assistance with numerous interlibrary loans and quiet places to write.

Roger Kimball has been gracious in taking a risk on this book, and his colleagues at Encounter Books—Sam Schneider, Lauren Miklos, Katherine Wong, and Heather Ohle—have been wonderfully professional in pushing it forward to completion. Christine Taylor and Nancy Evans at Wilsted & Taylor Publishing Services have been encouraging guides in finalizing the manuscript. My thanks also go to Anndrea Ellison for preparing the index.

Above all, I am grateful to my best friend and wife of thirty-one years, Karen, and to my five daughters, for their patience and support during my long work on this book. The publication of this book at this time is made more joyful by the additions of our sons-in-law, Jack Hummel and Zachary Crippen, to our family.

· NOTES ·

Introduction

1. Tribe, "The Supreme Court, 1972 Term," at 2. See also Elizabeth N. Moore, "Moral Sentiments in Judicial Opinions on Abortion," at 633 ("*Roe* invalidated every abortion statute then in effect in the United States, and, in practical effect, legalized abortion on demand in this country.").

2. Friedman, "The Conflict over Constitutional Legitimacy," 16. See also Dellapenna, *Dispelling the Myths*, 746–747 ("The Supreme Court's haste to decide these cases . . . imposed a more extreme approach to abortion on the United States than is found in almost any other nation."); Maltz, *The Chief Justiceship of Warren Burger*, 19 ("*Roe v. Wade*, which struck down all existing state abortion laws. The opinion exemplifies Blackmun's work product. It is best described as ponderous—a fifty-page exegesis that is a veritable gold mine of information on the historical and moral dimensions of the abortion question. But its treatment of the legal issues is conclusory and generally unsatisfying . . .").

3. See Yarbrough, *Harry A. Blackmun*, 141, 273, 346; Greenhouse, *Becoming Justice Blackmun*, 50, 187 ("Blackmun, always thin-skinned, was hypersensitive to slights from Burger . . ."). See also Note from Harry Blackmun to Potter Stewart and returned to Blackmun, January 16, 1973, Harry A. Blackmun Papers, Library of Congress, Box 151, Folder 3 ("Potter Who knows? I doubt now that they will be announced tomorrow. He [Burger] says he may write. I hope for Monday, the 22nd at the *latest*. They [the abortion decisions] *must* come down H." and marked "I wholeheartedly agree. P.S." with circle around "They *must* come down").

4. Yarbrough, *Harry A. Blackmun*, 217.

5. *Roe v. Wade*, 410 U.S. 113 (1973).

6. Balkin, ed., *What* Roe v. Wade *Should Have Said*, 3.

7. Ibid.

8. Chemerinsky, "Rationalizing the Abortion Debate," 107.

9. Cass Sunstein, in Balkin, ed., *What* Roe v. Wade *Should Have Said*, at 249.

10. Garrow, "*Roe v. Wade* Revisited," 80.

11. Ibid.

12. For example, on January 31, 1973, the Wisconsin attorney general sent a letter to all Wisconsin district attorneys, with his "advisory opinion" that the abortion decisions "have effectively rendered unconstitutional and unenforceable the Wisconsin abortion statute." See *Larkin v. McCann*, 368 F.Supp. 1352 (E.D. 1974).

13. Lois Wille, "Chicago's Abortion Clinics: Battle for Business Heats Up," *Chicago Daily News*, October 20, 1973.

14. Garrow, *Liberty and Sexuality*, 603–604n5 (citing Lawrence Lader, "The Abortion Revolution," *The Humanist* (May/June 1973): 4–7).

15. Steiner, ed., *The Abortion Dispute and the American System*, 13. Justice Lewis F. Powell's biographer, John Jeffries, noted that "No one foresaw a complete about-face." Jeffries, *Justice Lewis F. Powell, Jr.*, 333.

16. "Abortion on Demand," *Time*, January 29, 1973, p. 46. See Garrow, *Liberty and Sexuality*, 588.

17. David Brooks, "Roe's Birth, and Death," *New York Times*, April 21, 2005, available at http://www.nytimes.com/2005/04/21/opinion/21brooks.html?pagewanted=printe&position=.

18. *Roe*, 410 U.S. at 153.

19. Ibid., at 158.

20. Ibid., at 165.

21. Ibid.

22. *Roe*, 410 U.S. at 192. See also *Roe*, 410 U.S. at 153 (stating the emotional factors a physician might consider). Chief Justice Burger explicitly affirmed the broadest definition of "health" as "well-being" in his concurrence in *Doe v. Bolton*, 410 U.S. 179, 207–208 (1973). He wrote that the term "health" should be used "in its broadest medical context" (ibid.) and immediately cited the Court's discussion of "health" in *United States v. Vuitch*, 402 U.S. 62, 71–72 (1971), where the Court adopted what it called "the general usage and modern understanding of the word, 'health,' which includes psychological as well as physical well-being" and then cited a definition from *Webster's Dictionary*, "state of being . . . sound in body or mind." Ibid. at 72.

23. See Samuel W. Calhoun, "Stopping Philadelphia Abortion Provider Kermit Gosnell"; Forsythe and Kehr, "A Road Map through the Supreme Court's Back Alley."

24. See, e.g., "Abortion: The High Court Has Ruled" (editorial), *Family Planning Perspectives*, 5 (Winter 1973): at i ("Even New York's law appears to be overbroad in proscribing all abortions after 24 weeks except to preserve the woman's life, since the Court has held that an exception must also be made for preservation of the woman's health (interpreted very broadly).").

25. See, e.g., Wardle, *The Abortion Privacy Doctrine*; Uddo, "A Wink from the Bench."

26. Glendon, "From Culture Wars to Building a Culture of Life," 4. See also Glendon, *Abortion and Divorce in Western Law*, at 2. See also R. Beck, "The Essential Holding of *Casey*," 713, 723 and n. 62 (emphasizing the *Doe* health exception).

27. See chapter 4, notes 4–5, and accompanying text.

28. See the list posted by the National Committee for a Human Life Amendment at www.nchla.org/issues.asp?ID=46.

29. See "Human Life Amendment" at http://en.wikipedia.org/wiki/ Human_Life_Amendment.

30. *Roe*, 410 U.S. at 154.

31. See Wardle, *The Abortion Privacy Doctrine*; Wasserman, "Implications of the Abortion Decisions."

32. See, e.g., Greenberg, *Dred Scott and the Dangers of a Political Court*, 258 ("*Roe* in substance declared that state laws that prohibited abortions early on in a woman's pregnancy were unconstitutional, but that state laws which prohibited late-term abortions were constitutionally permissible."); Murphy, *Wild Bill*, 458 ("While the mother had an unlimited right to get an abortion in the first three months of pregnancy, and the state had the right to prevent an abortion in the last three months to protect the fetus, in the middle trimester a state could only regulate the decision to get an abortion based on the need to protect the health and life of the mother."); Hutchinson, *The Man Who Once Was Whizzer White*, 8 ("*Roe v. Wade* in 1973, which established a constitutional right for women in early pregnancy to choose between abortion and giving birth."); G. Edward White, *Intervention and Detachment: Essays in Legal History and Jurisprudence* (Oxford 1994), 98 (originally published as "The Integrity of Holmes' Jurisprudence," *Hofstra Law Review* 10 (1982): 633 ("*Roe v. Wade*'s guidelines for abortion, which allow a mother unrestricted autonomy to terminate a pregnancy in the first trimester . . .")) Bernard Schwartz, *The Ascent of Pragmatism*, 24 ("Blackmun wrote an opinion striking down the abortion law—first on limited grounds and then, in a revised draft, with a categorical holding on the right to an abortion during the early stages of pregnancy."); "Supreme Court Allows Early-Stage Abortions," headline, *Washington Post*, January 23, 1973; "Justices Allow Early Abortions," headline, *Washington Evening Star*, January 22, 1973; "High Court Rules Abortions Legal First Six Months," headline, Associated Press, January 23, 1973; clippings contained in Harry A. Blackmun Papers, Library of Congress, Box 151, Folder 11.

33. See *Colautti v. Franklin*, 439 U.S. 379 (1979); *Thornburgh v. American College of Obstetricians and Gynecologists*, 737 F.2d 283, 299 (3d Cir. 1984), aff'd, 476 U.S. 747 (1986); *Schultz v. Douglas*, 567 F.Supp. 522, 526 (D. Neb. 1981); *Margaret S. v. Edwards*, 488 F.Supp. 181, 196 (E.D.La. 1980).

34. See *Colautti v. Franklin*, 439 U.S. 379, 394 (1979) ("The contested

provisions in those cases [*Vuitch* and *Doe v. Bolton*] had been interpreted to allow the physician to make his determination in the light of all attendant circumstances—psychological and emotional as well as physical—that might be relevant to the well-being of the patient. The present statute does not afford broad discretion to the physician.").

35. See, e.g., *Planned Parenthood of Southeastern Pennsylvania v. Casey*, 505 U.S. 833, 844 (1992) (describing *Roe* as "holding that the Constitution protects a woman's right to terminate her pregnancy in its early stages") (plurality opinion of Justices O'Connor, Souter, and Kennedy); Ibid. at 923 ("five members of this Court today recognize that 'the Constitution protects a woman's right to terminate her pregnancy in its early stages.' ") (opinion of Justice Blackmun).

36. See Linton, "Enforcement of State Abortion Statutes after *Roe*"; Quay, "Justifiable Abortion," Pts. 1 and 2. Between 1967 and the end of 1970, "two states and the District of Columbia allowed abortion to preserve the life" or health (broadly construed) of the mother; thirteen states adopted the Model Penal Code model bill, and "four states allowed abortion on demand but set limits in terms of the age of the fetus," for a total of nineteen states and the District of Columbia. Linton, "Enforcement of State Abortion Statutes after *Roe*," at 159–161.

37. See Dellapenna, *Dispelling the Myths*; Keown, *Abortion, Doctors and the Law*; Dellapenna, "The History of Abortion"; Forsythe, "Homicide of the Unborn Child."

38. See Dellapenna, *Dispelling the Myths*, at 600, 624–631; Forsythe, "The Effective Enforcement of Abortion Law before *Roe v. Wade*," 193–194; Linton, "Enforcement of State Abortion Statutes after *Roe*," 157, 158–161, 255–259. See also, e.g., *State v. Menillo*, 168 Conn. 266, 362 A.2d 962 (1975) (Connecticut prosecution against non-physician), vacated and remanded, *Connecticut v. Menillo*, 423 U.S. 9 (1975); *State v. Sulman*, 165 Conn. 556, 339 A.2d 62 (1973) (prosecution against licensed physician for 1969 abortion); *Cheaney v. State*, 259 Ind. 138, 285 N.E.2d 265 (Ind. 1972), cert. denied, *Cheaney v. Indiana*, 410 U.S. 991 (1973); *People v. Bricker*, 389 Mich. 524, 208 N.W.2d 172 (1973); *State v. Hultgren*, 295 Minn. 299, 204 N.W.2d 197 (1973); *State v. Norflett*, 67 N.J. 268, 237 A.2d 609 (1975); *Commonwealth v. Jackson*, 454 Pa. 429, 312 A.2d 13 (1973).

39. 1973 R.I. Pub. Laws 68–70, ch. 15, sec. 2 (annotated at R.I. Gen. Laws secs. 11-3-1 to -5 (1981)); 1975 R.I. Pub. Laws 624, ch. 231, sec. 1 (codified at R.I. Gen. Laws sec. 11-23-5 (1981)). *Doe v. Israel*, 358 F.Supp. 1193 (D.R.I. 1973) (striking Rhode Island's law), aff'd, 482 F.2d 156 (1st Cir. 1973), cert. denied, 416 U.S. 993 (1973).

40. *Statistical Abstract of the United States* (101st ed., 1980), 60 (figure 2.3).

41. See Survey of American Attitudes toward Abortion, May 17–18, 2009, http://pollingcompany.com/viewPage.asp?pid=184 (accessed June 14, 2012).

Chapter One

1. Rehnquist letter to Harry Blackmun, July 16, 1987, original, with onionskin of Blackmun's reply of July 20, 1987, Harry A. Blackmun Papers, Library of Congress, Box 151, Folder 3, and Box 1407, Folder 13.

2. Justice Harry Blackmun, "Memorandum to the Conference," May 31, 1972, in Blackmun Papers, Box 151, Folder 3.

3. Rehnquist letter to Blackmun, July 16, 1987, original, with onionskin of Blackmun's reply, Blackmun Papers, Box 151, Folder 3, and Box 1407, Folder 13.

4. James F. Simon, *The Center Holds*, 85–86 and at 308n86 (noting author interview with Justice Blackmun on May 7, 1991).

5. On April 19, 1971, three days before the Justices decided to hear *Roe* and *Doe*, they reversed a federal court abortion decision from Wisconsin and sent the case back "for reconsideration in light of *Younger v. Harris*, 401 U.S. 37. . . .": *McCann v. Babbitz*, 402 U.S. 903 (1971); Garrow, *Liberty and Sexuality*, 487. Justice Willam O. Douglas, who strongly opposed *Younger*, was the sole dissenter from the order in *McCann*. A number of lower federal courts had dismissed federal challenges to state abortion laws under *Younger*. See, e.g., *Landreth v. Hopkins*, 331 F.Supp. 920 (N.D. Fl. September 22, 1971). Other judges decided that *Younger* did not apply if no state prosecutions were pending when a federal case was filed. The day after *Younger* was decided, Justice Douglas, in another abortion case from Illinois, *Doe v. Scott*, drafted a denial of a stay of the lower court decision, concluding that *Younger* was not relevant because there were "no allegations of pending prosecutions." Douglas wrote: "The problems presented by *Younger v. Harris* (decided Feb. 23, 1971) of enjoining a pending prosecution are not present in this case—there are no allegations of pending prosecutions." *Scott v. Doe* application for stay OT 70 (marked 1st draft: Feb. 24, 1971), William O. Douglas Papers, Library of Congress, Box 1500. *Roe* and *Doe* would present a different version on that same theme. See also the concern about *Younger* as a procedural hurdle expressed in Sigworth, "Abortion Laws in the Federal Courts," 130, 135n29 (written sometime between July and November 1971).

6. Woodward and Armstrong, *The Brethren*, 165–169.

7. See William J. Brennan, "A Tribute to Norman Dorsen," *Harvard Civil Rights–Civil Liberties Law Review* 27 (1992): 309. Dorsen (1930–) was a board member of Roy Lucas's James Madison Constitutional Law Center, and joined Lucas on other abortion case appeals.

8. Six-page Memo from "REG 1/5/71" re "No. 808, OT 1970 *Roe v. Wade*," Harry A. Blackmun Papers, Library of Congress, Box 151, Folder 9. His "Discussion" recommended: "This case should clearly be held for the *Dombrowski* cases and for *Vuitch*, No. 84, OT 1970" which involved "injunctive relief" and "declaratory relief" (emphasis in original).

9. Memo from "REG" to Justice Blackmun, January 5, 1971, Blackmun Papers, Box 151, Folder 9.

10. Thirty-two-page "Bench memo" from "JTR 12/10/71," Blackmun Papers, Box 151, Folder 9.

11. Justice William J. Brennan, "Memorandum re: Abortion Cases," December 30, 1971, in William J. Brennan Papers, Library of Congress, Box I: 285, Folder 9. See also "Opinions of William J. Brennan, October Term, 1971," Brennan Papers, Box II: 6, Folder 14 (October Term 1971), pp. 39, 40 ("In Conference, according to Justice Brennan's notes, it seemed to be generally agreed that the jurisdictional and other procedural hurdles to reaching the merits could be overcome in one way or another."). This document was compiled by Justice Brennan's clerks in May–June 1972.

12. Transcript, First *Roe* Argument, at 3. There are errors in the existing transcripts of the four oral arguments in *Roe v. Wade* and *Doe v. Bolton*. Due to the relative inaccessibility of the official transcripts, and because of the inaccuracies in available copies of the transcripts of the arguments in *Roe* and *Doe*, I have posted copies of the transcripts on the Americans United for Life website: the two arguments in *Roe* are posted at http://www.aul.org/roe-v-wade-transcripts/ and the two arguments in *Doe* at http://www.aul.org/doe-v-bolton-transcripts/. These posted copies are based on a close comparison of the official transcripts with the audios. The audios are posted on the Oyez website at www.oyez.org. The transcripts of the *Roe* and *Doe* arguments are posted at www.oyez.org, though I have corrected inaccuracies in the Oyez transcripts in those I have posted online. I hope that these contribute to scholarly and popular education. Here and below, my citations to the oral arguments are to the copies posted online.

13. *Mitchum v. Foster*, 407 U.S. 225 (1972). Justice Stewart wrote the opinion for the Court in which all Justices joined. Chief Justice Burger wrote a concurring opinion joined by Justices White and Blackmun, 407 U.S. at 243.

14. Woodward and Armstrong, *The Brethren*, at 169.

15. *Poe v. Ullman*, 367 U.S. 497 (1961).

16. See also Schroeder, Note, "Keeping Police Out of the Bedroom," at 1045.

17. *Poe*, 367 U.S. at 509 (Brennan, J., concurring in the judgment).

18. *Poe*, 367 U.S. at 509 (Douglas, J., dissenting); 367 U.S. at 522 (Harlan, J., dissenting). Harlan wrote:

> the intimacy of husband and wife is necessarily an essential and accepted feature of the institution of marriage, an institution which the State not only must allow, but which always and in every age it has fostered and protected. It is one thing when the State exerts its power either to forbid extra-marital sexuality altogether, or to say who may marry, but it is quite another when, having acknowledged a marriage and the intimacies inherent in it, it undertakes to regulate by means of the criminal law the details of that intimacy. (*Poe*, 367 U.S. at 553)

19. *Poe*, 367 U.S. at 552–553. See also Garrow, *Liberty and Sexuality*, at 195.

20. *Griswold v. Connecticut*, 381 U.S. 479 (1965).

21. See Lucas, "Federal Constitutional Limitations," 730. The Roy Lucas Abortion Litigation Papers are housed in the Olin Memorial Library at Wesleyan University, Middletown, Connecticut, http://www.wesleyan.edu/library/schome/FAs/LU1000-187.xml.

22. *Griswold*, 381 U.S. at 480.

23. Ibid., at 486.

24. Ibid., at 493. Douglas also quoted *Snyder v. Massachusetts*, 291 U.S. 97, 105 (1934), where Justice Cardozo wrote, "The Commonwealth of Massachusetts is free to regulate the procedure of its courts in accordance with its own conception of policy and fairness unless in so doing it offends some principle of justice so rooted in the traditions and conscience of our people as to be ranked as fundamental." This standard was relied upon in the Louisiana federal abortion case in upholding the Louisiana abortion law against a constitutional attack. *Rosen v. Louisiana State Board of Medical Examiners*, 318 F.Supp. 1217, 1223 (E.D. La. 1970).

25. Stern and Wermiel, *Justice Brennan*, at 279.

26. Ibid. at 284.

27. Ibid.

28. *Griswold*, 381 U.S. at 486–499.

29. Justice White, who would dissent in the abortion decisions, agreed with the result of invalidating that Connecticut law, but did not join Douglas's opinion. White's opinion could be seen as adopting the narrowest plausible reason for striking down the law. Connecticut defended the statute on the rationale that it helped to inhibit "promiscuous or illicit sexual relationships, be they premarital or extramarital." Although White agreed that that could be "a permissible and legitimate legislative goal," he concluded: "I wholly fail to see how the ban on the use of contraceptives by married couples in any way reinforces the State's ban on illicit sexual relationships." *Griswold v. Connecticut*, 381 U.S. at 505.

30. Dellapenna, *Dispelling the Myths*.

31. See the analysis of the opinions and Justice Harlan's papers in Schroeder, Note, "Keeping Police Out of the Bedroom." Bernard Schwartz has observed that "[i]t may be doubted, however, that the *Griswold* Court would have included the right to an abortion within this new right. At the *Griswold* conference, Chief Justice Warren had stated, 'I can't say . . . that the state has no legitimate interest (that could apply to abortion laws)'—implying that he thought such laws were valid." Bernard Schwartz, *The Ascent of Pragmatism*, at 409.

32. See the transcript reprinted in Mersky and Duffy, eds., *A Documentary History:* Griswold v. Connecticut ("Document 13," page unnumbered, 4 pages before the end—Emerson rebuttal). Hear the audio and see the transcript at http://www.oyez.org/cases/1960–1969/1964/1964_496. There is a discrepancy between the transcript in Mersky and the transcript posted at www.oyez.org.

33. Emerson, "Nine Justices in Search of a Doctrine," 232 ("Undoubtedly the

government could encourage birth control by many means other than strict compulsion, but a line between encouragement and coercion would have to be worked out. On the same view of the scope of the right to privacy, the way would be open for an attack upon significant aspects of the abortion laws.").

34. Clark, "Religion, Morality, and Abortion."

35. See e.g., *YWCA v. Kugler*, 342 F.Supp. 1048, 1066 and n. 75 (D. N.J. 1972) (citing Clark); *Poe v. Menghini*, 339 F.Supp. 986, 992 (D. Kan. 1972) (citing Clark); *Roe v. Wade*, 314 F.Supp. 1217, 1222 and n. 13 (N.D. Tex. 1970) (citing Clark); *Steinberg v. Brown*, 321 F.Supp. 741, 752 (N.D. Ohio 1970) (Green, dissenting, citing Clark twice); *Doe v. Scott*, 321 F.Supp. 1385, 1390nn26–27 (N.D. Ill. 1971) (citing Clark twice); *Rosen v. Louisiana State Board of Medical Examiners*, 318 F.Supp. 1217, 1236–1237n8 (E.D. La. 1970) (Cassibry, dissenting, citing Clark); *Babbitz v. McCann*, 310 F.Supp. 293, 300 (E.D. Wis. 1970) (citing Clark). See also Garrow, *Liberty and Sexuality*, at 481.

36. *United States v. Vuitch*, 402 U.S. 62, 79n2 (1971) (Douglas, J., dissenting).

37. *Doe v. Bolton*, 410 U.S. 179, at 217 (1973). See also the emphasis given Clark's essay in David Garrow's history: Garrow, *Liberty and Sexuality*, at 372, 416 ("Tom C. Clark's law review endorsement of applying *Griswold* to abortion"), 441, 446, 453, 468, 478, 481, 500, 501, 502, 536, 541, 550.

38. Clark, "Religion, Morality, and Abortion," at 7.

39. Ibid., at 10.

40. *Keeler v. Superior Court*, 2 Cal.3d 619 (1970). See Webb, Comment, "Is the Intentional Killing of an Unborn Child Homicide?" (describing the legislative history).

41. See, e.g., *Tiner v. State*, 239 Ark. 819, 394 S.W.2d 608 (1965) (upholding manslaughter conviction for killing an "unborn quick child" that was stillborn after injury, in violation of Ark. Stat. Ann. sec. 41-2223 (Repl. 1964)). See also Maledon, Note, "The Law and the Unborn Child"; Comment, "The Role of the Law of Homicide in Fetal Destruction."

42. Clark, "Religion, Morality, and Abortion," at 6.

43. Ibid., at 8.

44. See Dellapenna, *Dispelling the Myths*, at 342–370; Dyer, *Champion of Women and the Unborn*; Dyer, *The Physicians' Crusade against Abortion*; Witherspoon, "Reexamining *Roe*."

45. Clark, "Religion, Morality, and Abortion," at 9.

46. See Dellapenna, *Dispelling the Myths*, at 315–325; Linton, "*Planned Parenthood v. Casey*: The Flight from Reason," at 120 ("Appendix B: The Legal Consensus on the Beginning of Life").

47. Gronlund, *Supreme Court Justice Tom C. Clark*, 268 ("I was surprised to discover during my research in [April] 1969 he wrote an article entitled 'Religion, Morality and Abortion: A Constitutional Appraisal' . . . to support his belief that 'it is readily apparent at this point that a uniform scheme

concerning abortion is highly desirous.' He is calling for action, not by the judicial branch of the government—'courts cannot reach out to reform society'—but by state and federal legislators.").

48. Garrow, *Liberty and Sexuality*, at 416.

49. Ibid., at 564 (quoting Roy Lucas letter to Sarah Weddington, July 23, 1972).

50. *Eisenstadt v. Baird*, 405 U.S. 438 (1972).

51. Ibid., at 453 (emphasis in original).

52. Lazarus, *Closed Chambers*, at 364.

53. *Eisenstadt v. Baird*, 405 U.S. 438, 453 (1972). See Van Alstyne, Essay Review, "The Fate of Constitutional Ipse Dixits."

54. Justice William J. Brennan, "Memorandum re: Abortion Cases," December 30, 1971, in William J. Brennan Papers, Library of Congress, Box I: 285, Folder 9.

55. Lazarus, *Closed Chambers*, at 365.

56. Ibid.

57. Stern and Wermiel, *Justice Brennan*, at 343.

58. Eisler, *A Justice for All*, at 226.

59. *Eisenstadt v. Baird*, 405 U.S. 438.

60. *Abele v. Markle*, 342 F.Supp. 800 (D. Conn. 1972).

61. Saletan, "Unbecoming Justice Blackmun."

62. *Vuitch v. Furr*, 482 A.2d 811 (D.C. Ct. App. 1984). See Margaret Engel, "Doctor Faces License Battle," *Washington Post*, November 11, 1984, at B1; Margaret Engel, "Dr. Vuitch Surrenders D.C. License," *Washington Post*, December 21, 1984, at B1.

63. Garrow, *Liberty and Sexuality*, at 383.

64. *United States v. Vuitch*, 402 U.S. 62 (1971).

65. Jeffrey Rosen, *The Supreme Court*, at 171; Garrow, *Liberty and Sexuality*, at 478–479.

66. Garrow, *Liberty and Sexuality*, at 242.

67. *Griswold v. Connecticut*, 381 U.S. 479, 501 (1965).

68. Yarbrough, *John Marshall Harlan*, at 314.

69. Van Alstyne, "The Enduring Example of John Marshall Harlan," at 121–123.

70. Jeffrey Rosen, *The Supreme Court*, at 160 (Harlan's "conception of privacy was more carefully defined than Douglas's."). See also McConnell, "The Right to Die and the Jurisprudence of Tradition."

71. Fried, "The Conservatism of Justice Harlan," at 51–52.

72. Ibid., at 51–52 and n. 121.

73. Ibid., at 44. See also Fried's account of Harlan in Fried, *Order and Law*, at 72–75. See also Van Alstyne, "The Enduring Example of John Marshall Harlan," at 122–123.

74. In addition, David Garrow quotes notes from the Court's conference in the *Vuitch* case in January 1971, where Chief Justice Burger indicated that "he definitely rejected Dorsen's contention that a woman has an 'absolute right to decide what happens to her own body.' " Garrow, *Liberty and Sexuality*,

at 479, 844n5. At that point, "Hugo Black agreed with the Chief Justice. . . . There was 'no right to an abortion' and [Judge] Gesell 'has no right as a judge to create that right.'" Ibid. at 479.

75. Maltz, *The Chief Justiceship of Warren Burger*, at 246.

76. Garrow, *Liberty and Sexuality*, at 357. See Lucas, "Federal Constitutional Limitations."

77. Garrow, *Liberty and Sexuality*, at 521.

78. Ibid., at 510–511.

79. "Opinions of William J. Brennan, Jr. October Term 1971," William J. Brennan Papers, Library of Congress, Box II: 6, Folder 14 (October Term 1971), pp. XXXIX, LI ("The future of abortion laws obviously lay with Justice Blackmun, whose previous waverings gave no assurance of the votes he would finally cast. Justice Brennan at the end of the Term was, nonetheless, prepared to lay three-to-one odds that Justice Blackmun would eventually abandon the opinions he had written in *Wade* and *Bolton*."); "Opinions of William J. Brennan, Jr. October Term 1972," Box II: 6, Folder 16, pp. LVIII ("When the 1971 Term ended on June 29, 1972, and these cases had been formally laid over for reargument before a full Court including the newly appointed Justices Rehnquist and Powell, it is fair to say that it looked extremely doubtful that there would be a majority for the position that restrictive abortion laws are unconstitutional. See Notes, October Term 1971, pp. XXIX–LIV.").

80. *Roe v. Wade*, 404 U.S. 981 (U.S. December 7, 1971) ("Motion of appellee to postpone oral argument denied"). See also Garrow, *Liberty and Sexuality*, at 521 ("without dissent"); Bernard Schwartz, *The Unpublished Opinions of the Burger Court*, at 87.

81. Bernard Schwartz, *The Unpublished Opinions of the Burger Court*, at 86.

82. Quoted in Garrow, *Liberty and Sexuality*, at 531. See also ibid. at 521, 859n72 (citing Douglas Conference Notes, William O. Douglas Papers, Library of Congress, Box 1588, and Brennan Conference Notes, William J. Brennan Papers, Library of Congress, Box 418, 419). See also Bernard Schwartz, *The Unpublished Opinions of the Burger Court*, at 86.

83. Garrow, *Liberty and Sexuality*, at 531–533; Stern and Wermiel, *Justice Brennan*, at 370; Bernard Schwartz, *The Ascent of Pragmatism*, at 297–310.

84. One-page clerk memo from "KRR" to Douglas, December 17, 1971, William O. Douglas Papers, Library of Congress, Box 1589, Folder 2 (suggesting cases mis-assigned, including *Roe* and *Doe*); Stern and Wermiel, *Justice Brennan*, at 370.

85. Justice William J. Brennan, "Memorandum re: Abortion Cases," December 30, 1971, in William J. Brennan Papers, Library of Congress, Box I: 285, Folder 9.

86. Stern and Wermiel, *Justice Brennan*, at 369.

87. Brennan letter to Douglas, December 30, 1971, in William J. Brennan Papers, Library of Congress, Box I: 285, Folder 9.

88. Harry Blackmun letter to Chief, dated January 18, 1972, 1 page ("I nominate for reargument the two abortion cases . . ."), Lewis F. Powell, Jr. Papers, Box 5-150, Powell Archives, Washington and Lee University School of Law, Lexington, Virginia.

89. James F. Simon, *The Center Holds*, at 92.

90. Stern and Wermiel, *Justice Brennan*, at 371. See also Hutchinson, *The Man Who Once Was Whizzer White*, at 366 ("A major reason for putting the cases over [to be reargued] was the chilly reception that Blackmun's draft opinions received even from those on his side, favoring invalidation of the law."); Garrow, *Liberty and Sexuality*, at 548 ("Blackmun's *Roe* draft was an almost wholly unremarkable document. Ten of its seventeen pages were devoted, as Blackmun's cover note indicated, to questions of standing and jurisdiction. Only on page eleven did he reach the merits, and just as he said, it discussed the Texas antiabortion law only within the context of whether the statute's language was inadequately clear.").

91. Potter Stewart Papers, MS 1367, Box 268, Folder 3194, Manuscripts and Archives, Yale University Library.

92. White "1st Draft" dissent in *Roe v. Wade*, May 29, 1972, 3 pages, William J. Brennan Papers, Library of Congress, Box I: 285, Folder 7.

93. Bernard Schwartz, *The Ascent of Pragmatism*, at 303.

94. Garrow, *Liberty and Sexuality*, at 552.

95. Blackmun, "Memorandum to the Conference," May 31, 1972, Harry A. Blackmun Papers, Library of Congress, Box 151, Folder 3 ("You will recall that when we were canvassing the list for possible candidates for reargument when the bench would be full, I suggested that, although the Texas case perhaps might come down, the Georgia case should go over. . . . I have now concluded, somewhat reluctantly, that reargument in *both* cases at an early date in the next term, would perhaps be advisable. . . . I therefore conclude, and move, that both cases go over the Term.") (emphasis in original). The same memo is contained in the William J. Brennan Papers, Library of Congress, Box I: 285, Folder 7.

96. See, e.g., Justice Thurgood Marshall, May 31, 1972, letter to Justice Blackmun: "Like Bill Brennan, I, too, am opposed to reargument of these cases." Potter Stewart Papers, MS 1367, Box 268, Folder 3194, Yale University Library.

97. William O. Douglas Papers, Library of Congress, Box 1590, Folder 5. Brennan's handwritten note is also quoted by Jeffries, *Justice Lewis F. Powell, Jr.*, at 337, and cited by Urofsky, ed., *The Douglas Papers*, at 184n2 ("Brennan was as mad as WOD [William O. Douglas], and in a handwritten note he informed him not only of his anger at Burger's tactic, but also that Potter Stewart was equally outraged and prepared to make an issue of it."). Brennan's note is also quoted, though inaccurately, by Garrow, *Liberty and Sexuality*, at 556. Garrow inserts "months" after "nine." "Months" is not in the original note. It makes more sense to assume that "hold for nine" means

Justices, not months. Garrow, ibid. at 555–556, says that this Brennan note was written "within a day or two" of Burger's May 31 Memo.

98. Powell, Memo to the Conference re "Abortion Cases," June 1, 1972 ("I certainly do not know how I would vote if the cases are reargued."), William J. Brennan Papers, Library of Congress, Box I: 285, Folder 7. See also the William O. Douglas Papers, Library of Congress, Box 1590, Folder 5 (with same letter).

99. James F. Simon, *The Center Holds*, at 102; Garrow, *Liberty and Sexuality*, at 556.

100. James F. Simon, *The Center Holds*, at 104.

101. *Roe v. Wade*, 408 U.S. 919 (June 26, 1972).

102. Garrow, *Liberty and Sexuality*, at 557.

103. "Abortion Cases Creating Friction on High Court," *New York Times*, July 5, 1972 ("William O. Douglas . . . reportedly drafted—but did not release—an opinion charging that Chief Justice Burger had improperly assumed the authority to assign, which ultimately led to the delay.")

104. Garrow, *Liberty and Sexuality*, at 558.

105. *Cheaney v. State*, 259 Ind. 138, 285 N.E.2d 265 (July 24, 1972) (opinion by Justice Donald Hunter).

106. Letter from Indiana Supreme Court Associate Justice Donald H. Hunter to Douglas, October 17, 1972, with copy of Hunter's opinion in *Cheaney v. State*, 259 Ind. 138, 285 N.E.2d 265 (July 24, 1972), William O. Douglas Papers, Box 1590, Folder 6. The same letter was sent to Justice Blackmun: Harry A. Blackmun Papers, Library of Congress, Box 152, Folder 3.

107. Garrow, *Liberty and Sexuality*, at 558–559.

108. Garrow, "The Brains behind Blackmun"; George Freeman memo to Harry Blackmun. See also Scott, Note, "Quickening in the Common Law."

109. Potter Stewart Papers, MS 1367, Box 268, Folder 3194, Yale University Library.

110. That is true for the Mersky series and the Kurland and Casper volume on *Roe*. See Mersky and Hartman, eds., *A Documentary History*: Roe v. Wade; Kurland and Casper, eds., *Landmark Briefs and Arguments*. See also Irons and Guitton, eds., *May It Please the Court*.

111. See Mersky and Hartman, eds., *A Documentary History*: Roe v. Wade.

112. Garrow, *Liberty and Sexuality*, at 527 ("Beasley's remarkably vibrant and high-pitched voice gave her presentation an energetic and articulate air that outshone the three speakers who had preceded her."); ibid. at 527–528 ("other supporters conceded privately that Dorothy Beasley probably had been the most impressive speaker of the four.").

113. Fried, *Order and Law*, at 218n18. Chief Justice Hughes addressed the organization several times while he was Chief Justice. James F. Simon, *FDR and Chief Justice Hughes*, at 286, 336, 385. Chief Justice Vinson addressed the group in 1949. Stevens, *Five Chiefs*, 78. See also Barnard, "An Analysis and Criticism of the Model Penal Code Provisions"; Miller and Wintrode, Note, "A New Approach to Old Crimes."

114. *Roe v. Wade*, 410 U.S., at 165.

115. *Doe*, 410 U.S. at 192.

116. Garrow, *Liberty and Sexuality*, at 550.

117. Blackmun, "Memo to the Conference," December 21, 1972, Harry A. Blackmun Papers, Library of Congress, Box 151, Folder 6.

118. Justice Brennan letter to Justice Blackmun, December 13, 1972, Blackmun Papers, Box 151, Folder 8.

119. Blackmun, "Memo to the Conference," December 21, 1972, Blackmun Papers, Box 151, Folder 6.

120. Blackmun, "Memo to the Conference," January 16, 1973 (emphasis added), Blackmun Papers, Box 151, Folder 3.

121. Clerk memo to Powell, January 16, 1973, Lewis F. Powell Papers, Washington and Lee University School of Law, Box 5-150.

Chapter Two

1. Quoted in Greenhouse, *Becoming Justice Blackmun*, at 93, 94 (quoting Blackmun's outline for a new draft of the *Doe v. Bolton* opinion in October 1972).

2. Dellapenna, *Dispelling the Myths*, at 453.

3. Humphries, "The Movement to Legalize Abortion"; Dellapenna, *Dispelling the Myths*, at 495–516.

4. See Humphries, "The Movement to Legalize Abortion" ("the abortion movement did not suddenly emerge in the sixties as the unique expression of even this minority's concerns. The movement can be traced to the international family planning and American birth control movements, whose attention was focused on the eradication of poverty and oversized families.").

5. See Meehan, "The Road to Abortion, Part I." The *Eugenics Review* (London), vol. 50, no. 4 (January 1959), 261, reported that Glanville Williams had been elected a fellow of the Eugenics Society "during the past quarter." The British Eugenics Society did not use the name "British" in its title. It is now called the Galton Institute.

6. Dellapenna, *Dispelling the Myths*, at 586.

7. Humphries, "The Movement to Legalize Abortion."

8. Meehan, "The Road to Abortion: Part I."

9. Ibid.

10. *Abele v. Markle*, 342 F.Supp. 800, 803–804 (D. Conn. 1972).

11. Ibid.

12. Manuscript accompanying letter of Richard A. Schwartz to Justice Brennan, December 27, 1971, William J. Brennan Papers, Library of Congress, Box I: 285, Folder 8. The article was eventually published as Richard A. Schwartz, "The Social Effects of Legal Abortion."

13. *United States v. Vuitch*, 402 U.S. 62, 80n4 (1971) (Douglas, J., dissenting).

14. *Brown v. Board of Education*, 347 U.S. 483 (1954).

15. Dellapenna, *Dispelling the Myths*, at 636 and n. 47 (citing Laura Kalman, *The Strange Career of Legal Liberalism* (1996), 2 ("trust in the potential of courts,

particularly the Supreme Court, to bring about 'those specific social reforms that affect large groups of people . . . policy change with national impact.'"). "The attitude of the Warren Court carried over for at least a decade after Earl Warren retired." Dellapenna, *Dispelling the Myths*, at 636. See also Paulsen, "The Worst Constitutional Decision of All Time," 1022 ("Viewed from the perspective of thirty years' distance, *Roe* seems almost quaint—a relic of an era in which courts (and especially the Supreme Court) understood their role as being to make law; to resolve social issues; to prescribe rules for the nation. The Supreme Court Justices in 1973 were, in a sense (at least to a degree), prisoners of their own era, trapped in a set of assumptions about the judicial role that were broadly accepted at the time, but are now regarded as largely a fad (like lava lamps or bell-bottoms).").

16. *Roe v. Wade*, 410 U.S. 113, 116 (1973).

17. *Roe*, 410 U.S. at 165.

18. At the 1955 Planned Parenthood conference, Dr. Alfred Kinsey told the attendees: "at the risk of being repetitious, I would remind the group that we have found the highest frequency of induced abortion in the group, which, in general, most frequently uses contraceptives." Calderone, ed., *Abortion in the United States*, 157. In 1979, Dr. Malcolm Potts, the first medical director of the International Planned Parenthood Federation—and one of the authors of the seven medical sources cited in *Roe*—predicted that "as people turn to contraception, there will be a rise, not a fall, in the abortion rate." Malcolm Potts, "Fertility Rights," *The Guardian*, April 25, 1979.

19. Stern and Wermiel, *Justice Brennan*, at 283.

20. Clark, "Religion, Morality, and Abortion," at 1.

21. *Stanley v. Georgia*, 394 U.S. 557 (1969).

22. Ibid., at 559.

23. Ibid., at 567.

24. Garrow, *Liberty and Sexuality*.

25. Meehan, "The Road to Abortion, Part I," at 13.

26. Ibid., at 13n4.

27. Hall, ed., *Abortion in a Changing World*.

28. Garrow, *Liberty and Sexuality*, at 355, 380.

29. Ibid., at 204, 314, 463.

30. Ibid., at 809n25.

31. Meehan, "The Road to Abortion: Part I," at 13.

32. The conference proceedings were published as Calderone, ed., *Abortion in the United States*. Edwin Schur, a Yale law school student who attended, had recently published an article titled "The Abortion Racket" in *The Nation*, in which Schur referred to "abortion's skyrocketing death rate—an annual American loss of somewhere between three thousand and eight thousand women's lives." Schur, "The Abortion Racket." Schur later published several books as an influential sociologist.

33. Calderone, "Illegal Abortion as a Public Health Problem," at 949.

34. Table 1 is reproduced in *Legal Ramifications of the Human Life Amendment,*

Hearings before the Subcommittee on the Constitution of the Committee on the Judiciary, U.S. Senate, 98th Cong., 1st Sess. (1983), 188. See also *Abortion— Part 2: Hearing before the Subcommittee on Constitutional Amendments of the Committee of the Judiciary of the United States Senate on S.J. Res. 119 and S.J. Res. 120*, 93rd Cong., 2nd Sess. (1976), 107 (April 25, 1974, statement of Dr. Andre Hellegers, Professor of Obstetrics and Gynecology, Georgetown University).

35. Table 2 is reproduced from Cooke et al., eds., *The Terrible Choice*, 47.

36. Judges, *Hard Choices, Lost Voices*, at 78 (citing the American Public Health Association as recognizing the figure of 193 deaths for 1965).

37. Hellman and Pritchard, eds., *Williams Obstetrics*, at 520.

38. Quoted in Fred Graham, "Fetus Defects Pose Abortion Dilemma," *New York Times*, September 7, 1967, at 38.

39. Tietze and Lewit, "Legal Abortion," at 23. Tietze claimed in 1969 "in all likelihood it was under 1000" without citation or authority. Tietze and Lewit, "Abortion," at 23.

40. Hall, "Commentary," at 228.

41. Ibid.

42. Garrow, *Liberty and Sexuality*, at 281–284.

43. Lucas, "Federal Constitutional Limitations," at 730 ("Until recently, mishandled criminal abortions claimed the lives of an estimated ten thousand American women each year.") (citing Bates, "The Abortion Mill"; Lader; Fisher, "Criminal Abortion"; Leavy and Kummer).

44. *CBS Reports*, April 1965. See http://www.cbsnews.com/video/watch/?id= 3204142n.

45. Leavy and Kummer, "Criminal Abortion: A Failure of Law."

46. Lucas' Jurisdictional Statement in *Roe v. Wade*, at 6n25, in Mersky and Hartman, eds., *A Documentary History*: Roe v. Wade, 1:40.

47. Compare Jurisdictional Statement, 16n25, in Mersky and Hartman, eds., *A Documentary History*: Roe v. Wade, at 1:40, with Brief of Appellants, 22n19, in ibid., 1:158.

48. Guttmacher, "Therapeutic Abortion."

49. Garrow, *Liberty and Sexuality*, at 277. See also Barnard, "An Analysis and Criticism of the Model Penal Code Provisions"; Miller and Wintrode, Note, "A New Approach to Old Crimes."

50. Linton, "Enforcement of State Abortion Statutes after *Roe*," at 159n7.

51. Garrow, *Liberty and Sexuality*, at 329–330.

52. Ibid., at 330.

53. See http://en.wikipedia.org/wiki/Sherri_Finkbine. See, e.g., Elizabeth N. Moore, "Moral Sentiments in Judicial Opinions on Abortion" (and the emphasis she puts on the Finkbine case). Lader devoted an entire chapter to the incident in his 1966 book, *Abortion*.

54. Garrow, *Liberty and Sexuality*, at 289 ("Fifty-four percent of men said Finkbine had done the right thing, 30 percent the wrong thing; among women the two percentages were 50 and 33.").

55. Ibid., at 307.
56. Ibid., at 384 (Richard Lamm's formulation), 513 (citing *New York Times* coverage in October 1971 of a national poll finding "a full *50 percent* now saying that during the early stages of pregnancy, the choice should be left to a woman in consultation with her doctor.").
57. Ibid., at 562.
58. Ibid., at 562, citing August 1972 poll.
59. Ibid., at 302–303.
60. Ibid.
61. Blake, "Abortion and Public Opinion". For some reason, Blake looked at the opinion of white Americans only. Five of the six polls were conducted after 1965, and the last three Gallup Polls in 1968 and 1969 included a fourth question that Blake drafted herself. The National Fertility Study poll surveyed married white women only. The 1962 poll was conducted in the midst of the media focus on Sherrie Finkbine's dilemma.
62. Blake, "Abortion and Public Opinion," at 542 (emphasis added).
63. Moody and Carmen, *Abortion Counseling and Social Change*, at 102–104.
64. Garrow, *Liberty and Sexuality*, at 605.
65. See Linton, "*Planned Parenthood v. Casey*: The Flight from Reason," at 24. See also Linton, "Enforcement of State Abortion Statutes after *Roe*," at 159–161nn9–10.
66. Garrow, *Liberty and Sexuality*, at 307.
67. Ibid., at 507. See also "Antiabortion Forces Demonstrate a Growing Influence in State Legislatures across the Country," *New York Times*, June 28, 1971, p. 21.
68. Garrow, *Liberty and Sexuality*, at 482.
69. Ibid., at 482–487.
70. Lucas, "Federal Constitutional Limitations," at 730.
71. Memorandum from Jimmye Kimmey [Executive Director of the Association for the Study of Abortion] to Harriet F. Pilpel [Counsel to the ASA] et al., July 22, 1968, Roy Lucas Abortion Litigation Papers, Box 16, Olin Memorial Library, Wesleyan University. The board of directors of the ASA in July 1968, as indicated by the letterhead, included Louis M. Hellman, M.D., chairman, Robert E. Hall, M.D., president, Joseph Fletcher, S.T.D., vice president, Alan F. Guttmacher, M.D., vice president, Cyril C. Means, Jr., Stewart R. Mott, Harold Rosen, Ph.D., M.D., Keith P. Russell, M.D., the Hon. Percy E. Sutton, Esq., and Christopher Tietze, M.D. Lucas sought funding for the test case over the following months of 1968 from Stewart Mott and the Playboy Foundation, among others. The test case "ad hoc group" included Jimmye Kimmey and Dr. Robert Hall from the ASA, and "Mel Wulf [Legal Director of the American Civil Liberties Union], Harriet Pilpel, Cyril Means, and Professor Norman Dorsen of NYU Law School." Lucas letter of October 18, 1968, to Mr. Ann Israel, Roy Lucas Abortion Litigation Papers, Box 16. A memorandum on the litigation strategy prepared by Roy Lucas for the board of directors of the ASA, sometime in

the latter half of 1968 and before September 1968, outlined a strategy for declaratory relief based on physician discretion to make medical decisions. Roy Lucas Abortion Litigation Papers, Box 16.

72. *People v. Belous*, 71 Cal.2d 954, 458 P.2d 194, 80 Cal.Rptr. 354 (1969). For an effective critique of the *Belous* decision, see McGrew, Comment, "To Be or Not to Be."

73. Garrow, *Liberty and Sexuality*, at 813n45. Three months after *Belous*, Cyril Means recorded an encounter with Chief Justice Traynor at a bar association meeting in a letter to Roy Lucas, Marcia Lowry, and Nancy Stearns from the San Francisco Hilton on December 29, 1969. Means wrote: "Moments one would like to live over again: 1. Last night, when Chief Justice Traynor slapped me on the shoulder and said, "That was a *wonderful* article!" (emphasis in original). Roy Lucas Abortion Litigation Papers, Box 1, Olin Memorial Library, Wesleyan University.

74. *Babbitz v. McCann*, 310 F.Supp. 293 (E.D. Wis. March 5, 1970).

75. *Abele v. Markle*, 342 F.Supp. 800 (D. Conn. 1972), appeal docketed, No. 72–56 (USSC); *Abele v. Markle*, 351 F.Supp. 224 (D. Conn. 1972); *Doe v. Bolton*, 319 F.Supp. 1048 (N.D. Ga. 1970), *Doe v. Scott*, 321 F.Supp. 1385 (N.D. Ill. 1971), appeal docketed, No. 70–105 (U.S. 1971); *Poe v. Menghini*, 339 F.Supp. 986 (D. Kan. 1972); *YWCA v. Kugler*, 342 F.Supp. 1048 (D. N.J. 1972), *Babbitz v. McCann*, 310 F.Supp. 293 (E.D. Wis. 1970), appeal dismissed, 400 U.S. 1 (1970).

76. *Crossen v. Attorney General of Kentucky*, 344 F.Supp. 587 (E.D. Ky. 1972), vacated and remanded, 410 U.S. 950 (1973); *Rosen v. Louisiana State Board of Medical Examiners*, 318 F.Supp. 1217 (E.D. La. 1970); *Corkey v. Edwards*, 322 F.Supp. 1248 (W.D.N.C. 1971), vacated and remanded, 410 U.S. 950 (1973); *Steinberg v. Brown*, 321 F.Supp. 741 (N.D. Ohio 1970); *Doe v. Rampton*, No. C-234-70 (D. Utah 1971), vacated and remanded, 410 U.S. 950 (1973).

77. *People v. Belous*, 71 Cal.2d 954, 458 P.2d 194, 80 Cal.Rptr. 354 (1969); *State v. Barquet*, 262 So.2d 431 (Fla. 1972).

78. *Roe*, 410 U.S. at 154–155. *Cheaney v. State*, 259 Ind. 138, 285 N.E.2d 265 (July 24, 1972), appeal docketed, No. 72-6002, *Cheaney v. Indiana* (U.S.); *Spears v. Mississippi*, 257 So.2d 876 (Miss. 1972); *State v. Munson*, 86 S.D. 663, 201 N.W.2d 123 (S.D. 1972), appeal docketed, No. 72-631 (U.S. 1971), vacated and remanded, *Munson v. South Dakota*, 410 U.S. 950 (1973).

79. Five federal decisions upheld the constitutionality of state laws, while seven struck them down on various grounds. *Finding constitutional: Crossen v. Attorney General*, 344 F.Supp. 587 (E.D. Ky. 1972), vacated and remanded, 410 U.S. 950 (1973); *Rosen v. Board of Medical Examiners*, 318 F.Supp. 1217 (E.D. La. 1970), vacated and remanded, 412 U.S. 902 (1973); *Corkey v. Edwards*, 322 F.Supp. 1248 (W.D. N.C. 1971), vacated and remanded, 410 U.S. 950 (1973); *Steinberg v. Brown*, 321 F.Supp. 741 (N.D. Ohio 1970); *Doe v. Rampton*, No. C-234-70 (D. Utah 1971), vacated and remanded, 410 U.S. 950 (1973).

Finding unconstitutional: Abele v. Markle, 342 F.Supp. 800 (D. Conn. 1972), judgment vacated and cause remanded for consideration of question of mootness, 410 U.S. 951, reh'g den., 411 U.S. 940 (1973); *Abele v. Markle*, 351 F.Supp. 224 (D. Conn. 1972), vacated and remanded, 410 U.S. 951 (1973); *Doe v. Bolton*, 319 F.Supp. 1048 (N.D. Ga. 1970), aff'd as modified, 410 U.S. 179 (1973); *Doe v. Scott*, 321 F.Supp. 1385 (N.D. Ill. 1971), vacated and remanded sub. nom., *Hanrahan v. Doe*, 410 U.S. 950 (1973); *Poe v. Menghini*, 339 U.S. 986 (D. Kan. 1972); *YWCA of Princeton, N.J. v. Kugler*, 342 F.Supp. 1048 (D.N.J. 1972), vacated and remanded, 475 F.2d 1398 (3d Cir. 1973), judgment reinstated, Civil No. 264-70 (D.N.J. July 24 1973), aff'd mem. Op., 493 F.2d 1402 (3d Cir. 1974); *Roe v. Wade*, 314 F.Supp. 1217 (N.D. Tex. 1970), aff'd in part, rev'd in part, 410 U.S. 113 (1973); *Babbitz v. McCann*, 310 F.Supp. 293 (E.D. Wis. 1970), appeal dismissed, 400 U.S. 1 (1970).

Sixteen state decisions upheld the constitutionality of state laws, while five struck them down: *Finding constitutional: Nelson v. Planned Parenthood Center of Tucson, Inc.*, 19 Ariz.App. 142, 505 P.2d 580 (1973); *Cheaney v. State*, 259 Ind. 138, 285 N.E.2d 265 (1972), cert. den. sub nom., *Cheaney v. Indiana*, 410 U.S. 991 (1973); *State v. Abodeely*, 179 N.W.2d 347 (Iowa 1970), appeal dismissed, cert. den., 402 U.S. 936 (1971); *Sasaki v. Commonwealth*, 485 S.W.2d 897 (Ky. 1972), vacated and remanded, sub. nom., *Sasaki v. Kentucky*, 410 U.S. 951 (1973); *State v. Campbell*, 263 La. 1058, 270 So.2d 506 (1972); *State v. Scott*, 260 La. 190, 255 So.2d 736 (1971); *State v. Shirley*, 256 La. 665, 237 So.2d 676 (1970); *State v. Pesson*, 256 La. 201, 235 So.2d 568 (1970); *State v. Moretti*, 52 N.J. 182, 244 A.2d 499 (1968); *State v. Kruze*, No. 72-11, (Oh. March 10, 1972), dismissing appeal for want of a substantial constitutional question, vacated and remanded sub. nom., *Kruze v. Ohio*, 410 U.S. 951 (1973); *Spears v. State*, 257 So.2d 876 (Miss. 1972) (per curiam), cert. denied, 409 U.S. 1106 (1973); *Rodgers v. Danforth*, 486 S.W.2d 258 (Mo. 1972); *Byrn v. New York City Health and Hospitals Corp.*, 31 N.Y.2d 194, 286 N.E.2d 887, 335 N.Y.S.2d 390 (1972), appeal dismissed, 410 U.S. 949 (1973) (challenge by guardian ad litem for class of unborn children to the constitutionality of statute permitting abortion on demand through the twenty-fourth week of gestation); *State v. Munson*, 86 S.D. 663, 201 N.W.2d 123 (1972), vacated and remanded sub. nom., *Munson v. South Dakota*, 410 U.S. 950 (1973); *Thompson v. State*, 493 S.W.2d 913 (Tex. Crim. App. 1971), vacated and remanded sub. nom., *Thompson v. Texas*, 410 U.S. 950 (1973); *State v. Bartlett*, 128 Vt. 618, 270 A.2d 168 (1970).

Finding unconstitutional: People v. Belous, 71 Cal.2d 954, 458 P.2d 194, 80 Cal.Rptr. 354 (1969) (on vagueness grounds); *People v. Barksdale*, 3 Cal.3d 320, 503 P.2d 257, 105 Cal.Rptr. 1 (1972) (vagueness); *State v. Barquet*, 262 So.2d 431 (Fla. 1972) (vagueness); *State v. Nixon*, 42 Mich.App. 332, 201 N.W.2d 635 (1972), on remand, 50 Mich.App. 38, 212 N.W.2d 607 (1973) (arbitrary and unreasonable to prohibit a physician from performing an abortion where the woman herself is not subject to prosecution); *Beecham v. Leahy*, 130 Vt. 164, 287 A.2d 836 (1972) (arbitrary and unreasonable to pro-

hibit a physician from performing an abortion where the woman herself is
not subject to prosecution). I am grateful to Paul Linton for compiling this
tally.

80. A number of other courts dismissed federal court challenges on jurisdictional
or procedural grounds: *Hall v. Lefkowitz*, 305 F.Supp. 1030 (S.D.N.Y.)
(mooted by repeal of New York abortion law in 1970); *Doe v. Randall*,
314 F.Supp. 32 (D. Minn. 1970); *Doe v. Dunbar*, 320 F.Supp. 1297 (D.
Colo. 1970); *Landreth v. Hopkins*, 331 F.Supp. 920 (N.D. Fl. 1971); *Planned
Parenthood v. Nelson*, 327 F.Supp. 1290 (D. Az. 1971); *Ryan v. Specter*, 321
F.Supp. 1109 (E.D. Pa. 1971), 332 F.Supp. 26 (1971); *Rodgers v. Danforth*,
Civ. No. 18630-2 (W.D. Mo. 1970), appeal docketed, No. 70–89 (US
1970), vacated and remanded, 410 U.S. 949 (1973) (abstention).

81. The November 1969 decision in *Vuitch* cited the California Supreme Court's
September decision in *Belous*, and the March 5, 1970, Wisconsin decision in
Babbitz cited *Belous* and *Vuitch*. The *Belous* decision held that a 150-year-old
law that had been applied by courts in dozens of cases was unconstitutionally
"vague," the same conclusion that the D.C. court came to regarding the
D.C. law that had been enforced since 1901. The *Babbitz* decision held that
there was a constitutional right to abortion but only *before quickening*.

82. Dellapenna, *Dispelling the Myths*, at 568–569, 585–587. See also Dyer, *Champion of Women and the Unborn*; Dyer, *The Physicians' Crusade against Abortion*.

83. Dellapenna, *Dispelling the Myths*, at 568–569.

84. Ibid., at 565 and n. 254 (citing Calderone, Heffernan, Moore, Russell).
Guttmacher had previously written books that suggested that abortion was
tantamount to homicide. Guttmacher, *Into This Universe*, 46 (quoting Sir
Thomas Percival: "to extinguish the first spark of life is a crime of the same
nature, both against our Maker and society, as to destroy an infant, a child,
or a man"); Guttmacher, *Birth Control and Love*, 12 ("Fertilization, then, has
taken place; a baby has been conceived.").

85. Dellapenna, *Dispelling the Myths*, at 570.

86. Quoted in Garrow, *Liberty and Sexuality*, at 279.

87. Ibid., at 333; Greenhouse and Siegel, *Before* Roe v. Wade, at 25–28.

88. American Medical Association, "Position on Abortion."

89. Greenhouse and Siegel, *Before* Roe v. Wade, at 26.

90. Fletcher and Evans, "Maternal Bonding."

91. Tietze and Lewit, "Abortion."

92. Transcript, Second *Doe* Argument, at 6. See supra, chapter 1, note 12.

93. Tietze and Lewit, "Abortion," at 21.

94. Ibid., at 22 (emphasis added).

95. Dellapenna, *Dispelling the Myths*, at 244.

96. Ibid., 57.

97. Ibid., 56.

98. Ibid., at 211–228 ("The Reception of the Common Law on Abortion
and Infanticide in the American Colonies"), at 231 ("The evidence seems

irrefutable that around 1800 abortion was a serious common law crime in England, certainly after quickening and perhaps before quickening as well."); Scott, Note, "Quickening in the Common Law." See also Roden, "*Roe v. Wade* and the Common Law."

99. Dellapenna, *Dispelling the Myths*, at 313 ("And the evidence is overwhelming that the protection of the life of the unborn child (as they termed it) was the primary purpose underlying these statutes."); ibid. at 321 ("[I]n the United States, as in Japan, numerous jurists described the purpose of this legislation as the protection of the unborn child from destruction.").

100. Dellapenna, *Dispelling the Myths*, at 185 ("Legal records of the time indicate that both forms of abortion [injury techniques and ingestion techniques] were capital felonies regardless of consent or (more typically) lack of consent by the woman undergoing the abortion attempt."). "Extensive research has turned up indictments or appeals of felony for abortions dating back more than eight centuries. Abortionists were punished by hanging, imprisonment, and outlawry for the killing of the child, admittedly for abortions without the consent of the mother, but also without any requirement that the child be born alive before dying. Included among these was at least one case that resulted in the imprisonment of two men for the abortion of an unborn child apparently of one month's gestation. By the sixteenth century, abortionists were convicted for unequivocally voluntary abortion." Ibid. at 126–127.

101. Transcript, Second *Roe* Argument, at 12.

102. Dellapenna, *Dispelling the Myths*, at 322–324, 358–370. See also Dyer, *Champion of Women and the Unborn*; Dyer, *The Physicians' Crusade against Abortion.*

103. Hurwitz, "Jon O. Newman and the Abortion Decisions."

104. Garrow, *Liberty and Sexuality*, at 577.

105. Greenhouse and Siegel, *Before* Roe v. Wade, at 36–44.

106. Garrow, *Liberty and Sexuality*, at 336.

107. Ibid., at 393–394.

108. Greenhouse, *Becoming Justice Blackmun*, at 74–75.

109. Recounted in Lisa Shaw Roy, "Roe and the New Frontier," at 340; Jeffries, *Justice Lewis F. Powell, Jr.*, at 347. Powell was also influenced by his daughter, Molly. See Jeffries, ibid. See Letter of Justice Powell to Molly, June 3, 1985 (after the Supreme Court had agreed to hear *Thornburgh v. American College of Obstetricians and Gynecologists*, and marked "File in 84-495"), Lewis F. Powell Papers, Washington and Lee University School of Law, Box 268 ("At your suggestion, I have checked the Pennsylvania Abortion case granted for next Term and you are right that one of the numerous parties is Planned Parenthood of Pennsylvania. Although I do not think the views or activities of my daughters would disqualify me in this case, I appreciate your sensitivity in preferring not to become a board member in Utah. At your suggestion, I also talked to Penny and she will follow your example.").

110. See Juan Williams, *Thurgood Marshall*, at 354 ("Marshall was sympathetic

to this perspective from his experience as an advocate for poor blacks. Going back to his days in Baltimore and Harlem, he had heard stories about penniless black women who suffered or died at the hands of any hack willing to perform an illegal abortion. In the justices' conferences Marshall asserted that poor women needed to be able to have legal abortions since rich women could get around state laws by going to private clinics or leaving the country.").

Chapter Three

1. Transcript, First *Roe* Argument, at 16. Historian David Garrow has noted that "[p]ublished versions of the Roe transcript contain a modest number of errors that can be detected only when a listener carefully compares the transcript to the actual audio recording of the argument." Garrow, *Liberty and Sexuality*, 859n70. The errors in the published transcripts are, in fact, more significant. See supra, chapter 1, note 12.

2. Transcript, First *Doe* Argument, at 18.

3. Sarah Weddington recounted this incident in a banquet address on February 28, 1976, at the Western Regional Conference on Abortion, Denver, Colorado; it is published as the Introduction in Hern and Andrikopoulos, eds., *Abortion in the Seventies*, 277–279; See also Garrow, *Liberty and Sexuality*, at 443–444 ("The most reassuring moment, she said, came when Sarah Hughes looked down, made eye contact and 'gave me a reassuring smile' and then 'winked at me as if to say, "It's going to be all right."'"); Uddo, "A Wink from the Bench," at 398.

4. Garrow, *Liberty and Sexuality*, at 440.

5. Ibid.

6. Ibid., at 484.

7. Ibid.

8. Transcript, First *Roe* Argument. See also Faux, Roe v. Wade: *The Untold Story*, at 243.

9. Robin Pogrebin, "Breyer Invited to Make a Case for Architecture," *New York Times*, October 6, 2011, A4.

10. For an engaging account of the history of the Supreme Court and oral arguments, see Cushman, *Courtwatchers*.

11. Transcript, First *Doe* Argument, at 19.

12. The development of the factual record in the federal trial court in the Georgia case, including the critical question of Georgia's interest in its statute, might have been advanced by a guardian for the unborn child who attempted to present evidence. Ferdinand Buckley, an accomplished attorney in Atlanta, attempted to intervene to act as a guardian, but this was denied by the federal court. Such a guardian ad litem, Dr. Bart Heffernan (an obstetrician-gynecologist), was allowed to intervene in the Illinois case, *Doe v. Scott*, 321 F.Supp. 1385 (N.D. Ill. 1971), but no evidentiary hearing was held.

13. The jurisdiction of the three-judge district court relied on 28 U.S.C. 1343(3)

(1964 ed). Direct appeal to the Supreme Court of the three-judge district court's final judgment denying a permanent injunction rested on 28 U.S.C. 1253 (1964 ed). Congress changed the three-judge district court jurisdiction in 1976. Three-judge District Courts were convened pursuant to 28 U.S.C. 2281 (1970). This was repealed by the act of August 12, 1976, Public Law 94-381, section 1, 90 Stat. 1119. See 439 U.S. at 381n2.

14. Transcript, Second *Roe* Argument, at 9.
15. Two cases with better records included the Louisiana case *Rosen*, and the second Connecticut decision in *Abele v. Markle. Rosen v. Louisiana State Board of Medical Examiners*, 318 F.Supp. 1217, appeal docketed (U.S. Nov. 27, 1970). See the description of pending abortion cases in Sigworth, "Abortion Laws in the Federal Courts," at 130, 135, and n. 29.
16. Justice Harry Blackmun letter to Chief Justice William Rehnquist, July 20, 1987, Harry A. Blackmun Papers, Library of Congress, Box 151, Folder 3; Rehnquist letter to Blackmun, July 16, 1987, original, with onionskin of Blackmun reply, Blackmun Papers, Box 1407, Folder 13.
17. Transcript, First *Doe* Argument, at 23.
18. Garrow, *Liberty and Sexuality*, at 445 ("Then, no more than week [sic] before the scheduled hearing, Sandra called Margie Hames from Oklahoma. . . . Sandra also said she had felt fetal movement in her now four- to five-month pregnancy and that experience had convinced her that she no longer wanted an abortion."); Dellapenna, *Dispelling the Myths*, at 682–683.
19. Transcript, First *Doe* Argument, at 3 ("did not obtain the abortion, however, because she did not have the cash to deposit and pay her hospital bill in advance."). See also Dellapenna, *Dispelling the Myths*, at 683. Thirty-four years after the arguments, Margie Pitts Hames's representation about Mary Doe's (Sandra Cano's) intentions was contradicted by Sandra Cano's testimony before the Subcommittee on the Constitution, Civil Rights, and Property Rights of the Senate Committee on the Judiciary on June 23, 2005.
20. *Abele v. Markle*, 342 F.Supp. 800 (D. Conn. 1972).
21. Richard Gregory Morgan, "*Roe v. Wade* and the Lesson of Pre-*Roe* Case Law."
22. *Kleppe v. New Mexico*, 426 U.S. 529, 546 (1976) (quoting *Public Affairs Associates Inc. v. Rickover*, 369 U.S. 111, 113 (1962)).
23. *Castaneda v. Partida*, 430 U.S. 482, 499 (1977).
24. *Poe v. Ullman*, 367 U.S. 497, 509 (1961) ("I am not convinced, on this skimpy record, that these appellants as individuals are truly caught in an inescapable dilemma.").
25. Transcript of Argument in *United States v. Vuitch*, No. 84, OT 1970, 34 (Chief Justice Burger: "In this evolving developing stage of medical knowledge on the subject . . . how would we have any basis to pass on that, absent a record of testimony as to what is the present state of medical knowledge on the time and the term?").
26. *United States v. Vuitch*, 402 U.S. 62, 73 (1971).

27. Mersky and Hartman, *A Documentary History:* Roe v. Wade, 1:15 (Jurisdictional Statement).

28. Ibid., 1:17–18.

29. Justice William J. Brennan, "Memorandum re: Abortion Cases," December 30, 1971, in William J. Brennan Papers, Library of Congress, Manuscript Division, Box I: 285, Folder 9. See supra chapter 1, n. 10 and accompanying text. See also R. Beck, "Self-Conscious Dicta."

30. Transcript, First *Roe* Argument, at 8.

31. Hear the audio of the first argument in *Roe* at http://www.oyez.org/cases/1970–1979/1971/1971_70_18.

32. Transcript, First *Doe* Argument, at 26.

33. Urofsky, ed., *The Douglas Letters*, 184n1. See Chief Justice Warren Burger, "Memo to the Conference, re Abortion Cases," May 31, 1972, Lewis F. Powell Papers, Box 5-150 ("Perhaps my problem arises from the mediocre to poor help from counsel. On reargument, I would propose we appoint amici for both sides. . . .").

34. James F. Simon, *The Center Holds*, at 90.

35. Transcript, Second *Doe* argument, at 3.

36. Transcript, First *Doe* argument, at 6.

37. Mersky and Hartman, eds., *A Documentary History:* Roe v. Wade, 2:116 (Brief of Alan Charles, citing Leavy and Kummer, "Criminal Abortion: Human Hardship"). See also *People v. Belous*, 71 Cal.2d 954, 965–966, 458 P.2d 194, 80 Cal. Rptr. 354 (1969).

38. Transcript, First *Roe* argument, at 7.

39. *Griswold v. Connecticut*, 381 U.S. 479, 493 (1965) (citations omitted) (quoting *Snyder v. Massachusetts*, 291 U.S. 97, 105 (1934) and *Powell v. Alabama*, 287 U.S. 45, 67 (1932) (internal citations omitted)). This analysis was also cited by one federal judge, dissenting in the abortion case, *YWCA v. Kugler*, 342 F.Supp. 1048, 1080 (D. N.J. 1972).

40. Dellapenna, *Dispelling the Myths*, at 144, 1004.

41. See Dellapenna, *Dispelling the Myths*, at 14–15 ("Blackmun relied heavily and uncritically on Means' history, citing Means (and no other historian) no less than seven times." (citing *Roe v. Wade*, 410 U.S. at 136–139)).

42. Dellapenna, *Dispelling the Myths*, at 143–152, 187–189, 195–211, 275–288. See also Rafferty, Roe v. Wade: *The Birth of a Constitutional Right*; Linton, "*Planned Parenthood v. Casey*: The Flight from Reason," at 110nn35–36; Witherspoon, "Reexamining *Roe*."

43. Transcript, First *Roe* argument, at 7.

44. Dellapenna, *Dispelling the Myths*, chapter 1, 3–56. See also Kenny, *Abortion*, 181 ("The traditional forms of abortion had been infanticide and abandonment.").

45. Linton, "*Planned Parenthood v. Casey*: The Flight from Reason," at 110nn35–36 (citing court decisions).

46. Dellapenna, *Dispelling the Myths*, chapters 3 and 4, 125–228.

47. Transcript, First *Doe* argument, at 15.

48. Forsythe, "Homicide of the Unborn Child."

49. Ibid. A number of modern state courts have also recognized the evidentiary nature of these rules. *Hughes v. State*, 868 P.2d 730, 732–733 (Ok. Crim. App. 1994); *Commonwealth v. Lawrence*, 404 Mass. 378, 536 N.E.2d 571, 575–576 (1989); *Commonwealth v. Cass*, 392 Mass. 799, 467 N.E.2d 1324, 1328–1339 (1984); *People v. Greer*, 79 Ill.2d 103, 402 N.E.2d 203, 207–208 (1980); *State v. Holcomb*, 956 S.W.2d 286 (Mo. App. 1997).

50. Guttmacher, *Into This Universe*, at 23, 43–47.

51. Means, "The Law of New York Concerning Abortion," at 424 ("At common law, of course, there were only three criteria: conception, quickening, and live birth. Viability was never mentioned by common-law judges or treatise writers.")

52. Or, at least, that's the conventional story about Holmes's opinion for the Massachusetts Supreme Judicial Court in the *Dietrich v. Inhabitants of Northhampton*, 138 Mass. 14, 52 Am. Rep. 242 (1884). In fact, Holmes never used the word *viability*, and referred instead to "separate existence," which may well have referred to quickening. In any case, Holmes's opinion influenced American law until the middle of the twentieth century. See Roden, "Prenatal Tort Law"; Scott, Note, "Quickening in the Common Law." For a critique of Holmes's opinion, see Forsythe, "The Legacy of Oliver Wendell Holmes."

53. Dellapenna, *Dispelling the Myths*, at 254–287. See also Dyer, *Champion of Women and the Unborn*; Dyer, *The Physicians' Crusade against Abortion*. See also Rafferty, Roe v. Wade: *The Birth of a Constitutional Right*, at 163–174 ("quick with child" originally meant simply "alive" without regard to whether the mother had felt fetal movements).

54. Transcript, First *Doe* argument, at 6.

55. Dellapenna, *Dispelling the Myths*, at 237.

56. See, generally, Forsythe, "Homicide of the Unborn Child."

57. Dellapenna, *Dispelling the Myths*, at 99–110.

58. Transcript, Second *Roe* Argument, at 18.

59. This was demonstrated in English law as long ago as the 1848 case of *Regina v. West*, 2 C. & K. 784, 175 Eng. Rep. 329, 330 (1848) (applying the common law, not any statute). The born-alive rule meant that the law treated the unborn child as a human being at any point in pregnancy. Killing a child at even two months of pregnancy could be charged as a homicide as long as the child died outside the womb, even if the child died from prematurity. That distinction between dying inside or outside was due to the need for clear evidence at a time of high infant mortality and primitive medicine.

60. Transcript, Second *Roe* Argument, at 11. In the first *Roe* oral argument, Weddington had this exchange with Justice Stewart:

> JUSTICE STEWART: Does the Texas law in other areas of the law give rights to unborn children—in the areas of trusts, estates and wills, or any of the other . . .

MRS. WEDDINGTON: No, Your Honor, only . . . *only if they are born alive*. We have—the Supreme Court of Texas recently has held in one case that there is an action for prenatal injuries at any stage prior to birth, but only upon the condition that it be born alive. The same is true of our property law. The child must be born alive. And I think there is a distinction between those children which are ultimately born; and *I think it is appropriate to give them retroactive rights. But I think that's a completely different question from whether or not they had rights at the time they were still in the womb.* (emphasis added)

61. See Mersky and Hartman, eds., *A Documentary History:* Roe v. Wade, 2:459 (Brief of Americans United for Life); ibid., 3:3 (Brief of Association of Texas Diocesan Attorneys); ibid., 3:171 (Brief of Certain Physicians, Professors, and Fellows of the American College of Obstetricians and Gynecologists); ibid., 3:285 (Brief of National Right to Life Committee).

62. Transcript, First *Doe* Argument, at 25.

63. See *Roe*, 410 U.S. at 162–163 (interest in "potentiality of human life . . . grows in substantiality as the woman approaches term. . . .").

64. Wohlers, *Women and Abortion*; Dellapenna, *Dispelling the Myths*, at 299–302; Linton, "Enforcement of State Abortion Statutes after *Roe*," at 163–164n31 ("Although more than one-third of the states . . . have enacted statutes prohibiting a woman from aborting herself or consenting to an abortion performed on her by another, no prosecutions have been reported under any of these statutes. Nationwide, research has disclosed only two cases in which a woman has been charged with participating in her own abortion." (citing *Commonwealth v. Weible*, 45 Pa. Super. 207 (1911); *Crissman v. State*, 245 S.W.2d 438 (Tex. Crim. App. 1922)). No American court has upheld the conviction of a woman for self-abortion or consenting to an abortion performed on her by another. And with the exception of *Weible* and *Crissman*, there is no record of any woman having been charged with either offense as a principal or as an accessory.").

65. Dellapenna, *Dispelling the Myths*, at 299 and n. 300.

66. Ibid., at 300–301.

67. Lord Ellenborough's Act, 43 Geo. III ch. 58 (1803). Keown, *Abortion, Doctors and the Law*. See also Dellapenna, *Dispelling the Myths*, at 243–262.

68. Transcript, Second *Doe* Argument, at 14.

69. Transcript, First *Doe* Argument, at 13.

70. Dellapenna, *Dispelling the Myths*, at 135 ("And the courts in these cases [in the 1200s] spoke unequivocally in terms of the killing of a child, and not just in terms of a crime against the mother. The common law, in its early centuries, treated abortion as a crime in principle because it involved the killing of an unborn child—a tradition that continued with elaboration, but without interruption, until *Roe* changed it." (citing "Agnes's Appeal, an appeal of felony brought in 1200")).

71. See Horan, Forsythe, and Grant, "Two Ships Passing in the Night," at 276

("The Roman law reflected the legal axiom, *conceptus pro iam nato habetur*, under which the unborn child was to be treated like a born person whenever some benefit to the child was at stake. This maxim was adopted by the English common law at least by the [eighteenth century].").

72. *Bonbrest v. Katz*, 65 F.Supp. 138, 140 (D.D.C. 1946).

73. *Smith v. Brennan*, 31 N.J. 353, 362, 157 A.2d 497, 502 (1960).

74. Transcript, First *Doe* argument, at 15.

75. Transcript, First *Roe* argument, at 17.

76. Transcript, First *Roe* argument, at 20.

77. Dellapenna, *Dispelling the Myths*, at 271. See also Witherspoon, "Reexamining *Roe*," at 42–44.

78. Transcript, Second *Roe* Argument, at 10–11.

79. Transcript, Second *Roe* Argument, at 11.

80. *Steinberg v. Brown*, 321 F.Supp. 741, 746 (N.D. Ohio 1970) ("Once human life has commenced, the constitutional protections found in the Fifth and Fourteenth Amendments impose upon the state the duty of safeguarding it.").

81. Judge Clarie in his dissenting opinion in *Abele v. Markle*, 342 F.Supp. 800, 815 (D. Conn. 1972).

82. Paulsen, "The Plausibility of Personhood."

83. Transcript, Second *Roe* Argument, at 22.

84. Dellapenna, *Dispelling the Myths*, at 275.

85. Ibid., at 430.

86. Ibid., 315.

87. Ibid., 279 ("English physicians had advocated therapeutic abortions at least as early as 1756, although no authorization was enacted in England for such abortions until 1829. Arguments for these exceptions were grounded on appeals to a maternal right of self-defense, not on a rejection of fetal personhood. The 'self-defense' argument was made explicitly in the United States at least as early as 1866.").

88. See Dellapenna, ibid.; Linton, "*Planned Parenthood v. Casey*: The Flight from Reason," at 110nn35–36; Witherspoon, "Reexamining *Roe*."

89. Transcript, Second *Doe* Argument, at 18.

90. Transcript, Second *Doe* Argument, at 18.

91. Means, "The Law of New York Concerning Abortion," at 450ff.

92. Transcript, Second *Roe* Argument, at 14.

93. Transcript, Second *Doe* Argument, at 12.

94. Transcript, Second *Doe* Argument, at 13.

95. Transcript, Second *Doe* Argument, at 16.

96. Linton, "Enforcement of State Abortion Statutes after *Roe*," at 157, 163–164n31; Linton, "The Legal Status of Abortion" (2007); Dellapenna, *Dispelling the Myths*, at 695. Public referenda proposing abortion "reforms" along the lines of the Model Penal Code proposal for abortion "reform" had been rejected six times. Dellapenna, *Dispelling the Myths*, at 634–635, 674, 774. See also Dellapenna, *Dispelling the Myths*, at 594 ("The Model Penal Code and Limited Reform").

97. Transcript, First *Doe* Argument, at 15.

98. Transcript, Second *Doe* Argument, at 14.

99. Transcript, First *Doe* Argument, at 15; Transcript, Second *Doe* Argument, at 16.

100. Transcript, Second *Doe* Argument, at 16.

101. *Roe*, 410 U.S. at 157–158n54 ("When Texas urges that a fetus is entitled to Fourteenth Amendment protection as a person, it faces a dilemma. Neither in Texas nor in any other State are all abortions prohibited. Despite broad proscription, an exception always exists. The exception contained in Art. 1196 [the Texas statute], for an abortion procured or attempted by medical advice for the purpose of saving the life of the mother, is typical. But if the fetus is a person who is not to be deprived of life without due process of law, and if the mother's condition is the sole determinant, does not the Texas exception appear to be out of line with the Amendment's command? . . . If the fetus is a person, why is the woman not a principal or an accomplice? . . . If the fetus is a person, may the penalties be different?").

Chapter Four

1. Dellapenna, *Dispelling the Myths*, at 593. "Williams seized upon Holmes' concept of 'viability' to ground his arbitrary line." Ibid. at 588.

2. Blackmun letter of December 4, 1972, Lewis F. Powell, Jr., Papers, Washington and Lee University School of Law, Box 5-150.

3. Report of the Grand Jury at 99–100, In re County Investigating Grand Jury XXIII, Misc. No. 0009901-2008 (Pa. Com. Pl. Jan. 14, 2011), available at http://www.phila.gov/districtattorney/PDFs/GrandJuryWomensMedical .pdf. See also Samuel W. Calhoun, "Stopping Philadelphia Abortion Provider Kermit Gosnell"; Forsythe and Kehr, "A Road Map through the Supreme Court's Back Alley."

4. Sweden allows for abortion by request up to eighteen weeks. The state of Western Australia allows abortion by request up to twenty weeks, but no other state in Australia allows abortion beyond twelve weeks. Five countries have abortion by request up to fourteen weeks—Austria, Cambodia, France, Germany, and Romania.

    For Sweden: The Abortion Act, 1974:595 (2005) (Swed.) Unofficial translation by Ministry of Health and Social Affairs, Sweden. Available at http://www.sweden.gov.se/content/1/c6/06/28/70/4755c9dc.pdf.

    For Australia: Natasha Cica, *Abortion Law in Australia*, Law and Bills Digest Group, August 31, 1998, http://www.aph.gov.au/library/pubs/rp/1998-99/99rp01.htm.

    For Fourteen-Week Countries: Center for Reproductive Rights, *The World's Abortion Laws*, Fact Sheet (2008), at 2, available at http://www .reproductiverights.org/sites/crr.civicactions.net/files/pub_fac_abortion laws2008.pdf.

5. The United States is one of approximately 10 nations (out of 195) that allows abortion after fourteen weeks (Canada, China, the Netherlands, North Korea, Singapore, Sweden, United Kingdom, United States, Vietnam,

Western Australia (a state of Australia)) and one of only 4 (with Canada, North Korea, and China) that allows abortion for any reason after fetal viability. See Center for Reproductive Rights, *The World's Abortion Laws*, Fact Sheet (2008), available at http://www.reproductiverights.org/sites/crr.civicactions.net/files/pub_fac_abortionlaws2008.pdf; United Nations Department of Economic and Social Affairs Population Division, "World Abortion Policies 2011," March 2011, available at http://www.un.org/esa/population/publications/2011abortion/2011wallchart.pdf.

See also R. Beck, "The Essential Holding of *Casey*," at 722 and n. 58 (quoting authorities). The United Kingdom limits abortion to twenty-four weeks; see *Abortion Statistics, England and Wales: 2010*, available at http://www.dh.gov.uk/prod_consum_dh/groups/dh_digitalassets/documents/digitalasset/dh_127202.pdf.

6. Professor Randy Beck has analyzed the history of the viability rule in three studies: R. Beck, "Self-Conscious Dicta"; R. Beck, "*Gonzales, Casey* and the Viability Rule"; R. Beck, "The Essential Holding of *Casey*."

7. *Roe v. Wade*, 410 U.S. at 160 (1973) ("Viability is usually placed at about seven months (28 weeks) but may occur earlier, even at 24 weeks."). See also Judge Newman's opinion in *Abele v. Markle*, 351 F.Supp. 224, 232n10 (D. Conn. 1972) ("what appears to be the medical consensus [is] that the fetus normally becomes viable approximately 28 weeks after conception.").

8. Bernard Schwartz, *The Unpublished Opinions of the Burger Court*, at 83.

9. Ibid., 148; R. Beck, "Self-Conscious Dicta."

10. Some prominent scholars have suggested that a narrower decision based on vagueness might have avoided a lot of problems. Bernard Schwartz (1923–1997): "Had the original Blackmun draft come down as the Court opinion . . . a narrow decision striking down a state law for vagueness. . . . The subsequent schism that has been a major factor in American life might have been postponed or avoided—or possibly mitigated by its relegation to political rather than legal resolution." Bernard Schwartz, *The Unpublished Opinions of the Burger Court*, 83. John Hart Ely: "A plausible narrower basis of decision, that of vagueness, is brushed aside in the rush toward broader ground." Ely, "The Wages of Crying Wolf," 922.

11. Garrow, *Liberty and Sexuality*, at 549–551; R. Beck, "Self-Conscious Dicta."

12. Brennan letter to Blackmun, May 18, 1972, Potter Stewart Papers, Yale University Library, MS 1367, Box 268, Folder 3194.

13. Garrow, *Liberty and Sexuality*, at 549.

14. Memorandum from George Freeman to Justice Blackmun, August 11, 1972, Harry A. Blackmun Papers, Library of Congress, Box 152, Folder 5. Garrow cites this memo as an example of the broad decision-making that Blackmun delegated to his clerks. Garrow, "The Brains behind Blackmun." See also R. Beck, "Self-Conscious Dicta," at 519n71.

15. Bernard Schwartz, *The Ascent of Pragmatism*, at 306 ("The second draft also adopted the time approach followed in the final opinion. However, it used the first trimester of pregnancy alone as the line between invalid and valid state power."); R. Beck, "Self-Conscious Dicta," at 519.

16. *Abele v. Markle*, 351 F.Supp. 224 (D. Conn. 1972). See Garrow, *Liberty and Sexuality*, at 544, 568, 574, 583, 597 (noting impact of Newman); R. Beck, "The Essential Holding of *Casey*," 723 (emphasizing impact of Newman); Hurwitz, "Jon O. Newman and the Abortion Decisions" (emphasizing impact of Newman).

17. *Abele v. Markle*, 351 F.Supp. 224 (D. Conn. 1972). Judge Newman had written a previous opinion concurring in the invalidation of the original Connecticut statute earlier in 1972. *Abele v. Markle*, 342 F.Supp. 800, 805–809 (D. Conn. 1972) (Newman, J., concurring in the result). Newman conducted a cursory review of the legislative intent of the 1860 Connecticut abortion prohibition (which eliminated the quickening distinction). Dellapenna, *Dispelling the Myths*, at 316n11. Judge Newman overlooked the history of the common law and the first Connecticut statutory prohibition of abortion in 1821 as well as the obvious influence of the American Medical Association and medical developments in eliminating the quickening distinction to extend legal protection of the unborn child throughout pregnancy. Reading Connecticut law through the lens of Cyril Means, Newman disparaged the legislative intent to protect the unborn child and suggested that the intent was only to protect the mother's health. See also Dellapenna, *Dispelling the Myths*, at 221–224 (examining the Connecticut colonial case of *Rex v. Hallowell*, suggesting that "even pre-quickening abortions were considered serious crimes in colonial Connecticut") and at 270–271 (examining the purposes of the Connecticut statute of 1821).

18. For recent reaffirmation of Newman's influence, see Garrow, "*Roe v. Wade* Revisited," at 71, 78–79. A copy of Newman's opinion of September 20, 1972, can be found in the William J. Brennan Papers, Library of Congress, Box I: 285, Folder 8.

19. Lewis F. Powell, Jr., Papers, Washington and Lee University School of Law, Box 5-150.

20. Hurwitz, "Jon O. Newman and the Abortion Decisions."

21. *Abele v. Markle*, 351 F.Supp. 224, 232 (D. Conn. 1972).

22. Ibid. (citation omitted).

23. See ibid. Newman did not, for example, recognize, as Blackstone expressly stated, that the born-alive rule had been applied to uphold a homicide charge in the case of a child who was born alive, before viability, and died outside the womb. See Forsythe, "Homicide of the Unborn Child," at 585 (quoting Blackstone, *Commentaries on the Laws of England*, 4:198); ibid. at 589n21 and accompanying text. This was confirmed by the English case of *Regina v. West*, 2 C. & K. 784, 175 Eng. Rep. 329 (1848) and by numerous common law authorities. Forsythe, "Homicide of the Unborn Child," at 591 nn134–135 and accompanying text.

24. *Abele v. Markle*, 351 F.Supp. 224, 232 (D. Conn. 1972).

25. Prosser, *Law of Torts*, at 337–338.

26. See chapter 9. See also R. Beck, "The Essential Holding of *Casey*," at 732–734 (criticizing Newman's focus on viability).

27. *Abele v. Markle*, 342 F.Supp. at 805–809 (Newman, J., concurring in the

result). See Garrow, *Liberty and Sexuality*, at 544 (noting Newman's opinion "that relied heavily upon the work of Cyril Means"). For an exhaustive critique of Means's spurious history, see Dellapenna, *Dispelling the Myths*, at 13–14 and chapters 3–6.

28. Newman's clerk, Andrew Hurwitz, interviewed at the Supreme Court that fall and went on to clerk for Justice Stewart in 1973–1974; according to Hurwitz, he was known by Stewart—who interviewed Hurwitz that fall— as the clerk who wrote *Abele v. Markle*. Thirty years later, Hurwitz wrote a law review article to show Newman's influence on *Roe v. Wade*. Hurwitz, "Jon O. Newman and the Abortion Decisions," at 238–239n55. See also Greenhouse, *Becoming Justice Blackmun*, at 96. President Obama nominated Justice Hurwitz to the U.S. Court of Appeals for the Ninth Circuit in 2011–2012.

29. Bernard Schwartz, *The Ascent of Pragmatism*, at 305; R. Beck, "The Essential Holding of *Casey*," at 722–723.

30. Bernard Schwartz, *The Ascent of Pragmatism*, at 306.

31. Blackmun, fifty-page Draft, marked "circulated 11/22/72," William J. Brennan Papers, Library of Congress, Box I: 285, Folder 9, at 48.

32. Ibid.

33. Ibid.

34. Garrow, *Liberty and Sexuality*, at 572 and nn. 113–114. Garrow refers to a law student from the University of Texas who happened to be a "sympathetic friend" of fellow University of Texas graduates Sarah Weddington and her husband, Ron, and was "clerking for Justice Powell and working on Roe and Doe." Ibid. at 572. The only clerk who fits that description was Powell's clerk Larry Hammond.

35. Lewis F. Powell, Jr., Papers, Washington and Lee University School of Law, Box 5-150. Hurwitz, "Jon O. Newman and the Abortion Decisions," at 244.

36. Hammond Memo, Lewis F. Powell, Jr., Papers, Washington and Lee University School of Law, Box 5-150; R. Beck, "Self-Conscious Dicta."

37. Hammond Memo, Lewis F. Powell, Jr., Papers, Washington and Lee University School of Law, Box 5-150.

38. Lewis F. Powell, Jr., Papers, Washington and Lee University School of Law, Box 5-150. Emphasis added.

39. Lewis F. Powell, Jr., Papers, Washington and Lee University School of Law, Box 5-150. See also Hurwitz, "Jon O. Newman and the Abortion Decisions."

40. R. Beck, "Self-Conscious Dicta"; R. Beck, "The Essential Holding of *Casey*."

41. Leval, "Judging under the Constitution," at 1263.

42. Blackmun, letter of December 4, 1972, Lewis F. Powell, Jr., Papers, Washington and Lee University School of Law, Box 5-150 (emphasis added).

43. Garrow, "Revelations on the Road to *Roe*."

44. Blackmun, "Memo to the Conference," December 11, 1972, Harry A. Blackmun Papers, Library of Congress, Box 151, Folder 4 (emphasis added).

45. Lewis F. Powell, draft letter to Harry A. Blackmun re Abortion Cases, December 13, 1972, 1 page, Lewis F. Powell, Jr., Papers, Washington and Lee University School of Law, Box 5-150.

46. Ibid.

47. See Garrow, "Revelations on the Road to *Roe*," at 80, 83 ("Powell left his letter to Blackmun unsent, perhaps in the belief that Marshall's and Brennan's expressions of support had already made the point, or perhaps because he reiterated his views face-to-face.").

48. See ibid.

49. *Doe*, 410 U.S. 179, 215 (1973) (Douglas, J., concurring) ("While childbirth endangers the lives of some women, voluntary abortion at any time and place regardless of medical standards would impinge on a rightful concern of society. The woman's health is part of that concern; as is the life of the fetus after quickening.").

50. Letter from Justice Brennan to Justice Blackmun, December 13, 1972, 3 pages, Harry A. Blackmun Papers, Library of Congress, Box 151, Folder 8; R. Beck, "Self-Conscious Dicta," 524–525 (quoting Brennan letter of December 13, 1972).

51. James F. Simon, *The Center Holds*, at 113; Garrow, *Liberty and Sexuality*, at 583. Years later, Professor Tushnet severely criticized the viability rule. Tushnet, "Two Notes on the Jurisprudence of Privacy."

52. Memo from Larry A. Hammond to Powell, December 12, 1972, Lewis F. Powell, Jr., Papers, Washington and Lee University School of Law, Box 5-150. Quoted in Yarbrough, *Harry A. Blackmun*, at 221.

53. Blackmun, "Memo to the Conference, Re: Abortion Cases," December 15, 1972, Lewis F. Powell, Jr., Papers, Washington and Lee University School of Law, Box 5-150.

54. Memo from Powell to Hammond, December 27, 1972, Lewis F. Powell, Jr., Papers, Washington and Lee University School of Law, Box 5-150.

55. Memo from Powell to Hammond, January 3, 1973, Lewis F. Powell, Jr., Papers, Washington and Lee University School of Law, Box 5-150.

56. Hurwitz, "Jon O. Newman and the Abortion Decisions," at 244.

57. Marshall letter of December 12, 1972, Lewis F. Powell, Jr., Papers, Washington and Lee University School of Law, Box 5-150.

58. Dellapenna, *Dispelling the Myths*, at 589–590, 594, 1274.

59. Stewart Memo to Blackmun, December 14, 1972, Powell Papers, Box 5-150; R. Beck, "Self-Conscious Dicta."

60. Transcript, Second *Doe* Argument, at 9–10. Compare the audio at http://www.oyez.org/cases/1970-1979/1971/1971_70_40.

61. Transcript, Second *Doe* Argument, at 17.

62. Garrow, *Liberty and Sexuality*, at 445 ("Then, no more than week [*sic*] before the scheduling hearing, Sandra called Margie Hames . . . equally if not more important, Sandra also said she had felt fetal movement in her now four- to five-month pregnancy and that experience had convinced her that she no longer wanted an abortion.").

63. Transcript, First *Doe* Argument, at 6.

64. Transcript, Second *Doe* Argument, at 4.

65. *Roe*, 410 U.S. at 151 (emphasis added).

66. Greenhouse, *Becoming Justice Blackmun*, at 96. Greenhouse cites no document. Yarbrough, *Harry A. Blackmun*, at 220–222 (citing "Bezanson to Blackmun, November 29, 1972, Blackmun Papers, in-house online *Roe* and *Doe* files"). Blackmun's clerk, Randy Bezanson, wrote a three-page memo to Blackmun on November 29, 1972, which stated "Justice Powell's suggestion seems to view the relevant state interests too narrowly, and disregards the state's interest in assuring that the medical procedures employed will be safe. . . . The fetus is pretty large at 4 or 5 or 6 months, although it may not be 'viable.' I would imagine, and your opinion suggests to me, that the medical risks which attend abortion of a fetus increase as the size of the fetus increases. Thus the state's interests may increase vis-à-vis this factor before 'viability.'" Harry A. Blackmun Papers, Library of Congress, Box 151, Folder 8.

67. See Dellapenna, *Dispelling the Myths*, at 592; Tushnet, "Two Notes on the Jurisprudence of Privacy" (criticizing viability); R. Beck, "*Gonzales, Casey* and the Viability Rule" (emphasizing the arbitrary nature of viability limitation). See Forsythe and Presser, "Restoring Self-Government on Abortion," at 313–316 (summarizing the legal critics and criticism).

68. Ely, "The Wages of Crying Wolf," at 924.

69. Forsythe, "Homicide of the Unborn Child."

70. Ibid.

71. Dellapenna, *Dispelling the Myths*, at 463–466.

72. *Dietrich v. Inhabitants of Northampton*, 138 Mass. 14, 52 Am. Rep. 242 (1884). A legal commentator in 1962 described the significance of the case: "In *Dietrich v. Inhabitants of Northampton*, probably the first recorded case wherein recovery for injuries sustained before birth was sought, the Supreme Judicial Court of Massachusetts held that no remedy could be granted. Justices Holmes . . . based the decision on (1) the lack of precedent; and (2) the child's lack of an existence separate and distinct from the mother. Where the question of prenatal injuries arose elsewhere, the precedent set by the *Dietrich* case was followed. . . ." Note, "The Extension of Prenatal Injury Doctrine to Nonviable Infants," at 362.

73. Dellapenna, *Dispelling the Myths*, at 463. "The earliest legal use of the concept, although not the term itself, was by Holmes in his Dietrich opinion." Ibid. at 467–468n121 for citations; see Roden, "Prenatal Tort Law."

74. *Torigian v. Watertown News Co.*, 352 Mass. 446, 225 N.E.2d 926, 927 (1967) ("In the case at bar, where the fetus was not viable, we must decide whether there is a sound distinction from the situation where the fetus is viable. . . . [cit. omit.] In the vast majority of cases where the present issue has arisen, recovery has been allowed. [citing 8 cases] To the extent that the views of textwriters and legal commentators have come to our attention, they are unanimously of the view that nonviability of a fetus should not bar recovery. [cit. omit.] The grounds which have been most frequently urged against allowing recovery are lack of precedent, the avoidance of speculation or

conjecture, and the encouragement of fictitious claims. There is no longer lack of precedent. The advancement of medical science should take care of most of these arguments. The element of speculation is not present to any greater extent than in the usual tort claim where medical evidence is offered and the issue of causation must be weighed with great care. [cit. omit.] The opportunity for fraudulent claims can be faced by the courts as in other types of cases. [cit. omit.] We are not impressed with the soundness of the arguments against recovery. They should not prevail against logic and justice. We hold that the plaintiff's intestate was a 'person' within the meaning of G. L. c. 229, § 2, as amended."). See also Dellapenna, *Dispelling the Myths*, at 588n137, 463–475; Forsythe, "The Legacy of Oliver Wendell Holmes."

75. Hopkin, Note, "*Roe v. Wade* and the Traditional Legal Standards Concerning Pregnancy," at 724.

76. Note, "The Extension of Prenatal Injury Doctrine to Nonviable Infants."

77. Ibid., 364.

78. *Smith v. Brennan*, 31 N.J. 353, 362, 157 A.2d 497, 502 (1960).

79. Note, "The Extension of Prenatal Injury Doctrine to Nonviable Infants," at 367.

80. Ely, "The Wages of Crying Wolf," 922; See Linton, "*Planned Parenthood v. Casey*: The Flight from Reason," at 47–49nn141–145; Bopp and Coleson, "The Right to Abortion," at 246–282; Kadar, "The Law of Tortious Prenatal Death Since *Roe v. Wade*," at 652–653 ("the discussion [in *Roe*] was perfunctory, and unfortunately largely inaccurate and should not be relied upon as the correct view of the law at the time of *Roe v. Wade*."); Hopkin, Note, "*Roe v. Wade* and the Traditional Legal Standards Concerning Pregnancy," at 724.

81. Linton, "*Planned Parenthood v. Casey*: The Flight from Reason," at 47–49nn141–145. See also Linton, "The Legal Status of the Unborn Child under State Law."

82. Linton, "*Planned Parenthood v. Casey*: The Flight from Reason," at 51–58.

83. Ibid., at 49–51 and nn. 148–151.

84. See the chart in chapter 9. See also *Hamilton v. Scott*, 97 So.3d 728 (Ala. May 18, 2012).

85. Mersky and Hartman, eds., *A Documentary History:* Roe v. Wade, 2:3 ("Brief of the American College of Obstetricians and Gynecologists et al.").

86. See "Position Statement on Abortion," of the American Psychiatric Association, December 12–13, 1969, quoted in "Brief of the American College of Obstetricians and Gynecologists, et al.," in Mersky and Hartman, eds., *A Documentary History:* Roe v. Wade, 2:21. In addition, the Uniform Abortion Act adopted by the American Bar Association in 1972, drafted by the National Conference of Commissioners on Uniform State Laws, allowed abortion up to twenty weeks (and thereafter for broad reasons). "No-Fault Divorce Act and 'Nonarrest' Custody Bill Are Opposed by the House of Delegates in New Orleans," *American Bar Association Journal* 58 (1972): 380.

87. Tent. Draft No. 9, 1959, cited in Maledon, Note, "The Law and the Unborn Child," at 370.

88. See Linton, "*Planned Parenthood v. Casey*: The Flight from Reason," at 24 ("At the time *Roe* was decided, thirty States allowed abortion only to save the life of the mother; two States and the District of Columbia allowed abortion to save the life or preserve the health of the mother; one State allowed abortion to save the mother's life or to terminate a pregnancy resulting from rape; thirteen States had adopted [the Model Penal Code] or some variant thereof, allowing abortion under specified circumstances; and four States allowed abortion on demand, but set limits in terms of the age of the fetus. No State allowed unrestricted abortion throughout pregnancy, as *Roe* effectively does.").

89. *Roe*, 410 U.S. at 165 ("That opinion and this one, of course, are to be read together.").

90. *Doe*, 410 U.S. at 192 (emphasis added).

91. Glendon, "From Culture Wars to Building a Culture of Life," at 5. See also Paulsen, "The Worst Constitutional Decision of All Time," at 995–996n4 ("'Health,' however, is a legal term of art in the abortion context. *Roe*'s 'life or health' exception to permissible abortion regulation was explained in *Roe*'s companion case of *Doe v. Bolton* as including a wish to abort for 'family' or 'emotional' reasons and vested the appropriate medical judgment in the agreement of the woman and the physician performing the abortion that these considerations permitted an abortion even of a viable unborn child. . . . The result of this stylized definition of 'health' is that, because of the 'health' exception to abortion regulation in the last trimester, the mother may choose abortion for essentially any personal, family, or emotional reason, even in the last three months of pregnancy.").

92. See *Women's Medical Professional Corp. v. Voinovich*, 130 F.3d 187, 209–210 (6th Cir. 1997) ("importance of giving the physician discretion to decide whether an abortion is necessary"; finding health exception in state statute was too restrictive, unconstitutionally limited "the physician's discretion to determine whether an abortion is necessary to preserve the woman's health . . ."), cert. denied, 523 U.S. 1036 (1998). See also Tierney, "Post-Viability Abortion Bans and the Limits of the Health Exception"; Wassom, Comment, "The Exception That Swallowed the Rule?" However, after the Supreme Court's decision in 2007 in *Gonzales v. Carhart*, approximately eleven states have enacted a prohibition of abortion after twenty weeks.

93. See, e.g., *Planned Parenthood v. Heed*, 390 F.3d 53, 59 (1st Cir. 2004) ("a statute regulating abortion must contain a health exception in order to survive constitutional challenge"), rev'd on other grounds, *Ayotte v. Planned Parenthood*, 546 U.S. 320 (2006); *Planned Parenthood v. Owens*, 287 F.3d 910, 918 (10th Cir. 2002) ("the current state of the law is that state abortion regulations must provide an exception for the protection of the health of pregnant women. . . .").

94. This is basically what happened in 2005 in the New Hampshire parental notice case, *Ayotte v. Planned Parenthood*, 546 U.S. 320 (2006). The First Circuit applied the "health" exception to strike down New Hampshire's parental notice law, stating "a statute regulating abortion must contain a health exception in order to survive constitutional challenge." *Planned Parenthood v. Heed*, 390 F.3d 53, 59 (1st Cir. 2004). The Supreme Court in *Ayotte* overturned the First Circuit and reinstated the law for other reasons, without, however, clarifying the "health" definition. *Ayotte v. Planned Parenthood*, 546 U.S. 320, 327–338 (2006) ("a State may not restrict access to abortions that are 'necessary, in appropriate medical judgment, for preservation of the life or health of the mother'"). As the First Circuit's opinion indicates, no state regulation of abortion can stand if the *Doe* definition of "health" is required in state regulations because it vests the provider with complete discretion to ignore the law.

95. See, e.g., *Thornburgh v. American College of Obstetricians and Gynecologists*, 737 F.2d 283, 299 (3d Cir. 1984) ("It is clear from the Supreme Court cases that 'health' is to be broadly defined" (citing *Doe v. Bolton*)), aff'd, 476 U.S. 747 (1986); *Women's Medical Professional Corp. v. Voinovich*, 130 F.3d 187, 209–210 (6th Cir. 1997) ("importance of giving the physician discretion to decide whether an abortion is necessary"; finding health exception unconstitutionally limited "the physician's discretion to determine whether an abortion is necessary to preserve the woman's health. . . ."), cert. denied, 523 U.S. 1036 (1998).

96. R. Beck, "*Gonzales, Casey* and the Viability Rule."

97. *Planned Parenthood v. Casey*, 505 U.S. 833, 870 (1992) ("We conclude the line should be drawn at viability, so that before that time the woman has a right to choose to terminate her pregnancy. We adhere to this principle for two reasons. First, as we have said, is the doctrine of stare decisis. Any judicial act of line-drawing may seem somewhat arbitrary, but *Roe* was a reasoned statement, elaborated with great care.").

Chapter Five

1. Reid, Ryan, and Benirschke, *Principles and Management of Human Reproduction*, at 274.

2. Clerk Memo from "RLJ" to Justice Douglas, October 27, 1971, 1 p., William O. Douglas Papers, Library of Congress, Box 1590, Folder 5.

3. Marie McCullough, "More Trouble for Abortion Doctor, This Time in Pennsylvania," *Philadelphia Inquirer*, July 21, 2010, available at: http://articles.philly.com/2010-07-21/news/24967879_1_steven-chase-brigham -abortion-clinics-medical-license.

4. Second Amended Complaint, *Zallie v. Brigham*, #CAM-L-5528–04 (Superior Court of New Jersey, Law Division, Camden County October 18, 2001).

5. See Forsythe and Presser, "The Tragic Failure of *Roe v. Wade*"; Horan, Forsythe, and Grant, "Two Ships Passing in the Night"; Fried, *Order and*

Law, at 80–81 (calling *Roe* "a relentless series of non sequiturs and ipse dixits.").

6. An early critique of the medical statistics relied on by the Justices is Destro, "Abortion and the Constitution," at 1295–1303. See also Friendly, "The Courts and Social Policy" (criticizing the Court's reliance in *Roe* on data that was not part of the record); Miller and Barron, "The Supreme Court, the Adversary System, and the Flow of Information," at 1189–1201 (criticizing the Court's reliance in *Roe* on data that was not part of the record).

7. *Roe v. Wade*, 410 U.S. 113, 163 (1973) ("the State's important and legitimate interest in the health of the mother" becomes "compelling . . . in the light of present medical knowledge . . . at approximately the end of the first trimester. This is so because of the now-established medical fact, referred to above at 149, that until the end of the first trimester mortality in abortion may be less than mortality in normal childbirth. It follows that, from and after this point, a State may regulate the abortion procedure to the extent that the regulation reasonably relates to the preservation and protection of maternal health.")

8. Dellapenna, *Dispelling the Myths*, chapter 1, 29–56.

9. Ibid., 89–124.

10. Dellapenna identifies the "real breakthrough" with "the invention in the 1880s of Thorolf Hager's dilator that made the dilation and curettage procedure (a 'D & C') safe and accurate. . . . Sometime around 1890, the D & C began to be used to initiate abortions, but only around World War I did it become a common means [of] inducing abortions, use[d] by non-medical abortionists as well as by physicians." Dellapenna, *Dispelling the Myths*, at 333.

11. Ibid., 332–337, 453–454nn11–13.

12. Thorp, Hartmann, and Shadigian, "Long-Term Physical and Psychological Health Consequences of Induced Abortion."

13. Ibid.

14. Ibid.

15. Ibid.

16. Ibid.

17. See Shadigian and Bauer, "Pregnancy-Associated Death" (citing Reardon, Ney, Scheuren, et al., "Deaths Associated with Pregnancy Outcome"; Gissler et al., "Pregnancy-Associated Deaths in Finland 1987–1994"; Gissler et al., "Injury, Deaths, Suicides and Homicides"; Gissler and Hemminki, "Pregnancy-Related Violent Deaths.").

18. See, e.g., *ACOG Executive Board statement May 1968*: "It is emphasized that the inherent risk of such an abortion is not fully appreciated both by many in the profession and certainly not by the public. . . . The public should realize that in countries or societies that permit abortion on demand, many, if not the majority, are performed in physicians' offices. Under these circumstances it is reasonable to conclude that the mortality from this operation may exceed the maternal mortality of the United States and Canada while the incidence of serious complications is substantial." Quoted in Hilgers, "The Medical Hazards of Legally Induced Abortion," at 58.

ACOG Minority Report issued May 1969: "The inherent risks of a therapeutic abortion are serious and may be life-threatening; this fact should be fully appreciated by both the medical profession and the public. In nations where abortion may be obtained on demand, a considerable morbidity and mortality have been reported." Ibid., at 59.

19. See, e.g., *Royal College of Obstetricians and Gynaecologists (RCOG) March 1966 Statement:* "Those without specialist knowledge, and these include members of the medical profession, are influenced in adopting what they regard as a humanitarian attitude to the induction of abortion by a failure to appreciate what is involved. They tend to regard induction of abortion as a trivial operation free from risk. In fact, even to the expert working in the best conditions, the removal of an early pregnancy after dilating the cervix can be difficult, and is not infrequently accompanied by serious complications. This is particularly true in the case of the woman pregnant for the first time. . . . For women who have a serious medical indication for termination of pregnancy, induction of abortion is extremely hazardous and its risks need to be weighed carefully against those involved in leaving the pregnancy undisturbed. Even for the relatively healthy woman, however, the dangers are considerable." "Legalized Abortion: Report by the Council of the Royal College of Obstetricians and Gynaecologists," *British Medical Journal* 1 (April 2, 1966): 850–854, at 851. Quoted in Hilgers, "The Medical Hazards of Legally Induced Abortion," at 59.

RCOG 1970 Statement: "The risks of any of the currently available methods of terminating pregnancy, which involve general anesthesia, have always been recognized by gynaecologists but have been dismissed by others as non-existent and imaginary. The long-term hazards to physical well-being require follow-up studies which so far have not been undertaken in this country. Nevertheless, reports from other countries where abortion on demand has been the rule for several years show that late physical ill-effects are not uncommon." Ibid., at 59.

RCOG Consultants Report (1970): "Eight maternal deaths occurred in relation to 27,331 terminations of pregnancy during the year 1968–69. This gives a mortality rate of 0.3 per thousand (30/100,000), which is higher than the maternal mortality rate (including abortions, criminal or otherwise) for all the pregnancies in England and Wales at the comparable time. A statement issued by the Secretary of State of Parliament on 4 February 1970, reveals a similar state of affairs in respect to about 54,000 induced abortions notified from all sources during 1969; among these there were 15 maternal deaths." Ibid., at 60.

20. See, e.g., *Medical Society of the State of New York March 1970 Statement:* "The Medical Society of the State of New York would like to caution all physicians that an abortion performed after the twelfth week of gestation is fraught with tremendous danger." Ibid. at 59.

21. Tietze and Lehfeldt, "Legal Abortion in Eastern Europe." See also Group for the Advancement of Psychiatry, *The Right to Abortion*, at 7 (citing Garrett Hardin's 1964 speech at the University of California, Berkeley: "Hardin

points out that in Hungary, where legal abortion is readily available (and where the vacuum technique has been introduced), the death rate in more than a quarter of a million cases is less than 6 per 100,000. This contrasts with 17 deaths per 100,000 in the U.S. resulting from the removal of tonsils and adenoids, and with 24 deaths per 100,000 in the U.S. resulting from childbirth and its complications.") A copy of this report is contained in the William O. Douglas Papers, Library of Congress, Box 1508. Tietze later became a member of the board of directors of the Association for the Study of Abortion (ASA), funded by John D. Rockefeller III, and, in 1973, Tietze was awarded, along with his wife, Sarah Lewit, the Margaret Sanger Award from Planned Parenthood Federation of America (PPFA). See http://en.wikipedia.org/wiki/Margaret_Sanger_Awards#1981.

22. See *People v. Belous*, 80 Cal. Rptr. 354, 458 P.2d 194, 200–201n7 (1969) (stating "[i]t is now safer for a woman to have a hospital therapeutic abortion during the first trimester than to bear a child," citing Tietze and Lehfeldt, "Legal Abortion in Eastern Europe"; Kolblova, "Legal Abortion in Czechoslovakia"; Mehland, "Combating Illegal Abortion in the Socialist Countries of Europe," and admitting "[t]here are, of course, no comparable data in the United States."); *Babbitz v. McCann*, 310 F.Supp. 293, 301 (E.D. Wis. 1970) (citing *Belous* decision, not any medical study); *Poe v. Menghini*, 339 F.Supp. 986, 994n24 (D. Kan. 1972) (stating that "Plaintiffs' evidence indicates that the abortion procedure is among the safest of surgical procedures," citing without reference a "survey" that abortion is "2.7 times safer than childbirth"); *YWCA v. Kugler*, 342 F.Supp. 1048, 1074 and n. 112 (D. N.J. 1972) (stating that "abortion in the first trimester . . . is almost seven times safer than carrying the pregnancy to term" citing Tietze, "Mortality with Contraception and Induced Abortion"); *Abele v. Markle*, 342 F.Supp. 800, 801n6 (D. Conn. 1972) (stating risk of childbirth "[s]ubstantially greater than abortion in the first three months of pregnancy," citing the decisions in *YWCA v. Kugler, Belous*, and Tietze (1969)).

23. Justice Peter's opinion in *People v. Belous*, 458 P.2d 194, 199n7 (1969).

24. Tietze and Lehfeldt, "Legal Abortion in Eastern Europe"; Kolblova, "Legal Abortion in Czechoslovakia"; Mehland, "Combating Illegal Abortion in the Socialist Countries of Europe."

25. Garrow, *Liberty and Sexuality*, at 492–493.

26. Ibid., at 500.

27. The fifteen papers cited by Roy Lucas in Section IV of his Supplemental Appendix (nos. 43–56) are: Bumpass and Westoff, "The 'Perfect Contraceptive' Population"; Lerner, "Geographic Distribution of Need"; Muller, "Socioeconomic Outcomes of Restricted Access to Abortion"; Forssman and Thuwe, "One Hundred and Twenty Children Born"; Hall, "Abortion in American Hospitals"; Hall, "Therapeutic Abortion, Sterilization, and Contraception"; Margolis, "Therapeutic Abortion Follow-Up Study"; Walter, "Psychologic and Emotional Consequences of Elective Abortion"; Eastman and Hellman, *Williams Obstetrics*, 1085; Tietze, "Mortality

with Contraception and Induced Abortion"; Tietze, "Abortion Laws and Abortion Practices in Europe"; Margolis and Overstreet, "Legal Abortion without Hospitalization"; H. Harvey and B. Pyle, "On the Healthiness of Four Thousand Abortions in a Free-Standing Clinic" (unpublished); Goldsmith and Margolis, "Aspiration Abortion without Cervical Dilation"; Penfield, "Abortion under Paracervical Block."

The Lucas Supplemental Appendix is not reprinted in Mersky and Hartman, eds., *A Documentary History:* Roe v. Wade. It is available in the U.S. Supreme Court Library, access to which is limited to Supreme Court bar members.

28. "Peer-review" is a standard requirement of the best medical journals. It means that, as part of the editorial process before publication, the manuscript is read and critically analyzed and revised by reviewers, sometimes anonymous, who are experts in the particular area of the technical medical issues.

29. Justice William J. Brennan, "Memorandum re: Abortion Cases," December 30, 1971, in William J. Brennan Papers, Library of Congress, Box I: 285, Folder 9.

30. Transcript, First *Roe* Argument, at 22 (Jay Floyd: "There have been statistics furnished to this Court in various briefs from various groups, and from medical societies of different groups of physicians and gynecologists. . . . These statistics have not shown me, for instance—for example, that abortion is safer than normal childbirth. They have not shown me that there are not emotional problems that are very important, resulting from an abortion."); ibid. at 25 (Jay Floyd: "Now as I previously informed the Court, the statistics—or the people who prepare the statistics, and the different statistics are . . . not in conformity in connection with the medical aspects of abortion; that is, whether or not it's safer. There are some statistics that say it is and statistics that say it's not.").

31. Transcript, First *Doe* Argument, at 14. Hear the audio at www.oyez.org.

32. Transcript, Second *Doe* Argument, at 6.

33. *Black's Law Dictionary*, 986 (rev. 4th ed., 1968) ("The act by which a court, in conducting a trial, or framing its decision, will, of its own motion, and without the production of evidence, recognize the existence and truth of certain facts, having a bearing on the controversy at bar, which, from their nature, are not properly the subject of testimony, or which are universally regarded as established by common notoriety. . . .").

34. *Roe*, 410 U.S. at 149n44.

35. *Doe*, 410 U.S. at 190.

36. Tietze and Lehfeldt, "Legal Abortion in Eastern Europe"; Tietze, "Mortality with Contraception and Induced Abortion," 6–8; Tietze, "United States: Therapeutic Abortions, 1963–1968," 5–7; Potts, "Postconceptive Control of Fertility," 967; "Abortion Mortality—New York City," *Morbidity and Mortality Weekly Report* 20 (June 12, 1971): 208–209; Mehland, "Combating Illegal Abortion in the Socialist Countries of Europe"; Kolblova, "Legal Abortion in Czechoslovakia."

37. None of the seven sources was cited in the "Brief of the American College of Obstetricians and Gynecologists," in Mersky and Hartman, eds., *A Documentary History: Roe v. Wade*, 2:18. Tietze's 1969 article was cited by a number of briefs, including Lucas's Supplemental Appendix in Doe, the Charles brief on behalf of the National Legal Program on Health Problems of the Poor (Mersky and Hartman, eds., *A Documentary History: Roe v. Wade*, 2:98), Planned Parenthood Federation of America's first brief (ibid., 2:282). The New York City data was included in an appendix of the brief of State Communities Aid Association (ibid., 2:393ff.) and cited in Planned Parenthood Federation of America's Supplemental brief (ibid., 2:337–338).

38. They first appear as "Rider 16" amending the fifth draft opinion of the same date. See William O. Douglas Papers, Library of Congress, Box 1589, Folder 3 (6th draft in *Doe v. Bolton*, dated January 24, 1972, Rider 16 attached), Box 1590, Folder 4.

39. Five of the articles are then cited: the New York City data ("Abortion Mortality—New York City," *Morbidity and Mortality Weekly Report* 20 (June 12, 1971): 208, 209); the 1969 Tietze article; Tietze and Lehfeldt, "Legal Abortion in Eastern Europe"; Kolblova, "Legal Abortion in Czechoslovakia," and Mehland, "Combating Illegal Abortion in the Socialist Countries of Europe." Three of them had been cited by the California Supreme Court in *Belous*. See note 24 above and accompanying text.

40. *Doe*, 410 U.S. at 216–217n5 (Douglas, J., concurring).

41. Blackmun letter to Douglas, May 1972, William O. Douglas Papers, Library of Congress; One-page memo on New York City data to Blackmun with Blackmun handwritten edits, Harry A. Blackmun Papers, Library of Congress, Box 151, Folder 8.

42. See "Memorandum to the Conference, November 21, 1972, Re: No. 70-18—*Roe v. Wade*" with "1972 fall edition," 34n44, Blackmun Papers, Box 151, Folder 6.

43. *Roe*, 410 U.S. at 149 (emphasis added).

44. Ibid., at 163.

45. Ibid., at 163 (emphasis added).

46. Tietze and Lehfeldt, "Legal Abortion in Eastern Europe."

47. Watson Bowes, M.D., also pointed out the following flaws with the Tietze and Lehfeldt paper: "Abortion mortality varied widely among the European countries: from 6/100,000 in Czechoslovakia where abortions were performed largely on healthy women to 68/100,000 in Sweden where abortions were performed largely for medical indications. These abortion mortality rates were compared to maternal mortality from complications of pregnancy and childbirth (exclusive of induced abortion) in the years 1952–1957 in a number of European and Western countries ranging from 24/100,000 in white women in the U.S. to 175/100,000 in women in Japan. There were very few comparative data for induced abortion mortality and pregnancy-related mortality from the same country: in Sweden abortion mortality was 68/100,000 and childbirth mortality was 31–55/100,000.

There were no comparative data in populations matched for age, socio-economic status and medical complications." Author interview; analysis on file with the author.

48. See, e.g., *YWCA v. Kugler*, 342 F.Supp. 1048, 1074n112 (D. N.J. 1972) (quoting from Tietze, "Mortality with Contraception and Induced Abortion," 6, "Maternal Mortality . . . from childbirth . . . 20 deaths per 100,000 pregnancies. . . . Mortality associated with legal abortions performed in hospitals, at an early stage of gestation: 3 deaths per 100,000 abortions, based on current statistics from eastern Europe. . . ."); *Rosen v. Louisiana State Board of Medical Examiners*, 318 F.Supp. 1217, 1227n10 (E.D. La. 1970) (citing Tietze).

49. Tietze, "Mortality with Contraception and Induced Abortion" (Japan, Czechoslovakia, Hungary). This is sometimes mis-cited as "Morality with Contraception . . .". See, e.g., *Abele v. Markle*, 342 F.Supp. 800, 802n6 (D. Conn. 1972) (citing "Tietze, Morality [*sic*] with Conception [*sic*] and Induced Abortion . . .").

50. "This paper's conclusion was based on the numbers shown in Table 1, which in turn were dependent on the maternal mortality rate of 20/100,000 and the legal abortion mortality rate of 3/100,000. Tietze derived the rate of 20 deaths per 100,000 pregnancies in three steps:

1. starting from the rate of 18 deaths per 100,000 live births in U.S. in 1964–66 (he did not provide citation for the data), then
2. increased this rate by one third based on data from U.K. to account for deaths "associated" with pregnancy and childbirth (again no citation for the U.K. data, so it is not known what is the time period for the U.K. data), bringing the rate to 24/100,000, and then
3. decreased the rate one sixth to account for spontaneous fetal deaths (again no citation for the one-sixth rate, and it is not known when and where this data was taken from), thereby getting the 20/100,000 rate.

"The legal abortion mortality rate of 3/100,000 was derived from abortion numbers in Czechoslovakia, Hungary and Slovenia in 1957–1967, with citation from a Planned Parenthood publication (in press).

"Hence, Tietze is mixing and matching numbers from different countries (U.S., U.K., Czechoslovakia, Hungary, Slovenia and who knows where) and from different time period (1964–66, 1957–67, and who knows when). As indicated in comment 3 above, vigorous data analysis on abortion mortality requires comparative analysis with data adjusted for factors such as country, age, socio-economic status and medical complications etc. Absent such vigorous analysis, . . . Tietze is playing magic with the numbers here, and Tietze's methodology indicates that his research is of poor quality, if not outright useless." Analysis of Hon-Man Lee on file with the author.

51. Instead, Tietze cites another paper, "in press," which purports to provide data on abortion mortality in "Czechoslovakia, Hungary, and Slovenia, 1957–1967," though even that is for abortions "performed in hospital, at an

early stage of gestation": Tietze, "Abortion Laws and Abortion Practices in Europe."

52. Tietze, "United States: Therapeutic Abortions, 1963–1968," at 7.

53. Ibid. (emphasis added).

54. Potts, "Postconceptive Control of Fertility," at 967. Potts wrote in the 1970 book *Abortion*: "The illegal abortionist has played an essential role in the evolution of modern industrial urban living, with its lower birth rates, intensive education, and nuclear family system." Potts, Diggory, and Peel, *Abortion*, at 272.

55. Potts claims that "it is well-established that, when an operation is carried out early in pregnancy in a situation where it is legal on social as well as medical grounds and where the operation is common and the surgeons are experienced, then the mortality is substantially lower than that of childbirth." Potts, "Postconceptive Control of Fertility," at 967 (citing Table 2 on "Legal Abortion Mortality," which purports to have data for Denmark, Sweden, England and Wales, Yugoslavia, Japan, Czechoslovakia, and Hungary.) He cites a mortality rate in England of 36/100,000, for "surgeons in the NHS who perform a few abortions," and a rate of 14.2/100,000 for "the few surgeons who do many abortions in private practice." (ibid., 967). But there is no reference to any published paper, let alone a peer-reviewed one. Like Tietze, Potts cites a study by Lindahl on abortion in Sweden, but no such study is listed in the references. With no citation of authority of any kind, Potts states:

> Death rates for illegal abortions are difficult to establish because neither the numerator nor the denominator can be established with accuracy, but it is unlikely that the death rate attributable to criminal abortion is less than 50 or 100/100,000 illegal abortions and it is likely that, in many communities, the death rate for clandestine abortions may reach or exceed 1,000/100,000. (Ibid., 968)

For the death rate from illegal abortions in Sweden, he cites a 1950 paper—again, unpublished in any medical journal, let alone being a peer-reviewed study. He asserts that "twenty-eight per cent of 352 illegal abortions studied in Sweden were admitted to hospital" and there were "six deaths (1.7%)." But he notes that "as the data were obtained from imprisoned abortionists, [citing a 1950 Swedish Department of Interior Report] fatal complications were probably over-represented and, in developed countries, the death rate from illegal abortions may be one in 1,000 or less." (ibid., 968). Again, he gives no citation for that assertion. Most of his assertions on data are undocumented. He compares Sweden to Chile and the death rate in "developed" countries versus "developing" countries, and uses Chile as an example of the latter, asserting an "annual death rate attributable to abortion per 100,000 women aged 15–44 is over 20, which is between 20-fold and 40-fold the rate found in developed countries, where contraception is widely used, hospital facilities are better, and abortion, whether legal or illegal, is more likely to be induced by a medically qualified practitioner" (ibid., 968) and then claims that in "a developed country with good contraceptive usage and adequate hospital care, abortions (whether legal or illegal) kill one woman or less per 100,000 of the total population in the age group 15–44 per year." Again, he provides no citation. Finally, Potts addresses "risks of abortion in the total pattern of fertility control" in four rather disjointed paragraphs. No reference is made to specific short-term risks or to any long-term risks from abortion. He refers to a 1969 report from Britain (unpublished in a medical journal and not peer-reviewed) entitled "Report on Confidential Enquiries into Maternal Deaths in England and Wales, 1964–66." And he asserts that "deaths from abortion, nearly all of which are induced, have come to represent the largest single cause of maternal mortality in Britain," citing a specific figure of 133 of 597 deaths "attributable to abortion." He then shifts to advocating contraception and sterilization to reduce "risk to life." In regard to the comparison of mortality from abortion and childbirth, Potts thus provides virtually no data that can be analyzed or verified.

56. See, e.g., Siener and Mahoney, "Coordination of Outpatient Services," at 48 (percent of patients lost to followup); Pakter, O'Hare, Nelson, and Svigir, "A Review of Two Years' Experience in New York City," at 47, 63.

57. Kolblova, "Legal Abortion in Czechoslovakia."

58. Ibid. (citing a 1965 paper published by Cernoch).

59. Justice Blackmun's final citation, of Lader's book *Abortion*, was nothing if not ironic. Lader's third chapter, pp. 17–23, was on the safety of hospital abortion in the first trimester, and the Court had just struck down Georgia's hospitalization requirement and created a right to abortion that extended to viability and beyond. Lader cited "data" from the Soviet Bloc countries and Scandinavia. None of the studies he cites was peer-reviewed, and the data were "reported" second-hand through comments made in American journals by Hall, Rosen, and Gold. Some of the data came from Lader's own "survey," which was not peer-reviewed. See Lader, *Abortion*, at 180. Lader began to mouth the mantra. Based on this back-of-the-envelope "data" on hospital abortion in the first trimester, Lader concluded "it is safer to have a hospital abortion than to have a baby." Ibid. at 18.

60. Willson's *Obstetrics and Gynecology*, 4th ed. (1971), never cites this claim, nor Hellman and Pritchard, eds., *Williams Obstetrics*, 14th ed. (1971), nor *Novak's Textbook of Gynecology*, 8th ed. (1970), nor Danforth's *Textbook of Obstetrics and Gynecology*, 2nd ed. (1971), nor Greenhill's *Obstetrics*, 14th ed.

61. *Doe*, 410 U.S. at 208.

62. Clerk RLJ Memo to Justice Douglas, Box 1590, Folder 5.

63. One-page memo on New York City abortion data, Harry A. Blackmun Papers, Library of Congress, Box 151, Folder 8.

64. Yarbrough, *Harry A. Blackmun*, at 143, 152, 346; Greenhouse, *Becoming Justice Blackmun*, at 107.

65. *Roe*, 410 U.S. at 149n44.

66. U.S. Circuit Court Judge Henry J. Friendly, reputed to be the greatest federal judge in the 1970s who never made it to the Supreme Court, pointedly criticized the Justices for their reliance in *Roe* on social science and medical data that was not part of the record:

> [T]he main lesson I wish to draw from the abortion cases relates to procedure—the use of social data offered by appellants and amici curiae for the first time in the Supreme Court itself. . . . The Court's conclusion in *Roe* that "mortality rates for women undergoing early abortions, where the procedure is legal, appear to be as lower as or lower than the rates for normal childbirth" rested entirely on materials not of record in the trial court, and that conclusion constituted the underpinning for the holding that the asserted interest of the state "in protecting the woman from an inherently hazardous procedure" during the first trimester did not exist. . . . If an administrative agency, even in a rulemaking proceeding, had used similar materials without having given the parties a fair opportunity to criticize or controvert them at the hearing stage, reversal would have come swiftly and inexorably. . . . The Court should set an example of proper procedure and not follow a course which it would condemn if pursued by any other tribunal. (Friendly, "The Courts and Social Policy," at 36–37)

67. See note 77 infra.
68. See Thorp, "Public Health Impact." The problem with the mechanical comparison of the maternal mortality rate and the abortion mortality rate was first presented to the Supreme Court in 2006 in an amicus curiae brief filed by the American Center for Law and Justice in *Gonzales v. Carhart*, 550 U.S. 124 (2007), *Gonzales v. Planned Parenthood Federation of America*, 2005 U.S. Briefs 1382.
69. Letter of Julie Louise Gerberding, M.D., M.P.H., Director, Centers for Disease Control, July 20, 2004, reprinted in Brief Amicus Curiae of the American Center for Law and Justice in *Gonzales v. Carhart*, 550 U.S. 124 (2007), *Gonzales v. Planned Parenthood Federation of America*, 2005 U.S. Briefs 1382. See also Thorp, "Public Health Impact."
70. See, e.g., Chang et al., "Pregnancy-Related Mortality Surveillance" ("Pregnancy-related mortality ratios were calculated by using the number of deaths . . . (numerator) and live-birth data (denominator) . . ."").
71. This is explained in a brief filed in the Supreme Court in 2006 in *Gonzales v. Carhart*:

> For example, a woman who dies from an ectopic pregnancy will count as a maternal death but will not count for purposes of the live birth total. Even though many women survive ectopic pregnancies, the supposed maternal mortality rate for all ectopic pregnancies will be infinitely high. There will be *some* maternal

deaths in the numerator but *no* live births in the denominator, yielding an infinitely large fraction. Obviously, this is erroneous. Moreover, this error will distort the overall maternal mortality rate by adding to the numerator (deaths) while not adding to the denominator (live births). Notably, ectopic pregnancies are the leading cause of deaths in the first trimester. See, e.g., www.cdc.gov/mmwr/preview/mmwrhtml/00035709.htm (Current Trends Ectopic Pregnancy—United States, 1990–92 (CDC Jan. 27, 1995)). Hence, this is no trivial distortion. And the far greater number of women who survive an ectopic pregnancy will not be counted at all. Women who suffer miscarriages and die from associated complications will likewise be counted as maternal deaths, but neither they nor the vastly larger number of women who survive miscarriages will count toward the baseline, which requires live birth. The abortion mortality rate, by contrast, counts all abortion procedures, thus maintaining a fuller base (denominator) for rate computation. *See* www.cdc.gov/mmwr/preview/mmwr.html/ss5212a1.htm (Abortion Surveillance—United States 2000 (CDC Nov. 28, 2003)) (hereinafter, "Abortion Surveillance 2000") ("National case-fatality rates were calculated as the number of known legal induced abortion-related deaths per 100,000 reported legal induced abortions").

See Brief of American Center for Law and Justice, in *Gonzales v. Carhart, Gonzales v. Planned Parenthood Federation of America*, 2005 U.S. Briefs 1382.

72. Letter of Julie Louise Gerberding, M.D., M.P.H., Director, Centers for Disease Control, July 20, 2004, reprinted in Brief Amicus Curiae of the American Center for Law and Justice, in *Gonzales v. Carhart*, 550 U.S. 124 (2007), *Gonzales v. Planned Parenthood Federation of America*, 2005 U.S. Briefs 1382.

73. A peer-reviewed scientific study published in May 2012 in *PLoS ONE*, the online journal dedicated to "accelerating the publication of peer-reviewed science," looked at maternal mortality data in Chile over the fifty years between 1957 and 2007, and found that various factors, including education and childbirth delivery by skilled attendants, were important for reducing maternal mortality. The authors also found that legalized abortion was not a factor. Chile has long prohibited abortion. Even after Chile tightened its abortion prohibition in 1989, maternal mortality in Chile dropped significantly. See Koch, Thorp, Bravo, et al., "Women's Education Level."

74. Dellapenna, *Dispelling the Myths*, at 455.

75. Thorp, Hartmann and Shadigian, "Long-Term Physical and Psychological Health Consequences of Induced Abortion," at 76–77 ("Informed Consent Implications").

76. Dellapenna, *Dispelling the Myths*, at 455n15.

77. See, e.g., the websites of the National Abortion Federation, the Alan

Guttmacher Institute, the American Civil Liberties Union, Planned Parenthood, the Kaiser Family Foundation, and abortion providers. The Kaiser Family Foundation, for example, cities an abortion mortality rate of "0.6 per 100,000 abortions," and, "[f]or comparison," a risk of maternal death from childbirth of "6.7 per 100,000 deliveries." See Fact Sheet: Abortion in the U.S. (Oct. 2002) (available at www.kff.org/womenshealth/loader.cfm?url=/commonspot/security/getfile.cfm&PageID=14090).

Chapter Six

1. Calderone, "Illegal Abortion as a Public Health Problem," at 949. For a more extensive treatment of some of the issues in this chapter, see Forsythe, "The Effective Enforcement of Abortion Law before *Roe v. Wade*."
2. Dellapenna, *Dispelling the Myths*, at 702.
3. "David [Tundermann] memo to Roy [Lucas], Re Legislative Purpose," August 5, 1971, Roy Lucas Abortion Litigation Papers, Box 13, Olin Memorial Library, Wesleyan University. The memo is also quoted by Garrow, *Liberty and Sexuality*, at 853–854n41, and by Dellapenna, *Dispelling the Myths*, at 683–684.
4. *Roe v. Wade*, 410 U.S. 113 (1973), at 150.
5. See generally, Maeda, ed., *The Fetus as a Patient '87*; Kurjak, ed., *The Fetus as a Patient*; Harrison, Golbus, and Filly, *The Unborn Patient*; Volpe, *Patient in the Womb*; Harrison, Adzick, Longaker, et al., "Successful Repair In Utero."
6. Schulman, "Treatment of the Embryo and the Fetus in the First Trimester."
7. See generally, Dellapenna, *Dispelling the Myths*; Forsythe, "Homicide of the Unborn Child."
8. Dellapenna, *Dispelling the Myths*, at 125–256 (chapters 3, 4, and 5).
9. Patricia G. Miller, *The Worst of Times*, at 19.
10. Transcript, First *Doe* Argument, at 6.
11. Forsythe, "Homicide of the Unborn Child."
12. It was reported in 1855 that "The signs of abortion, as obtained by an *examination of the female*, are not very certain in their character. It is seldom, indeed, that an examination of the living female is had, and especially at a period early enough to afford any valuable indications. When abortion occurs in the early months, it leaves but slight and evanescent traces behind it." Mohr, *Abortion in America*, at 72 (quoting Francis Wharton and Moreton Stille, *Treatise on Medical Jurisprudence* (1855), at 277). See also Forsythe, "Homicide of the Unborn Child."
13. Forsythe, "Homicide of the Unborn Child."
14. Ibid.; *Showery v. State*, 690 S.W.2d 689, 693–694 (Tex. Ct. App. 1985) (modern definition of live birth).
15. As late as the first decade of the twentieth century, conferences of the American Medical Association recorded expressions of frustration by physicians that the public still held to the notion that the life of the child began with quickening and that the truth that human life began with conception was not widely

understood. See, e.g., Dorsett, "Criminal Abortion in its Broadest Sense," 957 (recounting statement during discussion by R. W. Holmes, M.D., of Chicago: "The fact should be taught that life begins with conception and not with quickening. . . . Many now make themselves believe that there is no life until the movements are felt." Ibid. at 961 ("If our statutes are to accomplish the results they should we must first educate the public mind and morals to the belief that conception means human life, and that the interruption or destruction of that conception means murder just as much as if the child had been murdered with a bludgeon after it had been delivered into the world.").

16. Cf. Blackstone, *Commentaries on the Laws of England*, 1:125 (concluding in a section on "The Rights of Persons" that "[l]ife is the immediate gift of God, a right inherent by nature in every individual; and it begins in contemplation of law as soon as an infant is able to stir in the mother's womb" with Blackstone, *Commentaries on the Laws of England*, 4:198, in a section on "Public Wrongs": "To kill a child in it's [*sic*] mother's womb, is now no murder, but a great misprision: but if the child be born alive, and dieth by reason of the potion or bruises it received in the womb, it is murder in such as administered or gave them.").

17. See, e.g., Williams, *The Sanctity of Life and the Criminal Law*, at 152 ("Abortion before quickening was no crime."); Leavy, "Criminal Abortion: Facing the Facts," 355n1 (citing Williams, supra).

18. Dellapenna, *Dispelling the Myths*, at 200. See also Rafferty, *Roe v. Wade: The Birth of a Constitutional Right*.

19. Means, "The Law of New York Concerning Abortion"; Means, "The Phoenix of Abortional Freedom." NARAL was first the National Association for the Repeal of Abortion Law, then the National Abortion Rights Action League, and is now the National Abortion and Reproductive Rights Action League. See Wolfgang Saxon, "Cyril C. Means, 73, a Specialist in Laws Regarding Abortion," *New York Times*, October 6, 1992, http://www.nytimes.com/1992/10/06/nyregion/cyril-c-means-73-a-specialist-in-laws-regarding-abortion.html.

20. See Dellapenna, *Dispelling the Myths*; Rafferty, *Roe v. Wade: The Birth of a Constitutional Right*; Byrn, "An American Tragedy"; Destro, "Abortion and the Constitution"; Gavigan, "The Criminal Sanction as It Relates to Human Reproduction"; Forsythe, "Homicide of the Unborn Child."

21. *Rex v. de Bourton* [The Twinslayer's Case], Y.B. Mich. 1 Edw. 3, fl. 28 (K.B. 1327); *Rex v. Anonymous* [The Abortionist's Case], in Sir Anthony Fitzherbert, *Graunde Abridgement tit. Corone*, f. 268, p. 263 (1st ed. 1516) (K.B. 1348).

22. Dellapenna, *Dispelling the Myths*; Destro, "Abortion and the Constitution"; Byrn, "An American Tragedy."

23. Numerous cases of prosecution for abortion at common law date back to the 1200s. Dellapenna, *Dispelling the Myths*, at 130–140. See also Rafferty,

Roe v. Wade: *The Birth of a Constitutional Right*. There is stronger evidence, beginning in the 1500s, that elective abortion was treated as a crime. Dellapenna, *Dispelling the Myths*, at 177–178 (citing *R. v. Lichefeld*, K.B. 27/974, Rex. m.4 (1505). In two other cases, a man was indicted for encouraging a woman to take an abortifacient and a female abortionist was sentenced to death for performing an abortion by "witchcraft." Ibid. at 178–181 (citing *R. v. Wodlake*, K.B. 9/513/m.23, K.B. 9/513/j.23d (1530), K.B. 29/162/m.11d (1531); *R. v. Turnour*, Assize 35/23/29 (Essex 1581)). In the 1600s, a woman was indicted for self-abortion but received a general pardon. Ibid. at 193–194 (citing *R. v. Webb* (Q.B. 1602), Calender of Assize Rec., Surrey Indictments, Eliz. I, at 512 (no. 3146) (J. Cockburn ed. 1980)). As attorney general, Edward Coke prosecuted a man for murder after a child was born alive but died after an abortion. *Regina v. Sims*, 75 Eng. Rep. 1075 (Q.B. 1601). In 1732, there was a misdemeanor conviction for an abortion before quickening. Dellapenna, *Dispelling the Myths*, at 233–237 (citing case of *Rex v. Beare*, 2 *The Gentleman's Magazine* 931 (Aug. 1732)); see also Gavigan, "The Criminal Sanction as It Relates to Human Reproduction" (citing *Beare*).

24. Gavigan, "The Criminal Sanction as It Relates to Human Reproduction," at 23. Means ignored the medical context of the quickening and born-alive rules and completely misinterpreted the two fourteenth-century cases, The Twinslayer's Case and The Abortionist's Case, on which he based his whole theory. See Dellapenna, *Dispelling the Myths*, at 195–203; Gavigan, "The Criminal Sanction as It Relates to Human Reproduction," at 22–23.

25. *Roe*, 410 U.S. at 135, 136.

26. *Roe*, 410 U.S. at 140.

27. Three months after *Belous*, Cyril Means recorded an encounter with Chief Justice Traynor at a bar association meeting in a letter to Roy Lucas, Marcia Lowry, and Nancy Stearns from the San Francisco Hilton on December 29, 1969. Means wrote: "Moments one would like to live over again: 1. Last night, when Chief Justice Traynor slapped me on the shoulder and said, "That was a *wonderful* article!" (emphasis in original). Roy Lucas Abortion Litigation Papers, Box 1, Olin Memorial Library, Wesleyan University.

28. See also Rafferty, Roe v. Wade: *The Birth of a Constitutional Right*.

29. Justin Dyer, "Reckoning with *Roe v. Wade*," Public Discourse, January 24, 2011, www.thepublicdiscourse.com.

30. See generally, Keown, *Abortion, Doctors and the Law*; Dellapenna, *Dispelling the Myths*.

31. In addition to his misinterpretation of the common law, Means's second thesis, based on New York abortion law, was that "the sole historically demonstrable legislative purpose behind" nineteenth-century American abortion statutes "was the protection of pregnant women from the danger to their lives imposed by surgical or potional abortion. . . ." Means, "The Phoenix of Abortional Freedom," at 336. The Court in *Roe* adopted this proposition wholesale. In response to Means's conclusions, Sauer has

noted, "[i]t would be a gross distortion . . . to believe that all or even most nineteenth-century laws were mainly attempts to protect women's health. . . . The medical profession was in the forefront of the drive for more restrictive laws, and, while the dangers of abortion to a woman were almost unfailingly pointed out, the main concern of doctors was with the safety of the foetus." Sauer, "Attitudes to Abortion in America, 1800–1973," at 57–58.

32. Dellapenna, *Dispelling the Myths*, at 299–302.

33. See, e.g., *People v. Reinard*, 33 Cal.Rptr. 908, 912, 220 Cal.App.2d 720, 724 (Cal. Dist. Ct. App. 1963) ("The abortee is considered the victim of the crime."); *Basoff v. State*, 208 Md. 643, 654, 118 A.2d 917, 923 (1956) ("regarded by the law as a victim of the crime, rather than as a participant in it."); *Thompson v. United States*, 30 App.D.C. 352, 363 (1908) ("She is regarded as his victim, rather than an accomplice.").

34. Dellapenna, *Dispelling the Myths*, at 273.

35. See, e.g., *State v. Barnett*, 249 Or. 226, 228, 437 P.2d 821, 822 (Or. 1968); *Zutz v. State*, 52 Del. 492, 160 A.2d 727 (Del. 1967); *People v. Kutz*, 9 Cal.Rptr. 626, 187 Cal.App.2d 431 (Cal. Dist. Ct. App. 1961) (not an accomplice); *State v. Miller*, 364 Mo. 320, 261 S.W.2d 103 (Mo. 1953); *People v. Stone*, 89 Cal.App.2d 853, 202 P.2d 333 (Cal. Dist. Ct. App. 1949); *People v. Clapp*, 24 Cal.2d 835, 151 P.2d 237 (Cal. 1944); *Commonwealth v. Sierakowski*, 154 Pa.Super.Ct. 321, 327, 35 A.2d 790, 793 (Pa. 1944) ("not an accomplice or *particeps criminis*."); *People v. Blank*, 283 N.Y. 526, 29 N.E.2d 73 (N.Y. 1940); *State v. Burlingame*, 47 S.D. 332, 337, 198 N.W. 824, 826 (S.D. 1924) (regarded as victim rather an accomplice or participant); *State v. McCurtain*, 52 Utah 63, 172 P. 481 (Utah 1918); *Gray v. State*, 77 Tex. Crim. 221, 229, 178 S.W. 337, 341 (Tex. Crim. App. 1915) (not an accomplice); *Seifert v. State*, 160 Ind. 464, 67 N.E. 100 (Ind. 1903); *State v. Pearce*, 56 Minn. 226, 230, 57 N.W. 652, 653 (Minn. 1894) ("She was the victim of a cruel act."); *People v. McGonegal*, 136 N.Y. 62, 32 N.E. 616 (N.Y. 1892); *People v. Vedder*, 98 N.Y. 630, 632 (1885).

The only apparent exception was in Alabama, in *Trent v. State*, 15 Ala. App. 485, 73 So. 834 (Ala. Ct. App. 1916). As in the other cases, the woman's guilt was not the issue but whether her status as an accomplice prevented the introduction of evidence without corroboration. The court concluded, however, that the woman should be considered an accomplice because the statute would otherwise lose its moral force. This rationale, however, never influenced other states. See also *Dykes v. State*, 30 Ala.App. 129, 1 So.2d 754 (Ala. Ct. App. 1941); *Steed v. State*, 27 Ala.App. 263, 170 So. 489 (Ala. Ct. App. 1936).

36. Wohlers, *Women and Abortion*, at 2.

37. See, e.g., *Commonwealth v. Weible*, 45 Pa. Super. 207; 1911 Pa. Super. Lexis 24 (1911); *Crissman v. State*, 93 Tex. Crim. 15, 245 S.W.2d 438 (1922).

38. *State v. Barnett*, 249 Or. 226, 228, 437 P.2d 821, 822 (Or. 1968) ("The acts prohibited are those which are performed upon the mother rather than any

action taken by her. She is the object of the acts prohibited rather than the actor.").

39. See, e.g., *Commonwealth v. Weible*, 45 Pa. Super. 207; 1911 Pa. Super. Lexis 24 (1911); *Crissman v. State*, 93 Tex. Crim. 15, 245 S.W.2d 438 (1922). See Pollak, *The Criminality of Women*, at 45–46 ("The best illustration of the degree to which the criminal behavior of the abortee herself is disregarded by our law-enforcing agencies can be found in the proceedings against the Pacific Coast Abortion Ring . . . in the thirties. Not one of the women who had engaged the services of this organization seems to have been prosecuted, however."); Linton, "Enforcement of State Abortion Statutes after *Roe*," at 163–164n31 (citing *Commonwealth v. Weible*, 45 Pa. Super. 207 (1911); *Crissman v. State*, 245 S.W.2d 438 (Tex. Crim. App. 1922)).

Idaho apparently passed an abortion law in 1972 that penalized women's participation in abortion, but it was apparently never enforced. See *McCormack v. Heideman*, Case No. 4:11-cr-00397-BLW (D. Idaho September 23, 2011). So, at the time of *Roe*, only four states had court decisions or statutes treating the woman as an accomplice for the purpose of corroborating her testimony against the provider (Alabama, Idaho, Ohio, and Wisconsin), but none of these states prosecuted women. See *Dykes v. State*, 1 So.2d 754 (Ala. Ct. App. 1941); *Waite v. State*, 4 Ohio App. 451 (1915); *State v. Adams*, 43 N.W.2d 446 (Wis. 1950). Idaho Code § 18-606(2) (1972).

40. See, e.g., S.D. Compiled Laws Ann. § 22-17-2 (1967).

41. There were additional policy reasons, beyond the evidentiary necessities, to not treat women as accomplices. If a woman was considered an accomplice, she might be unable to recover for the negligence of an abortionist. And allowing such negligence suits, despite the fact that a woman had submitted to an abortion, would supplement the criminal law and aid law enforcement. Cf. Wohlers, *Women and Abortion*, at 8–10 (citing *Gaines v. Wolcott*, 119 Ga.App. 313, 167 S.E.2d 366 (Ga. Ct. App. 1969), aff'd, 225 Ga. 373, 169 S.E.2d 165 (Ga. 1969) (woman can sue abortionist for negligence); *Henrie v. Griffith*, 395 P.2d 809 (Okla. 1965); *Castronovo v. Murawsky*, 3 Ill.App.2d 168, 120 N.E.2d 871 (Ill. App. Ct. 1954) (woman cannot recover for negligence); *True v. Older*, 227 Minn. 154, 34 N.W.2d 200 (1948) (woman could recover); *Nash v. Meyer*, 54 Idaho 283, 31 P.2d 273 (Idaho 1934) (woman cannot recover for negligence); *Martin v. Morris*, 163 Tenn. 10, 42 S.W.2d 207 (Tenn. 1931) (woman cannot recover); *Andrews v. Coulter*, 163 Wash. 429, 1 P.2d 320 (Wash. 1931) (woman could not recover damages for abortion but could recover for negligent treatment after abortion); *Martin v. Hardesty*, 91 Ind.App. 239, 163 N.E. 610 (Ind. App. 1928) (estate could recover after abortion death); *Szadiwicz v. Cantor*, 257 Mass. 518, 154 N.E. 251 (Mass. 1926) (woman could not recover); *Milliken v. Heddesheimer*, 110 Ohio St. 381, 144 N.E. 264 (Ohio Ct. App. 1924) (woman's estate could recover); *Hunter v. Wheate*, 63 App.D.C. 206, 289 F. 604 (D.C. Cir. 1923) (woman could not recover even if she was not an accomplice); *Lembo v. Donnell*, 117 Me. 143, 103 A. 11 (Me. 1918) (woman could recover); *Larocque v. Couneim*, 87 N.Y.S.

625, 42 Misc. 613 (N.Y. Sup. Ct. 1904); *Wells v. New England Mutual Life Ins. Co.*, 191 Pa. 207, 43 A. 126 (Pa. 1899) (estate cannot recover); *Goldnamer v. O'Brien*, 98 Ky. 569 (1896) (cannot recover from person urging her to have abortion); *Miller v. Bayer*, 94 Wis. 123, 68 N.W. 869 (Wis. 1896) (woman could recover)).

42. See Reagan, "'About to Meet Her Maker,'" at 1244 ("[n]o evidence suggests that officials consciously designed their investigative procedures to harass women. . . .").

43. See Dellapenna, *Dispelling the Myths*, at 430–438; Olasky, *Abortion Rites*; Olasky, *The Press and Abortion*; Forsythe, "The Effective Enforcement of Abortion Law before *Roe v. Wade*"; Harris, "A Functional Study of Existing Abortion Laws," at 91n18.

44. Ibid.

45. "Illegal Operation Nets M.D. Three Years," *New York Journal-American*, May 5, 1950; "Three Doctors and 4 Others Plead Guilty of Abortion," *New York Tribune*, February 18, 1952; "Charges M.D., Hospitals Hush Abortion Cases," *New York Post*, December 10, 1953.

46. Amen, "Some Obstacles to Effective Legal Control of Criminal Abortions."

47. See *In re Lurie*, 263 App. Div. 660, 34 N.Y.S.2d 247 (N.Y. App. Div. 1942); *In re Madden*, 24 N.Y.S.2d 127 (N.Y. App. Div. 1940). See also Bennett and Amen, *A Presentment on the Suppression of Criminal Abortions*; Bates, "The Abortion Mill," at 163–166.

48. See *In re Abortion in Kings County*, 206 Misc. 830, 135 N.Y.S.2d 381 (1954); *Application of Grand Jury of Kings County*, 286 A.D. 270, 143 N.Y.S.2d 501 (1955).

49. Calderone, ed., *Abortion in the United States*, at 35.

50. Ibid., at 37.

51. See generally, Charles O'Hara, *Fundamentals of Criminal Investigation* (1956), 477 (Chapter 26: Abortion); Harry Soderman and John O'Connell, *Modern Criminal Investigation* (1952), 298 (Abortion); John Adam and J. Collyer Adam, *Criminal Investigation: A Practical Textbook* (1934), 447 (Abortion).

52. See, e.g., *People v. Buffum*, 40 Cal.2d 709, 256 P.2d 317 (Cal. 1953) (overturning two convictions for conspiracy to commit abortion in California when the abortions were performed in Mexico, over the dissent of Justice Shenk). There were publicized trials of abortionists in many states, including Massachusetts, New York, California, and Oregon. These included Dr. G. Lotrell Timanus of Baltimore; Dr. Roy Odell Knapp of Akron, Ohio; Dr. Robert Spencer in Ashland, Pennsylvania; Geraldine Rhoades in Sacramento in the 1950s; Sophie Miller in St. Louis in 1951; Mary Pagan in Cincinnati in 1953; Grace Schaumer in Wichita in 1954; Robert Spencer in Pennsylvania, Sidney Knight in Louisiana, Drs. Moretti, Morin, Molinaro, and Raymond in New Jersey, and Dr. Robert Livingston in 1972 (Garrow, *Liberty and Sexuality*, at 367); Mucie in Missouri; Leon Belous in California; and Laura Miner in San Diego. *Time*, March 12, 1956, at 46. In Detroit in August 1956, Dr. Ed Keemer "and three other physicians

were arrested in an abortion raid by city police." He was "convicted and sent to prison in 1959." Garrow, ibid., at 362. Nathan Rappaport (who authored an anonymous memoir, *The Abortionist*, under the pseudonym Dr. X) was imprisoned during the summer of 1971. John Shriver Gwynne was repeatedly arrested in California in 1970 (Garrow, ibid., at 433) and police raided Dr. Lee Kennan's clinic in Madison, Wisconsin, as late as April 1971 (Garrow, ibid., at 487–488). In Portland, Oregon, the famous Ruth Barnett (Bush) was repeatedly prosecuted. The notion that she practiced openly with no legal problems is contradicted by the plain facts. She was "first raided in 1951" and arrested again in 1956 and arrested and convicted in the summer of 1966. Her case went up to the Oregon Supreme Court in 1968, where her conviction was upheld. *State v. Barnett*, 249 Or. 226, 437 P.2d 821 (1968). See also Garrow, *Liberty and Sexuality*, at 362; Dellapenna, *Dispelling the Myths*, at 561–565; Forsythe, "The Effective Enforcement of Abortion Law."

53. Patricia G. Miller, *The Worst of Times*, at 9.

54. Ibid., at 32.

55. *Finding constitutional: Nelson v. Planned Parenthood*, 19 Ariz.App. 142, 505 P.2d 580 (Ariz. Ct. App. 1973); *Cheaney v. State*, 259 Ind. 138, 285 N.E.2d 265 (Ind. 1972); *State v. Abodeely*, 179 N.W.2d 347 (Iowa 1970); *Sasaki v. Commonwealth*, 485 S.W.2d 897 (Ky. 1972); *State v. Campbell*, 263 La. 1058, 270 So.2d 506 (La. 1972); *State v. Moretti*, 52 N.J. 182, 244 A.2d 499 (N.J. 1968); *State v. Kruze* (Ohio 1972), vacated and remanded, 410 U.S. 951 (1973); *Spears v. State*, 257 So.2d 876 (Miss. 1972); *Rodgers v. Danforth*, 486 S.W.2d 258 (Mo. 1972); *Byrn v. New York City*, 31 N.Y.2d 194, 286 N.E.2d 887 (N.Y. 1972); *State v. Munson*, 86 S.D. 663, 201 N.W.2d 123 (S.D. 1972); *Thompson v. State*, 493 S.W.2d 913 (Tex. Crim. App. 1971); *State v. Bartlett*, 128 Vt. 618, 270 A.2d 168 (Vt. 1970).

   Finding unconstitutional: People v. Belous, 71 Cal.2d 954, 458 P.2d 194 (Cal. 1969); *State v. Barquet*, 262 So.2d 431 (Fla. 1972); *People v. Nixon*, 42 Mich. App. 332, 201 N.W.2d 635 (1972), remanded, *People v. Nixon*, 389 Mich. 809, 387 N.W.2d 921 (1973); *Beecham v. Leahy*, 130 Vt. 164, 287 A.2d 836 (Vt. 1972).

56. See, e.g., *State v. Menillo*, 362 A.2d 962 (1975) (Connecticut prosecution against non-physician); *State v. Sulman*, 165 Conn. 556, 339 A.2d 62 (1973) (prosecution against licensed physician for 1969 abortion); *Cheaney v. State*, 285 N.E.2d 265 (Ind. 1972), vacated and remanded, 410 U.S. 951 (1973); *People v. Bricker*, 389 Mich. 524, 208 N.W.2d 172 (1973); *State v. Hultgren*, 295 Minn. 299, 204 N.W.2d 197 (1973); *State v. Norflett*, 67 N.J. 268, 337 A.2d 609 (1975); *Commonwealth v. Jackson*, 454 Pa. 429, 312 A.2d 13 (1973).

57. Savage, *Turning Right*, at 80.

58. *Statistical Abstract of the United States* (112th ed., 1992), 180 (Table No. 287) (83,000 forcible rapes in 1980, 102,600 in 1990; 23,000 murders in 1980, 23,400 in 1990; 566,000 robberies in 1980, 639,000 in 1990; 673,000 aggravated assaults in 1980, 1,055,000 in 1990).

59. See, e.g., Williams, *The Sanctity of Life and the Criminal Law*, at 212 ("The effect of the law is not to eliminate abortion but to drive it into the most

undesirable channels."); Leavy and Kummer, "Criminal Abortion: Human Hardship," 126 and n. 20 ("[f]or professional abortionists there exists a low rate of prosecution and an even lower rate of conviction"); Leavy, "Criminal Abortion: Facing the Facts," at 359.

60. Sedgwick, *Law Enforcement Planning*, 42. ("The technique [for determining the optimal amount of crime in society] involved identifying the physical and psychic harm from crime, the costs of apprehension and conviction, the costs of wrongful conviction and punishment, and the social costs of punishing criminals." Ibid. at 56.)

61. Andenaes, "General Prevention," at 180.

62. Reagan, "'About to Meet Her Maker.'"

63. Dellapenna, *Dispelling the Myths*, at 484 ("Abortion's very illegality leaves us with no means of determining its actual incidence."), 548–558 ("The Incidence of Abortion between 1950 and 1970"). A good overview is contained in Grisez, *Abortion: The Myths, the Realities, and the Arguments*, at 35–65.

64. Leavitt, *Brought to Bed*, 24.

65. Pollak, *The Criminality of Women*, at 45; Rosenberg, *The Hollow Hope*, at 353–355.

66. See Dellapenna, *Dispelling the Myths*, at 338–340, 484, 489–490, 1148; Olasky, *Abortion Rites*. For example, in 1903, a physician at the annual meeting of the Illinois Medical Society stated that criminal abortion was "startlingly frequent." Others opined that "every physician" is, at one time or another, approached to perform elective abortion. In 1904, at a Chicago Medical Society symposium, a physician estimated that "probably 6,000 to 10,000 abortions [are] induced in Chicago every year." Bacon, "Chicago Medical Society, Regular Meeting." In 1921, a physician speaking at the 34th Annual Meeting of the American Association of Obstetricians and Gynecologists and Abdominal Surgeons in St. Louis stated that it had been estimated that there were 80,000 criminal abortions annually in New York City. Others in 1921 suggested that criminal abortion was "practiced extensively."

67. National Committee on Maternal Health, *The Abortion Problem*, at 155 (Dr. Herman N. Bundesen). A 1991 review by Gerald Rosenberg listed more than twenty estimates of illegal abortions nationwide between 1936 and 1972. Nearly all of these estimates were by either abortion advocates or by newspapers and magazines without original research. Rosenberg unfortunately took them at face value, despite his concession: "while most students of illegal abortion agree that the number was substantial, they have differed markedly on the figures. By the mid-1960's, however, the range seemed to be settling around 1 million. For obvious reasons of partisanship and lack of hard data, these figures can only be taken as very rough estimates." Rosenberg, *The Hollow Hope*, at 353–355 (Appendix 6). See also Solinger, *The Abortionist*, at ix.

68. Grisez, *Abortion: The Myths, the Realities, and the Arguments*, at 35–42.

69. Taussig, *Abortion, Spontaneous and Induced*. Taussig's book was sponsored by the National Committee on Maternal Health, Inc. *Time* magazine blessed

his book as "authoritative" and concluded that his calculations resulted from "careful figuring." *Time*, March 6, 1936, at 52.

70. Olasky, *The Press and Abortion*, at 70.

71. At the April 1955 Conference at Arden House sponsored by the Planned Parenthood Federation of America, Guttmacher stated: "Taussig's book pulls out a nice round number, but when you try to analyze the formulae by which the number is derived, you could have substituted other values and gotten quite a different answer." Calderone, ed., *Abortion in the United States*, at 50.

72. National Committee on Maternal Health, *The Abortion Problem*, at 28.

73. As Dr. Robert E. Hall, president of the Association for the Study of Abortion (ASA), said in 1967: "I would quarrel with Niswander on only one point, namely, his perpetuation of Taussig's thirty-year-old claim that five thousand to ten thousand American women die every year as the result of criminal abortions. Whether this statistic was valid in 1936 I do not know, but it certainly is not now. There are in fact fewer than fifteen hundred total pregnancy deaths in this country per annum; very few others could go undetected and of these fifteen hundred probably no more than a third are the result of abortion. Even the 'unskilled' abortionist is evidently more skillful and/or more careful these days. Although criminal abortion is of course to be decried, the demand for its abolition cannot reasonably be based upon thirty-year-old mortality statistics." Hall, "Commentary," at 228.

74. National Committee on Maternal Health, *The Abortion Problem*, at 1.

75. Stix and Wiehl, "Abortion and the Public Health," at 623.

76. Calderone, ed., *Abortion in the United States*, at 39. Others also doubted the reliability of the Kinsey study. Potter, "Abortion in the United States," 94 ("The lower estimate is based on a ratio of 3.1 induced abortions per 100 pregnancies found by C. Kiser and P. K. Whelpton for their Indianapolis sample and also by D. G. Wiehl and K. Berry for a New York City sample. The upper limit is based on a ratio of 18.9 induced abortions per 100 pregnancies reported by the staff of the Institute of Sex Research [Kinsey] from their analysis of 5,293 women. The appropriateness of the upper limit is placed in doubt by an appendix in which Tietze analyzes the representativeness of the ISR respondents in relation to estimates of 1945 distributions for urban white women in the United States. Tietze concludes that the ISR respondents are usefully representative but his tables contradict this conclusion by showing not only gross differences with respect to age, education and marital status, but also and more important, tangible differences with respect to age-specific marital fertility.").

77. Calderone, ed., *Abortion in the United States*, at 180 ("Taking into account the probable trend of the abortion ratio since the interwar period, a plausible estimate of the frequency of induced abortion in the United States could be as low as 200,000 and as high as 1,200,000 per year, depending upon the assumptions made as to the incidence of abortion in the total population as compared with the restricted group for which statistical data are available,

and upon the assessment of the discretion and magnitude of bias inherent in each series of data. There is no objective basis for the selection of a particular figure between these two estimates as an approximation of the actual frequency.").

78. Ibid. at 37 ("Of course, we don't know what the total number of criminal abortions performed in the United States happens to be. . . .") (Dr. Harold Rosen); Ibid. at 18 ("The incidence of criminal abortions is not better known in Norway than in the United States, the figures we have being mostly based on estimations or guesswork.") (Dr. Bard Brekke); Ibid. at 50 ("I think we have all been penalized in our thinking by lack of actual knowledge about illegal abortion. . . . In the first place, there are no good figures that I know of that in any way depict the incidence. . . . [W]e talk a lot about the practice of illegal abortion and how it is carried on—again without any factual data.") (Alan Guttmacher); Ibid. at 70 ("We have absolutely no hope of getting reports . . . of illegal induced abortions unless the woman requires subsequent hospital care, and . . . not even with all of these.") (Carl Erhardt, director of Records and Statistics, Department of Health, New York City); Ibid. at 110 ("[T]he number of [illegal abortions] which we are aware of must be only a fraction of the problem, and it is doubtful if any combination of sources can give us reliable figures on this purposefully hidden area.") (Dr. Sophia Kleegman).

   See also Harold Rosen, ed., *Therapeutic Abortion*, at 3–6 (330,000 illegal abortions) (Dr. Russell Fisher); Harold Rosen, ed., *Abortion in America*, at 180 ("There are no accurate figures on the number of spontaneous and induced abortions that occur annually in the United States.") (Dr. Manfred Guttmacher); Cooke et al., eds., *The Terrible Choice*, at 40–46 (based on proceedings of the International Conference on Abortion, held in Washington, D.C., September 6–8, 1967) (figures on criminal abortion are "based on personal estimates"; "no way has yet been found of obtaining reliable statistics that would give an exact figure for the total population").

79. Leavy and Kummer, "Criminal Abortion: Human Hardship," at 124. This seems to have been taken from Taussig's unreliable 1935 estimate, which Taussig retracted in 1942.

80. Leavy and Kummer, "Criminal Abortion: Human Hardship," at 124n7 (citing Fisher, "Criminal Abortion," in Harold Rosen, ed., *Therapeutic Abortion*, 8). Rosen's 1954 book was republished with Fisher's chapter as Harold Rosen, ed., *Abortion in America: Medical, Psychiatric, Legal, Anthropological, and Religious Considerations*. Fisher's 1954 chapter was a reprint of his 1951 article, Fisher, "Criminal Abortion." In all of these reprints, Fisher wrote: "Taussig and others have concluded that the abortion death rate during the late 1920's was about 1.2%, and amounted to over 8,000 deaths per year. Later estimates indicated that 70–75% of all deaths from criminal abortion were due to septicemia. With present day antibiotics, it seems safe to conclude that the net mortality rate has decreased to approximately one-half of one percent. This means that there were between five and six thousand deaths

from abortion in the United States last year!" Harold Rosen, ed., *Abortion in America*, at 8–9.

81. Kopp, *Birth Control in Practice*. A number of subsequent researchers and historians have emphasized the probable bias of Kopp's sample. Pollak, *The Criminality of Women*, at 47; National Committee on Maternal Health, *The Abortion Problem*, at 5 (statement by Halbert Dunn, M.D., the chief statistician for Vital Statistics, Bureau of the Census, at the June 1942 conference); Grisez, *Abortion: The Myths, the Realities, and the Arguments*, at 37.

82. Stix, "A Study of Pregnancy Wastage"; Stix and Wiehl, "Abortion and the Public Health." See also Stix and Notestein, *Controlled Fertility*.

83. Gebhard et al., *Pregnancy, Birth and Abortion*.

84. Leavy and Kummer, "Criminal Abortion: Human Hardship," at 125 (citing Calderone, *Abortion in the United States*).

85. Calderone, "Illegal Abortion as a Public Health Problem," at 949.

86. Guttmacher, ed., *The Case for Legalized Abortion Now*, at 69, 71–72.

87. Rosenberg, *The Hollow Hope*, at 355 (citing Tietze, "Two Years' Experience with a Liberal Abortion Law").

88. Sklar and Berkov, "Abortion, Illegitimacy, and the American Birth Rate."

89. Calderone, "Illegal Abortion as a Public Health Problem." See also Syska, Hilgers, and O'Hare, "An Objective Model for Estimating Criminal Abortions" (Table 2) (citing National Center for Health Statistics data, showing drop in maternal deaths (from all causes) from 7,466 in 1940 to 2,697 in 1950 to 1,328 in 1960, to 684 in 1970 and 554 in 1972); Hilgers and O'Hare, "Abortion Related Maternal Mortality," at 69, 80 (Table 7); Hearings on S.J. Res. 119 and S.J. Res. 130 before the Subcommittee on Constitutional Amendments of the Committee on the Judiciary, U.S. Senate, 93rd Congress, 2nd Session (1976), 121 (Table 1) (statement of Dr. Andre Hellegers).

90. Crandall, "Three Decades of Empty Promises," at 17 (citing *Supplement to the Monthly Vital Statistics Report: Advance Reports*, Series 24, Compilations of Data on Natality, Mortality, Marriage, Divorce, and Induced Terminations of Pregnancy, No. 3, *Vital and Health Statistics*, National Center for Health Statistics (CDC), 1986).

91. See Syska, Hilger, and O'Hare, "An Objective Model for Estimating Criminal Abortions," at 168 (citing National Center for Health Statistics data, showing drop in maternal deaths *from all causes* from 7,466 in 1940 to 2,697 in 1950, to 1,328 in 1960, to 684 in 1970, to 554 in 1972); Moore and Randall, "Trends in Therapeutic Abortion."

92. Harold Rosen, ed., *Therapeutic Abortion*, at xvii. Even as Cameron purports to address the "needs" for "therapeutic" abortion, his description sweeps well beyond the traditional definition of "therapeutic" as meaning necessary to save the life of the woman.

93. See, e.g., Gold et al., "Therapeutic Abortions in New York City," at 969; Guttmacher, "The Shrinking Non-Psychiatric Indications for Therapeutic Abortion," at 12.

94. See, e.g., Guttmacher, "Therapeutic Abortion," at 119 ("Unrestricted therapeutic abortion leads to loose medical thinking. Flouting the abortion laws also acts as a springboard for unorthodox, borderline medical ethical practices."); Russell, "Changing Indications for Therapeutic Abortion."

95. Guttmacher, "Therapeutic Abortion," at 118. Furthermore, he said, "Legitimate hospitals accept in addition some cases in a quasi-legal bracket, but only accept those of crying necessity. The greater the incidence of abortion in a given institution, the greater the proportion from the quasi-group, for the truly legal cases have a more or less constant incidence all over the country." Ibid. at 119. Guttmacher was once director of the obstetrical department at Mount Sinai Hospital and a member of its therapeutic abortion committee.

   Under the notion of abortion as a part of the constitutional right of privacy, the physician is viewed as a contractual agent of the patient who submits to her request to implement her constitutional right. Contrast this with Guttmacher's sentiment in 1954: "I do not feel that the obstetrician-gynecologist is simply the patient's agent who presents her request for interruption of pregnancy without himself evaluating it. I think he should pass this request on to the hospital authorities . . . only if he is convinced of the wisdom of the request. If he thinks the procedure unjustified, it behooves the physician consulted to discuss the matter in great detail with the patient and to attempt to persuade her to his viewpoint. If he fails to do this he has no further responsibility in the case." Ibid. at 119.

96. Calderone, "Illegal Abortion as a Public Health Problem," at 948–949. See also Schaefer, "Pregnancy and Tuberculosis"; Schaefer, "Results Following Therapeutic Abortion in Pulmonary Tuberculosis." Leavy and Kummer wrote in 1962: "the advance of medical science has made rare the situation where illness in a pregnant woman cannot be treated so that her life is not immediately endangered by the pregnancy." Leavy and Kummer, "Criminal Abortion: Human Hardship," at 126 (citing Guttmacher, "The Shrinking Non-Psychiatric Indications for Therapeutic Abortion"). By the 1960s, it was widely acknowledged that, with advances in medical science, it was hardly ever necessary to perform an abortion to preserve a woman's life. Russell, "Changing Indications for Therapeutic Abortion." See also Daniel Callahan, "Abortion: Some Ethical Issues" ("Except in the now-rare instances of a direct threat to a woman's life, an abortion cures no known disease and relieves no medically classifiable illness."); "Abortion: The Doctor's Dilemma," 35 *Modern Medicine* 12, 14–16 (April 24, 1967) (quoting Dr. David Decker of Mayo Clinic based on poll of 40,000 American physicians in 1967: there were "few, if any, absolute medical indications for therapeutic abortion in the present state of medicine").

97. Miller, *The Worst of Times*, at 327.

98. Calderone, *Abortion in the United States*, at 65.

99. Ibid. at 37, 67–68. Solinger repeated these figures in *The Abortionist*, but without attribution, merely referring to "a study."

100. Calderone, "Illegal Abortion as a Public Health Problem," at 949 (emphasis added).

101. "The technique of the well-accredited criminal abortionist is usually good. They have to be good to stay in business, since otherwise they would be extremely vulnerable to police action." Guttmacher, *Babies by Choice or by Chance*, at 216.

102. See, e.g., Leavy, "Criminal Abortion: Facing the Facts," at 357 (between five and ten thousand annually) (citing Mills, "A Medicolegal Analysis of Abortion Statutes").

103. Burtchaell, *Rachel Weeping*, at 65. See also Garrow, "*Roe v. Wade* Revisited," 71, 77 (noting the correction of "a commonly-made abortion-rights error by rightly noting that in the years before *Roe* only a few hundred women per year died from illegal abortions, not the thousands upon thousands that some writers—[Cass] Sunstein in this volume says 'as many as 10,000' annually—wrongly claim").

104. Bernard N. Nathanson, *Aborting America*, at 193.

Chapter Seven

1. Quoted in Randolph, "Before *Roe v. Wade*: Judge Friendly's Draft Abortion Opinion," at 1060 (excerpt from Friendly's draft opinion). See, generally, Dorsen, *Henry Friendly*.

2. Quoted in B. Brodt and M. McCabe, "Abortion Investigation Set," *Chicago Tribune*, November 13, 1978, at 1. A more extensive treatment of cases of abortion morbidity and mortality from 1973–1992 can be found in Cunningham and Forsythe, "Is Abortion the 'First Right' for Women?"

3. The 63-page presentment and 281-page grand jury report are available online. See Report of the Grand Jury, In re County Investigating Grand Jury XXIII, Misc. No. 0009901-2008 (Pa. Com. Pl. Jan. 14, 2011), available at http://www.phila.gov/districtattorney/PDFs/GrandJuryWomensMedical .pdf. See also Melinda Henneberger, "Kermit Gosnell's Pro-Choice Enablers (Is This What an Industry that Self-Regulates Looks Like?)," *Politics Daily*, January 23, 2011, http://www.politicsdaily.com/2011/01/23/ kermit-gosnells-pro-choice-enablers-how-clinics-become-death-t/.

4. See Pamela Zekman and Pamela Warrick, "The Abortion Lottery," *Chicago Sun-Times*, November 14, 1978, at 11. See also Bopp and Coleson, "The Right to Abortion," 312–315 (summarizing the *Sun-Times* series).

5. "Abortionist Sentenced to Three Years in Prison," *Rocky Mountain News*, December 4, 1981; *Denver Post*, May 22, 1981.

6. Debbie Sontag, "Do Not Enter," *Miami Herald*, September 17, 1989, at 8. "In 1983, four women died from botched abortions at Hipolito Barreiro's notorious Biscayne Blvd. clinic called the Women's Care Center . . ." Ibid., at 22.

7. Inez Herron died on November 3, 1983, in Bakersfield (NRL News, November 23, 1986); Cora Mae Lewis died on December 3, 1983 (Los Angeles County Coroner Report #83-15079); Patricia Chacon died on March 3, 1984

(Los Angeles County Coroner Report #84-2948); Yvonne Tanner died on August 14, 1984 (Los Angeles County Superior Court #C-55-5261); Mary Pena died on December 16, 1984 (Los Angeles County Coroner Report #84-16016). See Department of Vital Statistics, California Vital Statistics: 1986 (Table A-2, "Maternal Deaths by Selected Causes of Death, California, 1960–1984 (By Place of Residence").

8. *Vuitch v. Furr*, 482 A.2d 811 (D.C. Ct. App. 1984). See Margaret Engel, "Doctor Faces License Battle," *Washington Post*, November 11, 1984, at B1; Margaret Engel, "Dr. Vuitch Surrenders D.C. License," *Washington Post*, December 21, 1984, at B1.

9. *Dept. of Professional Regulation v. Obasi*, No. 89-2096 (Ill. Dept. of Prof. Reg. October 25, 1989).

10. Erica Kae Richardson died on March 2, 1989 (*Prince George's Journal*, May 30, 1990); Gladys Estanislao died on May 23, 1989; Debra M. Gray died on July 15, 1989 (Aetha Hill, "Two Tragedies Raise Doubts about Suitland Clinic; Abortion Patient, Left Paralyzed, Files Suit," *Washington Post*, August 13, 1990, at A1).

11. Gil, "Clinic Can Resume First Trimester Abortions," *Louisville Courier Journal*, November 1, 1990, B1; Gil, "Doctor at Abortion Clinic Not Disciplined by Board," *Louisville Courier Journal*, May 17, 1991, at B1.

12. Belkin, "Manhattan Doctor Loses State License over Abortion Cases," *New York Times*, November 26, 1991, at A12.

13. *The State* (Columbia, S.C.), February 20, 1994, 1B. See *Greenville Women's Clinic v. Bryant*, 222 F.3d 157 (4th Cir. 2000), cert. denied, 531 U.S. 1191 (2001). The clinic director, Dr. Jesse Johnce Floyd, was involved in a notorious late-term abortion that sparked the Supreme Court case of *Anders v. Floyd*, 440 U.S. 445 (1979). For a full account of this case, see Noonan, *A Private Choice*. The South Carolina regulations of 1995 did not go into effect until April 2003. A second suit was filed against the South Carolina regulations after the Supreme Court denied cert in 2001 (531 U.S. 1191 (2001)). The district court ruled for the plaintiffs again, and the Fourth Circuit again reversed in 2002 (2002 U.S. App. Lexis 27311 (4th Cir. November 15, 2002)), and the Supreme Court again denied cert. on April 28, 2003. *Greenville Women's Clinic v. Comm'r, S.C. Dep't of Health and Envt.*, 538 U.S. 1008 (2003). *The State* (Columbia, S.C.), April 29, 2003, 1B. See also Peter Nyikos, "The Saga of the South Carolina Abortion Clinic Regulation Act," *Life and Learning* 15 (2005): 363, available at http://www.uffl.org/vol15/nyikos05.pdf.

14. *People v. Jose Gilberto Higuera*, 244 Mich.App. 429, 625 N.W.2d 444 (2001).

15. Carol Sowers, "Examiner Says Tool Cut Womb," *Arizona Republic*, February 7, 2001, at B5. The Arizona Board of Medical Examiners had held a hearing on January 18, 1996, regarding Biskind's abortion of a prior patient on February 16–17, 1995, who died after an abortion from an 8-centimeter vertical laceration. The transcript of the 1995 hearing was published in the *Arizona Republic* after the death of Louann Herron in 1998. *State v. Biskind*,

No. CR99-00198 (Ariz. Superior Court 2001). "Abortion Doc Guilty in Woman's Death," CBSNews.com, February 11, 2001, http://www.cbsnews.com/stories/2001/02/20/national/main273313.shtml; "Abortion Doctor Is Convicted of Manslaughter in Woman's Death," *Chicago Tribune*, February 21, 2001, sec. 1, p. 20, available at http://articles.chicagotribune.com/2001-02-21/news/0102210245_1_louanne-herron-carol-stuart-schadoff-dr-john-biskind.

16. "History of Trouble at Clinic," *Arizona Republic*, January 17, 1999. See also "Abortion Clinic Owner No Stranger to Lawsuits," January 18, 1999, at http://lubbockonline.com/stories/011899/LD0632.shtml (last visited May 25, 2012).

17. Julie Marquis, "Doctor Pleads Guilty in Death after Abortion," *Los Angeles Times*, April 6, 2000, at A3; Raymond Smith, "Plea Changed to Guilty in Abortion Case," *The Press-Enterprise* (Riverside, Calif.), April 6, 2000, at A1; Jason Van Derbeken, "Guilty Plea Entered in Fatal-Abortion Trial," *San Francisco Chronicle*, April 7, 2000, at A7. Steir "had been disciplined five times between 1984 and 1996 for serious infractions, although his medical license was never suspended. One doctor who reviewed the records of Steir's disciplinary proceedings stated that Steir 'never seems to be aware of the extensive damage he is causing these patients.'" Dellapenna, *Dispelling the Myths*, at 716.

18. *Arizona Republic*, January 30, 2002, B1 (Valley and State section), discussing the re-arrest of abortionist Brian Finkel near his home on Tuesday, January 29, 2002, on new charges that he sexually molested patients seeing him for an abortion. According to the article, Finkel was accused of sexually abusing sixty-seven women at his abortion clinic. Other women made similar allegations, perhaps as many as ninety victims. *State v. Finkel*, CR 2001-015515 (Maricopa County Crim. Ct.). See Carol Sowers, "Finkel Gets 35 Years," *Arizona Republic*, January 23, 2004, at B1.

19. Sean O'Sullivan, "$2.2 million Awarded in Abortion Death," *News Journal* (Wilmington, Del.), January 16, 2002, at 1B.

20. Consent Order, In the Matter of Krishna Raganna, Board of Healing Arts of the State of Kansas, Docket No. 50-H, February 14, 2005; Final Order, Board of Healing Arts of the State of Kansas, Docket No. 50-H-58, June 14, 2005. See http://www.ksbha.org/boardactions/Years/05bdact.html (last visited October 12, 2011); http://www.ksbha.org/boardactions/Documents/rajanna3.pdf.

21. "Doctor Charged with Performing Abortions after License Was Revoked for Botching the Procedures," *Associated Press*, December 24, 2004.

22. Michelle Burhenn, "Texas Authorities Have Questions for Abortion Doctor in Wichita," *Kansas City Star*, February 23, 2005, at B2; Michelle Burhenn, "Kansas Patient's Death Gets Attention," *Kansas City Star*, February 23, 2005, at B8; Steve Painter, "Texas Seeks Records of Tiller Patient Who Died," *Wichita Eagle*, February 22, 2005, at 1B.

23. Kelli Cook, "Doctor's License Suspended for Fourth Time," Central Florida News 13, cfnews13.com, Aug. 11, 2010.

24. Tiffany Hsu, "Abortion Clinics Operator Is Charged," *Los Angeles Times*, February 8, 2008, http://www.latimes.com/news/local/la-me-abortion8feb 08,0,35683.story?page=1 (last visited May 25, 2012) (detailing investigations of Laurence Reich going back to 1979).

25. "Abortion Doctor Gets 6 Months in Woman's Death," BostonHerald.com, September 15, 2010, http://www.bostonherald.com/news/regional/view .bg?articleid=1281536.

26. Jonathan Abrams, "Abortion Procedure Caused Death of Riverside Woman, Lawsuit Alleges," *Los Angeles Times*, June 21, 2007, http://articles .latimes.com/print/2007/jun/21/local/me-abortion21 (last visited May 25, 2012).

27. "Abortion Clinics Investigated for Dumping Waste and Patient Records," FoxNews.com, March 19, 2008. See also Right to Life of Michigan, *Abortion Abuses and State Regulatory Agency Failure* (November 2011), available at: http://media.rtl.org/pdf/legislation/Abortion_Clinic_Abuses_March_2012 .pdf.

28. *Medicaid Fraud Report* (National Association of Medicaid Fraud Control Units, Washington, D.C.), September/October 2010, at 16, available at: http:// www.namfcu.net/resources/medicaid-fraud-reports-newsletters/2010 -publications/10SeptOct.pdf.

29. Courtney Perkes, "Family Sues Doctor in Abortion Death," *Orange County Register*, August 16, 2010; Courtney Perkes, "Abortion Doctor Gives Up License Again over Death," *Orange County Register*, January 25, 2011, http:// www.ocregister.com/articles/rutland-285561–death-license.html (last visited May 25, 2012).

30. Dinah Wisenberg Brin, "Abortion Doctor Accused of Murder," *Wall Street Journal*, January 20, 2011, at A5 (reporting closing in 2010, license suspended early in 2010).

31. Michael J. Feeney et al., "Queens Clinic A1 Medicine Probed after Alexandra Nunez Is Fatally Injured while Undergoing Abortion," NYDailyNews.com, January 27, 2010, http://www.nydailynews.com/news/queens-clinic-a1 -medicine-probed-alexandra-nunez-fatally-injured-undergoing-abortion -article-1.460728.

32. See Maryland Board of Physicians, "Sanctions: September 2010," (2010), 1, available at http://www.mbp.state.md.us/forms/sep10sanctions.pdf.

33. See *Washington Post*, October 15, 2010, http://www.washingtonpost .com/wp-dyn/content/article/2010/10/13/AR2010101304278.html?hpid =sec-nation.

34. In 1994, the *Chicago Tribune* reported that Brigham had been performing abortions in Pensacola and had "in the last two years had his medical license suspended in New York and Georgia and restricted in New Jersey and California amid accusations of improper procedures. And in Pennsylvania in 1992, the doctor, Steven Chase Brigham, 37, retired from the practice of medicine in an agreement worked out with state prosecutors. In New Jersey last December, the state Board of Medical Examiners placed Brigham under a number of restrictions in his abortion clinic practice after two

patients accused him of severely injuring them in the course of performing abortions." "Florida Abortionist Has Troubled Past," *Chicago Tribune*, September 30, 1994, sec. 1, p. 18.

35. "Two Maryland Abortion Doctors Face Murder Charges," CNN, December 30, 2011, http://articles.cnn.com/2011-12-30/justice/justice _maryland-abortion-doctors-murder_1_steven-brigham-abortion-clinic -fetuses?_s=PM:JUSTICE; see also Division of Occupational and Professional Licensing, Utah Department of Commerce, Media Alert, "Division of Occupational and Professional Licensing Enters Stipulation and Order with Nicola Irene Riley over Unlawful Conduct Regarding Her Utah Medical Licenses" (Aug. 31, 2011), available at http://www.commerce.utah.gov/ releases/11-08-31_opl-nicola-riley-stipulation.pdf.

36. Anthony Colarossi, "Judge Denies Orlando-Area Abortion Doctor New Trial in $36 Million Malpractice Case," *Orlando Sentinel*, August 15, 2011, available at http://articles.orlandosentinel.com/2011-08-15/news/os -abortion-doctor-ruling-20110815_1_abortion-doctor-orlando-women-s -center-malpractice-case (last visited May 25, 2012).

37. "3 at Pennsylvania Abortion Clinic Face Drug Abuse Charges," Associated Press, July 26, 2011, http://www.foxnews.com/us/2011/07/26/3 -at-pennsylvania-abortion-clinic-face-drug-abuse-charges.

38. Peter Hermann, "Doctor Arraigned in Maryland on Murder Charges in Abortion Case," *Baltimore Sun*, January 6, 2012, http://www.baltimoresun.com/ news/breaking/bs-md-abortion-doctor-arraigned-20120106,0,1944360 .story (last visited May 25, 2012).

39. Alexis Shaw, "Chicago Woman's Family Lawyers Up after Abortion-Related Death," ABC News, July 24, 2012, http://abcnews.go.com/US/chicago -womans-family-lawyers-abortion-related-death/story?id=16845276# .UBF-cNWuUQg.

40. "Documents Shed Light on Woman's Death after Abortion," CBS Chicago, July 24, 2012, http://chicago.cbslocal.com/2012/07/24/documents -shed-light-on-womans-death-after-abortion/. A series of stories on Reaves's death is covered at CBS Chicago, http://chicago.cbslocal.com/tag/tonya -reaves/.

41. *Doe v. Bolton*, 410 U.S. 179, 192 (1973) ("the medical judgment may be exercised in the light of all factors—physical, emotional, psychological, familial, and the woman's age—relevant to the well-being of the patient. All these factors may relate to health. This allows the attending physician the room he needs to make his best medical judgment."); *Colautti v. Franklin*, 439 U.S. 379, 394 (1979) ("The contested provisions in those cases [*United States v. Vuitch*, 402 U.S. 62 (1971), and *Doe v. Bolton*] had been interpreted to allow the physician to make his determination in the light of all attendant circumstances—psychological and emotional as well as physical—that might be relevant to the well-being of the patient. The present statute does not afford broad discretion to the physician."); *Women's Medical Professional Corp. v. Voinovich*, 130 F.3d 187 (6th Cir. 1997) ("The Court suggested,

however, that it favored providing broad discretion to physicians to make determinations as to 'medical necessity' in the abortion context . . ."), cert. denied, 523 U.S. 1036 (1998).

42. See, e.g., Douglas's first draft opinion of December 21, 1971 ("The District Court [in *Doe v. Bolton*] made no findings on this phase of the case. Therefore the cause must be remanded to it. . . . There may be other facets of the case which will also warrant additional findings."). William O. Douglas Papers, Library of Congress, Box 1590, Folder 4, p. 11. Justice Blackmun's clerk wrote a Bench Memo (a common device to help the Justice prepare for oral argument) three days before the first argument and told him in a section about the "Facts": "The appellees claim that no facts were actually developed at the 'proceedings,' and I can't tell from the Appendix whether there was testimony taken, or not. What facts there are arose from answers by Doe to interrogatories served on her by Slayton, some of which she answered and some of which she refused to answer; and the complaint itself, I suppose. These are in the Appendix from page 55 on." Bench Memo from GTF to Justice Blackmun, December 10, 1971, p. 9, Harry A. Blackmun Papers, Library of Congress, Box 153, Folder 1.

43. Bernard Schwartz, *The Ascent of Pragmatism*, at 299 ("Douglas said that he was inclined 'to remand to the district court. . . .' . . . Blackmun also indicated interest in Douglas's approach. 'I would be perfectly willing to paint some standards and remand for findings as to how it operates: does it operate to deny equal protection by discriminating against the poor?'").

44. This is through the procedure of having "standing to assert the constitutional rights of their patients," as the "Brief of the American College of Obstetricians and Gynecologists" in *Roe v. Wade* phrased it. Reprinted in Mersky and Hartman, eds., *A Documentary History*: Roe v. Wade 2:29n. See *Singleton v. Wulff*, 428 U.S. 106 (1976); see also Wallace, "Why Third-Party Standing in Abortion Suits Deserves a Closer Look."

45. *Planned Parenthood v. Casey*, 505 U.S. 833 (1992). See Paulsen, "The Worst Constitutional Decision of All Time"; Linton, "*Planned Parenthood v. Casey*: The Flight from Reason."

46. *Stenberg v. Carhart*, 530 U.S. 912 (2000). See Gauthier, "*Stenberg v. Carhart*."

47. *Gonzales v. Carhart*, 550 U.S. 124 (2007). See Ladwein, Note, "Discerning the Meaning of *Gonzales v. Carhart*."

48. Bernard Schwartz, *The Ascent of Pragmatism*, at 299 ("Brennan has no doubts. He would affirm the decision below [in *Doe v. Bolton*] 'as far as it goes' but would also 'go further to strike down the three-doctor thing as too restrictive.' Stewart agreed with the last point.").

49. Ibid., at 299 ("Once again, Justice Blackmun's position was ambivalent. 'Medically,' he pointed out, 'this statute [Georgia's] is perfectly workable'"); Garrow, *Liberty and Sexuality*, at 530–531 (Blackmun at Thursday, December 16, 1971 conference: "until the Georgia law had been 'ruined' by the Atlanta panel's ruling, Georgia had had 'a fine statute,'" "strikes a balance that is fair").

50. These briefs are reprinted in Mersky and Hartman, eds., *A Documentary History:* Roe v. Wade.

51. Blackmun, "Memorandum to the Conference re No. 70-40—*Doe v. Bolton*," May 25, 1972, p. 2, Harry A. Blackmun Papers, Library of Congress, Box 152, Folder 7 (emphasis in original).

52. David G. Savage, "*Roe* Ruling: More Than Its Author Intended," *Los Angeles Times*, September 14, 2005, available at http://articles.latimes.com/2005/sep/14/nation/na-abortion14 (last visited May 25, 2012).

53. Garrow, *Liberty and Sexuality*, at 501. See Mersky and Hartman, eds., *A Documentary History:* Roe v. Wade, 2:8 (listing Decker and Pratt's names on the amicus brief filed in the Supreme Court on August 17, 1971 on behalf of the American College of Obstetricians and Gynecologists et al.)

54. "Brief of the American College of Obstetricians and Gynecologists et al.," in Mersky and Hartman, eds., *A Documentary History:* Roe v. Wade, 2:28.

55. *Connecticut v. Menillo*, 423 U.S. 9 (1975).

56. Potter Stewart Papers, Yale University Library, MS 1367, Box 302, Folder 3663.

57. Ibid.

58. Ibid. (emphasis added).

59. Transcript, First *Roe* Argument, at 7.

60. Hilgers, "The Medical Hazards of Legally Induced Abortion," at 57.

61. Transcript, Second *Doe* argument, at 8.

62. Stevens, *Five Chiefs*, at 204. See generally, Dorsen, *Henry Friendly*.

63. Randolph, "Before *Roe v. Wade*: Judge Friendly's Draft Abortion Opinion." Though his papers were open to the public, the existence of Judge Friendly's draft opinion was not publicized until 2006.

64. Clerk Memo from "RLJ" to Douglas, October 27, 1971, William O. Douglas Papers, Library of Congress, Box 1590, Folder 5; one-page memo to Blackmun (undated), Blackmun Papers, Box 151, Folder 8.

65. *United States v. Vuitch*, 402 U.S. 62, 79n4 (1971) (Douglas, J., dissenting) (citing Hall, "The Truth about Abortion in New York").

66. Hall, "The Truth about Abortion in New York."

67. Brennan memo to Blackmun, May 18, 1972, William O. Douglas Papers, Library of Congress, Box 1590, Folder 5.

68. See, e.g., Gordon, "Genetical, Social and Medical Aspects of Abortion," at 728–729.

69. See *Stenberg v. Carhart*, 530 U.S. 914, 958 (2000) (Kennedy, J., dissenting) (noting Carhart's lack of credentials).

70. Transcript, Second *Roe* argument, at 9.

71. Transcript, Second *Doe* argument, at 19.

72. Brief Amicus Curiae of [223] Certain Physicians, Professors and Fellows of the American College of Obstetrics and Gynecology, filed October 15, 1971, in Mersky and Hartman, eds., *A Documentary History:* Roe v. Wade, 3:171ff.

73. "How Safe Is Abortion?," *Lancet*, December 4, 1972, at 1239–1240 (referencing an article by Stallworthy at p. 1245 of the same issue).

74. "Latent Morbidity after Abortion," *British Medical Journal*, March 3, 1973, 506 (calling "long-term effects" of abortion "latent morbidity").

75. See Wardle, "Protecting the Rights of Conscience of Health Care Providers"; Wardle, "A Matter of Conscience."

76. See Smolin, "Cultural and Technological Obstacles to the Mainstreaming of Abortion"; Emily Bazelon, "The New Abortion Providers," *New York Times Magazine*, July 14, 2010, available at www.nytimes.com/2010/07/18/magazine/18abortion-t.html?_r=1&pagewanted=all; Harris, Cooper, Rasinski, et al., "Obstetricians-Gynecologists' Objections to and Willingness to Help Patients Obtain an Abortion."

77. *Roe*, 410 U.S. at 171.

78. Letter, Edward Press, State Public Health Officer, Oregon to Harry A. Blackmun, Oct. 9, 1973, Harry A. Blackmun Papers, Library of Congress, Box 152, Folder 2.

79. See, e.g., *Word v. Poelker*, 495 F.2d 1349 (8th Cir. 1974) (St. Louis regulations); *Hallmark Clinic v. North Carolina Dep't of Human Resources*, 380 F. Supp. 1153 (E.D.N.C. 1974) (North Carolina regulations); *Friendship Center v. Chicago Board of Health*, 367 F.Supp. 594 (N.D. Ill. November 16, 1973) (Chicago regulations); *Hodgson v. Anderson*, 378 F.Supp. 1008 (D. Minn. June 27, 1974); *Arnold v. Sendak*, 416 F.Supp. 22 (S.D. In. June 15, 1976).

80. Miner, "Two More Reports of Hysterectomies after Abortions at the Friendship Center," *Chicago Sun-Times*, March 24, 1973, at 12, col. 1 (noting three women undergoing hysterectomies in March 1973, after undergoing abortions at Friendship Medical Center).

81. B. Brodt and M. McCabe, "Abortion Investigation Set," *Chicago Tribune*, November 13, 1978.

82. Pamela Zekman, "Risky Abortions: Chicago Clinics Are Exposed," *Time*, November 27, 1978, at 52.

83. *Coe v. Gerstein*, 376 F.Supp. 695 (S.D. Fla. 1974) (striking Fla. Stat. Ann. sec. 458.22(2) (1972), requiring an "approved facility" in the first trimester), appeal dismissed (U.S. No. 73-1157); *Poe v. Gerstein*, 417 U.S. 281 (1974) (U.S. No. 73-1283).

84. *Friendship Medical Center v. Chicago Board of Health*, 367 F.Supp. 594 (N.D. Ill. 1973), rev'd, 505 F.2d 1141 (7th Cir. 1974), cert. denied, 420 U.S. 997 (1975).

85. *Sendak v. Arnold*, 429 U.S. 968, 968 (1976) (White, J., dissenting). Justice White issued a strong dissent, describing the law as "requiring 'first trimester abortions to be performed by a physician in a hospital or a licensed health facility . . . which offers the basic safeguards as provided by a hospital admission, and has immediate hospital backup . . .'"; Ind. Code sec. 35-1-58.5-2(a)(1) (1975).

86. In four cases from 1973 to 1983, the Justices struck down a series of health and safety regulations: *Doe v. Bolton*, 410 U.S. 179 (1973) (invalidating two-physician concurrence, residency requirement, hospitalization requirement); *Planned Parenthood v. Danforth*, 428 U.S. 52 (1976) (invalidating standard of care); *City of Akron v. Akron Center for Reproductive Health*, 462 U.S. 416

(1983) (invalidating second-trimester hospitalization requirement); *Planned Parenthood v. Ashcroft*, 462 U.S. 476 (1983) (invalidating second-trimester hospitalization requirement).

87. See Justice White's dissent in *Sendak v. Arnold*, 429 U.S. 968 (1976), pointing out how the lower federal court had relied on a literal reading of the language in *Roe*, 410 U.S. at 163, "without inquiring whether [the Indiana regulation] was a reasonable health regulation." Ibid. See also Uddo, "A Wink from the Bench."

88. The First Circuit in 1978 struck a Rhode Island law requiring that physicians performing abortions at a clinic have privileges to practice at an accessible hospital. In the Fifth Circuit, Florida's regulations of first-trimester abortions were challenged and struck down (*Florida Women's Clinic v. Smith*, 536 F.Supp. 1048 (S.D.Fla. 1982)). Alabama's clinic regulations were challenged shortly after *Roe* and invalidated (*Mobile Women's Medical Clinic v. Board of Commissioners of Mobile*, 426 F.Supp. 331 (D.C.Ala. 1977)). The Sixth Circuit struck down Kentucky's clinic regulations in 1976 (*Wolfe v. Schroering*, 541 F.2d 523 (6th Cir. 1976)). Eight years later, in 1984, the Sixth Circuit struck down Michigan clinic regulations (*Birth Control Center v. Reizen*, 743 F.2d 352 (6th Cir. 1984)). Staffing and physical regulation of facilities were declared unconstitutional because they would increase costs and thus prices. The circuit court also struck down a prohibition on abortions in clinics after the first trimester. The Seventh Circuit's decision in the Chicago case in 1974 quickly eliminated abortion clinic regulations in Chicago, and that decision applied to Illinois, Indiana, and Wisconsin. Indiana's abortion clinic regulations were eliminated in 1976 (*Sendak v. Arnold*, 416 F.Supp. 22 (D. Ind. 1976)). The Eighth Circuit struck down Minnesota's clinic regulations (*Hodgson v. Lawson*, 542 F.2d 1350 (8th Cir. 1976)) and St. Louis's clinic regulations in 1974 (*Word v. Poelker*, 495 F.2d 1349 (8th Cir. 1974)).

89. The Civil Rights Attorney's Fees Award Act of 1976, 42 U.S.C. sec. 1988 (1976).

90. See, e.g., *Mahoning Women's Center v. Hunter*, 447 U.S. 918 (1980) (vacating and remanding, 610 F.2d 456 (6th Cir. 1979), "for further consideration in light of *New York Gaslight Club, Inc. v. Carey*, [447 U.S. 54 (1980) (regarding fees)] and *Supreme Court of Virginia v. Consumers Union*, 446 U.S. 719 (1980)." Stewart, White, Rehnquist, and Stevens dissented. Ibid. at 918. See also *Aware Woman Clinic, Inc. v. City of Cocoa Beach, Florida*, 629 F.2d 1146 (5th Cir. 1980) (involving the invalidation of a Florida city's attempt to pass clinic regulations).

91. *Planned Parenthood v. Ashcroft*, 462 U.S. 476, 488n12 (1983).

92. Ibid. at 488n12.

93. *City of Akron v. Akron Center for Reproductive Health*, 462 U.S. 416 (1983).

94. Letter from Justice Powell to Justice Brennan, March 9, 1983, Harry A. Blackmun Papers, Library of Congress, Box 369, Folder 4.

95. Letter from Justice Brennan to Justice Powell, March 8, 1983, Blackmun Papers, Box 369, Folder 4.

96. Letter from Justice Blackmun to Justice Powell, March 8, 1983, Blackmun Papers, Box 369, Folder 4.

97. *Doe*, 410 U.S. at 197 ("despite the presence of rascals in the medical profession, as in all others, we trust that most physicians are 'good' ").

98. *City of Akron v. Akron Center for Reproductive Health*, 462 U.S. 416 at 431–432 (1983) (invalidating Akron ordinance section 1870.03, requiring second-trimester abortions to be performed in a "hospital"); *Planned Parenthood v. Ashcroft*, 462 U.S. 476, 481–482 and n. 6 (1983) (invalidating Mo. Stat. section 188.025, requiring all second-trimester abortions to be performed in a "hospital").

99. *Tucson Women's Clinic v. Eden*, 379 F.3d (9th Cir. 2004). Associated Press, "Arizona Abortion Clinic Regulations to Take Effect," October 28, 2010. See also Arizona Department of Health Services Director's Blog, Posts Tagged "Abortion," http://directorsblog.health.azdhs.gov/?tag=abortion.

100. The question of congressional authority is addressed in Goldberg, "The Commerce Clause and Federal Abortion Law" and Pushaw, "Does Congress Have the Constitutional Power to Prohibit Partial-Birth Abortion?"

101. Ring-Cassidy and Gentles, *Women's Health after Abortion*, at 10–12 (citing Royal College of Obstetricians and Gynaecologists (UK), "The Care of Women Requesting Induced Abortion: 4. Information for Women" (2000), www.rcog.org.uk/guidelines/induced_abortion.html). See also Niinimaki et al., "Immediate Complications after Medical Compared with Surgical Termination of Pregnancy" (based on registry data of all women in Finland undergoing induced abortion from 2000–2006 with gestational duration of sixty-three days or less, found "medical termination is associated with higher incidence of adverse events" than surgical abortion); Sykes, "Complications of Termination of Pregnancy"; Duthie, Hobson, Tait, et al., "Morbidity after Termination of Pregnancy in First Trimester" (finding 12 percent rate of morbidity).

102. See Thorp, "Public Health Impact."

103. Jones and Kost, "Underreporting of Induced and Spontaneous Abortion in the United States."

104. Only 13 percent of women use their private insurance for abortion coverage. Seventy-four percent pay out of pocket. Rachel Laser on the *Diane Rehms Show*, October 5, 2009.

105. See Reardon, Strahan, Thorp, and Shuping, "Deaths Associated with Abortion Compared with Childbirth," at 286–291; Gissler et al., "Methods for Identifying Pregnancy-Associated Deaths," at 451 (many abortion-related deaths were not identified from death certificates).

106. Cates, Smith, Rochat, et al., "Assessment of Surveillance and Vital Statistics Data," at 204.

107. See the U.S. Standard Certificate of Live Birth, revised November 2003, available at http://www.cdc.gov/nchs/nvss/vital_certificate_revisions.htm.

108. "Since 1969, CDC has conducted abortion surveillance to document the number and characteristics of women obtaining legal induced abortions in

the United States." Pazol, Zane, Parker, et al., "Abortion Surveillance—United States, 2008."

109. Reardon, Strahan, Thorp, and Shuping, "Deaths Associated with Abortion Compared to Childbirth."

110. Megan Twohey, "State Abortion Reports Full of Recording Gaps," *Chicago Tribune*, June 16, 2011, at C1.

111. American Medical Association, Council on Scientific Affairs, "Induced Termination of Pregnancy before and after *Roe v. Wade*."

112. The Alan Guttmacher Institute (AGI) reported that "[i]n 2008, 1.21 million abortions were performed" in the United States; http://www .guttmacher.org/pubs/fb_induced/abortion.html (last visited May 26, 2012). In 2008, Planned Parenthood reported that it performed 324,008 abortions, or 26.8 percent of the abortions reported that year. Fact Sheet, September 2010, http://www.planned-parenthood.org/files/PPFA/fact_ ppservices_2010-09-03.pdf (last visited May 26, 2012).

113. See Thorp, "Public Health Impact."

114. See, e.g., the story of Holly Patterson's death after an RU-486 abortion: "Monty Patterson Critical of Planned Parenthood's Practices after Daughter's Death," Huffington Post, December 6, 2011, http://www.huffingtonpost .com/2011/12/06/monty-patterson-abortion_n_1132644.html?icid=maing -grid7%7Cmaing10%7Cdl16%7Csec1_lnk3%7CC118271 ("She was instructed by Planned Parenthood to insert 800 micrograms of misoprostol vaginally the next day, and to do it at home, not at a clinic. That is double the approved dosage of misoprostol, and it was taken vaginally instead of orally.").

115. *Choice Inc. v. Greenstein*, 691 F.3d 710 (5th Cir. 2012).

Chapter Eight

1. Calderone, "Illegal Abortion as a Public Health Problem," at 951.

2. Healy, *A New Prescription for Women's Health*, at 237.

3. Thorp, Hartmann, and Shadigian, "Long-Term Physical and Psychological Health Consequences of Induced Abortion."

4. Dellapenna, *Dispelling the Myths*, at 722ff ("*Roe* in Light of World Trends").

5. See Thorp, "Public Health Impact."

6. See Mersky and Hartman, eds., *A Documentary History:* Roe v. Wade, 3:252 (Table Four (citing Olsen, Nielsen, Ostergaard, Banner, Kaye, Rovinsky, Choate, Midak, Kotasek, Bengtsson, Menzies, and Wagatsuma)).

7. "Long term means manifesting more than two months after the procedure." Shadigian, "Reviewing the Evidence, Breaking the Silence," at 64n.

8. Republished as Harold Rosen, ed., *Abortion in America*.

9. Harold Rosen, "Psychiatric Implications of Abortion."

10. Ibid., at 446.

11. Ibid., at 448.

12. "Brief of the American College of Obstetricians and Gynecologists, the American Psychiatric Association, et al."; "National Legal Program on Health Problems of the Poor"; and "New Women Lawyers," reprinted in Mersky and Hartman, eds., *A Documentary History:* Roe v. Wade, vol. 2.

13. Fleck, "Some Psychiatric Aspects of Abortion"; N. M. Simon, "Psychological and Emotional Indications for Therapeutic Abortion"; Margolis et al., "Therapeutic Abortion Follow-Up Study"; Notman et al., "Psychological Outcome in Patients Having Therapeutic Abortions," paper presented at the Third International Congress of Psychosomatic Problems in Obstetrics and Gynecology, London, 1970; Pike, "Therapeutic Abortion and Mental Health"; White, "Induced Abortions"; Whittington, "Evaluation of Therapeutic Abortion as an Element of Preventive Psychiatry."

14. Mersky and Hartman, eds., *A Documentary History: Roe v. Wade*, at 2:3, 18 (citing Aarons, "Therapeutic Abortion and the Psychiatrist" and Moritz and Thompson, "Septic Abortion").

15. Mersky and Hartman, eds., *A Documentary History: Roe v. Wade*, at 3:65–79.

16. See Siegfried, "Psychiatric Investigation of the Sequelae of Interruption of Pregnancy" (Siegfried interviewed sixty-one women, two years after abortion, and found 13 percent to have "serious self reproach."); Ekblad, "Induced Abortion on Psychiatric Grounds" (Ekblad interviewed 479 women prior to abortion and again two and a half to three years later. At followup, he found 10 percent felt that operation unpleasant; 14 percent had mild self-reproach; and 11 percent had serious self-reproach and self-regret.); D. Beck, "Interruption of Pregnancy and Guilt Feelings" (Beck interviewed fifty women four months after legal abortion and nine had suppressed remorse which was expressed as various psychosomatic symptoms.); Niswander and Patterson, "Psychologic Reaction to Therapeutic Abortion" (Niswander and Patterson interviewed seventeen women, eight months after abortion for rubella. Eleven of the seventeen reacted unfavorably and eight had long-term negative experience.).

17. See Thorp, "Public Health Impact."

18. Ibid.

19. Priscilla Coleman, *Evaluation of APA Report 2008*, p. 3 (on file with the author).

20. Royal College of Obstetricians and Gynaecologists (UK), *The Care of Women Requesting Induced Abortion* (2000). (Short-term risks include infection and damaged reproductive organs.)

21. Thorp, Hartmann, and Shadigian, "Long-Term Physical and Psychological Health Consequences of Induced Abortion," at 68.

22. Ibid. at 68.

23. Ibid.

24. Ibid. at 69.

25. Ibid. at 77.

26. Ibid. at 68.

27. Ibid. at 77.

28. Ibid. at 67 (Abstract).

29. Ibid. at 70.

30. Ibid.

31. Thorp, Hartmann, and Shadigian, "Long-Term Physical and Psychological Health Consequences of Induced Abortion"; Fergusson, Horwood, and

Ridder, "Abortion in Young Women and Subsequent Mental Health"; Fergusson, Horwood, and Boden, "Abortion and Mental Health Disorders"; Coleman, Coyle, Shuping, and Rue, "Induced Abortion and Anxiety, Mood, and Substance Abuse Disorders."

32. Thorp, Hartmann, and Shadigian, "Long-Term Physical and Psychological Health Consequences of Induced Abortion," at 74. See also Dellapenna, *Dispelling the Myths*, at 713–714n104 (and the numerous studies between 1987 and 2002 cited therein). For contrary studies, finding no significant negative psychological outcome, see ibid., at 714n106.

33. Thorp, Hartmann, and Shadigian, "Long-Term Physical and Psychological Health Consequences of Induced Abortion," at 76.

34. See Shadigian and Bauer, "Pregnancy-Associated Death" (citing Reardon, Ney, Scheuren, et al., "Deaths Associated with Pregnancy Outcome"; Gissler et al., "Pregnancy-Associated Deaths in Finland 1987–1994"). Gissler et al., "Injury, Deaths, Suicides and Homicides"; Gissler and Hemminki, "Pregnancy-Related Violent Deaths."

35. Because some studies show an association between abortion and ectopic (tubal) pregnancy, and between abortion and infertility (though not enough to lead to definitive conclusions), more studies need to be done in these areas. Thorp, Hartmann, and Shadigian, "Long-Term Physical and Psychological Health Consequences of Induced Abortion," at 70.

36. Ibid., at 75.

37. Ibid.

38. Ibid.

39. Ibid., at 70.

40. Donohue and Levitt, "The Impact of Legalized Abortion on Crime," at 387.

41. "U.S. Fares Badly in Early Births in Global Study," *New York Times*, May 3, 2012, A1, A4. See Thorp, Hartmann, and Shadigian, "Long-Term Physical and Psychological Health Consequences of Induced Abortion"; Rooney and Calhoun, "Induced Abortion and Risk of Later Premature Births."

42. Institute of Medicine (2006).

43. Calhoun, Shadigian, and Rooney, "Cost Consequences of Induced Abortion."

44. Shah and Zao, "Induced Termination of Pregnancy and Low Birthweight and Preterm Birth"; Swingle et al., "Abortion and the Risk of Subsequent Preterm Birth"; Freak-Poli, Chan, Gaeme, and Street, "Previous Abortion and Risk of Preterm Birth."

45. Anum, Brown, and Strauss, "Health Disparities in Risk for Cervical Insufficiency," at 2899.

46. Di Renzo, Giardina, Rosati, et al., "Maternal Risk Factors for Preterm Birth."

47. Thorp, "Public Health Impact," at 5.

48. Calhoun, Shadigian, and Rooney, "Cost Consequences of Induced Abortion."

49. See, generally, www.pregnancy.about.com/cs/placentaprevia/a/previa.html (last visited July 9, 2013).

50. Thorp, Hartmann, and Shadigian, "Long-Term Physical and Psychological Health Consequences of Induced Abortion," at 75.

51. Ibid.

52. Ibid., at 70–71.

53. Soderberg et al., "Emotional Distress Following Induced Abortion."

54. Fergusson, Horwood, and Ridder, "Abortion in Young Women and Subsequent Mental Health" (finding an association between abortion and long-term, increased risk of depression).

55. Thorp, Hartmann, and Shadigian, "Long-Term Physical and Psychological Health Consequences of Induced Abortion"; Fergusson, Horwood, and Ridder, "Abortion in Young Women and Subsequent Mental Health"; Fergusson, Horwood, and Boden, "Abortion and Mental Health Disorders"; Coleman, Coyle, Shuping, and Rue, "Induced Abortion and Anxiety, Mood, and Substance Abuse Disorders."

56. Mota, Burnett, and Sareen, "Associations between Abortion, Mental Disorders, and Suicidal Behaviour"; Gissler et al., "Injury, Deaths, Suicides and Homicides"; Gissler et al., "Suicides after Pregnancy in Finland, 1987–1994," 1433 (finding an association between abortion and suicide).

57. Thorp, Hartmann, and Shadigian, "Long-Term Physical and Psychological Health Consequences of Induced Abortion," at 70.

58. Cougle, Reardon, and Coleman, "Generalized Anxiety Following Unintended Pregnancies."

59. See Shadigian and Bauer, "Pregnancy-Associated Death"; Gissler et al., "Injury Deaths, Suicides and Homicides"; Gissler and Hemminki, "Pregnancy-Related Violent Deaths."

60. Bradshaw and Slade, "The Effects of Induced Abortion on Emotional Experiences and Relationships."

61. Broen et al., "Reasons for Induced Abortion."

62. See Letter to Office of the United Nations High Commissioner on Human Rights (November 27, 2009) (Attachment 2), available at: http://www.aaplog.org/international-issues/aaplog-objection-to-inclusion-of-universal-access-to-reproductive-healthcare-as-a-part-of-mdg-5-letter-to-un-high-commissioner-on-human-rights/. See, e.g., Broen et al., "Reasons for Induced Abortion," 36; Cougle, Reardon, and Coleman, "Generalized Anxiety Following Unintended Pregnancies"; Gissler et al., "Injury, Deaths, Suicides and Homicides"; Bradshaw and Slade, "The Effects of Induced Abortion on Emotional Experiences and Relationships"; Reardon, Cougle, Rue, et al., "Psychiatric Admissions of Low-Income Women Following Abortion and Childbirth."

63. Bradshaw and Slade, "The Effects of Induced Abortion on Emotional Experiences and Relationships."

64. Dellapenna, *Dispelling the Myths*, at 784n61 (citing Moira Plant, *Women, Drinking and Pregnancy* (1985); H. Amaro, B. Zuckerman, and H. Cabral, "Drug Use among Adolescent Mothers: Profile of Risk," *Pediatrics* 84 (1989): 144; D. A. Frank, "Cocaine Use during Pregnancy: Prevalence and Correlates," *Pediatrics* 82 (1988): 888; L. G. Keith et al., "Substance Abuse in

Pregnant Women: Recent Experience at the Perinatal Center for Chemical Dependence of Northwestern Memorial Hospital," *Obstetrics and Gynecology* 73 (1989): 715; A.S. Oro and S.D. Dixon, "Perinatal Cocaine and Methamphetamine Exposure: Maternal and Neonatal Correlates," *Journal of Pediatrics* 111 (1987): 571; K. Yamaguchi and D. Kandel, "Drug Use and Other Determinants of Premarital Pregnancy and Its Outcome: A Dynamic Analysis of Competing Life Events," *Journal of Marriage and the Family* 49 (1987): 257; Klassen and Wilsnack, "Sexual Experience and Drinking among Women"; E.R. Morrissey and M.A. Schuckit, "Stressful Life Events and Alcohol Problems among Women Seen at a Detoxification Center," *Journal of Studies on Alcohol* 39 (1978): 1559).

65. See Klassen and Wilsnack, "Sexual Experience and Drinking among Women."

66. Reardon, Coleman, and Cougle, "Substance Use Associated with Unintended Pregnancy Outcomes."

67. Ibid.; Reardon, Strahan, Thorp, and Shuping, "Deaths Associated with Abortion Compared to Childbirth," at 204 and nn. 91–92. Coleman, "Induced Abortion and Increased Risk of Substance Abuse"; Coleman, Reardon, Rue, and Cougle, "A History of Induced Abortion in Relation to Substance Use."

68. Centers for Disease Control and Prevention, *Health, United States, 2012*, Table 35, http://www.cdc.gov/nchs/data/hus/2012/0.35.pdf.

69. Thorp, Hartmann, and Shadigian, "Long-Term Physical and Psychological Health Consequences of Induced Abortion," at 67 (Abstract).

70. Gissler et al., "Suicides after Pregnancy in Finland, 1987–1994."

71. Coleman, Reardon, Rue and Cougle, "State-Funded Abortions versus Deliveries."

72. Reardon, Ney, Scheuren, et al., "Deaths Associated with Pregnancy Outcome."

73. Cougle, Reardon, and Coleman, "Depression Associated with Abortion and Childbirth."

74. Cougle, Reardon, and Coleman, "Generalized Anxiety Following Unintended Pregnancies." See also V. Rue, Coleman, J. Rue, and Reardon, "Induced Abortion and Traumatic Stress"; Reardon, Cougle, Rue, et al., "Psychiatric Admissions of Low-Income Women Following Abortion and Childbirth."

75. Fergusson, Horwood, and Ridder, "Abortion in Young Women and Subsequent Mental Health."

76. Ibid.

77. Coleman, "Resolution of Unwanted Pregnancy."

78. Mota, Burnett and Sareen, "Associations Between Abortion, Mental Disorders, and Suicidal Behaviour."

79. Sue Nathanson, *Soul Crisis*.

80. *Planned Parenthood v. Casey*, 505 U.S. 833, 882 (1992).

81. Bradshaw and Slade, "The Effects of Induced Abortion on Emotional Experiences and Relationships," at 941.

82. Coleman, "Abortion and Mental Health."

83. See the January 2012 issue of the *British Journal of Psychiatry* for letters critical of the September 2011 study by Coleman, along with Coleman's response (http://bjp.rcpsych.org/content/199/3/180.abstract/reply#bjrcpsych_el_34290) and the response of David Fergusson (http://bjp.rcpsych.org/content/199/3/180.abstract/reply#bjrcpsych_el_33839).

    Two recent studies found no increased risk, but have some methodological problems. Munk-Olson, Laursen, Pedersen, et al., "First-Time First-Trimester Induced Abortion." The Munk-Olson study excluded women within the age bracket that should have been included, without explanation. As the authors conceded, a significant percentage of women were included in both cohorts; these should have been excluded. The authors focused only on women who were hospitalized, and failed to look at women who were treated in other ways for mental disorders. There were limited control variables. Follow-up was limited to just twelve months, despite data for a longer followup being available in the Danish registries. The Royal College of Psychiatrists (December 2011) found no increased risk, but, like the 2008 APA Report, excluded peer-reviewed, controlled, statistically significant studies that found an increased risk.

84. Reeves, Kan, Key, et al., "Breast Cancer Risk in Relation to Abortion," at 1741 ("It is well established that pregnancies that end in a full term birth ultimately confer a protective effect on breast cancer risk."). See also Shadigian, "Reviewing the Evidence, Breaking the Silence"; Lanfranchi, "The Abortion-Breast Cancer Link."

85. See generally, Lanfranchi, "The Abortion-Breast Cancer Link."

86. Okobia and Bunker, "Epidemiological Risk Factors for Breast Cancer."

87. Thorp, Hartmann, and Shadigian, "Long-Term Physical and Psychological Health Consequences of Induced Abortion," at 76.

88. Ibid.

89. Ibid., at 76, 77.

90. Brind, Chinchilli, Severs, and Summy-Long, "Induced Abortion as an Independent Risk Factor for Breast Cancer"; Kindley, "The Fit between the Elements."

91. See generally, Lanfranchi, "The Abortion-Breast Cancer Link."

92. See M.C. Pike et al., "Oral Contraceptive Use and Early Abortion as Risk Factors for Breast Cancer in Young Women," *British Journal of Cancer* 43 (1981): 72; L.A. Brinton et al., "Reproductive Factors in the Etiology of Breast Cancer," *British Journal of Cancer* 47 (1983): 757; L. Rosenberg et al., "Breast Cancer in Relation to the Occurrence and Time of Induced and Spontaneous Abortion," *American Journal of Epidemiology* 127 (1988): 981; H.L. Howe et al., "Early Abortion and Breast Cancer Risk among Women under Age 40," *International Journal of Epidemiology* 18 (1989): 300; A.E. Laing et al., "Breast Cancer Risk Factors in African-American Women: The Howard University Tumor Registry Experience," *Journal of the National Medical Association* 85 (1993): 931; J.R. Daling et al., "Risk of Breast Cancer among Young Women: Relationship to Induced Abortion," *Journal of the*

National Cancer Institute 86 (1994): 1584; A. E. Laing et al., "Reproductive and Lifestyle Factors for Breast Cancer in African-American Women," *Genetic Epidemiology* 11 (1994): A3000 (abstract); E. White et al., "Breast Cancer among Young U.S. Women in Relation to Oral Contraceptive Use," *Journal of the National Cancer Institute* 86 (1995): 505; J. R. Daling et al., "Risk of Breast Cancer among White Women Following Induced Abortion," *American Journal of Epidemiology* 144 (1996): 373; P. A. Newcomb et al., "Pregnancy Termination in Relation to Risk of Breast Cancer," *Journal of the American Medical Association* 275 (1996): 283; A. H. Wu et al., "Menstrual and Reproductive Factors and Risk of Breast Cancer in Asian-Americans," *British Journal of Cancer* 73 (1996): 680; J. Palmer, "Induced and Spontaneous Abortion in Relation to Risk of Breast Cancer," *Cancer Causes and Control* 8 (1997): 841; P. M. Marcus et al., "Adolescent Reproductive Events and Subsequent Breast Cancer Risk," *American Journal of Public Health* 89 (1999): 1244; D. Lazovich et al., "Induced Abortion and Breast Cancer Risk," *Epidemiology* 11 (2000): 76; M. Mahue-Giangreco et al., "Induced Abortion, Miscarriage, and Breast Cancer Risk of Young Women," *Cancer Epidemiology Biomarkers and Prevention* 12 (2003): 209; K. Meeske et al., "Impact of Reproductive Factors and Lactation on Breast Carcinoma in Situ Risk," *International Journal of Cancer* 110 (2004): 103; J. R. Palmer et al., "A Prospective Study of Induced Abortion and Breast Cancer in African-American Women," *Cancer Causes and Control* 15 (2004): 105; K. Henderson, "Incomplete Pregnancy Is Not Associated with Breast Cancer Risk: The California Teachers Study," *Contraception* 77 (2008): 391; J. Dolle et al., "Risk Factors for Triple-Negative Breast Cancer in Women under the Age of 45 Years," *Cancer Epidemiological Biomarkers and Prevention* 18 (2009): 1157.

93. See M. Segi et al., "An Epidemiological Study on Cancer in Japan," *Japanese Journal of Cancer Research* 48 (suppl.) (1957): 1; F. Nishiyama, "The Epidemiology of Breast Cancer in Tokushima Prefecture," *Shikoku Ichi* 38 (1982): 333; M. Ewertz et al., "Risk of Breast Cancer in Relation to Reproductive Factors in Denmark," *British Journal of Cancer* 58 (1988): 99; E. Luporsi, in N. Andrieu et al., "Familial Risk, Abortion and Their Interactive Effect on the Risk of Breast Cancer—A Combined Analysis of Six Case-Control Studies," *British Journal of Cancer* 72 (1995): 744; D. G. Zaridze, in N. Andrieu et al., "Familial Risk, Abortion and Their Interactive Effect on the Risk of Breast Cancer—A Combined Analysis of Six Case-Control Studies," *British Journal of Cancer* 72 (1995): 744; L. Rosenberg et al., "Breast Cancer in Relation to the Occurrence and Time of Induced and Spontaneous Abortion," *American Journal of Epidemiology* 127 (1988): 981; H. L. Howe et al., "Early Abortion and Breast Cancer Risk among Women under Age 40," *International Journal of Epidemiology* 18 (1989): 300; A. E. Laing et al., "Breast Cancer Risk Factors in African-American Women: The Howard University Tumor Registry Experience," *Journal of the National Medical Association* 85 (1993): 931; J. R. Daling et al., "Risk of Breast Cancer among Young Women: Relationship to Induced Abortion," *Journal of the National*

Cancer Institute 86 (1994): 1584; A. E. Laing et al., "Reproductive and Life-style Factors for Breast Cancer in African-American Women," *Genetic Epidemiology* 11 (1994): A3000 (abstract); N. Andrieu et al., "Familial Risk, Abortion and Their Interactive Effect on the Risk of Breast Cancer—A Combined Analysis of Six Case-Control Studies," *British Journal of Cancer* 72 (1995): 744; E. White et al., "Breast Cancer among Young U.S. Women in Relation to Oral Contraceptive Use," *Journal of the National Cancer Institute* 86 (1995): 505; L. Bu et al., "Risk of Breast Cancer Associated with Induced Abortion in a Population at Low Risk of Breast Cancer," *American Journal of Epidemiology* 141 (1995): S85; L. Lipworth et al., "Abortion and the Risk of Breast Cancer: A Case-Control Study in Greece," *International Journal of Cancer* 61 (1995): 181; M. A. Rookus et al., "Breast Cancer Risk after an Induced Abortion, a Dutch Case-Control Study," *American Journal of Epidemiology* 141 (1995): S54 (abstract); J. R. Daling et al., "Risk of Breast Cancer among White Women Following Induced Abortion," *American Journal of Epidemiology* 144 (1996): 373; P. A. Newcomb et al., "Pregnancy Termination in Relation to Risk of Breast Cancer," *Journal of the American Medical Association* 275 (1996): 283; M. A. Rookus and F. E. Leeuwan, "Induced Abortion and Risk for Breast Cancer: Reporting (recall) Bias in a Dutch Case-Control Study," *Journal of the National Cancer Institute* 88 (1996): 1759; R. Talamini et al., "The Role of Reproductive and Menstrual Factors in Cancer of the Breast before and after Menopause," *European Journal of Cancer* 32 (1996): 303; A. Tavani et al., "Abortion and Breast Cancer Risk," *International Journal of Cancer* 65 (1996): 401; M. Melbye et al., "Induced Abortion and the Risk of Breast Cancer," *New England Journal of Medicine* 336 (1997): 81; F. Fioretti, "Risk Factors for Breast Cancer in Nulliparous Women," 79 *British Journal of Cancer* 1923 (1999); H. Becher et al., "Reproductive Factors and Familial Predisposition for Breast Cancer by Age 50 Years: A Case Control Family Study for Assessing Main Effects and Possible Gene-Environment Interaction," *International Journal of Epidemiology* 32 (2002): 38; N. Tehranian et al., "The Effect of Abortion on the Risk of Breast Cancer," (2006), available at http://hdl.handle.net/10755/163877; K. Naieni et al., "Risk Factors of Breast Cancer in North of Iran: A Case-Control in Mazandaran Province," *Asian Pacific Journal of Cancer Prevention* 8 (2007): 395; J. Lin et al., "A Case Control Study on Risk Factors of Breast Cancer among Women in Cixi," *Zhejiang Preventative Medicine* 20 (2008): 3; J. Dolle et al., "Risk Factors for Triple-Negative Breast Cancer in Women under the Age of 45 Years," *Cancer Epidemiological Biomarkers and Prevention* 18 (2009): 1157; V. Ozmen et al., "Breast Cancer Risk Factors in Turkish Women—A University Hospital Based Nested Case Control Study," *World Journal of Surgical Oncology* 7 (2009): 37; P. Xing et al., "A Case-control Study of Reproductive Factors Associated with Subtypes of Breast Cancer in Northeast China," *Medical Oncology* 27 (2010): 926; L. Khachatryan et al., "Influence of Diabetes Mellitus Type 2 and Prolonged Estrogen Exposure on Risk of Breast Cancer among Women in Armenia," *Health Care for Women International* 32 (2011):

953; A. R. Jiang et al., "Abortions and Breast Cancer Risk in Premenopausal and Postmenopausal Women in Jiangsu Province of China," *Asian Pacific Journal of Cancer Prevention* 13 (2012): 33; J. Lecarpentier et al., "Variation in Breast Cancer Risk Associated with Factors Related to Pregnancies According to Truncating Mutation Location, in the French National BRCA1 and BRCA2 Mutations Carrier Cohort (GENEPSO)," *Breast Cancer Research* 14 (2012): R99; C. Yanhua et al., "Reproductive Variables and Risk of Breast Malignant and Benign Tumours in Yunnan Province, China," *Asian Pacific Journal of Cancer Prevention* 13 (2012): 2179.

94. Daling et al., "Risk of Breast Cancer among Young Women." The women at the highest risk are those who abort their first pregnancy (thereby delaying a first full-term pregnancy) and have a family history of breast cancer. Daling's study focused on that high-risk group and found a strong association—100 percent of the women went on to have breast cancer. In contrast, those studies that mix that high-risk group with women who had spontaneous miscarriages seem to wash out the association.

95. Joe Gelman, "Findings Linking Cancer to Abortions a Well-Kept Secret," *Daily News* (Los Angeles, California), September 28, 1997, available at http://www.thefreelibrary.com/FINDINGS+LINKING+CANCER+TO+ABORTIONS+A+WELL-KEPT+SECRET-a083942541; also quoted in http://en.wikipedia.org/wiki/Abortion%E2%80%93breast_cancer_hypothesis#Daling)

96. Royal College of Obstetricians and Gynaecologists, *The Care of Women Requesting Induced Abortion* (April 2000).

97. For a critique of these two studies, see Lanfranchi, "The Abortion-Breast Cancer Link," at 81–84.

98. Melbye et al., "Induced Abortion and the Risk of Breast Cancer." See the critique by Brind, "Induced Abortion as an Independent Risk Factor for Breast Cancer: A Critical Review."

99. Beral et al., "Breast Cancer and Abortion."

100. See Lanfranchi, "The Abortion-Breast Cancer Link."

101. Kindley, "The Fit between the Elements."

102. Thorp, Hartmann, and Shadigian, "Long-Term Physical and Psychological Health Consequences of Induced Abortion," at 67 (Abstract).

103. *McCorvey v. Hill*, 385 F.3d 846 (5th Cir. 2004), cert. denied, 543 U.S. 1154 (2005); *Cano v. Baker*, 435 F.3d 1337 (11th Cir. 2006), cert. denied, 549 U.S. 972 (2006).

104. *McCorvey v. Hill*, 385 F.3d 846 (5th Cir. 2004), cert. denied, 543 U.S. 1154 (2005).

105. *McCorvey v. Hill*, 385 F.3d at 850–851.

106. Ibid., at 852–853.

Chapter Nine

1. Prosser, *Law of Torts*, at 335. As a leading lawyer in Minnesota in the 1950s and a federal appellate judge in the 1960s, Harry Blackmun knew

Professor William Prosser fairly well, at least on a professional basis. They had been members of the same firm and worked together on a case or two. Yarbrough, *Harry A. Blackmun*, 44–45. As dean of the University of Minnesota Law School, Prosser was usually referred to as Dean Prosser, and he was considered the leading authority on the law of torts in the United States in the 1960s. Ibid. at 44.

2. "Pampers Hello Baby—Pregnancy Calendar," http://www.youtube.com/watch?v=rjW8aAqrsOk&feature=relmfu.

3. Paul, *Origins*.

4. See Dellapenna, *Dispelling the Myths*; Forsythe, "Homicide of the Unborn Child"; Samuel Farr, *Elements of Medical Jurisprudence* (1787) (quoted supra in chapter 6, in text accompanying note 29). See also Dyer, *Champion of Women and the Unborn*; Dyer, *The Physicians' Crusade against Abortion*.

5. At that time, the journal was called the *Notre Dame Lawyer*.

6. Maledon, Note, "The Law and the Unborn Child."

7. Author interview.

8. *Roe v. Wade*, 410 U.S. 113 (1973), at 162nn65–66.

9. Maledon, Note, "The Law and the Unborn Child," at 351.

10. *Thellusson v. Woodford*, 31 Eng. Rep. 117, 164 (Ch. 1798).

11. *Black's Law Dictionary*, 619 (rev. 4th ed., 1968).

12. *Thellusson v. Woodford*, 31 Eng. Rep. at 163.

13. *In re Holthausen's Will*, 175 Misc. 1022, 26 N.Y.S.2d 140 (NY Surr. Ct. 1941).

14. Maledon, Note, "The Law and the Unborn Child," at 354.

15. Ibid., at 356.

16. Ibid., at 357.

17. *Kelly v. Gregory*, 282 App.Div. 542, 125 NYS.2d 696, 697 (1953).

18. Maledon, Note, "The Law and the Unborn Child," at 358n67.

19. *Leal v. CC Pitts Sand and Gravel*, 419 S.W.2d 820 (Tex. 1967).

20. *Yandell v. Delgado*, 471 S.W.2d 569 (Tex. October 6, 1971) (affirmed that "a cause of action does exist for prenatal injuries sustained at any prenatal stage provided the child is born alive and survives."). The injury occurred approximately six and a half months before the child was born.

21. *Sinkler v. Kneale*, 401 Pa. 267, 164 A.2d 93, 96 (1960).

22. Maledon, Note, "The Law and the Unborn Child," at 359n78 (*White v. Kup*, 458 P.2d 617 (Nev. 1969)).

23. Prosser, *Law of Torts*, at 898.

24. Maledon, Note, "The Law and the Unborn Child," at 360n81.

25. Ibid., at 358n72. For an updated survey of state protection of the unborn child, see also Linton, "The Legal Status of the Unborn Child under State Law."

26. *Torigian v. Watertown News Co.*, 352 Mass. 446, 225 N.E.2d 926, 927 (1967) (three and a half months gestation).

27. See Forsythe, "Homicide of the Unborn Child."

28. *People v. Keeler*, 2 Cal. 3d 619, 470 P.2d 617, 87 Cal. Rptr. 481 (1970).

29. Amicus briefs in support of the United States were filed in *Vuitch* by

William F. Colliton, M.D., and by Bart Heffernan, M.D. See William O. Douglas Papers, Library of Congress, Box 1508 and Box 1590, Folder 5 (Memo from clerk re amicus briefs).

30. See the critique of *Keeler*, in light of the prior decision in *People v. Chavez*, 77 Cal. App. 2d 621, 176 P.2d 92 (1947), in Comment, "The Role of the Law of Homicide in Fetal Destruction," at 664–666.

31. Kadar, "The Law of Tortious Prenatal Death Since *Roe v. Wade*," at 652–653.

32. Ibid., 654.

33. *Roe*, 410 U.S. at 156.

34. The legislative history of the California fetal homicide law is reviewed in Webb, Comment, "Is the Intentional Killing of an Unborn Child Homicide?"

35. See, e.g., *State v. Merrill*, 450 N.W.2d 318 (Minn.), cert. denied sub. nom., *Merrill v. Minnesota*, 496 U.S. 931 (1990).

36. Dellapenna, *Dispelling the Myths*, at 1083.

Chapter Ten

1. Quoted in Blake, "Elective Abortion and Our Reluctant Citizenry," at 465.

2. Lydia Saad, "Americans Still Split along 'Pro-Choice,' 'Pro-Life' Lines," May 23, 2011, http://www.gallup.com/poll/147734/Americans-Split-Along-Pro-Choice-Pro-Life-Lines.aspx.

3. Garrow, *Liberty and Sexuality*, at 562.

4. Ibid., at 605.

5. Bernard Schwartz, *The Ascent of Pragmatism*, at 308.

6. *Webster v. Reproductive Health Services*, 492 U.S. 490, 535 (1989) (Scalia, J., concurring in part, and concurring in the judgment) ("We can now look forward to at least another Term with carts full of mail from the public, and streets full of demonstrators, urging us—their unelected and life-tenured judges who have been awarded those extraordinary, undemocratic characteristics precisely in order that we might follow the law despite the popular will—to follow the popular will. Indeed, I expect we can look forward to even more of that than before, given our indecisive decision today.").

7. The examples are legion: "Supreme Court Allows Early-Stage Abortions," *Washington Post*, January 23, 1973; "Justices Allow Early Abortions," *Washington Evening Star*, January 22, 1973; "High Court Rules Abortions Legal First Six Months," Associated Press, January 23, 1973; clippings contained in Harry A. Blackmun Papers, Library of Congress, Box 151, Folder 11.

8. Garrow, *Liberty and Sexuality*, at 563, 577.

9. Ibid., at 310, 546.

10. Blake, "Elective Abortion and Our Reluctant Citizenry," at 465.

11. As sociologist Mary Ann Lamanna concluded from her study of polling data from the early 1970s through the early 1980s: "Almost 20% support the

prolife position, defined as forbidding abortion under any circumstances except to save the mother's life . . . [and] [a]bout 25% support prochoice as defined in Roe v. Wade." Quoted in McConnell, "How Not to Promote Serious Deliberation about Abortion," at 1200n43.

12. See "Abortion," http://www.gallup.com/poll/1576/abortion.aspx. "Over the years, the Gallup Poll and similar surveys consistently have shown that a substantial majority of all persons in the United States oppose abortion on demand, with a broad majority favoring an indications policy whereby abortion would be legal if certain conditions exist." Dellapenna, *Dispelling the Myths*, at 952; Forsythe and Presser, "The Tragic Failure of *Roe v. Wade*," at 124n201 (quoting January 1, 1990 *Los Angeles Times* nationwide survey indicating that "[a]bortion is opposed across America by [a ratio] of five to four, with women much more opposed than men.").

13. Dellapenna, *Dispelling the Myths*, at 953.

14. See www.gallup.com.

15. See www.pollingcompany.com.

16. *Stenberg v. Carhart*, 530 U.S. 914, 921 (2000) (Breyer, J. opinion) ("Taking account of these virtually irreconcilable points of view, aware that constitutional law must govern a society whose different members sincerely hold directly opposing views, and considering the matter in light of the Constitution's guarantees of fundamental individual liberty, this Court . . . has determined and then redetermined that the Constitution offers basic protection to the woman's right to choose."); Ibid. at 947 (O'Connor, J., concurring) ("The issue of abortion is one of the most contentious and controversial in contemporary American society. It presents extraordinarily difficult questions that, as the Court recognizes, involve 'virtually irreconcilable points of view.'").

17. McConnell, "How Not to Promote Serious Deliberation About Abortion," at 1200.

18. Hunter, *Before the Shooting Begins*, at 86–90; Dellapenna, *Dispelling the Myths*, at 970 (documenting data showing public confusion over abortion law and policy).

19. See Tierney, "Post-Viability Abortion Bans and the Limits of the Health Exception."

20. Ginsburg, "Speaking in a Judicial Voice," at 1199, 1205 (and similar quotes that Justice Ginsburg cited in footnote 129, p. 1205).

21. Glendon, *Abortion and Divorce in Western Law*, at 22.

22. McConnell, "How Not to Promote Serious Deliberation about Abortion," at 1198n40.

23. E.g., Collins, *When Everything Changed*, at 234 ("In January 1973, the Supreme Court ruled 7 to 2, in *Roe v. Wade*, that any attempt to interfere with a woman's right to abortion during the first three months of pregnancy was a violation of her constitutional right to privacy.").

24. O'Connor, *The Majesty of the Law*, at 45 ("Since the Court struck down as

unconstitutional limitations by states on abortions in the first three months of pregnancy, large numbers of people have taken regularly to the streets to demonstrate either their support of or their opposition to the decision.").

25. Ibid. at 244 ("When in the 1970s the Court struck down as unconstitutional limitations by states on abortions in the first three months of pregnancy, a new body of protestors took to the streets in opposition.").

26. David J. Garrow, "A Supreme Court Justice's Uneven Volume of Views," *Sunday Chicago Tribune Book Review*, April 27, 2003, Books Section, at 1.

Justice White observed in dissent in *Thornburg* that a health exception was required even after viability. *Thornburgh v. American College of Obstetricians and Gynecologists*, 476 U.S. 747, 808–809 (1986) ("The Court now holds that this compelling interest cannot justify *any* regulation that imposes a quantifiable medical risk upon the pregnant woman who seeks to abort a viable fetus.") (emphasis in original).

27. A 2004 law review article documented that the post-viability prohibitions on the books in three-fourths of the states were unenforceable due to federal court decisions. Tierney, "Post-Viability Abortion Bans and the Limits of the Health Exception."

28. Breyer, *Making Our Democracy Work*, 68.

29. *Women's Medical Professional Corp. v. Voinovich*, 130 F.3d 187 (6th Cir. 1997), cert. denied, 523 U.S. 1036 (1998).

30. *Stenberg v. Carthart*, 530 U.S. 914, 930 (2000). ("Since the law requires a health exception in order to validate even a postviablity abortion regulation, it at a minimum requires the same in respect to previability regulation. See *Casey*, supra at 880 (majority opinion) (assuming need for health exception previability).")

31. Rasmussen Reports, August 11–12, 2010.

32. "The survey of 1,000 Likely Voters was conducted on August 11–12, 2010 by Rasmussen Reports. The margin of sampling error is +/− 3 percentage points with a 95% level of confidence. Field work for all Rasmussen Reports surveys is conducted by Pulse Opinion Research, LLC."

33. Hunter, *Before the Shooting Begins*, at 88 (Figure 1).

34. *Gonzales v. Carhart*, 550 U.S. 124 (2007).

Chapter Eleven

1. Bergmann, *The Economic Emergence of Women*, at 46.

2. Daniel Callahan, "An Ethical Challenge to Prochoice Advocates," at 684.

3. *Roe v. Wade*, 410 U.S. 113 (1973), at 153.

4. *Roe*, 410 U.S. at 116.

5. *Griswold v. Connecticut*, 381 U.S. 479 (1965). In earlier drafts, Douglas referred to marriage as "the main font of the population problem; and education of each spouse in the ramification of that problem, the health of the wife, and the well-being of the family, is central to family functioning." William O. Douglas Papers, Library of Congress, Box 1347 (Folder marked "opinions") ("Desk Copy, not cir, April 22, 1965"), p. 5.

6. *Doe*, 410 U.S. at 214–215.

7. Woodward and Armstrong, *The Brethren*, at 167.

8. Dellapenna, *Dispelling the Myths*, at 702. "Maternal deaths annually almost certainly were less than 1,000 throughout the post-war years, and by the 1960s were probably less than 100 and perhaps as few as 25 per year after 1970." Ibid. at 550.

9. Dellapenna, *Dispelling the Myths*, at 702 (there is no basis for the claim that "legalizing abortion saved 1500 women's lives in its first decade." (commenting on Tietze, "The Public Health Effects of Legal Abortion in the United States").

10. A 1987 medical journal article concluded that, on average, fifteen women die from legal abortion annually. In isolation, fifteen may seem a lot or hardly any at all. It takes on more meaning when you compare it to national statistics for 1972. The CDC reported thirty-nine deaths from *illegal* abortion and twenty-four deaths from *legal* abortion in 1972, the last full year before abortion was legalized on demand, in every state. U.S. Public Health Service, Centers for Disease Control, Abortion Surveillance 61 (November 1980).

11. Calhoun et al., "Maternal and Neonatal Health and Abortion." See also Dellapenna, *Dispelling the Myths*, at 705–706 ("The American Medical Association reports a 90 percent decline in maternal deaths from childbirth in the 30 years since Roe was decided. . . . The overall decline in pregnancy-related deaths does not appear to have resulted from the availability of abortion. Consider that there have been greater declines in maternal mortality in the Irish Republic (where abortions are illegal and remain difficult to obtain) than in most areas of the United Kingdom (where abortion is available virtually on demand). The maternal morality rate in the Irish Republic now is 7:100,000, in England and Wales 11:100,000, in Scotland 14:100,000, and in Northern Ireland 7:100,000.").

12. Centers for Disease Control, "Abortion Surveillance—United States, 2001," *Morbidity and Mortality Weekly Report* 53, no. SS-9 (November 26, 2004): 32 (Table 19), available at http://www.cdc.gov/. Hundreds of women and young girls have died from legal abortion since *Roe*. See generally, Cunningham and Forsythe, "Is Abortion the 'First Right' for Women?" The states haphazardly collect data and report them to the Centers for Disease Control (CDC) and the National Center for Health Statistics (NCHS). Because the states do not uniformly collect data, and because there is no uniform federal system of data collection, there is no national, authoritative source of data collection on maternal deaths from legal abortion. There are a number of partial studies. One study by a CDC statistician found 213 "legal abortion-related" deaths between 1972 and 1985—an average of 15 per year— while 540 deaths were examined as "possibly abortion related." Koonin, Smith, Ramick, and Lawson, "Abortion Surveillance—United States, 1989" (between 1978–1987, 108 maternal deaths from legal abortion, 14 maternal deaths from illegal abortions); Atrash et al., "Legal Abortion in the U.S.," 59; Koonin, Smith, Ramick, and Green, "Abortion Surveillance—United

States, 1992"; Atrash, Cheek and Hogue, "Legal Abortion Mortality and General Anesthesia" (citing 193 deaths nationally between 1972 and 1985); Kafrissen, Grimes, Hogue, and Sacks, "Cluster of Abortion Deaths at a Single Facility"; Grimes, Kafrissen, O'Reilly and Binkin, "Fatal Hemorrhage from Legal Abortion in the United States" (citing 194 deaths nationally between 1972 and 1979); LeBolt, Grimes, and Cates, "Mortality from Abortion and Childbirth" (citing 138 deaths nationally between 1972 and 1978); Grimes, Cates, and Selik, "Fatal Septic Abortion in the United States, 1975–1977"; Cates, Smith, Rochat, et al., "Assessment of Surveillance and Vital Statistics Data" (citing 240 deaths, "legal," "illegal," and "spontaneous" between 1972 and 1975).

13. Lawson, Frye, Atrash, et al., "Abortion Mortality." Atrash et al., "Legal Abortion in the U.S." (213 legal abortion deaths 1973–1985); Atrash, Cheek, and Hogue, "Legal Abortion Mortality and General Anesthesia" (193 deaths 1972–1985); Grimes, Kafrissen, O'Reilly, and Binkin, "Fatal Hemorrhage from Legal Abortion in the United States" (194 deaths 1972–1979); LeBolt, Grimes, and Cates, "Mortality from Abortion and Childbirth" (138 deaths 1972–1978); Cates, Smith, Rochat, et al., "Assessment of Surveillance and Vital Statistics Data" (204 deaths 1972–1975, 104 from legal abortion).

CDC statistics rely on death certificates provided by the states. One CDC official was reported as saying, "There have always been problems identifying deaths secondary to abortion. Death certificates are not the best source of death information, and we've always had concerns we're not getting all the deaths through the death certificate system." Price, "Statistics May Be Misleading on Deaths Caused by Abortion," *Washington Times*, June 4, 1994, at A5. The official also stated that it is "likely" that many abortion-related deaths might not be reported. Ibid.

14. Compare the CDC's "Abortion Surveillance Report" for 1985 and for 2001. The 1985 Report stated that "the number of deaths related to legal abortions decreased 75%, from 24 deaths in 1972 to six deaths in 1985." CDC, "Abortion Surveillance, United States, 1984–1985," *Morbidity and Mortality Weekly Report* 38, no. SS-2 (September 1, 1989): 11–15. The 2001 Report indicated that 11 deaths from legal abortion actually occurred in 1985. CDC, "Abortion Surveillance—United States, 2001," *Morbidity and Mortality Weekly Report* 53, no. SS-9 (November 26, 2004): 32 (Table 19).

15. *Ravenell, Estate of v. Eastern Women's Center*, 1990 WL 467656 (N.Y. Sup. Ct.) ($1.2 million verdict).

16. Police ended their investigation after one day, saying the patient "was cared for by a licensed doctor in a licensed facility." "Woman Dies from Bleeding after Abortion," *Tallahassee Democrat*, June 30, 1994, at 1. For other cases, see *Ruckman, Estate of v. Barrett*, 1991 WL 444085 (Green Co., Mo. Cir. Ct.) ($25,000,000 verdict for abortion death); *Redding v. Bramwell*, 1990 WL 468158 (Cobb Co., Ga. Sup. Ct.) ($500,000 verdict for abortion death); *Poteat, Estate of v. Dern*, 1987 WL 232018 (Charleston Co. Com. Pl. Ct.) ($35,000 for abortion death).

17. The abortion provider's lawyer was quoted as saying, "This is a standard risk of

the procedure. . . . We don't believe this was below the standard of care nor do
we believe it is malpractice." Dalton, "Doctor Probed after Abortion Causes
Death, *San Diego Union*, December 13, 1994, at B1, B3.

18. See Samuel W. Calhoun, "Stopping Philadelphia Abortion Provider Kermit
Gosnell"; Forsythe and Kehr, "A Road Map through the Supreme Court's
Back Alley."

19. Dodds, Note, "Defending America's Children," at 733. See also Elshtain,
"*Roe v. Wade*: Speaking the Unspeakable," at 182 (since *Roe*, we've "seen . . .
[a] tremendous increase in child abuse and abandonment. That was supposed
to disappear when every child was 'wanted,' or don't you remember the
sunny publicity to this effect?").

20. Dellapenna, *Dispelling the Myths*, at 123 (citing Laura Sessions Stepp, "Infants
Now Murdered as Often as Teens: Actual Rate May Be Higher Experts
Say," *Washington Post*, December 10, 2002, at A3).

21. Dellapenna, *Dispelling the Myths*, at 124; Rick Hampson, "Saving Babies Left
to Die: States Providing Safe Landing for Abandoned Infants," *USA Today*,
February 11, 2000, reprinted in *The Ethics of Abortion*, edited by Baird and
Rosenbaum, at 34.

22. Waite and Gallagher, *The Case for Marriage*, at 135.

23. W. Bennett, *The Index of Leading Cultural Indicators*, at 74. The United States
has "experienced steadily rising rates of births out of wedlock and also births
to teenage mothers despite the large numbers of abortions; in fact, the United
States for some time has had the highest rate of births to teenage mothers of
any developed nation." Dellapenna, *Dispelling the Myths*, at 716–717n125.

24. Dellapenna, *Dispelling the Myths*, at 984.

25. "Health, United States, 1998, with Socioeconomic Status and Health
Chartbook," Department of Health and Human Services publication no.
(PHS) 98-1232, available at http://www.cdc.gov/nchs/data/hus/hus98ncb
.pdf.

26. Akerlof, Yellen, and Katz, "An Analysis of Out-of-Wedlock Childbearing in
the United States."

27. Crandall, "Three Decades of Empty Promises," at 16.

28. "The State of Our Unions, 2003: The Social Health of Marriage in America,"
p. 23, National Marriage Project, at Rutgers, http://marriage.rutgers.edu/
publications/SOOU/SOOU2003.pdf.

29. Thomas, "The Divorce Generation," *Wall Street Journal*, July 9–10, 2011,
C1, C2, citing data from the National Marriage Project.

30. See Child Trends Data Bank, "Family Structure," http://www.childtrends
databank.org/?q=node/231 ("From 1970 to 1996, the proportion of all
children under age 18 who were living with two married parents decreased
steadily from 85 to 68 percent. This share was stable during much of the late
1990s and into the 2000s, but by 2010 it was down to 66 percent. (Figure 1))."

31. Transcript and audio recording of the arguments are available online via the
Oyez project, at http://www.oyez.org/cases/1970–1979/1971/1971_70_18/
argument.

32. Ibid.

33. Dellapenna, *Dispelling the Myths*, at 438–448.

34. Cunningham and Forsythe, "Is Abortion the 'First Right' for Women?" at 154.

35. Linton, "*Planned Parenthood v. Casey*: The Flight from Reason," 44–45 and nn. 129–132.

36. David Leonhardt, *New York Times*, August 4, 2012, at p. B1.

37. See Cunningham and Forsythe, "Is Abortion the 'First Right' for Women?" at 154–155nn336–340. The first state law in the United States on women's work hours was enacted in Wisconsin in 1867; it restricted hours of working women per day and per week, and grew to seventeen states by 1900 and to thirty-four states by 1912. Luke, *Every Pregnant Woman's Guide to Preventing Premature Birth*, 172. The biggest impetus to women in the labor force in the twentieth century was World War II, when 4.5 million women entered the labor force.

38. Dellapenna, *Dispelling the Myths*, at 958, citing Fawn Vrazo, "*Roe* Ruling Reverberates in the Clashing of Symbols," *Philadelphia Inquirer*, January 24, 1993, at C1, C4.

39. See *Statistical Abstract of the United States*: 2004–2005 70 (124th ed., 2004) (Table 90). The CDC's last survey (2004) indicated that the repeat abortion rate in New York City is nearly 60 percent, and, among other things, Maryland residents have the highest percentage (71.4 percent) of repeat abortions. Centers for Disease Control, "Abortion Surveillance—United States, 2001," *Morbidity and Mortality Weekly Report* 53, no. SS-9 (November 26, 2004): 29 (Table 13); available at http://www.cdc.gov/nccdphp/drh/surv_abort.htm. See Wardle, "The Quandary of Pro-life Free Speech," at 961 (Appendix 2) (charting the repeat abortion rate between 1974–1990). By contrast, the repeat abortion rate in Canada is 29 percent, meaning that approximately 1 in 3 abortions are repeat abortions. Millar, Wadhera, and Henshaw, "Repeat Abortions in Canada, 1975–1993."

40. Abortion advocates claim that an abortion rate of 30 percent (of all pregnancies) "has not changed one whit from the time that the Constitution was enacted through the 1800's and through the 1900's." Wardle, "Time Enough," at 948. Yet, between *Roe* and 1989, "the number of [induced] abortions has more than doubled, the rate of [induced] abortion has nearly doubled, and the ratio of [induced] abortions has increased by over fifty percent." Ibid. at 948, 985. The first two decades after *Roe* legalized elective abortion nationwide saw a significant increase in the rate of repeat (two or more) abortions—from 15.2 percent to 42.9 percent. Ibid. at 985.

41. See Mersky and Hartman, eds., *A Documentary History:* Roe v. Wade, 1:180–183, 210, 241–245 (Brief of Appellants).

42. See Letter from Henry Fenwick, Playboy Foundation, to Roy Lucas, The Twentieth Century Fund, October 28, 1968, Roy Lucas Abortion Litigation Papers, Box 16, Olin Memorial Library, Wesleyan University.

43. Glendon, at 51–52; MacKinnon, "*Roe vs. Wade*: A Study in Male Ideology."

44. Hunter, *Before the Shooting Begins*; Cunningham and Forsythe, "Is Abortion

the 'First Right' for Women?"; Crain, "Judicial Restraint and the Non-Decision in *Webster v. Reproductive Health Services*," at 303n187 (quoting *Los Angeles Times*, Jan. 1, 1990, at 1, col. 2 (nationwide survey indicating that "[a]bortion is opposed across America by [a ratio] of five to four, with women much more opposed than men").

45. Cunningham and Forsythe, "Is Abortion the 'First Right' for Women?"; Bordlee, "Abortion-Alternative Legislation and the Law of the Gift," at 136–137 (citing the negative impact on relationships); Mathewes-Green, *Real Choices*.

46. Akerlof, Yellen, and Katz, "An Analysis of Out-of-Wedlock Childbearing in the United States."

47. Regan, "Getting Our Stories Straight," at 455.

48. Cunningham and Forsythe, "Is Abortion the 'First Right' for Women?" at 154.

49. Torres and Forrest, "Why Do Women Have Abortions?" at 170.

50. Wardle, "The Quandary of Pro-life Free Speech," at 949n596 (citing Torres and Forrest, "Why Do Women Have Abortions?" 170); Faria et al., "Women and Abortion," at 91 (detailing that 20 percent of aborting women surveyed give as reasons: no partner, relationship problems, or partner objects); Luker, *Taking Chances* (discussing the negative impact that the availability of abortion as a means of birth control has had on contraceptive responsibility, and noting that many men perceive a woman's decision to proceed with an unplanned pregnancy, despite legalized abortion, as manipulative).

51. See, e.g., Barnett et al., "Partnership after Induced Abortion" (which found a significant negative impact on the relationship with the woman's partner following abortion).

52. Cunningham and Forsythe, "Is Abortion the 'First Right' for Women?" at 154.

53. Magnet, ed., *Modern Sex*.

54. Donna St. George, "Many New or Expectant Mothers Die Violent Deaths," *Washington Post*, December 19, 2004, at A1 (first of three articles), http://www.washingtonpost.com/wp-dyn/articles/A10074-2004Dec18.html.

55. Ibid. See also Horon and Cheng, "Enhanced Surveillance for Pregnancy-Associated Mortality—Maryland, 1993–1998" ("Homicide, the leading cause of pregnancy-associated death, was responsible for 20.2% of all pregnancy-associated deaths." (examining data for the state of Maryland)); McFarlane et al., "Abuse During Pregnancy and Femicide."

56. See Shadigian and Bauer, "Pregnancy-Associated Death"; Rich Lowry, "From Fetus to Baby," December 21, 2004, http://townhall.com/columnists/richlowry/2004/12/21/from_fetus_to_baby ("According to the Washington Post, homicide is the leading cause of death in pregnant women. It is partly because the boyfriends or lovers decide they don't want the 'fetus.' "). As the *Post* put it in explaining one typical murder, the father " 'at first denied it was his child, then pressed for an abortion, then plotted murder.' 'It seems to me that these guys hope against hope for a miscarriage

or an abortion, but when everything else fails, they take the life of the woman to avoid having the baby,' Jack Levin of Northeastern University told the *Post*." Ibid. See Donna St. George, "Many New or Expectant Mothers Die Violent Deaths," *Washington Post*, December 19, 2004, at A1 (first of three articles), http://www.washingtonpost.com/wp-dyn/articles/A10074–2004Dec18.html; Donna St. George, "Violence Intersects Lives of Promise," *Washington Post*, December 20, 2004, at A1, http://www.washingtonpost.com/wp-dyn/articles/A12359–2004Dec19.html; Donna St. George, Mending Shattered Childhoods, *Washington Post*, December 21, 2004, at A1, http://www.washingtonpost.com/wp-dyn/articles/A14920–2004Dec20.html.

57. See Shadigian and Bauer, "Pregnancy-Associated Death."

58. Stith, "Her Choice, Her Problem."

59. Dellapenna, *Dispelling the Myths*, at 10n42.

60. V. M. Rue, Coleman, J. Rue, and Reardon, "Induced Abortion and Traumatic Stress" (finding that 64 percent felt pressured by others to choose the abortion).

61. See "Bath, N.Y. Man Waives Extradition Hearing; Faces Criminal Homicide and First Degree Murder Charges," *Daily Review* (Towanda, Pennsylvania), April 9, 2010, http://thedailyreview.com/news/bath-n-y-man-waives-extradition-hearing-faces-criminal-homicide-and-first-degree-murder-charges-1.724164.

62. "Man Accused of Beating Woman Who Refused to Have Abortion," *Waterbury Republican American*, June 11, 2010, http://www.rep-am.com/articles/2010/06/11/news/local/doc4c121ffeef035994207908.txt.

63. "N.J. Man Thomas Hill Raped Wife Because She Wouldn't Get Abortion, Say Cops," http://www.cbsnews.com/8301–504083_162–20015352–504083.html; Jason Nark, "Cops: She Won't Get Abortion, So He Rapes Her in Front of Kids," www.phillynews.com, September 1, 2010, http://articles.philly.com/2010–09–01/news/24975737_1_charges-of-sexual-assault-rapes-abortion.

64. See John Futty, "Man Accused of Forced-Abortion Attempt Pleads Guilty in Court," *Columbus Dispatch*, April 28, 2011, http://www.dispatch.com/content/stories/local/2011/04/28/guilty-plea-in-forced-abortion-attempt.html.

65. *The Mercury* (Pottstown, Pennsylvania), April 21, 2011, http://www.pottsmerc.com/articles/2011/04/21/news/srv0000011476405.txt.

66. Isabelle Zehnder, "Breaking News Update: Tragic Revelations in the Murder of Jennifer Morgan, 28, and Her Infant, Ema," December 24, 2009, http://www.examiner.com/article/breaking-news-update-tragic-revelations-the-murder-of-jennifer-morgan-28–and-her-infant-ema.

67. "Houston Sailor Held in Death of Woman Who Reportedly Refused Abortion," *Los Angeles Times*, December 7, 2011, http://latimesblogs.latimes.com/nationnow/2011/12/houston-sailor-arrested-in-death-of-ex-who-refused-abortion.html.

68. See "Man Charged in Decade-Old Murder of Pregnant Girlfriend," ABC7
.com, November 9, 2011, http://abclocal.go.com/kabc/story?section=news/
local/los_angeles&id=8425719 ("'He did not want to be a father so he
wanted to get rid of Crystal and the baby,' said L.A. County Sheriff's
Department Detective Dave Coleman.").

69. MacKinnon, *Feminism Unmodified*, at 101.

70. See Saftlas, Wallis, Shochet, et al., "Prevalence of Intimate Partner Violence
among an Abortion Clinic Population" (Abstract: "Overall, physical and
sexual intimate partner violence prevalence was 9.9% and 2.5%, respectively;
8.4% of those in a current relationship reported battering. Former partners
perpetrated more physical and sexual assaults than did current partners.
Violence severity increased with frequency. Abortion patients experience
high intimate partner violence rates, indicating the need for targeted
screening and community-based referral.").

71. Quoted in Cunningham and Forsythe, "Is Abortion the 'First Right' for
Women?" at 154.

72. Klick and Stratmann, "The Effect of Abortion Legalization on Sexual
Behavior."

73. Donohue and Levitt, "The Impact of Legalized Abortion on Crime," at 386n8
("the decline in births [after *Roe*] is far less than the number of abortions,
suggesting that the number of conceptions increased substantially—an
example of insurance leading to moral hazard. The insurance that abortion
provides against unwanted pregnancy induces more sexual conduct or
diminished protections against pregnancy in a way that substantially increases
the number of pregnancies.").

74. Klick and Stratmann, "The Effect of Abortion Legalization on Sexual
Behavior."

75. Levine, *Sex and Consequences*.

76. Klick and Stratmann, "The Effect of Abortion Legalization on Sexual
Behavior."

77. Bergmann, *The Economic Emergence of Women*, at 46.

78. See, e.g., Alvare, "*Gonzales v. Carhart*: Bringing Abortion Law Back";
Bachiochi, "Embodied Equality."

79. Bachiochi, "Embodied Equality," at 920.

80. Sidney Callahan, "Abortion and the Sexual Agenda," at 177.

81. Alvare, "*Gonzales v. Carhart*: Bringing Abortion Law Back," at 444.

82. Dellapenna, *Dispelling the Myths*, at 955n133.

83. Ibid., at 955.

84. Ibid., at 955n134 and 952n112.

85. Blunt and Steeper, *Turnaround on Abortion*.

86. Bachiochi, "Embodied Equality."

87. Jonathan Last, *Wall Street Journal*, June 18, 2011, C10. See also Last, *What to
Expect When No One's Expecting*.

88. Jonathan Last, *Wall Street Journal*, June 18, 2011, C10.

89. Jonathan V. Last, "The War Against Girls," *Wall Street Journal*, June 24, 2011,

http://online.wsj.com/article/SB10001424052702303657404576361691165
631366.html.

90. Sam Roberts, "U.S. Births Hint at Bias for Boys in Some Asians," *New York Times*, June 14, 2009, http://www.nytimes.com/2009/06/15/nyregion/15babies.html.

91. Thorp, "Public Health Impact"; Thorp, Hartmann, and Shadigian, "Long-Term Physical and Psychological Health Consequences of Induced Abortion."

92. See Last, *What to Expect When No One's Expecting*; Longman, *The Empty Cradle*; Wattenberg, *Fewer*.

93. Hudson and den Boer, *Bare Branches*; Claudia Kalb, "Girl or Boy? The New Science of Sex Selection," *Newsweek*, January 26, 2004, at 45–53.

Conclusion

1. *City of Akron v. Akron Center for Reproductive Health*, 462 U.S. 416, 465 (1983) (O'Connor, J., dissenting).

2. See ibid., 420n1 ("That case was considered with special care."); *Planned Parenthood v. Casey*, 505 U.S. 833, 870 (1992) (plurality opinion of Justices O'Connor, Kennedy, and Souter) ("Any judicial act of line-drawing may seem somewhat arbitrary, but *Roe* was a reasoned statement, elaborated with great care.").

3. Julian Simon, *The Ultimate Resource*; Simon and Kahn, eds., *The Resourceful Earth*. See also Last, *What to Expect When No One's Expecting*.

4. See the May 2012 Gallup Poll by Lydia Saad, "'Pro-Choice' Americans at Record-Low 41%," http://www.gallup.com/poll/154838/Pro-Choice-Americans-Record-Low.aspx. See also Hunter, *Before the Shooting Begins*; Wardle, "The Quandary of Pro-Life Free Speech" (Appendices).

5. In June 1972, Gallup conducted a poll that was reported in the *Washington Post* in August 1972, during the Supreme Court's summer recess and shortly after Justice Blackmun spent his time at the Mayo Clinic Library. The *Washington Post* article on the Gallup Poll reported: "Two out of three Americans think abortion should be a matter for decision solely between a woman and her physician, according to a recent survey conducted by The Gallup Organization." Greenhouse and Siegel, *Before Roe v. Wade*, at 207–208 ("Presumably, those justices who were at home in Washington, or who read an American newspaper elsewhere, were aware of this poll. Clearly, Justice Blackmun was; a copy of the *Washington Post* article reporting the polls results was in his *Roe v. Wade* file.")

6. "CNN/*ORC* Poll," http://i2.cdn.turner.com/cnn/2011/images/09/15/rel15e.pdf (Question 21 and 22 Combined).

7. Polling Company, 2009.

8. There were cases with significant factual records pending at the Court in the fall of 1972 from Connecticut, Louisiana, New York, New Jersey, and Ohio, all of which were dismissed by the Court after the abortion decisions

in February 1973. 410 U.S. 949–951 (1973). Rehearings in *Roe* and *Doe* were denied on February 26, 1973. 410 U.S. 959 (1973).

9. Shadigian and Bauer, "Pregnancy-Associated Death."

10. See, e.g., Radford and Shaw, "Beyond *Roe* and Abstract Rights." Cf. Thorp, "Public Health Impact."

11. On Ireland, see Calhoun et al., "Maternal and Neonatal Health and Abortion." On Chile, see Koch, Thorp, Bravo, et al., "Women's Education Level."

12. Dellapenna, *Dispelling the Myths*, at 749 ("The Emergence of the Fetus"); Ibid. at 754 ("Separate treatment of the fetus as a patient actually had begun as early as 1928. As late as 1970, however, the only intrauterine procedure undertaken with some prospect of success was intrauterine transfusion because of Rh sensitization.").

13. Bernard N. Nathanson, *The Hand of God*, at 140–141.

14. Warren Hern, at the Association of Planned Parenthood Physicians meeting, San Diego, October 26, 1978, quoted in John H. Richardson, "The Last Abortion Doctor," *Esquire*, August 5, 2009, available at: http://www.esquire .com/features/abortion-doctor-warren-hern-0909-6.

15. See Blunt and Steeper, *Turnaround on Abortion*.

16. Ridley, *The Rational Optimist*, at 7–8. See also See also Ben J. Wattenberg, "America's 21st-Century Population Edge," *Wall Street Journal*, May 24, 2012, at A15.

17. William McGurn, "The Not So Dismal Science: Humanitarians v. Economists," *Imprimis* 40 (March 2011). See also Ridley, *The Rational Optimist*; Julian Simon, *The Ultimate Resource*; Simon and Kahn, eds., *The Resourceful Earth*. Ron Bailey recently noted:

> Forty years ago, *The Limits to Growth*, a report to the Club of Rome, was released with great fanfare at a conference at the Smithsonian Institution. The study was based on a computer model developed by researchers at [MIT] and designed "to investigate five major trends of global concern—accelerating industrial development, rapid population growth, widespread malnutrition, depletion of nonrenewable resources, and a deteriorating environment." . . . In 1972, the *Limits* researchers estimated known global oil reserves at 455 billion barrels. Since then the world has produced very nearly 1 trillion barrels of oil and current known reserves hover around 1.2 trillion barrels, a 40-year supply at current consumption rates. With regard to natural gas supplies, the International Energy Agency last year issued a report asserting, "Conventional recoverable resources are equivalent to more than 120 years of current global consumption, while total recoverable resources could sustain today's production for over 250 years." (Ron Bailey, "The Limits of *The Limits to Growth*," April 18, 2012, available at www.reason.com)

18. See Stulberg et al., "Abortion Provision among Practicing Obstetrician-Gynecologists."

19. Emily Bazelon, "The New Abortion Providers," *New York Times Magazine*, July 14, 2010, www.nytimes.com/2010/07/18/magazine/18abortion-t.html?_r=1&pagewanted=all.

20. Thorp, "Public Health Impact," at 5.

21. See www.aaplog.org.

22. *Mack v. Carmack*, 79 So.3d 597 (Ala. 2011). See also *Hamilton v. Scott*, 97 So.3d 728 (Ala. 2012).

23. *Carranza v. United States*, 267 P.3d 912 (Utah 2011).

24. See the fifty-state analysis in Linton, "The Legal Status of Abortion" (2012) (updating Linton, "The Legal Status of Abortion" (2007)). Linton's summary is as follows: "In sum, no more than eleven States—Arizona, Arkansas, Louisiana, Michigan, North Dakota, Oklahoma, Rhode Island, South Dakota, Texas, West Virginia and Wisconsin—and possibly as few as eight—Arkansas, Louisiana, Michigan, North Dakota, Oklahoma, Rhode Island, South Dakota, and Wisconsin—would have enforceable statutes on the books that would prohibit most abortions in the event *Roe* and *Casey* were overruled. In the other thirty-nine States (and the District of Columbia), abortion would be legal for most or all reasons throughout pregnancy." Ibid. at 184. See also Linton, "*Planned Parenthood v. Casey*: The Flight from Reason," at 42n124; Forsythe and Presser, "Restoring Self-Government on Abortion," at 343ff. (Appendix 1); Dellapenna, *Dispelling the Myths*, at 976 ("what might be expected of legislatures?").

25. See Goldberg, "The Commerce Clause and Federal Abortion Law."

26. *Roe v. Wade*, 410 U.S. 113 (1973), at 165.

· BIBLIOGRAPHY ·

Aarons, Z. Alexander. "Therapeutic Abortion and the Psychiatrist." *American Journal of Psychiatry* 124 (1967): 745.

Abele v. Markle. 452 F.2d 1121 (2d Cir. 1971).

Abele v. Markle. 342 F.Supp. 800 (D. Conn. 1972).

Abele v. Markle, 351 F.Supp. 224 (D. Conn. 1972).

Akerlof, George A., Janet L. Yellen, and Michael L. Katz. "An Analysis of Out-of-Wedlock Childbearing in the United States." *Quarterly Journal of Economics* 111 (May 1996): 277.

Alvare, Helen. "*Gonzales v. Carhart*: Bringing Abortion Law Back into the Family Law Fold." *Montana Law Review* 69 (2008): 409.

Amen, John Harlan. "Some Obstacles to Effective Legal Control of Criminal Abortions." In *The Abortion Problem: Proceedings of the Conference Held under the Auspices of the National Committee on Maternal Health, Inc. at the New York Academy of Medicine, June 19th and 20th, 1942,* 134. National Committee on Maternal Health, Williams and Wilkins, 1944.

American Medical Association. "Position on Abortion." *Journal of the American Medical Association* 213 (1970): 359.

American Medical Association, Council on Scientific Affairs. "Induced Termination of Pregnancy before and after *Roe v. Wade*: Trends in the Mortality and Morbidity of Women." *Journal of the American Medical Association* 268 (1992): 3231–3239.

Andenaes, Johs. "General Prevention: Illusion or Reality?" *Journal of Criminal Law, Criminology and Police Science* 43 (1952): 176.

Anum, Emmanuel A., Haywood L. Brown, and Jerome F. Strauss. "Health Disparities in Risk for Cervical Insufficiency." *Human Reproduction* 25 (July 19, 2010): 2894.

Atrash, Hani K., et al. "Legal Abortion in the U.S.: Trends and Mortality." *Contemporary OB/GYN* 35 (February 1990): 58.

Atrash, H. K., T. G. Cheek, and C. J. Hogue. "Legal Abortion Mortality and General Anesthesia." *American Journal of Obstetrics and Gynecology* 158 (1988): 420.

Babbitz v. McCann. 310 F.Supp. 293 (E.D. Wis. 1970), appeal dismissed, 400 U.S. 1 (1970).

Bachiochi, Erika, ed. *The Cost of "Choice": Women Evaluate the Impact of Abortion.* 2004.

———. "Embodied Equality: Debunking Equal Protection Arguments for Abortion Rights." *Harvard Journal of Law and Public Policy* 34 (2011): 889.

Bacon, C. S. "Chicago Medical Society, Regular Meeting, Held November 23, 1904." *Journal of the American Medical Association* (December 17, 1904): 1889.

Baird, Robert M., and Stuart E. Rosenbaum, eds. *The Ethics of Abortion: Pro-Life vs. Pro-Choice.* 3rd ed. 2001.

Balkin, Jack, ed. *What* Roe v. Wade *Should Have Said: The Nation's Top Legal Experts Rewrite America's Most Controversial Decision.* 2007.

Barnard, Thomas H., Jr. "An Analysis and Criticism of the Model Penal Code Provisions on the Law of Abortion." *Western Reserve Law Review* 18 (1967): 540.

Barnett, Winfried, et al. "Partnership after Induced Abortion: A Prospective Controlled Study." *Archives of Sexual Behavior* 21 (1992): 443.

Barsh, Joanna, and Susie Cranston. *How Remarkable Women Lead.* 2010.

Bates, Jerome. "The Abortion Mill: An Institutional Study." *Journal of Criminal Law, Criminology, and Police Science* 45 (1954): 157.

Beck, D. "Interruption of Pregnancy and Guilt Feelings." *Schweizerische Medizinische Wochenschrift* 94 (1964): 357.

Beck, Randy. "The Essential Holding of *Casey*: Rethinking Viability." *UMKC Law Review* 75 (2007): 713.

———. "*Gonzales, Casey* and the Viability Rule." *Northwestern University Law Review* 103 (2009): 249.

———. "Self-Conscious Dicta: The Origins of *Roe v. Wade*'s Trimester Framework." *American Journal of Legal History* 51 (2011): 505.

Bennett, J., and J. Amen. *A Presentment on the Suppression of Criminal Abortions, By the Grand Jury for the Extraordinary Special and Trial Term.* New York Supreme Court, October 15, 1941.

Bennett, William. *The Index of Leading Cultural Indicators: Facts and Figures on the State of American Society.* 1994.

Beral, V., D. Bull, R. Doll, et al. "Breast Cancer and Abortion: Collaborative Reanalysis of Data from 53 Epidemiological Studies, Including 83,000 Women with Breast Cancer from 16 Countries." *Lancet* 363 (March 27, 2004): 1007.

Bergmann, Barbara R. *The Economic Emergence of Women.* Basic Books, 1986.

Black, Cathie. *Basic Black: The Essential Guide for Getting Ahead at Work (and in Life).* 2007.

Blackmun, Harry A., Papers. Library of Congress.

Blackstone, William. *Commentaries on the Laws of England.* 4 vols. 1765–1769; University of Chicago Press, 1979.

Blake, Judith. "Abortion and Public Opinion: The 1960–1970 Decade." *Science* n.s. 171 (February 12, 1971): 540.

———. "Elective Abortion and Our Reluctant Citizenry: Research on Public Opinion in the United States." In *The Abortion Experience: Psychological and Medical Impact,* edited by Howard J. Osofsky and Joy D. Osofsky, chapter 22. Harper and Row, 1973.

Blunt, Christopher, and Fred Steeper. *Turnaround on Abortion.* June 2007. Available at http://www.overbrookresearch.com/publications.html.

Bopp, James, Jr., and Richard E. Coleson. "The Right to Abortion: Anomalous, Absolute, and Ripe for Reversal." *BYU Journal of Public Law* 3 (1989): 181.

Bordlee, Dorinda. "Abortion-Alternative Legislation and the Law of the Gift." In *The Cost of "Choice": Women Evaluate the Impact of Abortion,* edited by Erika Bachiochi. 2004.

Bradshaw, Z., and P. Slade. "The Effects of Induced Abortion on Emotional Experiences and Relationships: A Critical Review of the Literature." *Clinical Psychology Review* 23 (2003): 929.

Brennan, William J. "A Tribute to Norman Dorsen." *Harvard Civil Rights–Civil Liberties Law Review* 27 (1992): 309.

Brennan, William J., Papers. Library of Congress.

Breyer, Stephen. *Making Our Democracy Work: A Judge's View.* Knopf, 2010.

Brind, Joel. "Induced Abortion as an Independent Risk Factor for Breast Cancer: A Critical Review of Recent Studies Based on Prospective Data." *Journal of American Physicians and Surgeons* 10 (2005): 105, http://www.jpands.org/vol10no4/brind.pdf.

Brind, Joel, Vernon M. Chinchilli, Walter B. Severs, and Joan Summy-Long. "Induced Abortion as an Independent Risk Factor for Breast Cancer: A Comprehensive Review and Meta-Analysis." *Journal of Epidemiology and Community Health* 50 (1996): 481.

Broen, A. N., et al. "Reasons for Induced Abortion and Their Relation to Women's Emotional Distress: A Prospective, Two-Year Follow-Up Study." *General Hospital Psychiatry* 27 (2005): 36.

Bumpass, Larry, and Charles F. Westoff. "The 'Perfect Contraceptive' Population." *Science* 169 (September 1970): 1177.

Burtchaell, James. *Rachel Weeping: And Other Essays on Abortion.* Life Cycle, 1990.

Byrn, Robert M. "An American Tragedy: The Supreme Court on Abortion." *Fordham Law Review* 41 (1973): 807.

Calderone, Mary, ed. *Abortion in the United States: A Conference Sponsored by the Planned Parenthood Federation of America, Inc.* 1958.

———. "Illegal Abortion as a Public Health Problem." *American Journal of Public Health* 50 (July 1960): 948.

Calhoun, B. C., E. Shadigian, and B. Rooney. "Cost Consequences of Induced Abortion as an Attributable Risk for Preterm Birth and Impact on Informed Consent." *Journal of Reproductive Medicine* 52 (October 2007): 929.

Calhoun, Byron, John M. Thorp, and Patrick S. Carroll. "Maternal and Neonatal Health and Abortion: The 40-Year Experience in Great Britain and Ireland." *Journal of American Physicians and Surgeons* 18 (2013): 42.

Calhoun, Samuel W. "Stopping Philadelphia Abortion Provider Kermit Gosnell and Preventing Others Like Him: An Outcome That Both Pro-Choicers and Pro-Lifers Should Support." *Villanova Law Review* 57 (2012): 1.

Callahan, Daniel. "Abortion: Some Ethical Issues." In *Abortion, Society and the Law*, edited by David F. Walbert and J. Douglas Butler, 96. 1973.

———. "An Ethical Challenge to Prochoice Advocates." *Commonweal*, 117, no. 20 (November 1990).

Callahan, Sidney. "Abortion and the Sexual Agenda." In *The Ethics of Abortion: Pro-Life vs. Pro-Choice*, edited by Robert M. Baird and Stuart E. Rosenbaum, 167. 3rd ed. 2001.

Carroll, Patrick. *Ireland's Gain: The Demographic Impact and Consequences for the Health of Women of the Abortion Laws in Ireland and Northern Ireland since 1968.* PAPRI (Pension and Population Research Institute), December 2011. Available at http://www.papriresearch.org/papriresearchpublished papers.html.

Cates, Willard, Jr., Jack C. Smith, Roger W. Rochat, et al. "Assessment of Surveillance and Vital Statistics Data for Monitoring Abortion Mortality, United States, 1972–1975." *American Journal of Epidemiology* 108 (September 1978): 200–206.

Chang, Jeani, et al. "Pregnancy-Related Mortality Surveillance—United States, 1991–1999." *Morbidity and Mortality Weekly Report* 52 (February 21, 2003). http://www.cdc.gov/mmwr/preview/mmwrhtml/ss5202a1.htm.

Chemerinsky, Erwin. "Rationalizing the Abortion Debate: Legal Rhetoric and the Abortion Controversy." *Buffalo Law Review* 31 (1982): 107.

Clark, Tom C. "Religion, Morality, and Abortion: A Constitutional Appraisal." *Loyola of Los Angeles Law Review* 2 (1969): 1.

Coleman, Priscilla K. "Abortion and Mental Health: Quantitative Synthesis and Analysis of Research Published 1995–2009." *British Journal of Psychiatry* 199 (September 2011): 180–186.

———. "Induced Abortion and Increased Risk of Substance Abuse: A Review of the Evidence." *Current Women's Health Reviews* 1 (2005): 21.

———. "Resolution of Unwanted Pregnancy during Adolescence through Abortion versus Childbirth: Individual and Family Predictors and Psychological Consequences." *Journal of Youth and Adolescence* 35 (2006): 903.

Coleman, P. K., C. T. Coyle, M. Shuping, and V. M. Rue. "Induced Abortion and Anxiety, Mood, and Substance Abuse Disorders: Isolating the Effects of Abortion in the National Comorbidity Survey." *Journal of Psychiatric Research* 43 (2009): 770. Corrigendum, *Journal of Psychiatric Research* 45 (2011): 1133.

Coleman, P. K., D. C. Reardon, V. M. Rue, and J. Cougle. "A History of Induced Abortion in Relation to Substance Use during Subsequent Pregnancies Carried to Term." *American Journal of Obstetrics and Gynecology* 187 (2002): 1673.

Coleman, P. K., D. C. Reardon, V. M. Rue, and J. Cougle. "State-Funded Abortions versus Deliveries: A Comparison of Outpatient Mental Health Claims over 4 Years." *American Journal of Orthopsychiatry* 73 (2002): 141.

Collins, Gail. *When Everything Changed: The Amazing Journey of American Women from 1960 to the Present.* 2009.

Comment. "The Role of the Law of Homicide in Fetal Destruction." *Iowa Law Review* 56 (1971): 658.

Cooke, Robert E., et al., eds. *The Terrible Choice: The Abortion Dilemma.* 1968.

Corkey v. Edwards. 322 F.Supp. 1248 (W.D.N.C. 1971), vacated and remanded, 410 U.S. 950 (1973).

Cougle, J. R., D. C. Reardon, and P. K. Coleman. "Generalized Anxiety Following Unintended Pregnancies Resolved through Childbirth and Abortion: A Cohort Study of the 1995 National Survey of Family Growth." *Journal of Anxiety Disorders* 19 (2005): 137.

———. "Depression Associated with Abortion and Childbirth: A Long-Term Analysis of the NLSY Cohort." *Medical Science Monitor* 9 (2003): 157.

Crain, Christopher A. "Judicial Restraint and the Non-Decision in *Webster v. Reproductive Health Services.*" *Harvard Journal of Law and Public Policy* 13 (1990): 263.

Crandall, Candace. "Three Decades of Empty Promises." In *The Cost of "Choice": Women Evaluate the Impact of Abortion,* edited by Erika Bachiochi, 17. 2004.

Cunningham, Paige Comstock, and Clarke Forsythe. "Is Abortion the 'First Right' for Women?" In *Abortion, Medicine, and the Law,* edited by J. Douglas Butler and David F. Walbert. 4th ed. 1992.

Cushman, Clare. *Courtwatchers: Eyewitness Accounts in Supreme Court History.* Rowman and Littlefield, 2011.

Daling, Janet, et al. "Risk of Breast Cancer among Young Women: Relationship to Induced Abortion." *Journal of the National Cancer Institute* 86 (November 1994): 1584.

Danforth, David N., et al., eds. *Textbook of Obstetrics and Gynecology.* 2nd ed. 1971.

Davies, D. Seaborne. "Child-Killing in English Law." *Modern Law Review* 1 (1937): 203.

Dellapenna, Joseph W. *Dispelling the Myths of Abortion History.* Carolina Academic Press, 2006.

———. "The History of Abortion: Technology, Morality and Law." *University of Pittsburgh Law Review* 40 (1979): 359.

Del Tufo, Robert J. "Recovery for Prenatal Torts: Actions for Wrongful Death." *Rutgers Law Review* 15 (1960): 61.

Destro, Robert. "Abortion and the Constitution: The Need for a Life-Protective Amendment." *California Law Review* 63 (1975): 1250.

Di Renzo, G. C., I. Giardina, A. Rosati, et al. "Maternal Risk Factors for Preterm Birth: A Country-Based Population Analysis." *European Journal of Obstetrics, Gynecology, and Reproductive Biology* 159 (December 2011): 342–346.

Dodds, Tracy Leigh. Note. "Defending America's Children: How the Current

System Gets It Wrong." *Harvard Journal of Law and Public Policy* 29 (2006): 719.

Doe v. Bolton, 319 F.Supp. 1048 (N.D. Ga. 1970), appeal docketed, 39 U.S.L.W. 333 (U.S. Nov. 14, 1970) (No. 971).

Doe v. Bolton, 410 U.S. 179 (1973).

Doe v. Scott, 321 F.Supp. 1385 (N.D. Ill. 1971).

Donohue, John J., and Steven D. Levitt. "The Impact of Legalized Abortion on Crime." *Quarterly Journal of Economics* 116 (May 2001): 379.

Dorsen, David M. *Henry Friendly: Greatest Judge of His Era.* Harvard University Press, 2012.

Dorsett, Walter. "Criminal Abortion in Its Broadest Sense." *Journal of the American Medical Association* 51 (September 19, 1908): 957.

Douglas, William O., Papers. Library of Congress.

Duthie, S. J., D. Hobson, I. A. Tait, et al. "Morbidity after Termination of Pregnancy in First Trimester." *Genitourinary Medicine* 63 (1987): 182.

Dyer, Frederick N. *The Physicians' Crusade against Abortion.* 1999, 2005.

———. *Champion of Women and the Unborn: Horatio Robinson Storer, M.D.* 1999.

Eastman, Nicholson J., and Louis M. Hellman. *Williams Obstetrics.* 13th ed. 1966.

Eisenstadt v. Baird. 405 U.S. 438 (1972).

Eisler, Kim Isaac. *A Justice for All: William J. Brennan, Jr., and the Decisions That Transformed America.* 1993.

Ekblad, M. "Induced Abortion on Psychiatric Grounds: A Follow-Up Study of 479 Women." *Acta Psychiatrica et Neurologica Scandinavica*, Suppl. 99 (1955): 1–238.

Elshtain, Jean Bethke. "*Roe v. Wade*: Speaking the Unspeakable." In *Great Cases in Constitutional Law*, edited by Robert P. George, 175. 2000.

Ely, John Hart. "The Wages of Crying Wolf: A Comment on *Roe v. Wade.*" *Yale Law Journal* 82 (1973): 920.

Emerson, Thomas. "Nine Justices in Search of a Doctrine." *Michigan Law Review* 64 (1965): 219.

Faria, Gearaldine, et al. "Women and Abortion: Attitudes, Social Networks, Decision-making." *Social Work in Health Care* 11 (Fall 1985): 85.

Faux, Marian. Roe v. Wade: *The Untold Story of the Landmark Supreme Court Decision That Made Abortion Legal.* 1988.

Fergusson, D. M., L. J. Horwood, and J. M. Boden. "Abortion and Mental Health Disorders: Evidence from a 30-Year Longitudinal Study." *British Journal of Psychiatry* 193 (2008): 444.

Fergusson, D. M., L. J. Horwood, and E. M. Ridder. "Abortion in Young Women and Subsequent Mental Health." *Journal of Child Psychology and Psychiatry* 47 (2006): 16.

Fisher, Russell S. "Criminal Abortion." *Journal of Crimnal Law, Criminology, and Police Science* 42 (1951): 242. Reprinted in Rosen, ed., *Therapeutic Abortion.*

Fleck, Stephen. "Some Psychiatric Aspects of Abortion." *Journal of Nervous and Mental Disease* 151 (1970): 42.

Fletcher, John C., and Mark I. Evans. "Maternal Bonding in Early Fetal Ultrasound Examination." *New England Journal of Medicine* 308 (February 17, 1983): 392.

Forssman, Hans, and Inga Thuwe. "One Hundred and Twenty Children Born after Application for Therapeutic Abortion Refused." In *Abortion and the Unwanted Child,* edited by Carl Reiterman. 1970.

Forsythe, Clarke D. "The Effective Enforcement of Abortion Law before *Roe v. Wade.*" In *The Silent Subject: Reflections on the Unborn in American Culture,* edited by Brad Stetson. Praeger, 1996.

———. "Homicide of the Unborn Child: The Born Alive Rule and Other Legal Anachronisms." *Valparaiso University Law Review* 21 (1987): 563.

———. "The Legacy of Oliver Wendell Holmes." Book review. *University of Detroit Mercy Law Review* 69 (1992): 677.

Forsythe, Clarke D., and Bradley N. Kehr. "A Road Map through the Supreme Court's Back Alley." *Villanova Law Review* 57 (2012): 45.

Forsythe, Clarke, and Stephen B. Presser. "The Tragic Failure of *Roe v. Wade*: Why Abortion Should be Returned to the States." *Texas Review of Law and Politics* 10 (2005): 87.

Forsythe, Clarke D., and Stephen B. Presser. "Restoring Self-Government on Abortion: A Federalism Amendment." *Texas Review of Law and Politics* 10 (2006): 301.

Foudress, Bruce W. Note. "*State v. Abodeely,* (Iowa 1970)." *Drake Law Review* 20 (1971): 666.

Freak-Poli, R., A. Chan, J. Gaeme, and J. Street. "Previous Abortion and Risk of Preterm Birth: A Population Study." *Journal of Maternal-Fetal Medicine* 22 (January 2009): 1.

Fried, Charles. "The Conservatism of Justice Harlan." *New York Law School Law Review* 36 (1991): 33.

———. *Order and Law: Arguing the Reagan Revolution—A Firsthand Account.* Simon and Schuster, 1991.

Friedman, Lawrence M. "The Conflict over Constitutional Legitimacy." In *The Abortion Dispute and the American System,* edited by Gilbert Y. Steiner. Brookings Institution, 1982.

Friendly, Henry J. "The Courts and Social Policy: Substance and Procedure." *University of Miami Law Review* 33 (1978): 21.

Garrow, David J. "The Brains behind Blackmun." *Legal Affairs* (May–June 2005): 26–34, http://www.legalaffairs.org/issues/May-June-2005/feature_garrow _mayjun05.msp.

———. *Liberty and Sexuality: The Right to Privacy and the Making of* Roe v. Wade. 1st ed. 1994.

———. "Revelations on the Road to *Roe.*" *American Lawyer* 22 (May 2000): 80–83.

———. Book Review. "*Roe v. Wade* Revisited." *Green Bag* 2nd ser., 9 (Autumn 2005): 71.

Gauthier, Aimee M. "*Stenberg v. Carhart*: Have the States Lost Their Power to Regulate Abortion?" *New England Law Review* 36 (2002): 625.

Gavigan, Shelley. "The Criminal Sanction as It Relates to Human Reproduction: The Genesis of the Statutory Prohibition of Abortion." *Journal of Legal History* 5 (1984): 20.

Gebhard, Paul H., Wardell B. Pomeroy, Clyde E. Martin, and Cornelia V. Christenson. *Pregnancy, Birth and Abortion.* 1958.

Ginsburg, Ruth Bader. "Speaking in a Judicial Voice." *New York University Law Review* 67 (1992): 1185.

Gissler, Mika, et al. "Injury, Deaths, Suicides and Homicides Associated with Pregnancy, Finland 1987–2000." *European Journal of Public Health* 15 (2005): 459.

———. "Methods for Identifying Pregnancy-Associated Deaths: Population-Based Data from Finland, 1987–2000." *Paediatric and Perinatal Epidemiology* 18 (2004): 448.

———. "Pregnancy-Associated Deaths in Finland, 1987–1994—Definition Problems and Benefits of Record Linkage." *Acta Obstetricia et Gynecologica Scandinavica* 76 (1997): 651.

———. "Suicides after Pregnancy in Finland, 1987–1994: Register Linkage Study." *British Medical Journal* 313 (1996): 1431.

Gissler, Mika, and Elina Hemminki. "Pregnancy-Related Violent Deaths." *Scandinavian Journal of Public Health* 27 (1999): 54.

Glendon, Mary Ann. *Abortion and Divorce in Western Law: American Failures, European Challenges.* 1987.

———. "From Culture Wars to Building a Culture of Life." In *The Cost of "Choice": Women Evaluate the Impact of Abortion,* edited by Erika Bachiochi, 3. 2004.

Gold, Edwin M., Carl L. Erhardt, Harold Jacobziner, and Frieda G. Nelson. "Therapeutic Abortions in New York City: A 20-Year Review." *American Journal of Public Health* 55 (July 1965): 964.

Goldberg, Jordan. "The Commerce Clause and Federal Abortion Law: Why Progressives Might Be Tempted to Embrace Federalism." *Fordham Law Review* 75 (2006): 301.

Goldsmith, S., and A. Margolis. "Aspiration Abortion without Cervical Dilation." *American Journal of Obstetrics and Gynecology* 110 (June 1971): 580.

Gordon, Hymie. "Genetical, Social and Medical Aspects of Abortion." *South African Medical Journal* 42 (July 1968): 721.

Greenberg, Ethan. *Dred Scott and the Dangers of a Political Court.* 2009.

Greenhill, J. P. *Obstetrics.* 13th ed. 1965.

Greenhouse, Linda. *Becoming Justice Blackmun: Harry Blackmun's Supreme Court Journey.* 2005.

Greenhouse, Linda, and Reva B. Siegel. *Before Roe v. Wade: Voices That Shaped the Abortion Debate before the Supreme Court's Ruling.* 2010.

Grimes, D. A., W. Cates, Jr., and R. M. Selik. "Fatal Septic Abortion in the United States, 1975–1977." *Obstetrics and Gynecology* 57 (June 1981): 739–744.

Grimes, D. A., M. E. Kafrissen, K. R. O'Reilly, and N. J. Binkin. "Fatal Hemorrhage from Legal Abortion in the United States." *Surgery, Gynecology, and Obstetrics* 157 (1983): 461.

Grisez, Germain. *Abortion: The Myths, the Realities, and the Arguments.* 1970.

Griswold v. Connecticut. 381 U.S. 479 (1965).

Gronlund, Mimi Clark. *Supreme Court Justice Tom C. Clark: A Life of Service.* University of Texas Press, 2010.

Group for the Advancement of Psychiatry. *The Right to Abortion: A Psychiatric View.* October 1969.

Guttmacher, Alan F., ed. *Babies by Choice or by Chance.* 1959.

————. *Birth Control and Love: The Complete Guide to Contraception and Fertility.* 2nd rev. ed. 1969.

————, ed. *The Case for Legalized Abortion Now.* 1967.

————. *Into This Universe: The Story of Human Birth.* Viking Press, 1937.

————. "The Shrinking Non-Psychiatric Indications for Therapeutic Abortion." In *Therapeutic Abortion: Medical, Psychiatric, Legal, and Anthropological Considerations,* edited by Harold Rosen. 1954.

————. "Therapeutic Abortion: The Doctor's Dilemma." *Journal of the Mount Sinai Hospital, New York* 21 (1954): 111.

Hall, Robert E., ed. *Abortion in a Changing World.* 1970.

————. "Abortion in American Hospitals." *American Journal of Public Health* 57 (November 1967): 1933.

————. "Commentary." In *Abortion and the Law,* edited by David T. Smith. Press of Case Western Reserve University, 1967.

————. "Therapeutic Abortion, Sterilization, and Contraception." *American Journal of Obstetrics and Gynecology* 91 (February 1965): 518.

————. "The Truth about Abortion in New York." *Columbia Forum* 13 (Winter 1970): 18.

Hall v. Lefkowitz. 305 F.Supp. 1030 (S.D.N.Y. 1969).

Harris, Lisa H., Alexandra Cooper, Kenneth A. Rasinski, et al. "Obstetrician-Gynecologists' Objections to and Willingness to Help Patients Obtain an Abortion." *Obstetrics and Gynecology* 118 (October 2011): 905.

Harris, Thomas E. "A Functional Study of Existing Abortion Laws." *Columbia Law Review* 35 (1935): 87.

Harrison, Michael R., N. Scott Adzick, Michael T. Longaker, et al. "Successful Repair In Utero of a Fetal Diaphragmatic Hernia after Removal of Herniated Viscera from the Left Thorax." *New England Journal of Medicine* 322 (1990): 1582.

Harrison, Michael R., Mitchell S. Golbus, and Roy A. Filly. *The Unborn Patient: Prenatal Diagnosis and Treatment.* 1984.

Healy, Bernadine. *A New Prescription for Women's Health: Getting the Best Medical Care in a Man's World.* 1995.

Hellman, Louis M., and Jack A. Pritchard, eds. *Williams Obstetrics.* 14th ed. 1971.

Hern, Warren M., and Bonnie Andrikopoulos, eds. *Abortion in the Seventies: Proceedings of the Western Regional Conference on Abortion, Denver, Colorado, February 27–29, 1976.* National Abortion Federation, 1977.

Hewlett, Sylvia Ann. *Creating a Life: Professional Women and the Quest for Children.* 2002.

———. *Off-Ramps and On-Ramps: Keeping Talented Women on the Road to Success.* 2007.

Hilgers, Thomas W. "The Medical Hazards of Legally Induced Abortion." In *Abortion and Social Justice*, edited by Thomas W. Hilgers and Dennis J. Horan. Sheed and Ward, 1972.

Hilgers, Thomas W., and Dennis O'Hare. "Abortion Related Maternal Mortality: An In-Depth Analysis." In *New Perspectives on Human Abortion*, edited by Thomas W. Hilgers, Dennis J. Horan, and David Mall, 69. 1981.

Hittinger, Russell. "Abortion before *Roe.*" *First Things* (October 1994); reprinted in *First Things* (March 2010).

Hochschild, Arlie. *The Second Shift: Working Parents and the Revolution at Home.* 1989.

Hopkin, William R., Jr. Note. "*Roe v. Wade* and the Traditional Legal Standards Concerning Pregnancy." *Temple Law Quarterly* 47 (1974): 715.

Horan, Dennis J., Clarke D. Forsythe, and Edward Grant. "Two Ships Passing in the Night: An Interpretavist Review of the White-Stevens Colloquy on *Roe v. Wade.*" *Saint Louis University Public Law Review* 6 (1987): 229.

Horon, Isabelle, and Diana Cheng. "Enhanced Surveillance for Pregnancy-Associated Mortality—Maryland, 1993–1998." *Journal of the American Medical Association* 285 (March 21, 2001): 1455.

Hudson, Valerie M., and Andrea M. den Boer. *Bare Branches: The Security Implications of Asia's Surplus Male Population.* 2004.

Humphries, Drew. "The Movement to Legalize Abortion: A Historical Account." In *Corrections and Punishment*, edited by David F. Greenberg, chapter 9. Sage Publications, 1977.

Hunter, James Davison. *Before the Shooting Begins: Searching for Democracy in America's Culture War.* Free Press, 1994.

Hurwitz, Andrew D. "Jon O. Newman and the Abortion Decisions, a Remarkable First Year." *New York Law School Law Review* 46 (2002–2003): 231.

Hutchinson, Dennis J. *The Man Who Once Was Whizzer White: A Portrait of Justice Byron R. White.* 1998.

Irons, Peter, and Stephanie Guitton, eds. *May It Please the Court: The Most Significant Oral Arguments Made before the Supreme Court since 1955.* Book and separate 6-cassette set. The New Press, 1993.

Jeffries, John C., Jr. *Justice Lewis F. Powell, Jr.: A Biography.* 1994.

Jones, R. K., and K. Kost. "Underreporting of Induced and Spontaneous Abortion in the United States: An Analysis of the 2002 National Survey of Family Growth." *Studies in Family Planning* 38 (2007): 187–197.

Judges, Donald P. *Hard Choices, Lost Voices: How the Abortion Conflict Has Divided America, Distorted Constitutional Rights, and Damaged the Courts.* 1993.

Kadar, David. "The Law of Tortious Prenatal Death Since *Roe v. Wade.*" *Missouri Law Review* 45 (1980): 639.

Kafrissen, Michael E., David A. Grimes, Carol J. Hogue, and Jeffrey J. Sacks. "Cluster of Abortion Deaths at a Single Facility." *Obstetrics and Gynecology* 68 (September 1986): 387.

Kenny, Mary. *Abortion: The Whole Story*. 1986.

Keown, John. *Abortion, Doctors and the Law: Some Aspects of the Legal Regulation of Abortion in England from 1803 to 1982*. Cambridge University Press, 1988.

Kindley, John. "The Fit between the Elements for an Informed Consent Cause of Action and the Scientific Evidence Linking Induced Abortion with Increased Breast Cancer Risk." *Wisconsin Law Review* 1998 (1998): 1595–1644.

Klassen, A.D., and S.C. Wilsnack. "Sexual Experience and Drinking among Women in a U.S. National Survey." *Archives of Sexual Behavior* 15 (1986): 363.

Klick, Jonathan, and Thomas Stratmann. "The Effect of Abortion Legalization on Sexual Behavior: Evidence from Sexually Transmitted Diseases." *Journal of Legal Studies* 32 (2003): 407.

Koch, Elard, John Thorp, Miguel Bravo, et al. "Women's Education Level, Maternal Health Facilities, Abortion Legislation and Maternal Deaths: A Natural Experiment in Chile from 1957 to 2007." *PLoS ONE* 7(5) (May 2012). Available at http://dx.plos.org/10.1371/journal.pone.0036613.

Kolblova, Vera. Letter to the Editor. "Legal Abortion in Czechoslovakia." *Journal of the American Medical Association* 196 (April 25, 1966): 371.

Koonin, Lisa M., Jack C. Smith, Merrell Ramick, and Clarice A. Green. "Abortion Surveillance—United States, 1992." *Morbidity and Mortality Weekly Report: CDC Surveillance Summaries* 45 (May 3, 1996): 1–36.

Koonin, Lisa M., J.C. Smith, M. Ramick, and H.W. Lawson. "Abortion Surveillance—United States, 1989." *Morbidity and Mortality Weekly Report: CDC Surveillance Summaries*, 41 (September 4, 1992): 1–33.

Kopp, Marie E. *Birth Control in Practice*. 1934.

Kurjak, Asim, ed. *The Fetus as a Patient: Proceedings of the First International Symposium*. Sveti Stefan, Yugoslavia, June 4–7, 1984. New York, 1985.

Kurland, Phillip B., and Gerhard Casper, eds. *Landmark Briefs and Arguments of the Supreme Court of the United States: Constitutional Law: Roe v. Wade*. 1973; University Publications of America, 1990.

Lader, Lawrence. *Abortion*. Beacon Press, 1966.

Ladwein, Peter M. Note. "Discerning the Meaning of *Gonzales v. Carhart*: The End of the Physician Veto and the Resulting Change in Abortion Jurisprudence." *Notre Dame Law Review* 83 (2008): 1847.

LaFache, Anthony J. "The New York Abortion Reform Law: Considerations, Applications and Legal Consequences—More Than We Bargained For?" *Albany Law Review* 35 (1971): 644.

Lanfranchi, Angela. "The Abortion-Breast Cancer Link: The Studies and the Science." In *The Cost of "Choice": Women Evaluate the Impact of Abortion*, edited by Erika Bachiochi, 72–86. 2004.

Last, Jonathan. *What to Expect When No One's Expecting: America's Coming Demographic Disaster*. Encounter Books, 2013.

Lawson, Herschel W., Alice Frye, Hani K. Atrash, et al. "Abortion Mortality, United States, 1972 through 1987." *American Journal of Obstetrics and Gynecology* 171 (November 1994): 1365.

Lazarus, Edward. *Closed Chambers: The First Eyewitness Account of the Epic Struggles inside the Supreme Court.* 1998.

Leavitt, Judith Walzer. *Brought to Bed: Child-Bearing in America, 1750–1950.* 1986.

Leavy, Zad. "Criminal Abortion: Facing the Facts." *Los Angeles Bar Bulletin* 34 (1959): 355.

Leavy, Zad, and Jerome Kummer. "Criminal Abortion: Human Hardship and Unyielding Laws." *Southern California Law Review* 35 (1962): 123.

LeBolt, Scot A., David A. Grimes, and Willard Cates. "Mortality from Abortion and Childbirth: Are the Populations Comparable?" *Journal of the American Medical Associaton* 248 (1982): 188.

Lerner, R. C. "Geographic Distribution of Need for Family Planning and Subsidized Services in the United States." *American Journal of Public Health* 60 (October 1970): 1945.

Leval, Pierre. "Judging under the Constitution: Dicta about Dicta." *New York University Law Review* 81 (2006): 1249.

Levine, Phillip B. *Sex and Consequences: Abortion, Public Policy, and the Economics of Fertility.* Princeton University Press, 2004.

Linton, Paul Benjamin. "Enforcement of State Abortion Statutes after *Roe*: A State-By-State Analysis." *University of Detroit Law Review* 67 (1990): 157.

———. "The Legal Status of Abortion in the States If *Roe v. Wade* Is Overruled." *Issues in Law and Medicine* 23 (2007): 3.

———. "The Legal Status of Abortion in the States If *Roe v. Wade* Is Overruled." *Issues in Law and Medicine* 27 (2012): 181.

———. "The Legal Status of the Unborn Child under State Law." *University of St. Thomas Journal of Law and Public Policy* 6 (2011): 141.

———. "*Planned Parenthood v. Casey*: The Flight from Reason in the Supreme Court." *Saint Louis University Public Law Review* 13 (1993): 15.

Longman, Phillip. *The Empty Cradle: How Falling Birthrates Threaten World Prosperity and What to Do About It.* 2004.

Lowe, Hugh. Note. "Abortion." *Texas Law Review* 48 (1970): 937.

Lucas, Roy. "Federal Constitutional Limitations on the Enforcement and Administration of State Abortion Statutes." *North Carolina Law Review* 46 (1968): 730.

Lucas, Roy, Abortion Litigation Papers. Olin Memorial Library, Special Collections and Archives, Wesleyan University, Middletown, Connecticut. http://www.wesleyan.edu/library/schome/FAs/LU1000-187.xml.

Luke, Barbara. *Every Pregnant Woman's Guide to Preventing Premature Birth.* 2002.

Luker, Kristin. *Taking Chances: Abortion and the Decision Not to Contracept.* 1975.

MacKinnon, Catharine A. *Feminism Unmodified: Discourses on Life and Law.* Harvard University Press, 1987.

———. "*Roe vs. Wade*: A Study in Male Ideology." In *Abortion: Moral and Legal Perspectives*, edited by J. Garfield and P. Hennessay. University of Massachusetts Press, 1984.

Maeda, K., ed. *The Fetus as a Patient '87: Proceedings of the Third International Sym-*

posium "The Fetus as a Patient." Matsue, Japan, July 20–23, 1987. New York, 1987.

Magnet, Myron, ed. *Modern Sex: Liberation and Its Discontents.* 2001.

Maledon, William J. Note. "The Law and the Unborn Child: The Legal and Logical Inconsistencies." *Notre Dame Lawyer* 46 (1971): 349.

Maltz, Earl M. *The Chief Justiceship of Warren Burger, 1969–1986.* University of South Carolina Press, 2000.

Margolis, A., et al. "Therapeutic Abortion Follow-Up Study." *American Journal of Obstetrics and Gynecology* 110 (May 15, 1971): 243.

Margolis, A.J., and E.W. Overstreet. "Legal Abortion without Hospitalization." *Obstetrics and Gynecology* 36 (September 1970): 479.

Mathewes-Green, Frederica. *Real Choices: Listening to Women; Looking for Alternatives to Abortion.* 1994, 1997.

McConnell, Michael W. "How Not to Promote Serious Deliberation about Abortion." *University of Chicago Law Review* 58 (1991): 1181.

———. "The Right to Die and the Jurisprudence of Tradition." *Utah Law Review* 1997 (1997): 665.

McFarlane, J., et al. "Abuse during Pregnancy and Femicide: Urgent Implications for Women's Health." *Obstetrics and Gynecology* 100 (2002): 27–36.

McGrew, Jane Lang. Comment. "To Be or Not to Be: The Constitutional Question of the California Abortion Law." *University of Pennsylvania Law Review* 118 (1970): 643.

Means, Cyril C., Jr. "The Law of New York Concerning Abortion and the Status of the Foetus, 1664–1968: A Case of Cessation of Constitutionality." *New York Law Forum* 14 (1968): 411.

———. "The Phoenix of Abortional Freedom: Is a Penumbral or Ninth-Amendment Right About to Arise from the Nineteenth-Century Legislative Ashes of a Fourteenth Century Common-Law Liberty?" *New York Law Forum* 17 (1971): 335.

Meehan, Mary. "The Road to Abortion, Part I: How Eugenics Birthed Population Control." *Human Life Review* (Fall 1998).

Mehland, K.H. "Combating Illegal Abortion in the Socialist Countries of Europe." *World Medical Journal* 12 (1966): 84.

Melbye, Mads, et al. "Induced Abortion and the Risk of Breast Cancer." *New England Journal of Medicine* 336 (1997): 81.

Mersky, Roy M., ed. *A Documentary History of the Legal Aspects of Abortion in the United States: Colautti v. Franklin.* 2000.

Mersky, Roy M., and Jill Duffy, eds. *A Documentary History of the Legal Aspects of Abortion in the United States: Griswold v. Connecticut.* 2001.

Mersky, Roy M., and Gary Hartman, eds. *A Documentary History of the Legal Aspects of Abortion in the United States: Roe v. Wade.* 3 vols. Fred B. Rothman and Co., 1993.

———. *A Documentary History of the Legal Aspects of Abortion in the United States: Stenberg v. Carhart.* 2003.

———. *A Documentary History of the Legal Aspects of Abortion in the United States: Webster v. Reproductive Health Services.* 1990.

Mersky, Roy M., and Kumar Percy Jayasuriya, eds. *A Documentary History of the Legal Aspects of Abortion in the United States: City of Akron v. Akron Center for Reproductive Health.* 2007.

Mersky, Roy M., and Suzanne F. Young, eds. *A Documentary History of the Legal Aspects of Abortion in the United States: Planned Parenthood v. Casey.* 1996.

Millar, W.J., S. Wadhera, and S.K. Henshaw. "Repeat Abortions in Canada, 1975–1993." *Family Planning Perspectives* 29 (January–February 1997): 20.

Miller, Arthur Selwyn, and Jerome A. Barron. "The Supreme Court, the Adversary System, and the Flow of Information to the Justices: A Preliminary Inquiry." *Virginia Law Review* 61 (1975): 1187.

Miller, E. Mike, and Donald E. Wintrode. Note. "A New Approach to Old Crimes: The Model Penal Code." *Notre Dame Lawyer* 39 (1964): 310.

Miller, Patricia G. *The Worst of Times.* 1993.

Mills, Don H. "A Medicolegal Analysis of Abortion Statutes." *Southern California Law Review* 31 (Winter 1958): 181.

Mohr, James C. *Abortion in America: The Origins and Evolution of National Policy, 1800–1900.* 1978.

Moody, Howard, and Arlene Carmen. *Abortion Counseling and Social Change, from Illegal Act to Medical Practice: The Story of the Clergy Consultation on Abortion.* Valley Forge: Judson Press, 1973.

Moore, Elizabeth N. "Moral Sentiments in Judicial Opinions on Abortion." *Santa Clara Law Review* 15 (1975): 591.

Moore, J.G., and J.H. Randall. "Trends in Therapeutic Abortion: A Review of 137 Cases." *American Journal of Obstetrics and Gynecology* 63 (January 1952): 28.

Morgan, Richard Gregory. "*Roe v. Wade* and the Lesson of Pre-*Roe* Case Law." *Michigan Law Review* 77 (1979): 1724.

Moritz, C.R., and N.J. Thompson. "Septic Abortion." *American Journal of Obstetrics and Gynecology* 95 (1966): 46.

Mota, N.P., M. Burnett, and J. Sareen. "Associations between Abortion, Mental Disorders, and Suicidal Behaviour in a Nationally Representative Sample." *Canadian Journal of Psychiatry* 55 (April 2010): 239.

Muller, C. "Socioeconomic Outcomes of Restricted Access to Abortion." *American Journal of Public Health* 61 (June 1971): 1110.

Munk-Olson, T., T.M. Laursen, C.B. Pedersen, et al. "First-Time First-Trimester Induced Abortion and Risk of Readmission to a Psychiatric Hospital in Women with a History of Treated Mental Disorder." *Archives of General Psychiatry* 69 (2012): 159.

Murphy, Bruce Allen. *Wild Bill: The Legend and Life of William O. Douglas: America's Most Controversial Supreme Court Justice.* 2003.

Nathanson, Bernard N. *Aborting America.* 1979.

———. *The Hand of God: A Journey from Death to Life by the Abortion Doctor Who Changed His Mind.* 1996.

Nathanson, Sue. *Soul Crisis: One Woman's Journey through Abortion to Renewal*. Signet, 1989.

National Committee on Maternal Health. *The Abortion Problem: Proceedings of the Conference Held under the Auspices of the National Committee on Maternal Health, Inc. at the New York Academy of Medicine, June 19th and 20th, 1942*. Williams and Wilkins, 1944.

Niinimaki, Maarit, et al. "Immediate Complications after Medical Compared with Surgical Termination of Pregnancy." *Obstetrics and Gynecology* 114 (October 2009): 795.

Niswander, Kenneth R., and Robert J. Patterson. "Psychologic Reaction to Therapeutic Abortion: 1. Subjective Patient Response." *Obstetrics and Gynecology* 29 (1967): 702.

Noonan, John. *A Private Choice: Abortion in America in the Seventies*. 1979.

Note. "The Extension of Prenatal Injury Doctrine to Nonviable Infants." *DePaul Law Review* 11 (1962): 361.

Novak's Textbook of Gynecology. 8th ed. 1970; 9th ed. 1975.

O'Connor, Sandra Day. *The Majesty of the Law: Reflections of a Supreme Court Justice*. 2003.

Okobia, M.N., and C.H. Bunker. "Epidemiological Risk Factors for Breast Cancer: A Review." *Nigerian Journal of Clinical Practice* 8 (2005): 35.

Olasky, Marvin. *Abortion Rites: A Social History of Abortion in America*. 1992.

———. *The Press and Abortion, 1838–1988*. 1988.

Pakter, J., D. O'Hare, F. Nelson, and M. Svigir. "A Review of Two Years' Experience in New York City with the Liberalized Abortion Law." In *The Abortion Experience: Psychological and Medical Impact*, edited by Howard J. Osofsky and Joy D. Osofsky, 47–72. Harper and Row, 1973.

Paul, Annie Murphy. *Origins: How the Nine Months before Birth Shape the Rest of Our Lives*. 2010.

Paulsen, Michael Stokes. "The Plausibility of Personhood." *Ohio State Law Journal* 74 (2012): 14.

———. "The Worst Constitutional Decision of All Time." *Notre Dame Law Review* 78 (2003): 995.

Pazol, K., S.B. Zane, W.Y. Parker, et al. "Abortion Surveillance—United States, 2008." *Morbidity and Mortality Weekly Report: CDC Surveillance Summaries* 60(SS15) (November 25, 2011): 1–41.

Penfield, A.J. "Abortion under Paracervical Block." *New York State Journal of Medicine* 71 (June 1971): 1185.

People v. Belous. 71 Cal.2d 954, 458 P.2d 194, 200, 80 Cal. Rptr. 354 (1969), cert. denied, 397 U.S. 915 (1970).

Petchesky, Rosalind Pollack. *Abortion and Woman's Choice: The State, Sexuality, and Reproductive Freedom*. Rev. ed. 1990.

Pike, C.C. "Therapeutic Abortion and Mental Health." *California Medicine* 111 (October 1969): 318.

Poe v. Menghini. 339 F.Supp. 986 (D. Kan. 1972).

Poe v. Ullman. 367 U.S. 497 (1961).

Pollak, Otto. *The Criminality of Women.* 1978.

Potter, Robert G., Jr. "Abortion in the United States." Book review. *Milbank Memorial Fund Quarterly* 37 (January 1959): 92.

Potts, D. M. "Postconceptive Control of Fertility." *International Journal of Gynaecology and Obstetrics* 8 (November 1970): 957.

Potts, Malcolm, Peter Diggory, and John Peel. *Abortion.* 1970.

Powell, Lewis F., Jr. Papers. Powell Archives, Washington and Lee University School of Law, Lexington, Virginia.

Prosser, William L. *Law of Torts.* 4th ed. 1971.

Pushaw, Robert J., Jr. "Does Congress Have the Constitutional Power to Prohibit Partial-Birth Abortion?" *Harvard Journal on Legislation* 42 (2005): 319.

Quay, Eugene. "Justifiable Abortion—Medical and Legal Foundations." Pts. 1 and 2. *Georgetown Law Journal* 49 (1960): 173; *Georgetown Law Journal* 49 (1961): 395.

Radford, Barbara, and Gina Shaw. "Beyond *Roe* and Abstract Rights: American Public Health and the Imperative for Abortion as a Part of Mainstream Medical Care." *Saint Louis University Public Law Review* 13 (1993): 207.

Rafferty, Philip. *Roe v. Wade: The Birth of a Constitutional Right.* Ann Arbor, Michigan: University Microfilms International Dissertation Information Service, 1992.

Randolph, A. Raymond. "Before *Roe v. Wade*: Judge Friendly's Draft Abortion Opinion." *Harvard Journal of Law and Public Policy* 29 (2006): 1035.

Reagan, Leslie J. "'About to Meet Her Maker': Women, Doctors, Dying Declarations, and the State's Investigation of Abortion, Chicago, 1867–1940." *Journal of American History* 77 (March 1991): 1240.

Reardon, David. "Abortion Decisions and the Duty to Screen: Clinical, Ethical, and Legal Implications of Predictive Risk Factors of Post-Abortion Maladjustment." *Journal of Contemporary Health Law and Policy* 20 (2003): 33.

Reardon, David, Priscilla Coleman, and Jesse Cougle. "Substance Use Associated with Unintended Pregnancy Outcomes in the National Longitudinal Survey of Youth." *American Journal of Drug and Alcohol Abuse* 26 (2004): 369.

Reardon, David C., Jesse R. Cougle, Vincent M. Rue, et al. "Psychiatric Admissions of Low-Income Women Following Abortion and Childbirth." *Canadian Medical Association Journal* 168 (2003): 1253–1256.

Reardon, D. C., P. G. Ney, F. Scheuren, et al. "Deaths Associated with Pregnancy Outcome: A Record Linkage Study of Low Income Women." *Southern Medical Journal* 95 (2002): 834.

Reardon, David C., Thomas W. Strahan, John M. Thorp, and Martha W. Shuping. "Deaths Associated with Abortion Compared to Childbirth—A Review of New and Old Data and the Medical and Legal Implications." *Journal of Contemporary Health Law and Policy* 20 (2004): 279.

Reeves, G. K., S. W. Kan, T. Key, et al. "Breast Cancer Risk in Relation to Abortion: Results from the EPIC Study." *International Journal of Cancer* 119 (October 1, 2006): 1741.

Regan, Milton C., Jr. "Getting Our Stories Straight: Narrative Autonomy and Feminist Commitments." *Indiana Law Journal* 72 (1997): 449, 455.

Reid, Duncan E., Kenneth J. Ryan, and Kurt Benirschke. *Principles and Management of Human Reproduction*. 1972.

Ridley, Matt. *The Rational Optimist: How Prosperity Evolves*. HarperCollins, 2010.

Ring-Cassidy, Elizabeth, and Ian Gentles. *Women's Health after Abortion: The Medical and Psychological Evidence*. deVeber Institute for Bioethics and Social Research, 2002.

Roden, Gregory J. "*Roe v. Wade* and the Common Law: Denying the Blessings of Liberty to Our Posterity." *University of West Los Angeles Law Review* 35 (2003): 212.

———. "Prenatal Tort Law and the Personhood of the Unborn Child: A Separate Legal Existence." *St. Thomas Law Review* 16 (Winter 2003): 207.

Rodgers v. Danforth. 486 S.W.2d 258 (Mo. 1972).

Roe v. Wade. 314 F.Supp. 1217 (N.D. Tex. 1970), appeal docketed, 39 U.S.L.W. 3229 (U.S. Oct. 6, 1970) (No. 808).

Roe v. Wade. 410 U.S. 113 (1973).

Rooney, B., and B. C. Calhoun. "Induced Abortion and Risk of Later Premature Births." *Journal of American Physicians and Surgeons* 8 (2003): 46.

Rosen, Harold, ed. *Abortion in America: Medical, Psychiatric, Legal, Anthropological, and Religious Considerations*. Beacon Press, 1967.

———. "Psychiatric Implications of Abortion: A Case Study in Social Hypocrisy." *Western Reserve Law Review* 17 (1965): 435.

———, ed. *Therapeutic Abortion: Medical, Psychiatric, Legal, Anthropological and Religious Considerations*. 1954.

Rosen, Jeffrey. *The Supreme Court: The Personalities and Rivalries That Defined America*. 2007.

Rosen v. Louisiana State Board of Medical Examiners. 318 F.Supp. 1217 (E.D. La. 1970).

Rosenberg, Gerald N. *The Hollow Hope: Can Courts Bring About Social Change?* 1991.

Roy, Lisa Shaw. "Roe and the New Frontier." *Harvard Journal of Law and Public Policy* 27 (2003–2004): 339.

Rue, V.M., P.K. Coleman, J. Rue, and D.C. Reardon. "Induced Abortion and Traumatic Stress: A Preliminary Comparison of American and Russian Women." *Medical Science Monitor* 10 (2004): SR5–SR16, www.medscimonit.com/pub/vol_10/no_10/4923.pdf.

Russell, Keith P. "Changing Indications for Therapeutic Abortion." *Journal of the American Medical Association* 151 (1953): 108.

Saftlas, Audrey F., Anne B. Wallis, Tara Shochet, et al. "Prevalence of Intimate Partner Violence among an Abortion Clinic Population." *American Journal of Public Health* 100 (August 2010): 1412.

Saletan, William. "Unbecoming Justice Blackmun." *Legal Affairs* (May–June 2005), http://www.legalaffairs.org/issues/May-June-2005/feature_saleton_mayjun05.msp.

Sauer, R. "Attitudes to Abortion in America, 1800–1973." *Population Studies* 28 (1974): 53.

Savage, David. *Turning Right: The Making of the Rehnquist Supreme Court*. 1992.

Schaefer, George. "Pregnancy and Tuberculosis: A Review of the Literature." *Obstetrical and Gynecological Survey* 6 (December 1951): 767.

———. "Results Following Therapeutic Abortion in Pulmonary Tuberculosis." *American Journal of Obstetrics and Gynecology* 63 (January 1952): 129.

Schroeder, Andrew B. Note. "Keeping Police Out of the Bedroom: Justice John Marshall Harlan, *Poe v. Ullman*, and the Limits of Conservative Privacy." *Virginia Law Review* 86 (2000): 1045.

Schulman, Joseph D. "Treatment of the Embryo and the Fetus in the First Trimester: Current Status and Future Prospects." *American Journal of Medical Genetics* 35 (1990): 197.

Schur, Edwin. "The Abortion Racket." *The Nation* 180 (March 5, 1955): 199.

Schwartz, Bernard. *The Ascent of Pragmatism: The Burger Court in Action.* 1990.

———. *The Unpublished Opinions of the Burger Court.* 1988.

Schwartz, Richard A. "The Social Effects of Legal Abortion." *American Journal of Public Health* 62 (October 1972): 1331.

Scott, Mark. Note. "Quickening in the Common Law: The Legal Precedent *Roe* Attempted and Failed to Use." *Michigan Law and Policy Review* 1 (1996): 199.

Sedgwick, Jeffrey Leigh. *Law Enforcement Planning: The Limits of an Economic Analysis.* 1984.

Shadigian, Elizabeth. "Reviewing the Evidence, Breaking the Silence: Long-Term Physical and Psychological Health Consequences of Induced Abortion." In *The Cost of "Choice": Women Evaluate the Impact of Abortion*, edited by Erika Bachiochi, 63. 2004.

Shadigian, Elizabeth M., and Samuel T. Bauer. "Pregnancy-Associated Death: A Qualitative Systematic Review of Homicide and Suicide." *Obstetrical and Gynecological Survey* 60 (2005): 183.

Shah, P.S., and J. Zao. "Induced Termination of Pregnancy and Low Birthweight and Preterm Birth: A Systematic Review and Meta-Analyses." *British Journal of Obstetrics and Gynaecology* 116 (October 2009): 1425.

Siegfried, S. "Psychiatric Investigation of the Sequelae of Interruption of Pregnancy." *Schweizer Archiv fur Neurologie und Psychiatrie* 67 (1951): 365.

Siener, Catherine H., and Elizabeth Mahoney. "Coordination of Outpatient Services for Patients Seeking Elective Abortion." *Clinical Obstetrics and Gynecology* 14 (March 1971): 48.

Sigworth, Heather. "Abortion Laws in the Federal Courts: The Supreme Court as Supreme Platonic Guardian." *Indiana Legal Forum* 5 (1971): 130.

Simon, James F. *FDR and Chief Justice Hughes: The President, the Supreme Court, and the Epic Battle over the New Deal.* 2012.

———. *The Center Holds: The Power Struggle inside the Rehnquist Court.* Simon and Schuster, 1995.

Simon, Julian. *The Ultimate Resource.* Princeton University Press, 1981.

Simon, Julian L., and Herman Kahn, eds. *The Resourceful Earth: A Response to Global 2000.* Basil Blackwell, 1984.

Simon, N.M. "Psychological and Emotional Indications for Therapeutic Abortion." *Seminars in Psychiatry* 2 (1970): 283.

Simon, Rita J., and Gloria Danziger. *Women's Movements in America: Their Successes, Disappointments, and Aspirations*. 1991.

Sklar, June, and Beth Berkov. "Abortion, Illegitimacy, and the American Birth Rate." *Science* 185 (September 13, 1974): 909.

Smolin, David. "Cultural and Technological Obstacles to the Mainstreaming of Abortion." *Saint Louis University Public Law Review* 13 (1993): 261.

Soderberg, Hanna, et al. "Emotional Distress Following Induced Abortion: A Study of Its Incidence and Determinants among Abortees in Malmo, Sweden." *European Journal of Obstetrics, Gynecology, and Reproductive Biology* 79 (1998): 173.

Solinger, Rickie. *The Abortionist: A Woman against the Law*. 1996.

State v. Munson. 86 S.D. 663, 201 N.W.2d 123 (S.D. 1972).

Steiner, Gilbert Y., ed. *The Abortion Dispute and the American System*. Brookings Institution, 1983.

Stern, Seth, and Stephen Wermiel. *Justice Brennan: Liberal Champion*. Houghton Mifflin Harcourt, 2010.

Stetson, Brad, ed. *The Silent Subject: Reflections on the Unborn in American Culture*. 1996.

Stevens, John Paul. *Five Chiefs: A Supreme Court Memoir*. 2011.

Stewart, Potter, Papers (MS 1367). Manuscripts and Archives, Yale University Library, New Haven, Connecticut.

Stith, Richard. "Her Choice, Her Problem: How Having a Choice Can Diminish Family Solidarity." *International Journal of the Jurisprudence of the Family* 2 (2011): 179.

Stix, Regine K. "A Study of Pregnancy Wastage." *Milbank Memorial Fund Quarterly* 13 (1935): 347.

Stix, Regine, and Frank Notestein. *Controlled Fertility: An Evaluation of Clinic Service*. 1940.

Stix, Regine K., and Dorothy G. Wiehl. "Abortion and the Public Health." *American Journal of Public Health* 28 (1938): 621.

Stulberg, Debra B., et al. "Abortion Provision among Practicing Obstetrician-Gynecologists." *Obstetrics and Gynecology* 118 (September 2011): 609.

Swingle, H. M., et al. "Abortion and the Risk of Subsequent Preterm Birth: A Systematic Review with Meta-Analyses." *Journal of Reproductive Medicine* 54 (February 2009): 95.

Sykes, P. "Complications of Termination of Pregnancy: A Retrospective Study of Admissions to Christchurch Women's Hospital 1989 and 1990." *New Zealand Medical Journal* 106 (March 10, 1993): 83.

Syska, Barbara J., Thomas W. Hilgers, and Dennis O'Hare. "An Objective Model for Estimating Criminal Abortions and Its Implications for Public Policy." In *New Perspectives on Human Abortion*, edited by Thomas W. Hilgers, Dennis J. Horan, and David Mall, 168. 1981.

Taussig, F. J. *Abortion, Spontaneous and Induced: Medical and Social Aspects*. C. V. Mosby, 1936.

Thorp, John M., Jr. "Public Health Impact of Legal Termination of Pregnancy in the US: 40 Years Later." *Scientifica* 2012 (2012). http://www.hindawi.com/journals/scientifica/2012/980812/.

Thorp, John, Katherine Hartmann, and Elizabeth Shadigian. "Long-Term Physical and Psychological Health Consequences of Induced Abortion: Review of the Evidence." *Obstetrical and Gynecological Survey* 58 (January 2003): 67.

Tierney, Michael J. "Post-Viability Abortion Bans and the Limits of the Health Exception." *Notre Dame Law Review* 80 (2004): 465.

Tietze, Christopher. "Abortion Laws and Abortion Practices in Europe." *Advances in Planned Parenthood* 5 (1969): 194.

———. "Mortality with Contraception and Induced Abortion." *Studies in Family Planning* 45 (September 1969): 6.

———. "The Public Health Effects of Legal Abortion in the United States." *Family Planning Perspectives* 16 (1984): 26.

———. "Two Years' Experience with a Liberal Abortion Law: Its Impact on Fertility Trends in New York City." *Family Planning Perspectives* 5 (1973): 36.

———. "United States: Therapeutic Abortions, 1963–1968." *Studies in Family Planning* 59 (1970): 5.

Tietze, Christopher, and Hans Lehfeldt. "Legal Abortion in Eastern Europe." *Journal of the American Medical Association* 175 (April 1961): 1149.

Tietze, Christopher, and Sarah Lewit. "Abortion." *Scientific American* 220 (January 1969): 3.

———. "Legal Abortion." *Scientific American* 236 (January 1977): 21.

Torres, Aida, and Jacqueline Darroch Forrest. "Why Do Women Have Abortions?" *Family Planning Perspectives* 20 (July/August 1988): 169.

Transcript of First Oral Argument in *Doe v. Bolton*, 410 U.S. 179 (1973). U.S. Supreme Court. December 13, 1971. Available at http://www.aul.org/doe-v-bolton-transcripts/.

Transcript of First Oral Argument in *Roe v. Wade*, 410 U.S. 113 (1973). U.S. Supreme Court. December 13, 1971. Available at http://www.aul.org/roe-v-wade-transcripts/.

Transcript of Reargument in *Doe v. Bolton*, 410 U.S. 179 (1973). U.S. Supreme Court. October 11, 1972. Available at http://www.aul.org/doe-v-bolton -transcripts/.

Transcript of Reargument in *Roe v. Wade*, 410 U.S. 113 (1973). U.S. Supreme Court. October 11, 1972. Available at http://www.aul.org/roe-v-wade -transcripts/.

Tribe, Laurence. "The Supreme Court, 1972 Term—Foreword: Toward a Model of Roles in the Due Process of Life and Law." *Harvard Law Review* 87 (1973): 1.

Trout, Monroe. "Therapeutic Abortion Laws Need Therapy." *Temple Law Review* 37 (1964): 172.

Tulkoff, Myer S. "Legal and Social Control of Abortion." *Kentucky Law Journal* 40 (1952): 410.

Tushnet, Mark. "Two Notes on the Jurisprudence of Privacy." *Constitutional Commentary* 8 (1991): 75.

Uddo, Basile. "A Wink from the Bench: The Federal Courts and Abortion." *Tulane Law Review* 53 (1979): 398.

Urofsky, Melvin I., ed. *The Douglas Letters*. 1987.

United States v. Vuitch. 305 F.Supp. 1032 (D.D.C. 1969), rev'd and remanded, 402 U.S. 62 (1971).

Van Alstyne, William W. "The Enduring Example of John Marshall Harlan: 'Virtue as Practice' in the Supreme Court." *New York Law School Law Review* 36 (1991): 109.

―――. Essay Review. "The Fate of Constitutional Ipse Dixits." *Journal of Legal Education* 33 (1983): 712.

Volpe, E. Peter. *Patient in the Womb*. 1984.

Waite, Linda J., and Maggie Gallagher. *The Case for Marriage: Why Married People are Happier, Healthier, and Better Off Financially*. 2000.

Wallace, Stephen J. "Why Third-Party Standing in Abortion Suits Deserves a Closer Look." *Notre Dame Law Review* 84 (2009): 1369.

Walter, G.S. "Psychologic and Emotional Consequences of Elective Abortion." *Obstetrics and Gynecology* 36 (September 1970): 482.

Wardle, Lynn D. *The Abortion Privacy Doctrine: A Compendium and Critique of Federal Court Abortion Cases*. 1980.

―――. "A Matter of Conscience: Legal Protection for the Rights of Conscience of Healthcare Providers." *Cambridge Quarterly of Healthcare Ethics* 2 (1993): 529.

―――. "Protecting the Rights of Conscience of Health Care Providers." *Journal of Legal Medicine* 14 (1993): 177–230.

―――. "The Quandary of Pro-Life Free Speech: A Lesson from the Abolitionists." *Albany Law Review* 62 (1999): 853.

―――. "Time Enough: *Webster v. Reproductive Health Services* and the Prudent Pace of Justice." *Florida Law Review* 41 (1989): 881.

Wasserman, Richard. Note. "Implications of the Abortion Decisions: Post *Roe* and *Doe* Litigation and Legislation." *Columbia Law Review* 74 (1974): 237.

Wassom, Brian D. Comment. "The Exception That Swallowed the Rule? *Women's Professional Corporation v. Voinovich* and the Mental Health Exception to Post-Viability Abortion Bans." *Case Western Reserve Law Review* 49 (1999): 799.

Wattenberg, Ben J. *Fewer: How the New Demography of Depopulation Will Shape Our Future*. 2004.

Webb, Borden D. Comment. "Is the Intentional Killing of an Unborn Child Homicide?" *Pacific Law Journal* 2 (1971): 170.

White, R. "Induced Abortions: A Survey of Their Psychiatric Implications, Complications and Indications." *Texas Reports on Biology and Medicine* 24 (1966): 531.

Whittington, H.G. "Evaluation of Therapeutic Abortion as an Element of Preventive Psychiatry." *American Journal of Psychiatry* 126 (1970): 1224.

Williams, Glanville. *The Sanctity of Life and the Criminal Law*. 1957.

Williams, Joan. *Unbending Gender: Why Family and Work Conflict and What to Do about It*. 2000.

Williams, Juan. *Thurgood Marshall: American Revolutionary*. 1998.

Willson, J. Robert, Clayton T. Beecham, and Elsie Reid Carrington. *Obstetrics and Gynecology*. 4th ed. 1971.

Willson, J. Robert, Clayton T. Beecham, Isador Forman, and Elsie Reid Carrington. *Obstetrics and Gynecology*. 1958.

Witherspoon, James S. "Reexamining *Roe*: Nineteenth-Century Abortion Statutes and the Fourteenth Amendment." *St. Mary's Law Journal* 17 (1985): 29.

Wohlers, Paul D. *Women and Abortion: Prospects of Criminal Charges*. The American Center for Bioethics, undated. Reprinted in *Legal Ramifications of the Human Life Amendment, Hearings before the Subcommittee on the Constitution of the Committee on the Judiciary*, U.S. Senate, 98th Cong., 1st Sess. (February 28, March 7, 1983), 233–242.

Woodward, Bob, and Scott Armstrong. *The Brethren: Inside the Supreme Court*. Simon and Schuster, 1979.

Yarbrough, Tinsley E. *Harry A. Blackmun: The Outsider Justice*. 2008.

———. *John Marshall Harlan: The Great Dissenter of the Warren Court*. 1992.

YWCA v. Kugler. 342 F.Supp. 1048 (February 29, 1972), aff'd without op, 493 F.2d 1402 (3d Cir. 1974), cert. denied, 415 U.S. 989 (1974).

· INDEX ·

Bold page numbers indicate illustrations.